COSPLAY: A HISTORY

THE BUILDERS, FANS,

AND MAKERS WHO BRING YOUR

FAVORITE STORIES TO LIFE

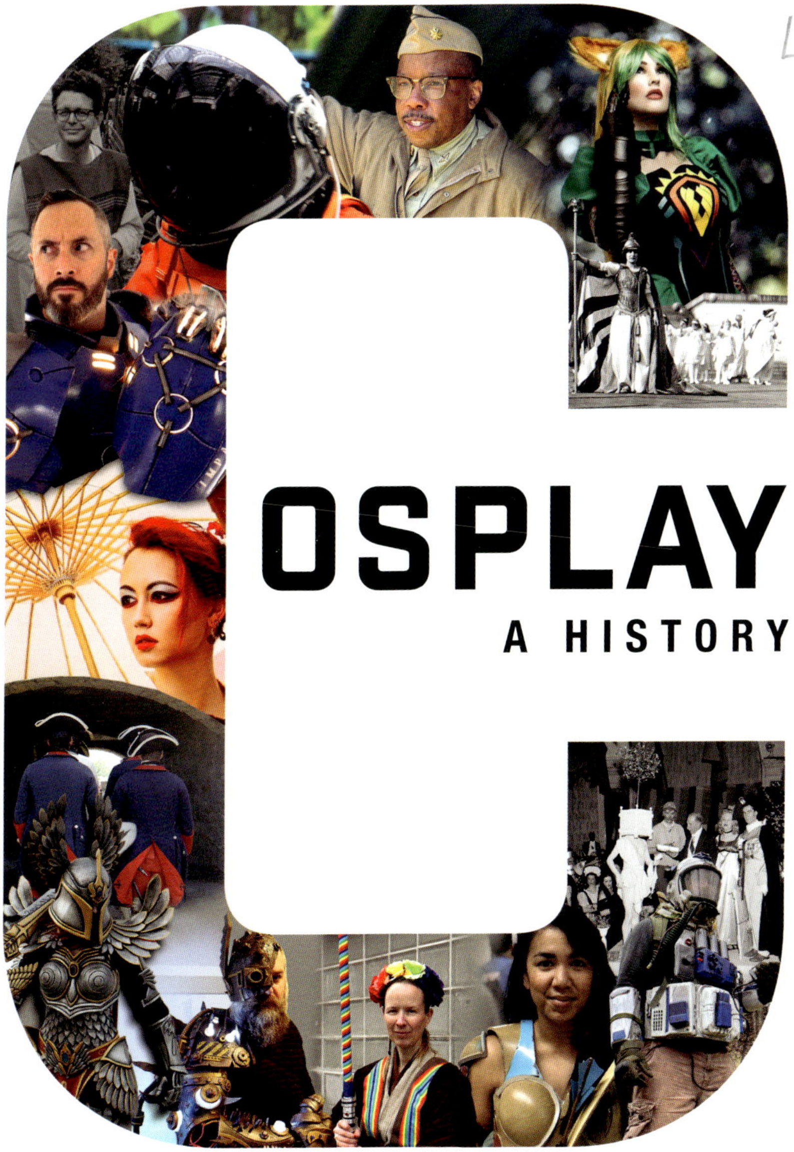

COSPLAY
A HISTORY

ANDREW LIPTAK
FOREWORD BY ADAM SAVAGE

LONDON SYDNEY **NEW YORK** TORONTO NEW DELHI

To Bram and Iris: I hope that you never lose the curiosity, excitement, joy, and wonder that I see in you every day.

1230 AVENUE OF THE AMERICAS, NEW YORK, NEW YORK 10020

Copyright © 2022 by Andrew Liptak

All rights reserved, including the right to reproduce this book or portions thereof in any form whatsoever. For information, address Saga Press Subsidiary Rights Department, 1230 Avenue of the Americas, New York, NY 10020.

First Saga Press trade paperback edition June 2022

SAGA PRESS and colophon are trademarks of Simon & Schuster, Inc.

For information about special discounts for bulk purchases, please contact Simon & Schuster Special Sales at 1-866-506-1949 or business@simonandschuster.com.

The Simon & Schuster Speakers Bureau can bring authors to your live event. For more information or to book an event, contact the Simon & Schuster Speakers Bureau at 1-866-248-3049 or visit our website at www.simonspeakers.com.

Interior design by Michelle Marchese

Manufactured in Canada

10 9 8 7 6 5 4 3 2 1

Library of Congress Cataloging-in-Publication Data is available.

ISBN 978-1-5344-5582-5
ISBN 978-1-5344-5584-9 (ebook)

CONTENTS

Foreword by Adam Savage — ix
Introduction — xi

PART 1
FANDOM AND CONVENTIONS — 1

Apollo Enthusiasts **3**

**11 Chapter 1
The Origins of Fandom**
Jules Verne **12** | The Vril-Ya Bazaar **13** | Mr. Skygack **15** | The Origins of Science-Fiction Fandom **17** | The First Worldcon **18**

**22 Chapter 2
Convention Masquerades**

**33 Chapter 3
Reliving Stories of the Past**

**36 Chapter 4
Beyond Worldcon**
Superheroes **36** | Costume-Con **38**

**40 Chapter 5
Trek Invasion**

**47 Chapter 6
The Summer of 1977**

**52 Chapter 7
Legions of Fans**
The Evolution of a Stormtrooper **53** | DIY **54** | The Birth of a Legion **57** | Building a Movement **62** | The Rebel Legion **63** | The 405th Infantry Division **66** | STARFLEET **68** | Screen Accuracy **68** | Community **70**

**72 Chapter 8
The Rise of Comic-Con**
The Early Years **73**

**78 Chapter 9
Costume Play**
The Rise of Anime **78** | Japanese Cosplay Explodes **81** | North American Fandom **83**

**87 Chapter 10
Mainstream Acceptance**

**95 Chapter 11
Identity**
#28DaysofBlackCosplay **98** | Identifying Gender **102** | Sexism in Cosplay **106** | Group Demographics **108** | Sex Appeal **109**

**113 Chapter 12
Protest Cosplay**
Women's Rights **115** | International Protests **117** | Criticisms and Complicated Histories **119** | Politics and Cosplay **122**

**123 Chapter 13
Charity**

PART 2
TRADITIONS   127

129 Chapter 14
Street Theatrics
Street Performance 129 | Fantasticals 132

136 Chapter 15
Bringing the Past to Life
Fort Ticonderoga 136

143 Chapter 16
Living in the Past
The Eglinton Tournament 143 | Reenacting 147

151 Chapter 17
Halloween
Origins 152 | Ragamuffin Days 154 | Holiday Industrial Complex 158 | Halloween Today 165 | Pipeline to Cosplay 166

PART 3
PRODUCTION   169

171 Chapter 18
Instruments of Storytelling
Clothing as a Storytelling Device 171 | The Origins of Costumes 175

179 Chapter 19
Do It Yourself

183 Chapter 20
The Act of Cosplaying
Performance 183 | Cosplay vs. Professionals 188 | Replication 190 | The Build 193 | Scaling up 194 | Cosplay Repair 197

202 Chapter 21
Selling Stuff Online
Major Retailers: eBay and Amazon 203 | Etsy 205 | Cosplay Companies 207 | ANOVOS and Denuo Novo 208 | Cosplay Supplies 211 | Ethics 213

216 Chapter 22
Technologies
Early Cosplay Technologies 216 | Pepakura 218 | EVA Foam 219 | 3D Printing 223 | Laser Cutting and CNC 230 | Electronics and Motors 231 | Makeup 233 | Direct Income Platforms 236

239 Chapter 23
Cycles of Costuming
Replenishment 247

249 Chapter 24
From Fan to Pro
Costume Design 251 | Prop Shops 253 | Imperial Boots 255

PART 4
LEGALITY/FRANCHISE SUPPORT — 257

259 Chapter 25
Fan Works

263 Chapter 26
Walking, Talking Copyright Violation: Intellectual Property
Legal Threats **263** | Studio Control and Contact **268** | Legality **269** | Cosplay Pros **273** | Pro Acting **275**

278 Chapter 27
Influencing Canon
Rose Bowl Parade **278** | Canonized **280** | The Rise of the Mercs **283**

PART 5
TECHNOLOGY — 291

295 Chapter 28
Hollywood

298 Chapter 29
Owning a Piece of History

301 Chapter 30
Internet Forums
Early Days **302** | The Replica Prop Forum **304** | ACP and Cosplay.com **307**

310 Chapter 31
Virtual Communities
Smartphones and Cameras **310** | Social Media **312** | Facebook Groups **317** | Instagram and TikTok **318** | YouTube **320** | Cosplay Music Videos **323** | Fragile Infrastructure **324** | Sharing Is Caring **329**

332 Chapter 32
Cosplay and COVID-19

337 Chapter 33
The Future
Media **337** | Technology **339** | Corporate Encouragement **340** | Cosplay Lite **343** | A Precarious Existence **345**

347 Chapter 34
Why We Troop

Acknowledgments — **351**

FOREWORD

BY ADAM SAVAGE

What the hell is cosplay, and how is it different from just putting on a costume? The answer seems tricky, but in my opinion, it's only tricky if you're thinking of cosplay as a hobby. It's not. Cosplay is expansive. It's a bona fide art form, and an inclusive one—there's precious little gatekeeping overall.

And "hobby" is an awful word. It slinks around our conversations, laden with negative connotations. It's often useless and has a strange implied relationship with work, in that a hobby could never be important like *work* is. Everyone agrees, I think, that hobbies are generally considered good. But we as a society tend to belittle them, and in doing so, we're sequestering some of the most interesting cultural knowledge into a bucket labeled "dumb stuff." I reject this way of thinking entirely. I'm in charge of the complex machine that is me, and if part of the maintenance of that machine means I find peace and solace and quietude in an activity like making, commissioning, rehearsing, adjusting, and performing in costume, that's *not* an insignificant thing.

For me, cosplay is most simply described as the practice of wearing a costume with the possibility that something important (aesthetically, emotionally, philosophically, socially, etc.) might happen during the wearing of that costume. Like all art, it can be produced and consumed in countless different ways, and like all art, cosplay is about transformation and transmission.

The transformation is real: putting on these costumes is frequently transformative and sometimes transcendent. We all like wearing things that make us feel good. I'm sure, reader, that you've experienced a positive emotional reaction to a particular piece of clothing: the warmth of a heavy coat, that shirt you know you look great in, or new sneakers that make walking feel fun again. Cosplay is the practice of seeking out that high, but multiplied by a thousand.

The transmission is equally real. The performative aspect of cosplay is intrinsic to its nature; cosplay is a social art form. This is a practice that happens *among* us. We are literally pouring our bodies into shapes and narratives that hold meaning for us, then finding each other at events and showing each other what we've done. This is maybe the most illuminating revelation I've had about cosplay: that it's theater. I love theater. It's where I got my start. Theater is among the oldest and most important arts, but cosplay is theater in which the line between audience and performer isn't blurred; it just doesn't exist. We're all here for the show. Finally, like all art, our participation in it invariably teaches us about ourselves.

Andrew has done a great service to the world by writing this book and treating this beautiful art with the seriousness it deserves, despite cosplay's penchant for absurdity.

INTRODUCTION

Think back to the film that you love the most. Or that television show you binged in its entirety over a weekend, the book you stayed up all night reading, or the video game you spent countless hours working to beat. Remember the feeling you had where you could be part of that story, living in that world, if you only closed your eyes?

That's the feeling that comes to life around the world as thousands of fans descend into their workshops, make their way to convention floors, scenic landscapes, or out onto the street to take candy from strangers. That feeling of love for a story is what motivates people to dress up as their favorite characters.

We are storytelling creatures, and for millennia, we've turned to props and costumes to help convey stories and our appreciation for them. Costuming has a long history, used in events from religious rites to theatrical performances to movies and television shows, to Halloween and fan conventions.

I've been dressing up in costumes since I was little. Like most kids of my generation, I used Halloween as an opportunity to imagine that I was someone else. The earliest costume that I remember wearing was Batman (my younger brother was Robin), but the first one that I put together out of fascination for the character was a white-armored stormtrooper from *Star Wars: A New Hope*.

My wish to become that stormtrooper was finally granted years later at my high school's end-of-the-year band concert. I'd played trumpet in my middle and high school bands for six years, and just about every day since I'd joined, I'd pestered the school's band director, Chris Rivers, to let us play the music from *Star Wars*. That spring he'd relented, and for months we'd been practicing arrangements of John Williams's music. As the concert approached, I realized that we could make it even cooler, beyond just playing the iconic music. We needed to bring *Star Wars* into the auditorium.

This concert was the culmination of my obsession with the franchise, which first took root in the spring of 1997, when my father brought me to the theater to see the special-edition rereleases of *A New Hope*, *The Empire Strikes Back*, and *Return of the Jedi*. I distinctly remember my twelve-year-old self staring out the window on the ride home after each screening, thinking about how cool the troopers looked and imagining how it might feel to wear such a costume.

With the special editions I was hooked, endlessly rewatching the trilogy on VHS, reading and rereading the tie-in novels, and dressing up as Luke Skywalker for Halloween. For years I fantasized about building my own suit of stormtrooper armor. I thought that my shop class might be an opportunity to craft something, but shaping sheet metal into elaborate curves proved a daunting task. So I scoured the internet for other ideas, discovering various forums and how-to sites, which showed that not only was it possible, but people *actually made* their own armor. It was while I was in high school that I came across some of those people: a group of fans that called itself the 501st Legion.

I first encountered the Legion in the pages of *Star Wars Insider*, which profiled the dedicated fans who dressed up as stormtroopers, scout troopers, and even Darth Vader. I knew that I needed to find out more about the group, and I was determined to invite them to that upcoming spring concert. With the blessing of Mr. Rivers—I'm sure at that point just to get me out of his office—I sent an email to my local chapter, the 501st New England Garrison, outlining the situation in the hope that just one of their members would respond.

Lo and behold, one did.

In 2003, Scott Allen resided in Rhode Island, a five-hour drive from central Vermont. He emailed me back, saying that he would be happy to attend the concert in armor. On the day of the concert, he showed up, plastic tote in tow, and for the first time, I got to see a real, live stormtrooper. As my classmates trickled into the music center before the concert, they gawked at the sight of this random guy clad in a gleaming white costume.

Onstage, we launched into John Williams's "The Imperial March," and Scott marched down the aisle in his armor. The audience went nuts.

That 2003 concert is my own personal origin story. Armed with a bonus from my job at a summer camp a month later, I mailed Scott a check. Weeks later, a big brown box showed up at my home, and I remember my astonishment as I pulled each gleaming piece of white plastic out, one by one.

My first-ever encounter with a stormtrooper, during my high school's end-of-year concert. We played music from *Star Wars*, and Rhode Island trooper Scott Allen showed up in armor. That evening changed my life.

Courtesy of Andrew Liptak

The suit came trimmed and ready to assemble. Within hours, I had put it together and was parading around the house in my own set of stormtrooper armor. I pulled it out for Halloween, skits at the summer camp, and the bookstore where I worked. I joined the 501st Legion, and midway through college, I flew out to Indianapolis for *Star Wars* Celebration III, where I was surrounded by tens of thousands of like-minded fans—not just *Star Wars* fans, but fellow 501st members. I went on to wear that armor for parades and festivals, for onstage appearances with "Weird Al" Yankovic, to escort Snoop Dogg through Times Square, and to visit Make-A-Wish recipients.

Plenty of costumes have followed that first suit of armor—a clone trooper from *Attack of the Clones*, another from *The Clone Wars* TV series and *Revenge of the Sith*, one of the new stormtroopers from *The Force Awakens*, a shoretrooper and General Merrick from *Rogue One*. I've branched out beyond *Star Wars* over the years: I've dressed up as Dr. Daniel Jackson from *Stargate SG-1*, Dr. House from the show *House, M.D.*, a Belter from *The Expanse*, and Sam Rockwell's lonely astronaut from *Moon*. My costume wish list has grown to include everything from rugged suits of power armor to fantastical space suits to casual jumpsuits. I'll get to them someday.

In the years since I constructed my first costume, I've found myself in the middle of a vibrant community that shares a passion for *Star Wars*, all things popular culture, and the craft of making costumes based on the characters that we see in books, comics, movies, television, and video games.

In 2016, *MythBusters* host Adam Savage went on a TED stage with a talk titled "My Love Letter to Cosplay," a thirteen-minute speech in which he recounted his own obsession with building costumes and the impact that they have on people. He described the revelation that he had while attending San Diego Comic-Con for the first time in 2002, dressed as No-Face from Hayao Miyazaki's 2001 film *Spirited Away*.

Adam Savage poses in a replica Space Shuttle space suit at New York Comic Con in 2018.

Courtesy of Andrew Liptak

During that convention, he dressed as the character and took on its voice and movements and was surprised when people interacted with him as though they were in the story. "This isn't a performer-audience relationship," he said in the talk—this is a different kind altogether, one in which the audience and costumer can interact in new ways. "*This is cosplay. We are, all of us on that floor, injecting ourselves into a narrative that meant something to us. And we're making it our own. We're connecting with something important inside of us. And the costumes are how we reveal ourselves to each other.*"[1]

Savage's talk highlights the core of what cosplay is: It's more than just dressing up as a favorite character. It's embodying part of a story, consuming it in a way that goes be-

---

1 Adam Savage, "My Love Letter to Cosplay," filmed July 15, 2016 in Vancouver, Canada, TED video, https://www.ted.com/talks/adam_savage_my_love_letter_to_cosplay.

G.I. Joe cosplayers at the 2019 Dragon Con in Atlanta, Georgia, pose for a group picture.

Courtesy of Andrew Liptak

yond passive participation. It is interactive, interpretive, and immersive, adding an additional dimension beyond the outfit. Cosplay, which *Merriam-Webster* defines as "the activity or practice of dressing up as a character from a work of fiction (such as a comic book, video game, or television show)," originates from the phrase "costume play" and has increasingly become a new way for fans around the world to engage with their favorite stories. Above all, it's a community.

Within the last decade, cosplay has exploded into mainstream culture. Shows like *Game of Thrones*, *The Walking Dead*, and *The Big Bang Theory* have turned genre stories into the latest watercooler talking points, and with that wave, obsessions that were once stigmatized are now commonplace. Costume contests are no longer relegated to bars on Halloween, as conventions ranging from San Diego Comic-Con to your local/regional one occur just about every weekend around the country, filled to capacity.

But despite its newfound popularity, cosplay isn't new. It's a hobby that's enjoyed a long and vibrant history for more than a century as fans have painstakingly brought their favorite characters to life.

INTRODUCTION

Building a costume can be a long, involved process that can encompass everything from designing patterns, sewing garments, and joining complex pieces of plastic and foam together. It can be as simple as pulling the right combination of clothes from your closet. It can require wiring and electricity. Builders can use a 3D printer to build parts or props; or a set of tools as basic as a razor blade, some foam, and hot glue. Cosplayers are painters, sculptors, mechanics, woodworkers, electricians, dressmakers, tailors, cobblers, leatherworkers, and blacksmiths, or perhaps none of these at all.

These costumers are an inherently creative group of individuals who work tirelessly to assemble their cosplays to bring their favorite characters to life. They might sink decades into a single costume, painstakingly getting each and every detail exactly right. They might build a new costume for each event they attend. Some cosplayers just want to have something to wear on Halloween, to the latest film premiere for their favorite franchise, or to their local convention.

Cosplay is also a vocation that lands firmly at the intersection of art, culture, and technology, utilizing both the latest advances in materials science and manufacturing, and age-old practices of sewing and metalwork. Plenty of cosplayers make their living by building and designing commissioned works, posing for photographers, or setting up online personas for fans. Some volunteer within their communities, bringing their enthusiasm for their characters to those in need. In all these cases, they're interpreting, engaging with, and building on the stories that they cherish.

But above all, it's an outlet for creative play and exhibition, and is a way to take part in something greater than themselves, to be part of a community of fellow builders.

The goal of this book is to dig into that rich history and subculture and answer a question central to the entire scene: Why do we take the time and effort to re-create the characters and moments from our favorite stories?

To answer that question, we're going to look at the communities that have come to practice and celebrate cosplay as we know it, delve into its early days, and explore how it's evolved over the course of decades thanks to conventions and new technologies. We'll examine what costumes mean for the people who wear them, what those cosplayers represent to those who own the properties that inspire them, and what the entire field of cosplay means to the entertainment industry in a rapidly changing world.

So, strap in, suit up, and don't forget to pack some extra glue and tape, just in case.

part one

Fandom and Conventions

On April 18, 1969, three months before their historic mission, astronauts Neil Armstrong and Buzz Aldrin practice in the space suits they'd later wear to walk on the moon.
Image: NASA

Adam Savage wearing a space suit commissioned from Ryan Nagata.
Courtesy of Norm Chan

APOLLO ENTHUSIASTS

"This thing is a masterpiece of replication," Adam Savage says, standing in the middle of a cluttered shop. He's wearing a white Apollo-era space suit costume constructed for him by designer and space suit builder Ryan Nagata. "Ryan makes what I consider the best Apollo replicas that are out there. His attention to detail astounds me."[1]

If there's one place where science fiction and history naturally intersect, it's the space race. The massive program that eventually brought astronauts to the moon was inherently dramatic—just like something out of science fiction, right down to the complicated space suits that the astronauts wore on the surface of the moon.

Space suits have their origins in the protective garments worn by aeronauts in the 1930s. Later, as airplanes came into common usage, engineers devised ways to supply pilots and crews with oxygen; and as they pushed the limits, pilots began to come up with new forms of protection. As aviator Wiley Post began to plan a solo flight around the world in the early 1930s, he teamed up with the Phillips Petroleum Company to create a pressurized suit that would help him survive the journey.

The suit itself was made out of rubber and came with a cylindrical metal helmet with

---

1 "Adam Savage's Apollo A7L Spacesuit Replica!" Adam Savage's Tested, filmed and edited by Joey Fameli, YouTube video, January 16, 2017, https://www.youtube.com/watch?v=p4vRNjur7nc.

a porthole in the center. It looked like something out of a science-fiction movie and was featured in one: 1935's *Air Hawks*. Post's goal was to drum up publicity for his exploits, and it worked. "The exposure highlights the dense network of media, perception, and human performance through which, and for which, pressure suits would thereafter be designed,"[2] wrote Nicholas de Monchaux in *Spacesuit: Fashioning Apollo*.

As this was happening, science fiction's modern sensibilities and iconography were beginning to develop in the pulp magazines that hit newsstands in the 1920s and 1930s. The term "space suit" appeared in the July 1929 issue of *Science Wonder Stories*[3] and in E. E. "Doc" Smith's story "Galactic Patrol" in the September 1937 issue of *Astounding Stories*; and "space helmet" turned up in M. W. Wellman's story "Disc-Men of Jupiter" in the September 1931 issue of the pulp science-fiction magazine *Wonder Stories*.[4]

Indeed, the suits that Post wore did something interesting. They helped link two concepts together: the practicality of a garment designed to help a person survive and the cool factor that captured the public's imagination. "In the opening credits of *Air Hawks*, when Post's name is flashed on the screen," Monchaux wrote, "it is superimposed on footage of the flier, pressure suit and all."[5]

In the postwar era, the suits that high-altitude fighter pilots and astronauts began to wear looked like something that one might have seen decades earlier on the covers of science-fiction pulp magazines and novels—and the public noticed. Monchaux cites news coverage that connected new pressure suits to science-fiction stories, and by the time NASA launched its Mercury, Gemini, and Apollo missions, the silver- (and later white) suited astronauts were quite familiar to the public.

Toy and costume companies produced their own versions of space-themed Halloween costumes in the 1950s and 1960s: Ben Cooper, Inc. produced a number of astronaut costumes, while the Ideal Toy Company released its S.T.A.R. (Space Travel and Reconnaissance) Team lineup, which included a fantastic-looking bubble helmet, water gun, utility belt, and boots for children to dress up in.[6]

---

2   Nicholas de Monchaux, *Spacesuit: Fashioning Apollo* (United Kingdom: MIT Press, 2011), 57.
3   Jeff Prucher, ed., *Brave New Words: The Oxford Dictionary of Science Fiction* (New York: Oxford University Press, 2007), 208.
4   Prucher, 202.
5   Prucher, 65.
6   "Star Team," Toys You Had: Remembering Toys from the 60s to 80s, accessed December 2, 2021, http://www.toysyouhad.com/Starteam.htm.

While there have been plenty of adult costumers who've suited up as any number of characters from science fiction and fantasy, the science fiction and real-world historical appeal cross over once again with the work of Ryan Nagata, an artist and maker who builds replica space suits for space enthusiasts and film productions alike.

"I made my first space suit costume when I was fourteen years old, after I saw the movie *Apollo 13*," Nagata explained. His interest was purely out of fascination with the suit itself, and he says that he didn't plan to get into the business of making the suits for a living. He ended up going to film school, "and that's where I picked up all the skills to make props and costumes."

After graduating, he worked as a director but kept making his own props on the side. Along the way, he decided that with all the skills he had acquired over the years, he could make a better space suit than he had back when he was fourteen. His first "high-fidelity" effort was one of the silver Mercury space suits, and he later helped *MythBusters* star Adam Savage with his own suit, which he wore on the show.

Ryan Nagata wearing one of his Gemini-era suits.

Courtesy of Ryan Nagata

Nagata noted that while there are some shops that produce costumes for Hollywood films, there really isn't a place where a collector can pick up an accurate space suit. As he began to produce his own replicas, people took notice. Savage was among the first to commission a space suit replica from him. Nagata's first convention with his creations was Spacefest in Tucson, Arizona, an annual event frequented by the surviving Apollo astronauts. The suits attracted considerable attention there. "I've just been doing it ever since," he explained.

When Nagata replicates real-world objects, he incorporates the same approach that historians employ when working to re-create the past, which many cosplayers have

A "Snoopy Cap" created by Ryan Nagata.
Courtesy of Ryan Nagata

adopted for building their own costumes: a strict attention to detail to get the replica to look as close as possible to the original.

He initially started his work by examining photographs of the Apollo-era suits. Eventually, however, the viral popularity of his suits on social media opened some doors, granting him access to the measurements for some of the original Apollo hardware produced by companies like ILC Dover. In other instances, he tracks down private collectors who might have a specific part, "and they'll send me measurements or even the piece."

Nagata notes that his work is still an artistic reconstruction: his suits aren't designed to be pressurized, and he has to make judgment calls on how to change things that would be too expensive or unnecessary to duplicate, given that they're never going into space like the originals.

"But I do think it's like you're stepping into that world when you put on the suit," Nagata says. "I think there's even a slightly stronger degree of reality because people actually went into space in these suits, whereas a costume suit was just in a movie."

Nagata noted that his own personal interest in costuming extends beyond NASA's space suits: he built his own *Star Trek* costumes and was interested in reenacting. "I think there's a romanticism that we have about World War II that we don't have for Vietnam, for obvious reasons, and I think with the space program, there's that same romanticism," he says. "There's a scene that sticks out for me the most in *Apollo 13*: the suit-up and launch sequence. It still makes me tear up every time I see it, and I think that the putting on the outfit is kind of a superhero costume. The closest thing to a superhero outfit in the real world might be a space suit. I think it definitely captures the romanticism of it."

Nagata noted that some of the astronauts felt the same way about their own suits when they wore them. After supplying an X-15 pressure suit costume to director Damien Chazelle for his 2018 film *First Man*, he met Space Shuttle astronaut Joe Engle, who was on set consulting for the film. According to Nagata, Engle loved the suit. "He said the X-15 suit was definitely the sexiest pressure suit that he ever wore, and that when he put it on, he felt like a real spaceman, like he'd seen in science fiction."

When I spoke with Savage a couple of years ago, he explained that space suits appealed to him "because I secretly want to be a superhero," noting that they satisfy his love of safety equipment and armor. "The space suit is the most amazing, because you're bringing your own mini Earth with you."[7] When it came to space suits, he explained that part of the appeal was from "the high-level details that tell the story that this was made by people. If you look at NASA hardware really close up, you really can sense that these aren't production-made items. They're one-offs, each one handmade by a machinist, designed by engineers."[8]

The suits that Nagata makes have that level of detail and, accordingly, don't come cheap: a replica Apollo suit that's fully kitted out for the moon can run a buyer anywhere from $22,000 to $25,000, and it can take months for Nagata to construct. Most buyers don't commission an entire space suit from him, however; an enthusiast might just want a set of gloves or a flight suit or a helmet. While the price point puts it out of range for your average cosplayer, Nagata notes that most of his clients aren't looking to suit up for a trip to Comic-Con. "A lot of the people who were [into NASA history] are older now, and they have money," he says. "I've made a lot of full suits for private collectors who always wanted one when they were a kid."

---

[7] Andrew Liptak, "Adam Savage on His Live Science Show, Cosplay, and 'Promoting the Joy in Making Things,'" *The Verge*, March 25, 2017, https://www.theverge.com/2017/3/25/15049064/adam-savage-brain-candy-live-cosplay-mythbusters-tested-building-interview.

[8] Andrew Liptak, "Adam Savage Explains Why Space Suits Are His Happy Place," *The Verge*, July 23, 2017, https://www.theverge.com/2017/7/23/16015448/adam-savage-spacesuits-cosplay-costuming-sdcc-2017.

There are other space suit costumes out on the market, but they tend to fall into two categories: cheaper ones aimed at Halloween revelers, and deluxe replicas that cost thousands of dollars, which Nagata says still aren't as detailed as his.

Other space fans, like Wayne Neumaier, have opted to build their own. Neumaier works in the aerospace industry as an engineer in Huntsville, Alabama; and while growing up, he began building his own costumes out of everything from discarded football helmets to sheet metal and soda bottles. After watching *Star Wars: Attack of the Clones*, he became interested in making costumes of his own and constructed his very own Jango Fett, then continued with V from *V for Vendetta* and one of the Ghostbusters. One of his dream costumes was a space suit. "I wanted to be an astronaut my whole life," he told me; to make one of the Apollo suits that went to the moon. He decided to re-create the A7-L model that Jim Lovell would have worn during the Apollo 13 mission.

Wayne Neumaier in his replica Apollo 13 space suit.
Courtesy of Wayne Neumaier

Like Nagata, he started by closely studying reference images, then set about sewing the bodysuit and procuring the connectors, helmet, and everything else that he needed. Eventually, he was allowed to take direct measurements from an A7 suit at the U.S. Space & Rocket Center's archives.[9] When he brought the costume to Dragon Con in 2013, he brought along an American flag to pose with and got an overwhelming reaction. "It was insane," he recounted. "I would argue that it was the most popular thing I have ever brought to Dragon Con, because everybody is familiar with the space program."

Space enthusiasts aren't limited to just NASA's Apollo-era gear, either. In September

---

9 Wayne Neumaier, "Apollo A7L Moon Suit Part 2: Examining the Real Space Suits!" 2StoryProps (website), February 2014, https://2storyprops.blogspot.com/2014/02/apollo-a7l-moon-suit-part-2-examining.html.

2017, SpaceX CEO Elon Musk unveiled the space suit that his company's astronauts would eventually wear,[10] a sleek, white-and-black suit that the company says was constructed in-house, and which included a 3D-printed helmet.[11]

As the head of carmaker Tesla and private rocket company SpaceX, Musk has attracted his own devoted fan base over the years; and some of those fans, like Neumaier, have built their own interpretations of his company's space suit,[12] designing their own 3D-printable versions that anyone with the right equipment could print out themselves.[13] Undoubtedly, as space becomes more accessible, and more private space companies enter the scene, cosplayers will follow suit and make replicas of their own.

In many ways, the efforts of space suit builders demonstrate a bridge between two adjacent but otherwise separate worlds: cosplay and living history. Space suits sit at the edge of science fiction and reality and thus serve two audiences: those enthralled with the romantic calling of space travel, and those who love the look and feel of something that was once just the stuff of science fiction.

---

10   Mike Wall, "Check Out SpaceX's New Spacesuit: Elon Musk Shares on Instagram," *Space*, September 13, 2017, https://www.space.com/38132-elon-musk-spacex-spacesuit-crew-dragon-photo.html.
11   "Dragon," SpaceX (website), accessed December 2, 2021, https://www.spacex.com/vehicles/dragon.
12   Dani Banner, "Creating a SpaceX Suit," Danban Studio (website), accessed December 2, 2021, https://danbanstudio.com/new-blog/2018/12/1/re-creating-the-spacex-iva-suit-1.
13   "SpaceX Helmet," by user Nathan720, Thingiverse (website), March 5, 2019, https://www.thingiverse.com/thing:3471482; "SpaceX Wearable Helmet from Dragon Crew," from seller Technologyrev, Etsy, accessed December 2, 2021, https://www.etsy.com/listing/692973250/space-x-wearable-helmet-from-dragon-crew.

1 THE ORIGINS OF FANDOM

At the end of June 1939, Forrest J. Ackerman and Myrtle R. Douglas boarded a train in California and set off for the first-ever World Science Fiction Convention at Caravan Hall in New York City. The event has since become one of the major foundations of the science-fiction community, an annual gathering of fans, writers, editors, and others involved in the science-fiction publishing field. While the gathering marked the start of one of fandom's main traditions, including guests of honor, panel discussions, and readers networking in person, Ackerman and Douglas helped inaugurate another mainstay: bringing their favorite fictional characters to life at a convention with a costume.

Forrest J. Ackerman and Myrtle Douglas pose at the 1939 World Science Fiction Convention
Courtesy of John L. Coker III

The practice of cosplay is widespread now, particularly among fan communities, but at the time it was almost unheard of, and Ackerman's and Douglas's costumes attracted a considerable amount of attention among the convention's attendees. While their costumes are widely recognized as the starting point for the entire cosplay movement, dressing up in costume to play a character with one's friends is not without historical precedent.

JULES VERNE

On April 2, 1877, science-fiction author Jules Verne and his family were enduring a difficult time: his wife, Honorine, was ill, and their teenage son Michel was a handful who had been shipped off to the Mettray Penal Colony in 1876 for six months, a reform school of sorts for delinquents. To provide a distraction from their troubles, Verne decided to throw an elaborate costume ball that would be a chance for the family and their neighbors to enjoy themselves.

Verne sent out nearly seven hundred invitations and told his publisher, Pierre-Jules Hetzel, that the event had his entire hometown of Amiens, France, in a state of excitement. The local paper, *Le Progrès de la Somme*, described the evening: "It was a truly magical sight, these splendid costumes sparkling beneath the chandeliers and almost blinding one in their contrast with the black formal coats worn by the sober."

Le Monde illustré wrote about the event days later: "The ball began at ten o'clock, and at that moment the sight was magical; the costumes, of remarkable richness, were sprin-

An engraving depicting Jules Verne's party, in which guests dressed up as characters from his books.

kled with news drawn from the works of the master of the house, to which he wished to render a brilliant homage by reproducing the different types created by his fertile imagination. Among the ladies, there were Indian costumes of great value and perfectly executed; the fashionable pieces provided a lot of subjects, including a lovely Marjoram. The men had Mexican, Chinese, Arab, Russian, etc. costumes."[1]

In his book *Jules Verne: An Exploratory Biography*, Herbert R. Lottman explains another feature seen throughout the evening: "Although the invitations didn't specifically call for it, many guests had the good sense to come dressed as characters from Verne novels (for example, as Hindu women—a reminder of Mrs. Aouda, the youngest widow in *Around the World in Eighty Days*)."[2] It's a good demonstration of the fandom that Verne had attracted over his career, and the passion that his books inspired in his readers.

▬ THE VRIL-YA BAZAAR

In 1871, English politician and writer Edward Bulwer-Lytton published an early science-fiction novel called *Vril: The Power of the Coming Race,* about a young miner who brings along a friend to explore a mine shaft and a recently exposed chasm. Midway through their descent, the companion is killed, and the miner discovers a vast subterranean world inhabited by angelic creatures called the Vril-ya, who show him around their city. Over the course of the book, he learns their language, discovers their telepathic abilities, and falls in love with one of their women before eventually returning to Earth's surface.

The book was a hit at the time and became influential in the budding science-fiction genre; when H. G. Wells published *The Time Machine* in 1895, reviewers compared it to Bulwer-Lytton's book. That popularity led the Royal Albert Hall to throw a Vril-themed party in 1891, which the historic concert hall has proclaimed as "the first ever sci-fi convention."[3]

Held March 5–10, 1891, the costume party was a fundraising event to support London's West End Hospital and the School of Massage and Electricity. "Visitors were encouraged to come in fancy dress, filling the Hall with various 'Coming Race' characters

---

1   "Un Bal Costumé Chez Jules Verne" [A Costume Ball at the Home of Jules Verne], *Le Monde illustré*, 21st year, no. 1044, April 14, 1877, https://laporteouverte.me/2016/11/13/un-bal-costume-chez-jules-verne.
2   Herbert R. Lottman, *Jules Verne: An Exploratory Biography* (New York: St. Martin's Press, 1996), 204.
3   Lydia Smith, "5–10 March 1891: Bovril and the First Ever Sci-Fi Convention, at the Royal Albert Hall," Royal Albert Hall (website), March 2, 2016, https://www.royalalberthall.com/about-the-hall/news/2016/march/5-10-march-1891-bovril-and-the-first-ever-sci-fi-convention-at-the-royal-albert-hall.

An illustration depicting the Royal Albert Hall's Vril-Ya Bazaar, proclaimed the first-ever sci-fi convention. *Image: Royal Albert Hall*

and generally 'exotically' costumed fans of the book." A young lady came dressed as Princess Zee, "wearing a black satin dress and silver flower tiara that glowed with electric lights," while others wore wings or were dressed in a range of foreign styles.[4] The building was decorated in Vril-ya style: "The hall was bedecked in flowers, palm leaves and ferns. A grand 'Pillar of the Vril-ya' was erected in the arena, modeled on Cleopatra's Needle. Vril-themed magic shows, a fortune telling dog, musical entertainment and grand feasts were held in the auditorium, while winged Vril-ya mannequins flew above." Vendors on-site sold trinkets and merchandise. The event appears to have been a bit ahead of its time—newspaper columnists were critical of it due to the outlandish costumes and the fantastical nature of its theme. And despite being extended for two days past its intended run, the

---

4   "'The Coming Race' and 'Vril-Ya' Bazaar and Fete, in Joint Aid of the West End Hospital, and the School of Massage and Electricity," Royal Albert Hall (website), https://memories.royalalberthall.com/content/coming-race-and-vril-ya-bazaar-and-fete-joint-aid-west-end-hospital-and-school-massage-and-1.

event had a significant dip in attendance after its opening day and was a financial disaster for its organizer, Dr. Herbert Tibbits, who ended up declaring bankruptcy.[5]

The Royal Albert Hall describes the event as a specific gathering inspired by a science-fiction story, and it does have many hallmarks of the conventions that we hold today, including vendors selling to attendees; elaborately decorated rooms meant to bring another world to life; and of course, fantastical costumes.

MR. SKYGACK

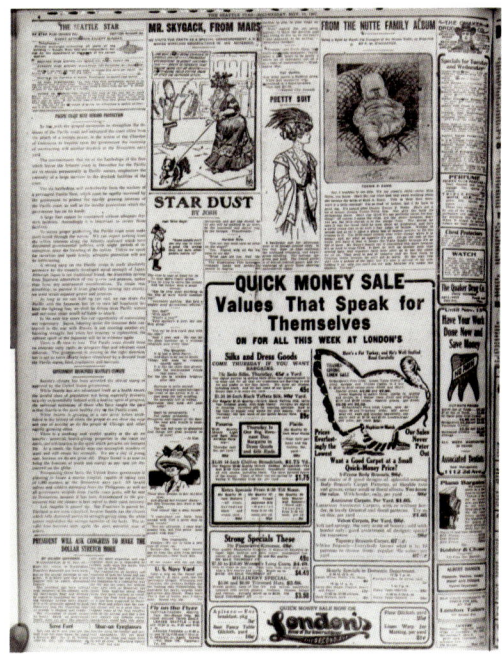

An installment of *Mr. Skygack, From Mars*, originally published on November 13, 1907, which provided plenty of costuming inspiration for early fans.

Costuming wasn't always limited to an event like a party or bazaar. Another early example of cosplay are the fans of a comic strip called *Mr. Skygack, From Mars*.

In 1907, writer Fred Schaefer and cartoonist A. D. Condo created the comic strip, which ran until 1911. It followed the observations of a hapless Martian who arrived on Earth to study humans, generally misinterpreting or misunderstanding the strange behaviors and actions of Earth's inhabitants. Condo depicted the titular Skygack as a humanoid alien, with an elongated, bristly head and large eyes, often dressed in a long smock. The cartoon's tagline summed up his mission: "He Visits the Earth as a Special Correspondent and Makes Wireless Observations in His Notebook." The *Encyclopedia of Science Fiction* describes the cartoon as "possibly the first sf comic, . . . almost certainly the first continuing depiction of an extraterrestrial being in comics form."[6]

---

5   Alex Palmer, "The Strange Story of the Vril-Ya Bazaar and Fete, the 'World's First Sci-Fi Convention,'" *Mental Floss*, May 31, 2021, https://www.mentalfloss.com/article/646499/first-sci-fi-convention-vril-ya-bazaar.
6   *The Encyclopedia of Science Fiction*, A D Condo (entry), updated May 24, 2017, http://www.sf-encyclopedia.com/entry/condo_a_d.

THE ORIGINS OF FANDOM   15

Newspapers across the country picked up the cartoon, and it drew a large fan base, inspiring some to try to re-create the character themselves. On December 19, 1908, the *Spokane Press* featured an illustration depicting a man named William A. Fell and his wife, who had attended a "mask skating carnival" as Mr. Skygack and Diana Dillpickles, another popular cartoon character. "Both the costumes closely followed those of the comic characters made familiar to the public through their appearance in the cartoons of Artist Condo."[7]

They weren't alone: just two years later, on March 8, 1910, the *Tacoma Times* ran an article on the front page: IMITATOR OF "MR. SKYGACK FROM MARS" IS ARRESTED.

"This startling news spread about town today and caused intense excitement, for no one is better known and more widely liked than is Mr. Skygack, whose odd picture and quaint sayings printed in the *Times* have made him a favorite in most every home in Tacoma. But it wasn't the real 'Mr. Skygack from Mars' who landed in the city jail. It was only an imitation of the original 'Mr. Skygack' and that's what caused the trouble."[8]

The costumer in question was Otto James, and he had worn the costume on Tacoma's Pacific Avenue earlier in the day to help advertise for a local skating rink. The police officers who arrested him determined that he had violated a city ordinance that banned costumes in public, and he was released after he paid his bail of ten dollars.

James wasn't responsible for building the costume. According to the paper, he had "borrowed the Skygack costume from a young lady who wore it at a masque ball recently and took the prize."[9]

Two years later, another Mr. Skygack popped up in the news. On May 24, 1912, the *Tacoma Times* ran a picture on its front page: WINS FIRST PRIZE AS "SKYGACK." A reader, August Olson, who lived sixty miles away in Monroe, Washington, had sent in a picture of a costume that he had worn in a local "masked ball," at which he earned first prize.[10] Like his cartoon counterpart, Olson wore a mask with an elongated head and big eyes, along with a long white smock. To top off the costume, he carried a notepad upon which to make his observations of the human race.

---

7   Luke Plunkett, "Cosplay Is Over 100 Years Old," *Kotaku*, May 16, 2016, https://cosplay.kotaku.com/cosplay-is-over-100-years-old-1777013405.
8   "Imitator of 'Mr. Skygack from Mars' Is Arrested," *Tacoma Times*, vol. VII, no. 67, March 8, 1910, 1, https://www.newspapers.com/image/68052071/?terms=skygack.
9   "Imitator of 'Mr. Skygack from Mars' Is Arrested."
10 "Wins First Prize as 'Skygack,' " *Tacoma Times*, vol. IX, no. 133, May 24, 1912, 1, https://www.newspapers.com/image/68080662/?terms=skygack.

The spate of Mr. Skygack costumes that made headlines in the United States underlines a couple of notable things. The cartoon was a recognizable story, and simple enough that individuals could put together a depiction of the character on their own. Their efforts were enough to garner coverage in the local papers and even win prizes in costume contests. These are also examples of instances where costumes were utilized outside of the usual theatrical production or Halloween celebration. They were used for amusement: for contests, or to attract attention as an advertisement.

But science fiction was about to become much bigger than a newspaper comic strip: it would become a world and community unto itself.

THE ORIGINS OF SCIENCE-FICTION FANDOM

Science fiction has a deep, rich past—one that sees its roots stretch back to ancient times. Fans and scholars often point to Mary Shelley's 1818 novel *Frankenstein: or, The Modern Prometheus* as its most recognizable origin point, followed by the works of authors like Edgar Allan Poe, Jules Verne, H. G. Wells, and many, many others. In the early twentieth century, one enterprising editor, Hugo Gernsback, founded *Amazing Stories* magazine, the first publication dedicated to the types of stories that would come to be known as "science fiction." Born in Luxembourg in 1884, Gernsback immigrated to the United States at age twenty and quickly set up a magazine called *Modern Electrics*, which featured articles and fiction geared toward radio enthusiasts, as well as parts that they could buy.

Gernsback was already a fan of a growing body of fiction featuring fantastic technologies written by authors such as Shelley, Wells, Verne, and Poe, and he began to include short, science-driven stories in his own publications, including his own serialized novel, *Ralph 124C 41+*.

Gernsback wasn't the first editor to solicit and include science fiction in his publications, but he recognized the appetite from technologically minded readers, who yearned to imagine what the future might hold—especially what gadgets they might someday use. To feed that appetite, he founded *Amazing Stories* in 1926.

Amazing Stories was a lightning strike in a primordial pond: a jolt of energy to the right set of ingredients. Its bold, garish covers and fantastical content attracted many would-be science-fiction writers and fans, and it quickly became a hit at newsstands.

Gernsback quickly added other serials to his lineup, such as *Air Wonder Stories*, *Science Wonder Quarterly*, and *Scientific Detective Monthly*. In his magazines, Gernsback introduced a useful feature for his readers: a letter column that allowed them to respond to stories or one another and locate nearby fans.

Gernsback wanted to build a durable audience that would remain engaged with his publications (and thus continue to buy them) and in 1934 launched a fan club called the Science Fiction League, with local chapters scattered around the world. The desire to meet and interact with other fans grew beyond Gernsback's network; groups like the Futurians in New York City and the Los Angeles Science Fantasy Society have their roots as his club's chapters, but eventually established their own identities. These groups brought together science-fiction fans for regular meetings to socialize, discuss their favorite stories, and critique one another's stories. Out of these fan clubs emerged some of the genre's foundational individuals, such as Isaac Asimov, Ray Bradbury, Frederik Pohl, C. L. Moore, and Forrest Ackerman, who encouraged and competed with one another to break into the growing field of magazines.

■ THE FIRST WORLDCON

The emergence of organized fandom led to larger gatherings: conventions that brought together hundreds of fans from all around the country, and eventually from around the world. The 1939 World Science Fiction Convention's organizers drew around two hundred fans and writers from all over the United States, including the likes of Asimov and Bradbury, as well as professionals like *Astounding Science Fiction* editor John W. Campbell Jr. Also among their numbers were fans like Ackerman and Douglas—who went by the Esperanto name Morojo—soon to revolutionize costuming with cosplay.

The pair hailed from Los Angeles, California, and had each been heavily involved in the local science-fiction scene. Ackerman was born in 1916 and fell in love with science fiction at age ten when his mother gave him a copy of Gernsback's *Amazing Stories*.

Ackerman jumped feet-first into fandom, quickly amassing a personal library of dozens of other science-fiction magazines. He began writing stories of his own, although he never seriously pursued a career as a science-fiction writer as other fans like Asimov and Bradbury did. Instead, he began writing letters to magazines and fellow fans. In the 1930s, he set up a fan club of his own—the Boys' Scientifiction Club, wrote for various science-fiction fanzines, and was an early member of the Los Angeles Science Fantasy Society. He's widely considered to have coined the abbreviation "sci-fi."

It was within this circle of science-fiction fans that he caught the eye of Myrtle Rebecca Douglas in 1937. They were both attendees of a world language meeting for the fictional language Esperanto, and they had a lot in common.

Douglas was a devoted science-fiction fan, and the two of them collaborated on a fanzine called *Imagination!*, the LASFS's official publication. Ackerman later recalled that she helped produce the printed edition: "She was a real pro in the typing, stenciling & mimeoing departments. An excellent proof-reader. And she was a staunch supporter of nonstoparagraphing & Ackermanese, god bless her—I say, fully conscious of the fact that she was an atheist."[11]

But she was also interested in costumes, and when she and Ackerman traveled across the country to attend the 1939 World Science Fiction Convention, she created two costumes for them to wear for the event. "She designed & executed my famous 'futuristicostume'—and her own—worn at the First World Science-Fiction Convention, the Nycon of 1939."[12] The costumes were based on a film that the pair had enjoyed: an adaptation of H. G. Wells's novel *Things to Come*. Ackerman's costume consisted of a green satin cape and a long-sleeved, button-down yellow shirt emblazoned with his nickname, 4SJ. In his memories of the convention, Ackerman noted that they had based the costume on Frank R. Paul's artwork and the film, and he described it as being like "mild-mannered Clark Kent, going into the telephone booth and coming out as Superman."[13]

In his book *Bradbury: An Illustrated Life*, Jerry Weist wrote that "this was really the beginning of costumes and the masquerade at conventions." The pair were surprised that they were the only people dressed up in costume, and [that] the reaction was one of confusion, according to Ray Bradbury's biographer, Sam Weller, who told me that "People asked them, 'What the heck are you doing?'"

"I just kind of thought everybody was going to come as spacemen or vampires or one thing or another," Weller recounts Ackerman saying in *The Ray Bradbury Chronicles: The Life*

---

11 Forrest J. Ackerman, "I Remember Morojo" (privately printed), February 11, 1965, http://efanzines.com/Morojo/Morojo-AnAppreciation-1965.pdf.
12 Ackerman, "I Remember Morojo."
13 Forrest J. Ackerman, "Through Time and Space with Forry Ackerman, Part 1," *Mimosa* (magazine), no. 16, December 1994, http://www.jophan.org/mimosa/m16/ackerman.htm.

of Ray Bradbury. "We walked through the streets of Manhattan with children crying and pointing: 'It's Flash Gordon! It's Buck Rogers!' "[14]

"I even got the nerve to go out to the World's Fair in it; they had a platform with a microphone, and if you were from Spain, or from Sweden or France or Germany or wherever, you could come up and greet the world in your native language. So I got this quixotic notion to go up and speak in Esperanto to the world, and say that I was a time traveler from the future, where we all spoke this language."[15]

In one picture, Ackerman is looking at the camera, a grin plastered across his face, dressed in high boots, uniform pants, and a textured vest over a collared shirt. The entire outfit makes him look like one of those characters from the covers of the pulp magazines. In another, Ackerman towers over Douglas, who is wearing an advanced-looking dress. In his memoir, *The Way the Future Was*, science-fiction editor Frederik Pohl recounted the scene: "We met Californians like Forrest J.

Forrest J. Ackerman poses for a picture at the first-ever World Science Fiction Convention. Made by his then-girlfriend, Myrtle Douglas, this outfit is considered to be the starting point of costuming within the science-fiction community.

Courtesy of John L. Coker III

Ackerman and his feminine sidekick Morojo, both of them stylishly dressed in fashions of the Twenty-First Century and turning heads in every cafeteria they entered."[16]

This moment is a notable one: while this wasn't the first gathering of fans, it was the first large-scale convention for which fans from all over the country assembled, demonstrating to all involved (and also those unable to attend) that they weren't alone in their interests. During these early days, science fiction's visual depictions came through the artwork that graced the cover of pulp magazines and the occasional science-fiction film,

---

14   Sam Weller, *The Ray Bradbury Chronicles: The Life of Ray Bradbury* (New York: HarperCollins, 2005), 95.
15   Ackerman, "Through Time and Space with Forry Ackerman, Part 1."
16   Frederik Pohl, *The Way the Future Was* (New York: Ballantine Books, 1978), 95–96.

like *Metropolis* or *Things to Come*. Moreover, while people certainly dressed up for costume parties and masquerade contests prior to this moment, the convention appears to be the first time that we see the two phenomena together.

What makes this moment even more significant is that it demonstrated that a fan's expression of their love of science fiction wasn't entirely text-based. While fans wrote their own magazines, artwork, stories, and letters to one another, each of which contributed to the original framework that is fandom, Douglas and Ackerman demonstrated that they could also express that fandom in the real world.

They wouldn't be alone.

2 CONVENTION MASQUERADES

While the first instance of a larger movement is a historic moment, a repeat performance is just as important: it ensures that the original experience wasn't a one-off. After Ackerman and Douglas's foray into costuming at the 1939 convention, fans ensured that costuming and costume masquerades would become a major part of future science-fiction conventions and Worldcons.

Once the first World Science Fiction Convention had concluded, the fan community quickly determined that the next would take place in Chicago on September 1–2, 1940. That year's convention, ChiCon, included a more robust schedule, including a Science Fiction Masquerade Party to be hosted by fans Jack Speer and Milton A. Rothman.

Fans from around the country, including Ackerman and Douglas, made their way to Chicago for the weekend's festivities. This time, the pair was joined by others who brought along their own costumes for the costume contest. "The notion had caught on," Ackerman later wrote. "And we now had about twenty-five fans in costume."[1] Their number included the likes of E. E. "Doc" Smith, author of the Lensman series, one of arguably the biggest series in the genre at the time, who dressed up as one of C. L. Moore's characters, Northwest Smith.

"The masquerade didn't start until nine o'clock p.m., faithful to the tradition that

---

1 Ackerman, "Through Time and Space with Forry Ackerman, Part 1."

convention events may not proceed on schedule," Harry Warner Jr. writes in his history of the early days of science-fiction fandom, *All Our Yesterdays: An Informal History of Science Fiction Fandom in the 1940s*. "Costumed fans walked one by one to the dais, and identified the characters they represented."

"The masquerade Sunday evening contained many fannish props that have survived throughout the years, water pistols were unholstered, and weapons described as dart guns—almost certainly primitive plonkers—were in use."[2]

Warner recounted some of the other costumes that made an appearance: author Cyril M. Kornbluth appeared as the Invisible Man, George Tullis showed up as L. Sprague de Camp's character Johnny Black, Jack Speer was Buck Rogers, Doc Smith's daughter Honey dressed up as her father's character Nurse MacDougall, and plenty of others. "Dave Kyle won first prize as Ming the Merciless, Emperor of Mongo," he wrote, while "[Robert] Lowndes in a pale orange robe took second award, as the Bar Senestro, of *The Blind Spot*."[3]

Ackerman and Douglas returned with the same costumes they had brought to New York the year before, but were prepared to add more. "Morojo (the leading femfan of the time) and I appeared at the costume affair in our original futuristicostumes," Ackerman wrote in a later remembrance, "and this time did a little skit together, doing dialog from HG Wells's film *Things to Come*."[4] The pair won third prize in the contest.

During the event, Ackerman realized that the group could potentially garner some additional attention for both the convention and the genre. "I thought, why waste the opportunity to garner some publicity for the convention and science fiction in general, so I gathered the gang together and we paraded thru the lamplit streets of Chicago to a newspaper office four or five blocks away."[5]

"I went up to him with a straight face," Ackerman wrote of a stranger. "He was looking at these Martians and other futuristic people, and wondered what in the world had hit him—so with a straight face, I said, 'Well, sir, we are time travelers. Tomorrow, we picked up your paper and we found this photograph of ourselves and

---

2   Harry Warner Jr., *All Our Yesterdays: An Informal History of Science Fiction Fandom in the 1940s* (Framingham: NESFA Press, 2004), 135–36.
3   Warner, *All Our Yesterdays*, 135.
4   "1940 – Chicon I, Chicago," from the Noreascon 3 program book, 1989, https://fancyclopedia.org/Chicon_I_Reminiscence_(Ackerman).
5   "1940-Chicon I, Chicago."

this interview. So we realized that we'd have to come back in our time machine to be interviewed!' "[6]

This supposed interview never made it into the paper.

The group's costumes did attract some unwanted attention, according to Warner. "Speer, in a golden radio helmet, flying belt vest, helium gun, and shorts, attracted the attention of a policeman. The officer first threatened to call a patrol wagon, then tossed in a heretical manner several auction originals to the street, and simmered down only when Speer proved his identity and business by means of cards showing him to be a federal employee."[7]

The third Worldcon took place in 1941 in Denver, and as with the two conventions that preceded it, costumes were once again part of the weekend. American science-fiction author Robert Heinlein was the convention's guest of honor, and he attended with his wife, Leslyn. In his biography, *Robert A. Heinlein: In Dialogue with His Century, Volume 1, 1907–1948: Learning Curve*, William H. Patterson Jr. wrote that the earlier conventions were a far cry from the major events that they have become today—thousands of guests taking part in numerous programming tracks—"with only two hundred or so people, Robert and Leslyn were highly visible."[8]

As in the prior convention, attendees (except for Heinlein, it seems) came prepared: Edward Everett "E. E." Evans ultimately took first prize in the contest, in an elaborately constructed "A Bird Man from Rhea" costume, which a fan named James LeRoy "Rusty" Hevelin described in a fanzine as "vividly colored, each feather being put on separately, and the eyes (cockeyed) were up in stalks." Walter J. "Doc" Daugherty took home the contest's second-place honor for his space suit costume cobbled together out of parts from the airplane factory where he was employed; one that Hevelin described as including a "plastiglass helmet, shoulder guards, ray gun, and a protuberance on the headpiece which was purported to be a means of thought expression. From the shoulder guards, a flowing black cloak fell down behind a suit of blue and gold."[9]

Ackerman and Douglas were also in attendance and brought new costumes to show off. Ackerman, who ended up getting the night's third prize, had teamed up with future

---

6 Ackerman, "Through Time and Space with Forry Ackerman, Part 1."
7 Warner, *All Our Yesterdays*, 137.
8 William H. Patterson Jr., *Robert A. Heinlein: In Dialogue with His Century, Volume 1, 1907–1948: Learning Curve* (New York: Tor Books , 2010), 279.
9 Warner, *All Our Yesterdays*, 137.

LEFT: At the 1941 World Science Fiction Convention in Denver, Colorado, E. E. Evans wowed fellow con-goers with his Bird Man costume, which featured thousands of feathers added to a mask.

RIGHT: Walter J. Daugherty poses at the World Science Fiction Convention in Denver, Colorado, in 1941. He worked at a defense manufacturer and was able to create his costume out of parts he'd fished out of the trash at his workplace.

Photos courtesy of John L. Coker III

monster maker and animator Ray Harryhausen, who created for him a grotesque mask that Hevelin described as "somewhat loose in the front and he achieved a rather grisly effect by purposeful breathing." Douglas was dressed as a member of the frog-like Akka from A. Merritt's novel *The Moon Pool*.[10]

Other costumers included Chet Cohen (dressed as a prophet from Heinlein's stories), Bill Deutsch (Dr. Pinero from Heinlein's story "Life-Line"), Cyril M. Kornbluth (a mad scientist), Erle M. Korshak (a skeleton), Damon Knight (John Star from Jack Williamson's *The Legion of Space*), Robert A. W. Lowndes (a zombie with a slashed throat), and Elmer Moukel (The Probable Man).

Heinlein, who had been caught off-guard by the costume contest, entered anyway, as "Adam Stink, the world's most lifelike robot," while Leslyn arrived at the contest dressed in "Oriental" garb as Queen Niafer of Cabell's *Figures of Earth*.[11]

---

10 Warner, *All Our Yesterdays*, 137.
11 Patterson Jr., *Robert Heinlein: In Dialogue with His Century*, 279.

CONVENTION MASQUERADES

After the contest, fans flocked to the winners and their costumes. "They were marveling over the greater wonders at the convention," Warner wrote, noting that there was much talk about "the fact that Daugherty would have been forced to pay $500 for the glass in his helmet if he hadn't salvaged it from the trash pile at his airplane factory, or the painstaking way in which each feather had been attached to the Evans costume."[12]

The onset of World War II put a damper on fan activities for the next couple of years, as a number of authors and fans were called to serve in the war. The planned 1942 Worldcon in Los Angeles, Pacificon I, was postponed because of fears over a Japanese invasion of America's West Coast—members voted to table the conference until the end of the war.[13] When it did finally come to a close, organizers began planning for a return in 1946. The convention's pre-event progress report prominently advertised the costume ball: "One of the highlights of interest at all Conventions is the Costume Ball, where everyone tries to outdo the others with the costumes of famous or outré characters from the stories you have read"; and specifically called back to Ackerman's and Douglas's costumes in the first Worldcon, not even a decade in the past. The organizers promised an even larger event: "This year we can expect bigger and better costumes than ever before," they wrote, "for we have had delicate little hints that many fen are planning finer and more elaborate and more bizarre costumes than ever before."[14]

The convention's program booklet advertised the masquerade for July 6, the final night of the con,[15] but that year's convention appears to have been a subdued affair: Ackerman, one of the chief organizers of the event, fell ill, and Warner recounts that the "masquerade ball that night was not much of a masquerade or a ball, on the whole."[16] Some fans dressed up, such as Paul Cater (future cowboy), Douglas (a snake woman), Evans (who reprised his Bird Man costume from the previous convention), Dale Hart (Gray Lensman, from E. E. "Doc" Smith's Lensman series), Nieson Himmel (a character from L. Sprague de Camp's novella *The Stolen Dormouse*), Pat Kenealy (Cthulhu from H. P. Lovecraft's mythos), Art Joquel (a wizard), Charles Lucas (the priest from S. Fowler

---

12   Warner, *All Our Yesterdays*, 144.
13   Warner, *All Our Yesterdays*, 205.
14   "Pacificon Fourth World Science Fiction Convention News," No. 2, June 1946, https://fanac.org/conpubs/Worldcon/Pacificon%20I/1946%20-%20Pacificon%20-%20PR%202.pdf#view=Fit.
15   "Pacificon Program Booklet," July 1946, https://fanac.org/conpubs/Worldcon/Pacificon%20I/Pacificon%20Program%20Book.pdf#view=Fit.
16   Warner, *All Our Yesterdays*, 327.

Members of Pacificon I in 1946: From left to right: [Unknown], [Unknown], Morojo, [Unknown], Walter J. Daugherty (cowboy hat), Eleanor O'Brien, Forrest J. Ackerman, Virginia Laney, Leslyn Heinlein, and Roland Dushington.

Courtesy of John L. Coker III

Wright's 1928 novel *The Island of Captain Sparrow*), Len Moffatt (Vincent the Vampire), and Ralph Rayburn Phillips (a Tibetan Buddhist). Several attendees were honored for their originality and creativity in crafting their costumes.

There doesn't appear to have been a masquerade at the 1947 Worldcon, Philcon I, or the following year at Torcon I in Toronto, but 1949's Cinvention in Cincinnati, Ohio, featured a masquerade that closed out the convention. By this point, fandom as a cultural institution and the conventions that had sprung forth from it were becoming regular, formalized events.

The members of Torcon held a formal fan survey that tried to take stock of the number of fans, their reading habits, interests, beliefs, and more, while also emphasizing the importance of bringing in new fans to the movement.[17] The conventions were becoming increasingly well-known, pulling in hundreds and thousands of dollars to fund their operations, and began to draw fans from not only the US but other countries as well. Cinvention had the distinction of hosting a televised half-hour program, which organizers billed as the "biggest event in the history of fandom."[18]

In the Worldcons that followed, the masquerade became a regular feature. In the program booklet for Philcon II in 1953, the organizers pointed to the masquerade as an ongoing tradition and "high point" within the convention circuit. That year marked the first time the convention held a formal award ceremony to honor the artists, fans, publications, and works that they had gathered to celebrate—an award that would eventually

---

17 "Torcon Report," edited and compiled by Edward N. McKeown, published by the House of York for the Torcon Society, Toronto, 1948, https://fanac.org/conpubs/Worldcon/Torcon%20I/Torcon%20Report.pdf#view=Fit.
18 "Science, Fantasy, and Science Fiction," *The Magazine of Facts and Fiction: The Cinvention Supplement to Vol. 2, No. 2*, 1950, https://fanac.org/conpubs/Worldcon/Cinvention/1949%20-%20Cinvention%20Post%20Con%20Report.pdf#view=Fit.

Olga Ley, appearing at the 1954 Worldcon, SFCon, in San Francisco, dressed as "Deep Space."

Olga Ley poses for a picture at the 1956 World Science Fiction Convention in New York City.

Photos courtesy of John L. Coker III

be called the Hugo Award, science fiction's highest honor. The festivities began on September 6 at seven p.m. and were followed by the convention's costume party, which ran until midnight. The night's festivities of course included a costume contest (for which winners would receive a year's subscription to a number of science-fiction magazines) as well as an appearance by Bob Courtleigh, the lead actor in NBC's sci-fi series *Atom Squad*. According to the program, he'd "attend in costume—but not to compete."[19]

The post-con report was glowing: "Last night with the Con spirit pervading the atmosphere bubblingly, the perennial masquerade, a convention tradition, was executed with the usual attitude of light-heartedness that has been the keynote for past masquerades." Leslie Perri, a longtime fan and writer, earned a callout for her portrayal of "The Lady in Red," as did an unnamed fan dressed as a BEM (Bug-Eyed Monster) "with a massive stomach," and a couple from Detroit dressed as Buck Rogers and Wilma. "There was no dearth of innovation either at the audience level, having dozens of cleverly worked up outfits and esoteric puns in costume," the newsletter's authors wrote.[20]

---

19   "Eleventh World Science Fiction Convention Program Book," Philadelphia, September 1953, https://fanac.org/conpubs/Worldcon/Philcon%20II/Philcon%202%20Program%20Book.pdf#view=Fit.
20   Dave Kyle, Harlan Ellison, George J. Viksnins, Karl Osen, Norman O. Browne, David Ish, ed., *Philcon Reporter*, published by and for the Eleventh World Science Fiction Convention, Philadelphia, September 1953, https://fanac.org/conpubs/Worldcon/Philcon%20II/Philcon%20Reporter%20Kyle,%20Ellison%20et%20al%201953-09-07%20Mon.pdf#view=Fit.

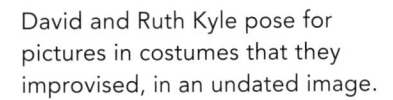

David and Ruth Kyle pose for pictures in costumes that they improvised, in an undated image.

Alex Eisenstein poses for a picture at Midwestcon sometime in the 1950s.

Photos courtesy of John L. Coker III

Like the conventions that hosted them, the costume masquerades and parties were growing. In his memoir . . . *Always a Fan*, author and editor Mike Resnick noted that while the costuming scene had started out as an informal part of the convention's programming, it began to take on a more prominent role as fans approached it more seriously. "Perhaps the first great costumer was Olga Ley, the wife of writer and scientist Willy Ley, who wore a series of stunning costumes in the late 1950s."[21]

Conventions that followed began to advertise masquerades as part of their programming: the ChiCon II flyer listed the "'Flying Saucers'—A Science-Fiction Masquerade" at midnight on August 31, 1952, hosted by "The Elves', Gnomes', and Little Men's Science-Fiction, Chowder and Marching Society of Berkeley, California."[22] In the lead-up to the event, the con's organizers noted that "one third of those attending the convention promised to be at the ball in costume, and most of the rest mentioned that they'd like to be there

---

21 Mike Resnick, . . . *Always a Fan: True Stories from a Life in Science Fiction* (Rockville: Wildside Press, 2009), 68.
22 "World Science Fiction Convention Program," Chicago, August 30, 1952, http://files.johnbray.org.uk/Documents/Fandom/Conventions/World/Worldcon/Chicon%20II/Program%20Book.pdf.

to see the fun dressed as Earthmen, circa 1952."[23] The event would come with a contest with "humorous prizes for the best costumes," as well as music and refreshments.

Notably, the organizers explained that people didn't have to go all out to make an elaborate costume. "Maybe the reason you voted that you wouldn't be at the masque in costume was because you visualized 'costume' as a $150 custom-draped spacesuit or a 20 foot snakeskin to make you look like Worsel of Velantia. Did you ever think that a costume need not be an elaborate rented affair? That you could be a slan in a business suit—provided you just gilded a few front strands of your hair? . . . A little ingenuity can make you a clever costume at little cost."[24]

The invitation also reveals some of the earlier, male-dominated tendencies of fandom, as women were encouraged to "be Bergey fems, but you'll have just as much fun in an evening dress wearing a hat called 'The Conquest of Space.' And has anyone thought of coming as a tesseract or that new Minsky attraction, the Moebius Strip?"[25] The innuendo is readily apparent.

SFCon, the 1954 World Science Fiction Convention in San Francisco, likewise advertised a masquerade.[26] "What a gala event we hope to make it," wrote Poul Anderson. "I have seen the three paintings by George Faraco, which will be given away as prizes for the best costumes. The first prize will be a large canvas, showing Earth seen from a space station; the other two are lunar landscapes."[27]

Pictures from the event include monsters, aliens, and others. Costumers like Olga Ley and Jessica Cramer turned up to the event wearing costumes inspired by the science-fiction genre; Ley dressed in black clothing adorned with silver stars as "Deep Space," while Cramer simply dressed up in a ball gown, her hair dusted with glitter to appear as "Miss Galaxy."[28]

In a convention progress report for Clevention a year later, the organizers reported that "fans have accepted the Masquerade Ball as an integral part of each convention and since

---

23 "Masquerade Theme 'Flying Saucers,'" *Who Comes to Science Fiction Conventions?*, Bulletin no. 3, June 1952, http://files.johnbray.org.uk/Documents/Fandom/Conventions/World/Worldcon/Chicon%20II/PR%203.pdf.
24 "Masquerade Theme 'Flying Saucers.'"
25 "Masquerade Theme 'Flying Saucers.'"
26 *SFCon Progress Report No. 1*, https://fanac.org/conpubs/Worldcon/SFCon/1954%20-%20SFCon%20-%20PR%201.pdf.
27 "Progress Report," *SFCon Progress Report #4*, San Francisco, August 1954, https://fanac.org/conpubs/Worldcon/SFCon/1954%20-%20SFCon%20-%20PR%204.pdf.
28 "Masquerade," *Clevention Progress Report #2*, 13th World Science Fiction Convention, Cleveland, September 1955, http://files.johnbray.org.uk/Documents/Fandom/Conventions/World/Worldcon/Clevention/PR%202.pdf.

each succeeding Masquerade has improved over its predecessor, we found no reason to bypass this highly delightful feature."[29] The organizers provided pictures of costumes from earlier conventions as inspiration for aspiring costumers.

The conventions that followed over the course of the rest of the decade—NyCon II (1956), Loncon I (1957), Solacon (1958), and Detention (1959)—all featured masquerades as social events, allowing con-goers to mingle and have fun after a day of attending panels and readings.

Astrid Bear, a longtime science-fiction fan and daughter of authors Poul and Karen Anderson, described fandom of the 1950s and 1960s as much less robust than its present-day configuration. Conventions at the time were "very small," she told me in an interview, and fans might have only one or two conventions to attend each year, rather than one almost every weekend throughout the year.

Dorothy J. Heydt and Astrid Bear pose as members of Starfleet from *Star Trek* at Westercon XXII in Santa Monica, California, in July 1969.

Courtesy of Meg Creelman

Fans were also different, she notes: "People tended to be generalists at the time. They'd be someone who read all the science-fiction magazines, and published a fanzine, and maybe also the costuming, and maybe also did some writing."

Bear says her family had long been interested in costuming. "I grew up going to science-fiction conventions, and my mother loved costuming—her mother made costumes for her when she was young—and had majored in theater arts at Catholic University." That background helped her with her own costumes in the early days of science-fiction fandom in the 1950s, "just for the fun of it, [and] then [she] got involved in the masquerade scene at the Worldcons."

By the 1960s, fans were spending more and more time on their costumes, Resnick

---

29 "Masquerade," https://fanac.org/conpubs/Worldcon/Clevention/1955%20-%20Clevention%20-%20PR%202.pdf .

explained in his book. "Fans spent considerable time—weeks, sometimes months—preparing their costumes," coming up with creative and vibrant outfits to bring with them. "Since the costumes were far less elaborate than by modern standards, a number of pros also participated. Perhaps the most famous was beloved old E. E. 'Doc' Smith coming to the 1962 Chicon masquerade as C. L. Moore's 'Northwest Smith.' "[30]

But as the event became a mainstay within science-fiction fandom, it was evolving into more than just a night of partying. The masquerade represented more than showing off a costume: it was about bringing the entire experience of the character to life. Contestants would enter their costume and would then go up onstage to perform before the gathered crowd: they might reenact a scene as their character or otherwise put on a performance or sketch. The event has remained central at the World Science Fiction Convention (now called Worldcon), as well as other cons throughout the world, with a formalized divisional system (broken up by age and skill level, ranging from novice to journeyman to master) and rules for participants.

Lensman author E. E. "Doc" Smith poses as Northwest Smith from C. L. Moore's short stories at the 1962 Worldcon, ChiCon III in Chicago, Illinois.

Courtesy of John L. Coker III

But the ways in which convention attendees were costuming was changing as well. For many of those early conventions, costuming was relegated to the costume party or masquerade, and attendees didn't necessarily go out in costume to panels or to interact with fans or their fellow costumers. "Hall costuming kind of started getting going in the late 1960s," Bear says. In contrast to the masquerade costumes, hall costumes were more casual and could be worn all day, like an officer from *Star Trek*. This came from a mindset of "making something interesting and unique and wearing it for more than a couple of hours," Bear says.

Over the course of the 1950s, '60s, and '70s, science-fiction fandom grew to become a global community with a shared love for the same stories. With that organization came regular events and traditions, which now included costuming, laying the groundwork for the cosplayers who would follow in the coming decades.

---

30   Resnick, . . . *Always a Fan*, 69.

3 RELIVING STORIES OF THE PAST

Poul Anderson at Medieval Tourney, Baycon, 1968.
Courtesy University of California, Riverside. Photo by Jay Kay Klein

While science fiction provided fandom with plenty of inspiration for futuristic characters, aliens, robots, and more, its members weren't interested in only what was to come: many were keenly interested in the distant past as well, and found inspiration in garments and stories from throughout history.

On May 1, 1966, a group of science-fiction and fantasy fans gathered at the home of Diana Paxson for a party in Berkeley, California. Those invited were told to expect a tournament, and that they were being summoned as "knights to defend in single combat the title of 'fairest' for their ladies."[1]

That event kicked off a major costuming and reenactment organization called the Society for Creative Anachronism (SCA), which is dedicated to "the research and re-creation of pre-seventeenth-century skills, arts, combat, culture, and employing knowledge of history to enrich the lives of participants through events, demonstrations, and other educational presentations and activities."[2]

---

1 "What Is the SCA?" Society for Creative Anachronism (website), accessed December 3, 2021, http://socsen.sca.org/what-is-the-sca.
2 "What Is the SCA?"

Paxson was part of a group of writers known as the Greyhaven, which included Marion Zimmer Bradley, Paul Edwin Zimmer, Poul Anderson, and a number of others. As Michael A. Cramer describes in his history of the organization, *Medieval Fantasy as Performance: The Society for Creative Anachronism and the Current Middle Ages*, Paxson's intention was less a show of historical accuracy and more performance "done in a tongue-in-cheek fashion, combining period elements with a modern sense of irony." Some people who attended the event showed up as knights, "but others as fantasy characters. There was even a Napoleonic officer, a Roman, and a hobbit."[3]

Cramer explains that the group was simply there to have a good time, and that "this tolerance of variety allowed members of the SCA to have experiences that were emotionally authentic, as they employed those faux medieval (and in this case classical) tropes they brought with them."[4] The party was a success, and Paxson held another one later that summer, then again the following year. They rented out parks to hold their tournaments, and by 1968, the group had incorporated into a formal organization with an established governance structure, and staged a tournament during that fall's World Science Fiction Convention.

That demonstration helped to raise the profile of the group, but it also helped change how con-goers thought about costumes. "People who were involved in the SCA were wearing their clothing all day, or maybe all weekend," Astrid Bear recalled. "I think that's another cross-pollination moment between the idea of just wearing something for a couple of hours at a masquerade versus wearing something fantastical or historical for the entire weekend." The convention's post-event report highlighted not only the *Star Trek* exhibit but also the SCA event: "The Medieval Tourney held on the Hotel lawn Monday afternoon was a riot of colorful costumes, banners, and pavilions, with enough swordplay to satisfy the most sanguine, and authentic medieval music presented live before the tourney. Later that night a medieval party hosted by the BayCon committee was enjoyed by many with much free beer and crazy medieval dancing."[5]

That same year, Marion Zimmer Bradley moved to New York, where she set up a new chapter of the SCA, the Eastern Kingdom, bringing it to a new coast. The following year, members set up the Middle Kingdom, centered in the Chicago area. Other such groups sprang up around the country in the years that followed, transforming the group

---

3   Michael A. Cramer, *Medieval Fantasy as Performance: The Society for Creative Anachronism and the Current Middle Ages* (Lanham, MD: Scarecrow Press, 2010), 2.
4   Cramer, *Medieval Fantasy as Performance*, 2.
5   "BayCon: A Report from the Chairmen," 26th World Science Fiction Convention (BayCon), 1968, https://fanac.org/conpubs/Worldcon/Baycon/Baycon%20-%20Report%20from%20the%20Chairman.pdf.

A member of the SCA takes part in a mock battle at Northeast Wars in Essex, Vermont, in 2009. *Courtesy of Andrew Liptak*

into a vibrant, sometimes cantankerous organization. Cramer points to arguments that it offered a utopian fantasy in which people would make up their own rules for an alternate society, one that cleaves closely to the story of medieval Europe. The group was also heavily influenced by fantasy literature and pop culture, and its development coincided with the rise in popularity of the fantasy RPG *Dungeons & Dragons*, bringing in its own players who wanted to act out their characters in the flesh.

Another movement preceded the SCA by a couple of years: the Renaissance fair. In 1963, Phyllis Patterson set up a theater and workshop in her backyard in Los Angeles as part of a summer drama class, after leaving work to take care of her infant son. With help from her husband, Ron, the project grew and became the Renaissance Pleasure Faire, in which they sought to re-create the atmosphere of the Renaissance era.[6]

Within a couple of years, hundreds of imitators popped up across the country as the model proved to be appealing as a destination for people looking for a slight relief from modern society. Both institutions, the SCA and the growing network of Renn Faires, provided that feeling of escape for fans: a place to escape from the real world and to draw them into a story informed by both history and fantasy.

---

[6] "Phyllis Patterson Dies at 82; Co-founder of Renaissance Pleasure Faire," *Los Angeles Times*, June 9, 2014, https://www.latimes.com/local/obituaries/la-me-phyllis-patterson-20140610-story.html.

RELIVING STORIES OF THE PAST

4 BEYOND WORLDCON

While costuming got its start within traditional science-fiction conventions, Worldcon provided opportunities for the form to break out beyond the confines of traditional programming. Now a well-established fixture within science-fiction fandom, it was beginning to attract talented individuals who were far more dedicated to the craft. By the 1980s, the masquerades were becoming so complicated that Worldcon had to establish some new rules, according to Mike Resnick: "The competition was divided into categories that still exist today [2009]: novice, journeyman, and master."[1]

Costuming also benefited from a growing body of visual media as Hollywood began to produce more science-fiction and fantasy films and television shows, while comic book companies like Marvel and DC were populating newsstands and wire racks with vividly drawn adventures of superheroes in comic book form.

SUPERHEROES

In the 1960s, superheroes were still a niche interest within science-fiction circles. While science fiction had been seen largely as a lowbrow, childish obsession, comics fandom occupied an even lower rung on the ladder. However, the two worlds would eventually

---

1 Mike Resnick, . . . *Always a fan: True Stories from a Life in Science Fiction* (Rockville: Wildside Press, 2009), 70.

collide: fans and writers Richard and Pat Lupoff appeared at the 1960 World Science Fiction Convention in Pittsburgh as Captain and Mary Marvel, possibly the first to suit up as comic characters at a convention. "Although Dick Lupoff admits that the costumes weren't of high quality," Daniel Peretti notes in *Superman in Myth and Folklore*, "he deems it a success: 'Everyone just clustered around and wanted to talk about the costumes and the characters they were based on.' "[2]

According to fanzine writer Bruce Pelz, in 1963, "although only a few of the LA fans collect comics, almost all of them are comics fans in that they read or have read comics and enjoyed doing so (though a large number would refuse to admit the fact)."[3]

Just a couple of years later, recalling the Lupoffs' appearance at Worldcon in costume, a group of LA-based fans attended the 1962 Chicago Worldcon as the Justice League. "The first problem was parceling out the roles. The little group of instigators quickly grabbed their favorite heroes before letting the rest of the LA crew in on the idea, but even the latecomers were reasonably happy with their roles, and there were even a number of characters left untaken."[4]

Dick and Pat Lupoff pose at Pittcon, the 1960 World Science Fiction Convention, as Captain and Mary Marvel.

Courtesy of Carol Resnick

From there, Bjo Trimble "took a stack of colored ditto carbons and copied full-page illustrations of the JSA characters, which I duplicated so we would have worksheets to build the costumes from," Pelz wrote. "For those such as myself who are quite incompetent at making costumes, Bjo included a checklist of costume materials and suggestions of where they could best be located."

The group eventually debuted eight members of the JLA: Black Canary, Dr. Fate, Dr. Mid-Nite, Green Lantern, Hawkman, Sandman, and Wonder Woman. "It turned out that others, too, had decided that comic characters were 'in' for that masquerade, as

---

2 Daniel Peretti, *Superman in Myth and Folklore* (Jackson: University Press of Mississippi, 2017), Chapter 6.
3 Roy Thomas, ed., *All-Star Companion Volume 4* (Raleigh: TwoMorrows Publishing, 2009), 125.
4 Thomas, *All-Star Companion*, 126.

BEYOND WORLDCON   37

other fans came as Batman, Robin, Prince Ibis, Taia, and another Flash, as well as a Flash Gordon group that took the 'Best Group' prize that we were trying for. It was a good year for comic heroes."[5]

▬ COSTUME-CON

Some fans were more interested in costuming than they were the rest of science fiction, and they wanted to have more dedicated time to explore the craft and experience of creating costumes. In 1979, fan and science-fiction writer Adrienne Martine-Barnes put together an ad in *MEGAMART* magazine: "Where are all those wonderful costumes shown off only once or twice at conventions or parties? Are they hanging in the closet, neglected? Now a unique opportunity can remedy the situation."[6]

She was proposing a new convention dedicated to costumes: COSTUME-MANIA, to be held January 25–27, 1980, at the Leamington Hotel in Miami, Florida. That particular event didn't end up taking place, but the efforts showed that there was a growing interest in costuming as a distinct branch of fandom. At the next year's Worldcon in Denver, costuming at the convention had become more prominent. "First, attendees at Denvention saw the inauguration of the now-legendary multiple-tier (Master-Journeyman-Novice-Young Fan) Division System for the costume competitions known as masquerades. Secondly, many costumers, who had been competing against each other for years, actually attempted to talk to each other for the first time in a friendly way after the masquerade. Third, the demand for costume programming was demonstrated when the 'How I Made My Masquerade Costume' panel ran over its time limit and continued informally in the hotel hallways after another panel took over the room."[7]

Speaking with other fans at the convention, Martine-Barnes decided to move forward with organizing another costume-oriented convention, to be called Costume-Con 1. The convention took place in Mission Bay, California, in January 1983, attracting around 140 attendees, with panels covering the ins and outs of making costumes. The program-

---

5   Thomas, *All-Star Companion*, 126.
6   Karen Schnaubelt, "The Genesis and Evolution of Costume-Con," for Costume-Con 7 program book (1989), revised by Betsy R. Marks Delaney, Costume-ConNections: Home of the Costume-Con Visual Archive (website), accessed December 4, 2021, http://www.costume-con.org/about-us/the-genesis-and-evolution-of-costume-con.
7   Schnaubelt, "Genesis and Evolution of Costume-Con."

ming for that first event included tutorials on how to use millinery wire, overcome one's fear of sewing, weather costumes, replicate costumes from film and television, and more.[8]

While it was designed as a single-year event, it was popular enough that its organizers ended up scheduling a second in San Jose, California, for 1984; and in 1985, the convention moved to Columbia, Maryland.

With the 1985 convention, the organizers set up an overarching organization to run it: the International Costumers' Guild, which is "dedicated to the promotion and education of costuming as an art form in all its aspects."[9] They also established competition guidelines and a regular newsletter. The convention continues to be run each year, providing this segment of fandom with their own space to collaborate.

Costuming had long since outgrown its roots as a niche activity within fandom: with its own dedicated conventions and tracks, costuming was now a pillar of the fan community, with its own institutions and traditions.

---

[8] "CC01 - Costume-Con 1: Program & Participants," Costume-ConNections: Home of the Costume-Con Visual Archive (website), accessed December 4, 2021, http://www.costume-con.org/costume-con-01-program-participants.

[9] "About the International Costumers' Guild," International Costumers' Guild, Inc. (website), accessed December 12, 2021, https://icggallery.org/the-icg.

5 TREK INVASION

From its inception, science-fiction fandom coalesced around print as fans organized through letter columns, fanzines, and local conventions. In the aftermath of the Second World War, new technologies brought the genre to new mediums. Television saw the rise of science-fiction shows like *Captain Video and His Video Rangers*, while advances in special effects allowed filmmakers to produce films like *Destination Moon* (based on Robert Heinlein's 1947 novel *Rocket Ship Galileo*), Stanley Kubrick and Arthur C. Clarke's *2001: A Space Odyssey,* and an adaptation of Pierre Boulle's *Planet of the Apes*.

In 1966, NBC first aired a television series that would alter science-fiction fandom forever: *Star Trek*. The inaugural season of twenty-nine episodes followed the adventures of Captain James T. Kirk and the crew of the *Starship Enterprise* as they visited new and unusual planets.

Fandom had seen nothing like it. In his editorial for the February 1967 issue of *Galaxy Science Fiction*, editor Frederik Pohl wrote about the reception that the series had received at the 1966 World Science Fiction Convention in Cleveland, Ohio: "The producers of a new science-fiction television show called *Star Trek* appeared, bearing pilot films, samples of costumes, a brace of writers and their own good selves. They were greeted with a great deal of enthusiasm from the fans and well they should have been, because a power of money had gone into some handsome sets, and a power of talent had been invested in preparing the scripts." Pohl noted that when the series aired later that fall, he had expected it to be worse than what he'd seen at the convention. The opposite was true: "The regular shows were just as good as the pilots! It looked as though there were finally going to be a regular science-fiction series on television that we wouldn't have to explain away as a cheap imitation of the real thing; something some of us might turn to for *enjoyment*."[1]

While Hollywood and the budding television industry had produced a number of science-fiction films and television shows prior to *Star Trek*, science-fiction fans were extremely critical. It's not hard to see why: the genre often requires considerable resources to create convincing sets, costumes, and special effects. Moreover, most fans weren't thrilled with the simplistic stories and characters that they saw. There were exceptions, of course: Rod Serling's *The Twilight Zone* and 1950's *Destination Moon* met their expectations, in part because they relied on writers who came out of the literary science-fiction scene.

Star Trek hit all the same buttons. In *Star Trek Lives!*, Jacqueline Lichtenberg, Sondra Marshak, and Joan Winston note that the series "used a totally different kind of writer in a totally different way. It reached out into the science-fiction community and pulled in writers who had spent their lifetimes perfecting a slant tailored to create a specific effect in a very narrow audience," they wrote. Writers hired for the series included Richard Matheson, Theodore Sturgeon, Fredric Brown, Harlan Ellison, Norman Spinrad, and Robert Bloch, all of whom were familiar to anyone reading science-fiction magazines at the time, and who "were famous for their proven ability to affect their readers very strongly."[2]

By the 1960s, fandom was beginning to change, due in part to Gene Roddenberry's series. Science fiction was no longer just content for pulp magazines: there were now science-fiction films, radio dramas, comics, and novels available to fans, and, accordingly, their interests became more specialized. "I think that goes back to when *Star Trek* came in," Astrid Bear explained to me. "There were people who came to science fiction for the first time because of *Star Trek*. It was this big, mainstream thing that wasn't incredibly popular, but it was well-known. When it was originally being aired, it was a little off the mainstream, but it still brought a tremendous influx of people into science fiction who had not been there before, and I think there are people who came into [fandom] with the identity as a *Star Trek* fan, that didn't branch out as much, and that made

---

1   Frederik Pohl, ed., *Galaxy Science Fiction*, vol. 25, no. 3, February 1, 1967, 5–6.
2   Jacqueline Lichtenberg, Sondra Marshak, and Joan Winston, *Star Trek Lives!* (New York: Bantam Books: 1975), 37.

Fans in *Star Trek* costume at art show, St. Louiscon, 1969.

Courtesy University of California, Riverside.
Photo by Jay Kay Klein

room for other people who were *Doctor Who* fans or *Battlestar Galactica* fans, more media-focused rather than media-and-literature."[3]

Star Trek wasn't a huge hit for NBC. In his editorial in *Galaxy Science Fiction*, Pohl had lamented the probability of cancellation during the show's first season and encouraged fans to write to NBC to show their support for the series. "Enjoy it while you can, fellows. As of yesterday the word was out: *Star Trek* will be off the air shortly after you read this. It just didn't make it in the ratings."[4] The series limped along with low ratings on NBC for two seasons before the network was ready to pull the plug, and it was the probability of the show's cancellation that galvanized fans into action. After a major letter-writing campaign, NBC gave the show another chance, airing a third season, and giving Roddenberry enough episodes to sell the series in syndication, where it became a cultural phenomenon through reruns. Through it, more people than ever found—and fell in love with—science fiction.

Star Trek and the rise of science-fiction television brought about another advantage over its print predecessors: visual reference. While costumers had previously relied on book covers, interior art, and comic book art to create their own costumes, the ones used in television and film productions were physical garments that the actors wore onscreen—and from which fans could easily reverse-engineer or replicate, either by cobbling together

---

3   Astrid Bear, in discussion with the author, January 2020.
4   Frederik Pohl, ed., *Galaxy Science Fiction*, 6.

something from existing garments or sewing up something on their own. *Star Trek*'s costumes were relatively simple, which gave it a distinct advantage over films with more complicated space suits or elaborate costumes: they were minimalist bright shirts, black collars, pants, boots, and a Starfleet insignia badge—all things an enthusiastic fan could scrounge up on their own.

While *Star Trek* certainly appealed to science-fiction fans, this new influx of bodies into fandom had its friction points. In Mark A. Altman and Edward Gross's *The Fifty-Year Mission: The Complete, Uncensored, Unauthorized Oral History of Star Trek: The First 25 Years,* Jacqueline Lichtenberg pointed to differences between the two camps of fans: "Fandom was composed of *readers*—other media just didn't connect. Thus at conventions, 'Trekkies' were socially shunned, and eventually *Trek* items were prohibited from being on the program schedule." In the same volume, *Star Trek* fans Bjo and John Trimble noted that "Science-fiction fandom, established since the 1940s, viewed the sudden invasion of *Star Trek* fans with alarm. Until the popularity of the show, most fans discovered SF via books and magazines."[5]

Two cosplayers pose as members of Starfleet at FAN EXPO Boston in 2021.

Courtesy of Andrew Liptak

In her book *Science Fiction Culture*, Camille Bacon-Smith writes that longtime fans were uneasy with the changes that *Star Trek* was bringing to the convention scene: this was a new group of fans joining the movement who came from a different storytelling tradition than those who had built it, a fandom that had come up through a culture of print media. "For fans who relate most strongly to the history of fandom as primarily a small, long-distance community of like-minded readers who created their own fanzines

---

5   Mark A. Altman and Edward Gross, *The Fifty-Year Mission: The Complete, Uncensored, Unauthorized Oral History of Star Trek: The First 25 Years* (New York: Thomas Dunne Books, 2016), 530.

Star Trek creator Gene Roddenberry dressed as a Romulan, along with an actress dressed as Andrea, from the episode "What Are Little Girls Made Of" at the 1966 Worldcon—Tricon—in Cleveland, Ohio.

Photos courtesy of John L. Coker III

to keep in touch with one another, the masquerade is a waste of resources. It draws an audience that this group perceives as primarily passive receivers of a produced show rather than the active participants these core members value."[6] In other instances, fans complained that "when you've seen one Luke Skywalker, you've seen them all—except at a masquerade, where there are probably five more waiting in the wings."[7]

That's an attitude that persists to this day. Before I went to my first literary convention, a mentor pulled me aside and told me not to bring my stormtrooper costume: It wasn't that type of convention, he explained. Science-fiction author Carrie Vaughn explained that when she started out, there was also a bit of resistance to cosplaying in the traditional convention circuit. "When I started going to the regional science fiction literary conventions [in the late 1990s], nobody dressed up except for the masquerade," she explained. "I don't know where [that reluctance] came from. There was just this perception that if you're going to be a serious author on panels talking about your books, then you don't dress up."[8]

---

6   Camille Bacon-Smith, *Science Fiction Culture* (Philadelphia: University of Pennsylvania Press, 1999), 56.
7   Evelyn C. Leeper, "LaCon II," Fanac (website), accessed January 19, 2022, https://fanac.org/conpubs/Worldcon/L.A.con%20II/LAcon%20II%20Evelyn%20Leeper%20con%20report.pdf.
8   Andrew Liptak, "Carrie Vaughn's Immersive Worlds," *Transfer Orbit* (newsletter), June 22, 2021, https://transfer-orbit.ghost.io/carrie-vaughn-questland-author-interview-fantasy-lotr-immersion.

Star Trek was also changing *who* was a fan. In *The History of Science Fiction*, Adam Roberts noted that the show's three lead male stars led "some critics [to] suggest that *Star Trek* is more responsible than any other SF text for the increase in female interest in the genre."[9]

Bear echoed that point. "Prior to *Star Trek* coming in, science fiction was definitely majority male, both in terms of writers and fans. It wasn't one hundred percent by any means," she recalled, "but if you look back at pictures taken at conventions and banquets, it would be 60:40, 70:30 men to women. *Star Trek* happened, and a lot of women came into us. The ratio of male to female fans changed and has never been as strongly male dominated as it was prior to that."

With that exclusion—outright or subtle—*Star Trek* fans helped to carve out their own spaces, producing their own fanzines and conventions. Fans in Newark, New Jersey, organized a small convention at the Newark Public Library in 1969, and in 1972, two fans named Devra Langsam and Elyse Rosenstein organized *Star Trek Lives!*, a convention dedicated entirely to the series. They planned for guest speakers, including science-fiction author Isaac Asimov and series creator Gene Roddenberry, as well as an art show, screenings of episodes, a display from NASA, and, critically, a costume call. After advertising the convention widely in local media, they expected around five hundred people to attend. Instead, three thousand people turned up to hear Gene Roddenberry speak and to meet fellow fans. The following year, six thousand people came, and in 1974, it was more than fifteen thousand.[10]

"The costume call was a gala affair, due largely to the enthusiasm of the fans," wrote Joan Winston in *Star Trek Lives!* "It must be thoroughly disquieting to ring for an elevator and have the doors fly open on a six-foot tall, Technicolor tribble . . . that says, 'What floor please?' One doesn't meet a talking ball of fluff every day. And that evening, we had a plethora of tribbles. Little kids in costumes Ma had made for them, and big kids in costumes they had made themselves. It was a fuzzy night. We also had an excess of Spocks, with over half of them female—strange for such a logical species."[11]

What *Star Trek* did was change the nature of fandom. For decades, it had been a

---

9 Adam Roberts, *The History of Science Fiction: Palgrave Histories of Literature* (United Kingdom: Palgrave Macmillan, 2005), 394.
10 Lichtenberg, Marshak, and Winston, *Star Trek Lives!*, 5.
11 Lichtenberg, Marshak, and Winston, *Star Trek Lives!*, 67.

community devoted to the written word of science fiction. With *Star Trek*, an entirely new generation of fans met science fiction for the first time, unencumbered by the traditional gatekeepers that reinforced the notion of what it was to be a science-fiction fan. The result was more women and fans of color picking up the mantle.

In many ways, it brought about a new type of fandom: people who were chiefly interested in a single science-fiction franchise. In doing so, it set the model for other fan communities of films like *Alien, Ghostbusters*, and *Star Wars*, who would in turn organize their own groups. It also helped to inject a new set of traditions and activities for fans: cosplay, fan art, and fan fiction, all activities that weren't part of the accepted social fabric of fandom until that point. In doing so, it helped to change people's conception about being a fan; it was no longer constrained to one type of person, but to a multitude, paving the way for entirely new organizations and social groups to form.

6 THE SUMMER OF 1977

While *Star Trek* galvanized the science-fiction community, no science-fiction film had quite the impact as a film that arrived in theaters in 1977: George Lucas's *Star Wars*.

Lucas, a film student who had just come off his second feature, *American Graffiti*, in 1973, had decided that he wanted to tackle a pulp science-fiction story next. Initially, he wanted to adapt *Flash Gordon,* but when he wasn't allowed to pick up the rights, he opted to create his own story.

His film followed the adventures of a senator-princess, a charismatic smuggler, and a farm boy who gets sucked into a titanic battle against an evil empire set on destroying anyone who stands in their way. Unlike other science-fiction films, which presented a polished look at the future, Lucas's story was set in a run-down world that felt lived-in, full of amazing aliens, gigantic starships, and never-before-seen special effects.

Star Wars was a hit with the public in part because of the efforts that Lucasfilm made to establish inroads with fans before the film's release. Steve Sansweet, who served as Lucasfilm's head of fan relations, explained that company officials had begun making the rounds at science-fiction conventions a year before the film hit theaters. "Charles Lippincott, who was the head of marketing and licensing, was a comic book fan himself, a fellow geek, and who knew people within the science-fiction and comic book communities," Sansweet says. "Charlie was the one who said, 'We've got to get the word out to

David Rhea poses as a stormtrooper from *Star Wars: A New Hope* in 1977 or 1978. After seeing the movie in theaters, he was hooked and wanted to make his own stormtrooper. Working off a picture in a magazine and a series of trips back to the theater, he constructed his own out of a football helmet, papier-mâché, and cardboard.

Courtesy of Cheryl Rhea

David Rhea poses as Boba Fett from *The Empire Strikes Back*.

Courtesy of Cheryl Rhea

the fan base about this movie, because I can't trust [20th Century] Fox to do it.'" They sold posters, established a fan club, and screened some early footage at conventions.

When *Star Wars* arrived in theaters in May 1977, it introduced science fiction to a much wider audience than traditional fandom—to the grumbling of some longtime literary science-fiction fans, who complained that it was a rip-off of Asimov's *Foundation* or Frank Herbert's *Dune*. Children flocked to theaters over and over, seeing the film dozens of times that summer, and, accordingly, wanted to reenact the adventures of Princess Leia Organa, Han Solo, and Luke Skywalker. While some could get away with using sticks as lightsabers and water pistols as blasters, others wanted more.

One of the most captivating aspects of the *Star Wars* franchise is its iconic costumes. Princess Leia's white senatorial gown and side hair buns, Han Solo's vest and blaster, Darth Vader's imposing black mask and cape, the glossy white-plated stormtrooper armor, and the bright-orange X-wing pilot suits proved to be enticing costumes for fans. Many saw the film and realized that they wanted costumes of their own that looked as much as possible like what they saw on the big screen.

48   COSPLAY: A HISTORY

In the 1970s, fans had limited options for nailing down the details of these costumes: commercially made costumes weren't generally available, so they resorted to watching the films over and over to jot down notes or sketch pictures, or tracking down occasional pictures that cropped up in posters and dedicated magazines like *Starlog*.

David Rhea was seventeen when he watched *Star Wars* for the first time in Yakima, Washington. "[I'm] a creative person. I've always made things—back in the *Star Trek* days, I made phasers and communicators out of wood, anything I could get my hands on. When *Star Wars* came out, I was hooked.

"I started thinking after it was out," he explained to me, "'I want to be a stormtrooper. How can I be a stormtrooper?'" He explained that at the time, there wasn't much in the way of reference photos, save for the occasional magazine. "I started buying those, and the other magazines, [which] didn't have very good pictures. I think I had two pictures of Darth Vader at a distance, and I had one or two of the stormtroopers, that was it."[1]

He began work nonetheless using the images that he had. First was the helmet. Rhea made his best guess with the face, hooking it onto an old football helmet, and finished the rest with papier-mâché, glue, and parts from his mother's hair dryer. He went back to the theater over and over again while he was building the costume. "I went to the movie with my notepad and pencil, and I'd go, 'Crap, I didn't write anything down.' It took a couple of times until I was able to get more details.

"I started working on the suits, using just cardboard, normal cardboard boxes. I wrapped them in crepe paper and glued it on so it was smooth. Then I put on tons and tons of polyurethane paint." After his stormtrooper was complete, Rhea moved on to make his own Darth Vader, and brought the costumes to his high school for Costume Day in September 1977. In early 1978, a local theater got in touch, asking if he'd be willing to help them advertise the rerelease of the film that spring, promising him and his stepsister free tickets. He made a third costume—a Jawa with working lights in its face. "We went and walked around the theater for probably a week or so and had a blast. Everyone wanted pictures and thought we were the real thing."

The costumes then sat for a couple of years until *The Empire Strikes Back* hit theaters in 1980. Rhea noted that with the film's release, there was a much larger fan community

---

[1] David Rhea, in conversation with author, May 2019.

for the franchise, and that the publicity for the sequel included better pictures. He improved on and built even more costumes—Luke Skywalker and his lightsaber; a better, light-equipped chest box for Darth Vader; Boba Fett. "We did more movie things, then were in a parade with some Girl Scouts. Anything I [could] do to wear the suit."

Rhea wasn't the only person to construct his own costume after multiple screenings. Sean Schoenke saw *Star Wars* as a college freshman in 1977 and returned more than a dozen times over the course of that summer. When one of his fellow record store employees announced that they were going to throw a *Star Wars*–themed birthday party, he hatched the idea to make his own costume.

Schoenke told Kristin Baver of StarWars.com that he had made other costumes over the years, including a Sgt. Pepper uniform to wear to a George Harrison concert. For Darth Vader, he looked for any images that he could find for reference and scrounged together parts from around his house. A black drape became his cape, he wired up his own chest box, and he constructed a helmet out of an army helmet and some broken sunglasses. When he debuted it at the party, "it was a hit," impressing his friends and guests.[2]

Star Wars also became a major merchandising hit. Lucasfilm granted licenses for costumes to companies such as Ben Cooper, Inc., which produced costumes in time for that year's Halloween; and Don Post, which made a line of deluxe helmets and costumes made of injection-molded vinyl from the 1970s to the late 1990s, allowing some fans to skip the steps needed to build a complicated helmet.

The film's vibrant world and characters were particularly attractive to fan costumers. Compared to earlier science-fiction films like *Logan's Run* or *Silent Running*, where characters wore stylized costumes or uniforms, Lucas's film looked completely natural, its costumes like actual clothing that people in its universe would wear.

It was relatable, and with a little effort, one could easily be Han Solo, Princess Leia, or Luke Skywalker. With a bit more effort, one could put together the more complicated costumes like the stormtrooper or Darth Vader. In the decades to come, that challenge would invite fans to tackle more complicated costumes that were almost indistinguishable from their onscreen counterparts. Science-fiction fans latched onto the film quickly: during 1977's World Science Fiction Convention, SunCon, fans dressed up as various

---

2   Kristin Baver, "Most Impressive Fans: The Story of What May Be the First Darth Vader Cosplay," *Star Wars* (website), July 12, 2017, https://www.starwars.com/news/most-impressive-fans-sean-schoenke-first-darth-vader-cosplay.

characters from the film,[3] including Chewbacca,[4] while characters like Princess Leia[5] popped up at subsequent conventions.

Sansweet notes that, broadly, *Star Wars* brings out a larger desire to see oneself in the world that Lucas had built. "George created a huge sandbox," he says, noting that he sees far more people creating work based on the property than some of the other ones out there, like *Star Trek, Battlestar Galactica*, or *Harry Potter*. "There's just this desire to take part in this giant sandbox and to play and have fun and to do things with fellow fans."

---

3   Debbie King, photographer, "Masquerade - ???, Seth Lady, Leia Organa, Obi-wan Kenobie, Wookie Smokeweed, Vader Raider, R2-D1, Cori Piratess," The Fanac Fan History Project (website), http://www.fanac.org/photohtm.php?worldcon/SunCon/w77m003.
4   Peggy Ann Dolan, photographer, "Elliott Shorter and Chewbacca Escorting Corey Seidman During the Banquet," caption by Ted Greenstone, updated by Amy Wolfthal and Joe Siclari, The Fanac Fan History Project (website), http://www.fanac.org/photohtm.php?worldcon/SunCon/w77m015.
5   "Princess Leia. ???" The Fanac Fan History Project (website), http://www.fanac.org/photohtm.php?worldcon/IguanaCon/w78m014.

7 LEGIONS OF FANS

In October 2019, an email landed in my inbox: "Congratulations, *The Rise of Skywalker* red carpet premiere attendee." I was one of a select group of members of the 501st Legion that Lucasfilm was inviting to take part in the world premiere of *The Rise of Skywalker*, the latest installment of George Lucas's *Star Wars* film series.

The moment was a culmination of years of costuming and collaboration between Lucasfilm and the fan community, and was a notable recognition for the club: a thank-you for supporting the franchise for decades. For me, it was a high point in a personal journey that has lasted as long as the 501st has been around—quite a memorable occasion as a fan.

Since its founding in 1997, the 501st Legion has become the largest organized *Star Wars* fan costuming organization in the world, numbering in the tens of thousands of members, who turn out to thousands of events every year, from major comic conventions to small library events to hospital visits. It's a group that came from humble origins: two fans who wanted to dress up in stormtrooper armor and have a bit of fun with their friends.

When I first encountered the 501st in 2003, I didn't fully understand the scale of the world I would soon find myself in: an international community of like-minded *Star Wars* fans who sported costumes from the franchise. The 501st Legion might have been dedicated to a single franchise, but its rise coincides with a massive sea change within popular culture, coming at a time when fandom was becoming more mainstream, internet communities had begun to thrive, and the companies that owned major franchises began to embrace the growing numbers of fans who suited up as their characters.

THE EVOLUTION OF A STORMTROOPER

As George Lucas began developing his science-fiction movie in the 1970s, he first worked with concept artist Ralph McQuarrie to create the visual look and feel of the universe. McQuarrie came up with the basis for costumes for the wide range of characters in the film, including the white-armored foot soldiers of the Empire. McQuarrie imagined them as the ultimate obedient soldiers for a fascist regime and designed them to look menacing, almost like skeletons.[1]

The task of producing the costumes fell to industrial designer Andrew Ainsworth and artist Nick Pemberton. Pemberton sculpted each part of the armor in clay, then turned the molds over to Ainsworth to produce. Ainsworth had begun building a company that manufactured plastic products, using a process known as thermoforming to heat and form sheets of plastic into various objects, like kayaks and fishponds.[2]

Ainsworth used the same process for the stormtrooper costumes: each mold was placed in a vacuum forming machine, which heats a sheet of plastic and pulls it down over a vacuum, forming each piece into the desired shape. In February 1976, director George Lucas and costume designer John Mollo were impressed with Ainsworth's prototypes and placed an order for fifty stormtrooper and forty X-wing pilot helmets out of high-density polyethylene (HDPE) and acrylonitrile butadiene styrene (ABS). With the film's production behind schedule, set designer John Barry tasked Ainsworth with building the rest of the armor for the costume.

"Stormtroopers were the nightmare costume," Mollo told J. W. Rinzler in *The Making of Star Wars: The Definitive Story Behind the Original Film*. Lucas was about to begin production in Tunisia, and the costumes weren't ready. "On top of all this, George announced that he was going to take some stormtroopers on location, and he wanted them to be in 'combat order,'" which meant additional components. Mollo

---

1 Brandon Alinger, *Star Wars: Costumes Original Trilogy* (San Francisco: Chronicle Books, 2014), 29.
2 "Our Story," Shepperton Design Studios + originalstormtrooper.com (website), accessed December 4, 2021, https://www.originalstormtrooper.com/our-story-19-w.asp.

and his team scavenged anything they could find: backpack frames, Tupperware, drainpipes, and more to create suitable backpacks for the troopers, and when Lucas asked for a rank marker, they used a motorcycle chest protector spray-painted orange to add to the kit. Once completed, Mollo shipped the armor costumes off to Tunisia for the start of production.[3]

When Lucasfilm began work on the film's sequel, *The Empire Strikes Back*, Mollo was able to reuse some of the original costumes. "With twenty-four Imperial stormtrooper costumes left over from *Star Wars*, John Mollo initially budgeted to refurbish the helmets and armor," wrote Ryder Windham and Adam Bray in *Stormtroopers: Beyond the Armor*. "The costumes' fastening systems, which had required ongoing repairs during the filming of *Star Wars*, were upgraded with more durable materials. Helmets and armor received fresh coats of white paint. The 'teeth' on the helmets, which had been painted gray for *Star Wars*, were painted black for *Empire*." Mollo and his team also pulled new suits of armor based on the originals, with some minor improvements.[4]

Return of the Jedi's production in 1982 required even more stormtroopers for some of the film's climactic battles. Lucasfilm hauled all of *The Empire Strikes Back* armor out of storage and manufactured another fifty suits.[5]

For the sequels, Mollo and his team built on the design language to introduce variants for specific planets, like the snowtrooper and scout trooper. In the years that followed, Lucasfilm would take the costumes out for publicity at major events like the Academy Awards in 1978, or the films' premieres as they hit theaters. Those new variants expanded what filmgoers saw onscreen and, in a more cynical take, allowed Lucasfilm to produce a number of new toys for eager fans.

DIY

In the 1980s, costumers took the next step toward making a better *Star Wars* costume. Though the films had left theaters, fans still wanted to suit up as one of the franchise's

---

3 J. W. Rinzler, *The Making of Star Wars: The Definitive Story Behind the Original Film* (New York: Ballantine Books, 2007), 138–39.
4 Ryder Windham and Adam Bray, *Star Wars Stormtroopers: Beyond the Armor* (New York: Harper Design, 2017), 48.
5 Windham and Bray, *Star Wars Stormtroopers*, 60.

iconic characters: the Imperial stormtrooper. Some of these costumers had greater ambitions than constructing Halloween costumes out of cardboard and scraps. They wanted a *real* stormtrooper costume. In the late 1980s, a company called Marco Enterprises developed its own set of stormtrooper armor, resculpting the entire suit from scratch based on what they saw in the film. The company's designers used the same process as the film's prop makers: they created molds, upon which they vacuum formed ABS plastic to shape each individual part.

According to StarWarsHelmets.com, a fan site dedicated to documenting the various types of fan-made armor, Marco was "the guy that really started the fan-made stormtrooper armor and helmet movement"[6] that was at the heart of what would become the larger *Star Wars* costuming scene. In the early 1990s, the company began selling the costume in kit form: buyers would get a box of parts and accessories, along with a set of directions. The armor eventually fell out of fashion, and the company reportedly "got into a bit of licensing trouble and had to quit production."[7]

Looking at the armor today, one can see it's not an accurate match to what's on-screen, but at the time, it was an impressive costume: one that transformed the user into a figure that might have stepped off the screen and into real life.

Marco's suit might have been the first, but it wouldn't be the last. A maker named Gerardo Follano sculpted a new suit of armor based on the Marco Enterprises armor, improving on the accuracy of the helmets and a couple of other components. In turn, a different sculptor developed another kit, known as the FX, which took off among early *Star Wars* costumers.

If you knew the right person, you could purchase it (mine cost me around $500–$600 in 2003), and in the mail you would receive a big brown box. Inside the box was the entire armored piece: the three parts that made up the helmet, decals, chest, back, shoulders, arms, abs, legs, and belt. The kits also included a holster and Velcro, which enabled an eager fan to assemble the suit in a little over an hour.

Looking back at that early set of armor, most 501st members and armor purists

---

6 "Marco Armor," Star Wars Helmets (website), accessed December 4, 2021, http://www.starwarshelmets.com/imperialfanMarco.htm.
7 Josh Ling, photographer, "Marco's Stormtrooper Armor," description by Chris Georgoulias, from the collection of Steve Sansweet, The Star Wars Collectors Archive (website), accessed December 4, 2021, http://theswca.com/images-repli/marco-stormtrooper.html.

A group of stormtroopers poses around Darth Vader at the Woburn Halloween Parade in Woburn, Massachusetts.

Courtesy of Andrew Liptak

would cringe. It was a fan sculpt: the chest wasn't *quite* the right shape, and the detailing on the abs was a bit off. The helmet was comically large, with an enormously wide frown, and had a flat top. But because Follano mass-produced the costume and shipped it all in one package (save for the shoes and black bodysuit), the kit was widely adopted around the world by 501st members until it was eventually phased out after more accurate armor became widely available.

Getting your own stormtrooper armor wasn't just a matter of finding the right kit. By the late 1990s, prop makers began putting up websites that helped steer people through the process of building their own armor. One of the most influential sites was Jeff Allen's Studio Creations, on which he provided detailed instructions for how to construct your own armor from scratch.

"Basically, it started out as a Mindspring account," Allen told me. "I started with writing a tutorial for building a stormtrooper, and that's what a lot of people in the early days saw."[8]

---

8   Jeff Allen, in conversation with the author, January 2020.

Whereas before one might have had to trawl through Usenet threads and obscure websites, Allen laid out the entire process for building one's own suit of armor—stormtrooper and more. His "Definitive Stormtrooper Costume How-To"[9] broke the process down into a number of steps: making a body cast, sculpting armor, making plaster molds, building a vacuum form table, vacuum forming armor, and assembling and detailing the armor. It took a daunting concept and broke it down into smaller, achievable steps. When I came across the site shortly after Allen launched it in the late '90s, I didn't have the technical wherewithal to make it myself, but it was a valuable resource for understanding how the armor worked and what went into making it.

"I've always been an artist of all trades," Allen explained. "Sculpting, painting, drawing, and all that in high school. At some point, I was like, filmmaking looks really good, and fun. So I started delving into that in my senior year in high school. If I did film, I wanted to do science-fiction films because of *Star Wars* and *Close Encounters of the Third Kind*. I thought, maybe I could use my art skills to create my own costumes and sets for my own films and cut some of the cost. I went down that path, but at the same time, I was going to conventions like the Atlanta Fantasy Fair and Dixie Trek, local big conventions, where I ran into people wearing the costumes for fun."[10]

▬ THE BIRTH OF A LEGION

In 1994, Albin Johnson was recovering from an accident that had cost him his left leg. The experience was a traumatic one for Johnson, who wrote that after numerous operations and an amputation, he'd "lost some of the steam in [his] life."[11] When he eventually returned to work, he and his friend and coworker Tom Crews began reminiscing about a shared interest: *Star Wars*, particularly the white-armored stormtroopers. "The stormtroopers were the original space commandoes, bad asses in gleaming white armor, soulless black eyes, and snarling grimaces on their faces."[12]

With the films set to return to theaters for the twentieth anniversary of the first film's

---

9   "Definitive Stormtrooper Costume How-To: Introduction," Studio Creations (website), accessed December 4, 2021, https://www.studiocreations.com/howto/stormtrooper/index.html.
10 Jeff Allen, in conversation with the author, January 2020.
11 Albin Johnson, "501st Legion History: 1997," Albin Johnson (website), accessed December 4, 2021, https://albinjohnson.com/trooper-tk210-journal/history-of-the-501st/501st-legion-history-1997.
12 Johnson, "501st Legion History."

LEFT: Albin Johnson suited up in his stormtrooper armor in the spring of 1997.

RIGHT: Dressed as a stormtrooper, Albin Johnson trooped at a screening of *The Empire Strikes Back* special edition in the spring of 1997.

Photos courtesy of Albin Johnson

release, Crews and Johnson became obsessed with the idea of dressing up as the film's iconic stormtroopers. "After a while we wondered: How would one possibly obtain armor like that? Does it even exist? Could someone make it?"[13] Those questions sent Johnson and Crews down a rabbit hole on the internet, and they eventually located a phone number in a Usenet group. "I plunked down a LOT of money and ordered a set," Johnson recalled. "In two weeks, the stuff arrived. With a lot of trouble, I managed to get it all together and whaddya know? Suddenly there was a stormtrooper walking around in the real world."[14] Johnson brought it out to a local screening of *The Empire Strikes Back*.

"I knew this was my chance to make a splash with my new toy," Johnson said. "I remember marching into the shabby little movie theater where they were showing it. I was nervous as hell—you couldn't see anything in that helmet, and it was so uncomfortable. Would this thing even look real? Am I making an idiot out of myself? You would have thought Godzilla walked into the lobby from the reaction I got. Screams went up from

---

13 Johnson, "501st Legion History."
14 Johnson, "501st Legion History."

the crowd as they freaked out over an actual stormtrooper stalking the room. Kids came up and began poking me, fan-boys fawned over me, and inevitably a drunk asshole would try to show off in front of his girlfriend by taunting me."[15]

The armor was a hit, but mostly a curiosity to moviegoers at the theater. But when he attended a screening of *Return of the Jedi* with Crews, Johnson discovered that there was strength in numbers. "The instant we stepped out together the difference was obvious. Same screams, same adoration. Only this time, people kept their distance. If we posted near a doorway, people walked by respectfully and waved. Stark contrast to the poking treatment I'd gotten before. No longer did they see me as a museum exhibit on display—we had the appearance of a unit of troopers placed there to guard something."[16]

Cheralyn Lambeth dressed as a scout trooper at a *Return of the Jedi* special edition premiere in Greensboro, North Carolina, in the summer of 1997.

Courtesy of Cheralyn Lambeth

Johnson and Crews weren't the only fans who dressed up in costumes for the rerelease. Future 501st member and archivist Cheralyn Lambeth[17] explained that she had loved costumes as a kid and ended up attending UNC-Chapel Hill, where she told me she studied film and television, then the Juilliard School's Professional Production Program. She was also a passionate *Star Wars* fan, and when the special editions came out, she constructed a scout trooper costume out of cardboard and wore it to the premiere of *Return of the Jedi* in summer 1997 in Greensboro, North Carolina.

---

15   Johnson, "501st Legion History."
16   Johnson, "501st Legion History."
17   Cheralyn Lambeth, "My first set of (cardboard!) biker scout armor at a premiere of Return of the Jedi Special Edition in Greensboro, NC, Summer 1997," Facebook, January 2, 2020, https://www.facebook.com/photo.php?fbid=10157204677714055&set=a.10157204648509055&type=3.

LEGIONS OF FANS

Albin Johnson trooping at a comic book store.

Courtesy of Albin Johnson

As the trilogy left theaters, Johnson faced the prospect of putting the armor away, and mulled over the fact that if you had more troopers in one place, the excitement from bystanders went up exponentially. "After two weeks of terrorizing movie-goers Tom and I decided it was time to branch out," Johnson wrote for StarWars.com. "We were on to something and we wanted to see what else stormtroopers could do. It was time to book gigs at the State Fair and the local comic shops. But the lessons I learned in those first few weeks of trooping would stick with me. And in particular those two concepts would percolate in my head, making me wonder: what was possible with an army of stormtroopers?"[18]

They soon booked a gig with a local comic book store, with a bonus: the store had rented a Darth Vader costume for a promotion, and they were joined by a high school fan who had constructed his own suit of Boba Fett armor. They were soon invited to other businesses to help support a *Star Wars* gaming tournament, a daycare graduation ceremony, video store events, and other occasions. They accompanied Peter Mayhew for an appearance at another comic book store, setting the stage for the close relationship that the Legion would have with many of the franchise's actors and crew as they moved through the convention circuit.[19]

Recognizing that there were likely other people out there who shared their interests, Crews and Johnson set about building a website to showcase their adventures: they posted pictures of their *Star Wars* alter egos, TK-210 and TK-512 (so named for the unfortunate TK-421 in *A New Hope*), as though they were stationed aboard the Death Star. They were regular guys, complaining about life in the Imperial military. "I got an email from a bloke in Canada named Scott McArthur. He said he'd seen my web page

---

18   Albin Johnson, "The Birth of the 501st Legion Part One: Studies in Trooping," *Star Wars* (website), August 17, 2012, https://web.archive.org/web/20141208015634/https://www.starwars.com/news/the-birth-of-the-501st-legion-part-one-studies-in-trooping.
19   Albin Johnson, "The Birth of the 501st Legion, Part 3: Let the Wookiee Win," *Star Wars* (website), September 27, 2012, https://web.archive.org/web/20210306081030/https://www.starwars.com/news/the-birth-of-the-501st-legion-part-3-let-the-wookiee-win.

Members of the 501st Legion pose for a picture during Dragon Con in Atlanta, Georgia, in 1998. Already at that point, the group included more than just stormtroopers: it featured a wider range of *Star Wars* Imperial cosplayers.

Courtesy of Albin Johnson

and loved it. In fact, he had a stormtrooper costume of his own!"[20] Johnson added him to the page. More stormtroopers emailed him, sharing their pictures for the site, which he dutifully posted with humorous captions.

Johnson soon realized that he had something interesting on his hands: a fan group of his own, made up of people who shared an extremely specific interest in *Star Wars*. The website slowly grew as more people joined Johnson's ranks. He settled on a name, something suitably military-like: the 501st Legion, inspired by his father's own story of being a pilot during the Second World War.[21] He imagined it as Darth Vader's personal army—the elite soldiers that the Dark Lord of the Sith himself would call upon for the most dangerous of missions.

In 1998, Johnson assembled the first gathering of the 501st Legion at Dragon Con in Atlanta, Georgia. Amid their ranks were more than just stormtroopers: their members now sported other costumes from the Imperial military, including a TIE pilot, Imperial officer, sand trooper, bounty hunters, and Darth Vader. "Dragon Con was the first ever meeting of the 501st Squad in person," Johnson wrote.

But the idea of an organized costume club was new, and the assembled members were skeptical at first. "No one was buying it. Some of them even made fun of it. I couldn't GIVE away membership back then. Even Anthony Daniels thought we were idiots, judging by the way he looked at us."

---

20 Albin Johnson, "The Birth of the 501st Legion, Part 5: Build It and They Will Come," *Star Wars* (website), November 20, 2012, https://www.starwars.com/news/the-birth-of-the-501st-legion-part-five-build-it-and-they-will-come.
21 Johnson, "The Birth of the 501st Legion, Part 5."

Early members of the 501st taking part in the costume contest at Dragon Con in Atlanta, Georgia, in 1998.

Members of the 501st Legion pose for a picture outside at Dragon Con in Atlanta, Georgia, in 1998.

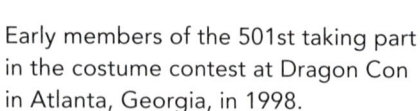

Photos courtesy of Albin Johnson

▄▄ BUILDING A MOVEMENT

Johnson persisted with his idea. A number of them had come to enter Dragon Con's costume contest, and he encouraged them to enter together.

Lambeth was in that inaugural group of costumers in 1998 dressed as Princess Leia. She explained that the group had entered the convention's *Star Wars* contest and re-created the opening *Tantive IV* scene from *A New Hope*. "We were a huge hit," she explained to me. "Everybody loved all the stormtroopers; we walked in and the crowd just exploded. It was a great moment."[22]

The moment convinced Johnson that he was on the right track. "Right there we re-captured the intensity of that well-known scene and demonstrated how effective several stormtroopers could be in a presentation. It really encouraged me to work harder on the 501st concept."[23] The moment inspired Lambeth to keep at it, and she ended up replacing her cardboard armor with a set of plastic armor.

Ultimately, Johnson's vision prevailed, and his group began to come together. In 1999, the long-awaited continuation of the *Star Wars* franchise, *The Phantom Menace*, hit theaters, bringing with it a new flood of interest in the films and costumes. Lucasfilm held its first official convention, *Star Wars* Celebration, which brought together members

---

22 Cheralyn Lambeth in conversation with the author, January 2020.
23 Albin Johnson, "501st Legion History: 1998," Albin Johnson (website), accessed December 3, 2021, https://albinjohnson.com/trooper-tk210-journal/history-of-the-501st/501st-legion-history-1998.

of Johnson's website for the first time. Johnson noted that by the end of the year, the group claimed 147 members from seven different countries.[24]

It only expanded from there, forming regional units called Garrisons, which allowed members to gather locally so they could help one another build costumes and take part in nearby events. These allowed the group to grow and strengthen itself across the world, giving individual members an accessible foothold and helping them feel like part of a much larger whole.

Over time, the group grew in number. Members sent in pictures to the official *Star Wars* magazine, *Star Wars Insider*, and slowly, Lucasfilm began to realize that they had a large body of devoted fans. Johnson explained that the first real meeting between his members and Lucasfilm officials came during Celebration II, the second official *Star Wars* convention, held in 2002 in Denver, Colorado. Johnson noted that he offered up the group's services to Lucasfilm for the convention: quasi-security (in appearance only) for line control and similar light tasks. It was the start of a major relationship that persists to the present day, one of benefit to both parties.

THE REBEL LEGION

The 501st Legion isn't the only major *Star Wars* costuming group out there. While members of Johnson's group initially featured costumes from the franchise's villains, a fledgling group opted to focus exclusively on the franchise's heroes.

That vote prompted a handful of members—Tony Troxell, Richard Fairbrother, Ed O'Connell, Ken Ograyensek, and Doug Fesko—to launch a counterpart to the 501st in 2001: the Rebel Legion, which quickly grew.[25] By 2005, the new group counted more than fifteen hundred members among its ranks.

The Rebel Legion provided an outlet for a range of heroic characters: Rebel pilots and Rebel Fleet troopers, "face characters" (characters with a specific name or appearance), and Jedi Knights. Like the 501st, membership came with requirements: a list of mandatory components (Costume Reference Library) that ensured a uniform look

---

24 Albin Johnson, "501st Legion History: 1999," Albin Johnson (website), December 3, 2021, https://albinjohnson.com/trooper-tk210-journal/history-of-the-501st/501st-legion-history-1999.
25 Donna Keeley, "Celebrating the Good Guys: The History of the Rebel Legion," *Star Wars* (website), June 26, 2015, https://www.starwars.com/news/history-of-the-rebel-legion-part-1.

For *The Phantom Menace*, Albin Johnson ditched his original stormtrooper costume and dressed up as a Jedi Knight.

Courtesy of Albin Johnson

across the Legion's growing ranks. The Rebel Legion also encouraged a certain level of creativity from their members, who came up with an in-universe name and backstory for their characters, turning the entire exercise into more than just costume replication.

"When I first started out," Johnson told me at Dragon Con 2019, "it was a very selfish motivation, that I wanted to be a part of *Star Wars*. I wanted to live in the skin of *Star Wars*. Costuming was never anything that I was super interested in. But when the rereleases came out, I just found a strange hunger to get into it in a way that I'd never done before. The idea of dressing up as a stormtrooper was like a salvation to me, from feeling cut off from *Star Wars*. With the bucket, you can be anonymous, and with the armor, you are a fully immersive character, and with my leg, I felt like there were no outward appearances. Me being an amputee . . . my initial expectations for costuming were basically just wanting to be in the *Star Wars* universe.

"Fast-forward all these years and the level of complexity and sophistication is infinitely light-years away from where we first started," he explained. "We were taking the baby steps of trying to learn what you do in costume in public: How do you entertain the public? Because after the initial sight of the costume, a lot of that excitement dies out. So I would

OPPOSITE PAGE, FROM LEFT
1: Members of the Rebel Legion's Alderaan Base pose for a picture during the 2019 Rutland Halloween Parade. *Courtesy of Andrew Liptak*
2: Members of the New England and Canadian garrisons pose at Burlington Kids Day in Vermont in 2009. *Courtesy of Andrew Liptak*
3: Members of the 405th Infantry Division gather at Halo: Outpost Discovery. *Courtesy of Anthony Ortiz*
4: Members of the 405th Infantry Division gather at Dragon Con in 2018. *Courtesy of Samuel A. Famoyegun of SF Design*

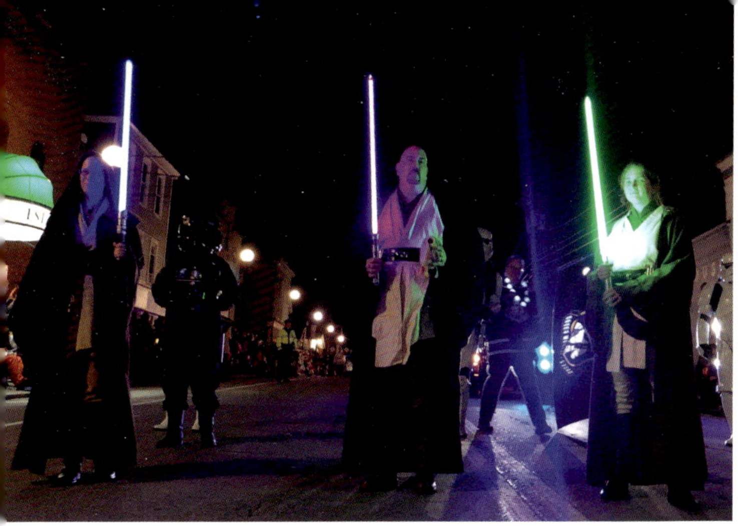

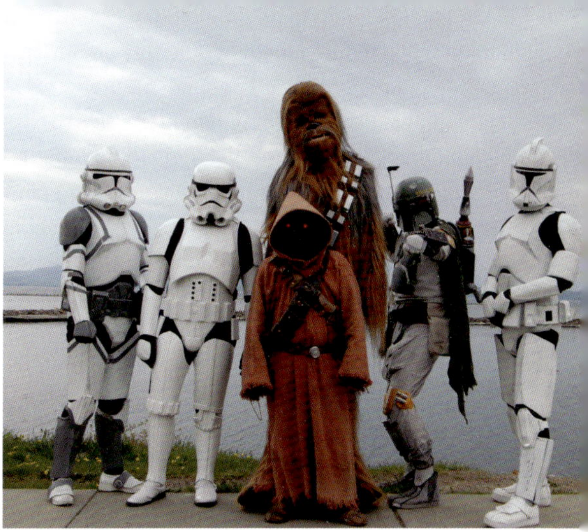

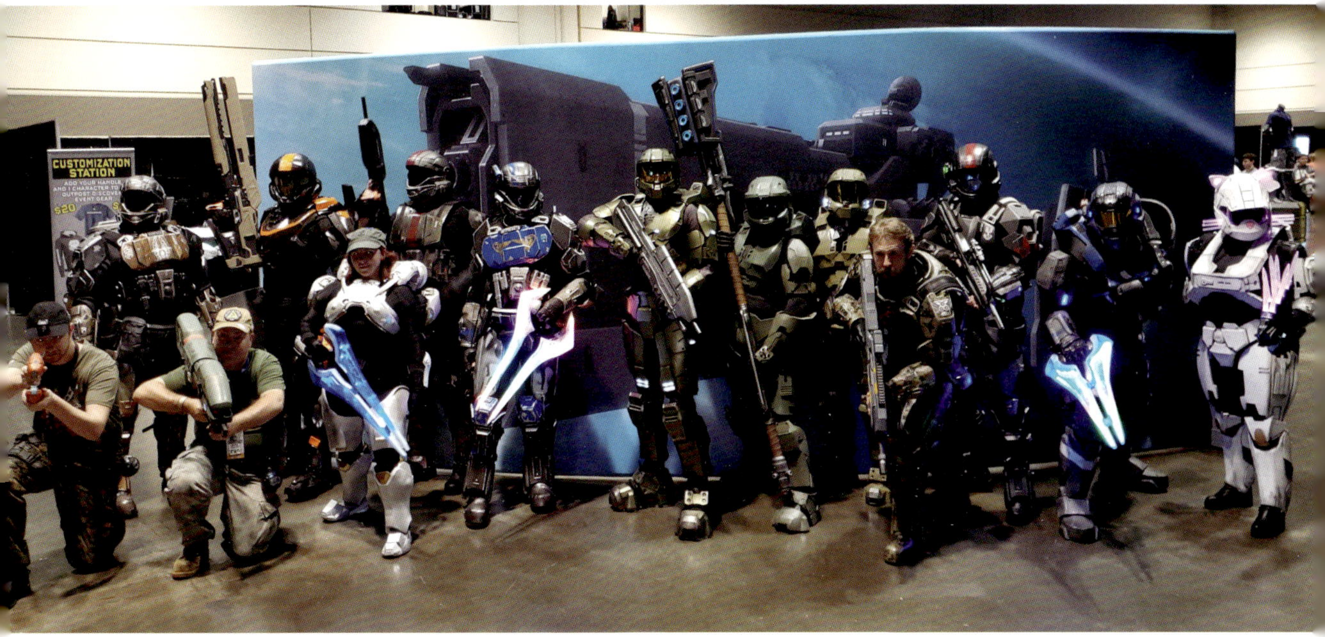
CUSTOMIZATION STATION

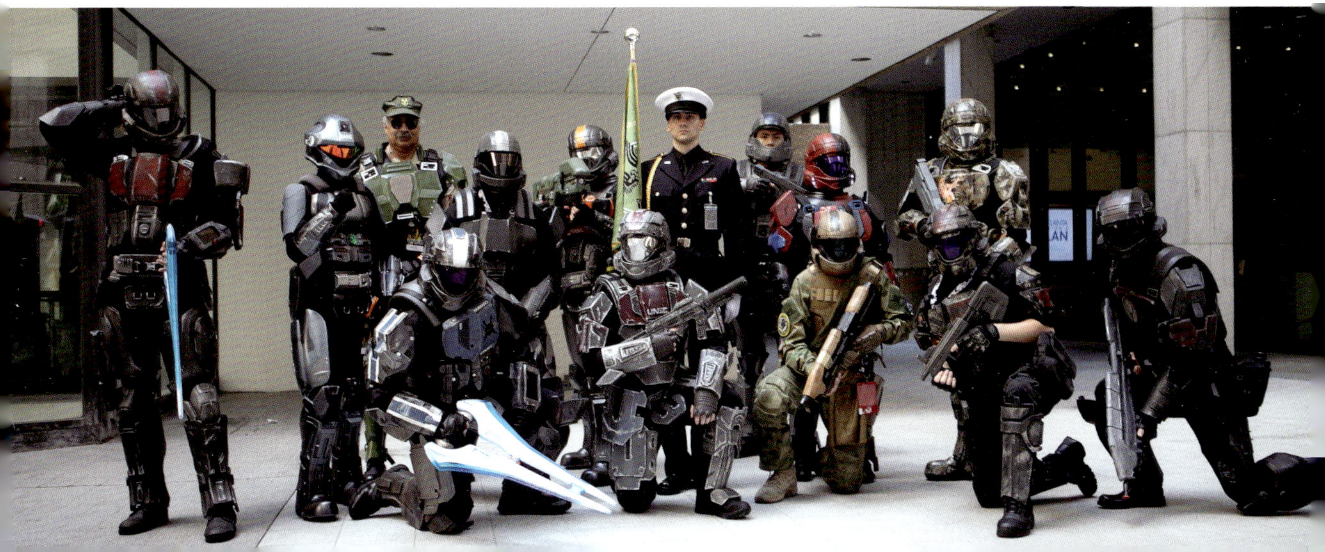

devise little electronic boxes that I rigged as rebel spy detectors, and I'd hit a button and light it up if someone in a movie theater line looked like they were sporting. Early on, it was so primitive in terms of what we knew, what we could do with costuming, and how we got there. How do we get the costumes? Who supplies them? How can you modify them to where you can survive in them for longer than an hour? It's almost akin to the first manned space mission—how do we get this guy into space and keep them alive? After we figure that out, then you can think about putting a space station up there."

The 501st Legion provides Lucasfilm with a massive pool of eager volunteers who possess costumes that are equal (even superior) to the ones that were seen in the original films—people who could be called upon to help with a variety of tasks, such as commercials, public appearances, and, eventually, supporting roles in the films and television shows themselves.

THE 405TH INFANTRY DIVISION

When video game studio Bungie launched its military science-fiction title *Halo: Combat Evolved* in 2001, the Xbox exclusive quickly found an audience; and in the twenty years since that first installment, an entire franchise of video game sequels and spin-offs has followed, along with books, comics, and even serialized online shows. Millions of players have worn the armor of Master Chief, *Halo*'s central character, a power-armored super soldier, as he shoots his way through the ranks of enemy aliens known as the Covenant.

For nearly as long as the game's been around, fans have worked to figure out how to replicate Master Chief's iconic armor. Robert Letts, the division identity officer for the 405th Infantry Division, told me that the costuming group got its start when a fan named Adam Grumbo started a message forum called MjolnirArmor in 2007, designed to guide interested cosplayers in building the *Halo* universe's various costumes. It eventually became a formal costuming club that now counts thousands of fans around the world as its members. "The goal in those early days," Letts explained, "was to provide as many resources as possible to help people create their own costumes from the *Halo* universe." The forums, he said, were a good way to help newcomers navigate some of the complicated costume parts and share with one another their appreciation of the game franchise and its lore.[26]

---

26 Robert Letts, in conversation with the author, October 2021.

After a major site hack, Letts explained that the group experienced a bit of a slowdown, which prompted the group to reorganize and rethink its mission. The group's leadership went to Art Andrews, the owner of the Replica Prop Forum, or RPF, who acquired it as part of his company. The various organizational changes, Letts says, "have proven to be best for the organization as a whole and truly allowed the 405th to flourish and grow." The site overhauled its resources for new members and has continued to grow. In 2019, the organization partnered with Microsoft's 343 Industries to appear at the company's traveling Halo: Outpost Discovery event, and its members have contributed to the company's Halo Museum at its headquarters.

In many ways, it's a group similar to organizations like the 501st: a global body designed to "promote the development of artistic skill and the honing of artistic talent through the creation of Halo costumes and props,"[27] in the pursuit of celebrating the world and its characters. There are some differences, however. The organization doesn't require members to own a costume; fans can join as non-costuming members who participate in the forums and attend various events, while members with costumes must meet various standards that the club sets down. "Type D/Deployed Membership" status is reserved for those who own a costume; while members in the three upper tiers (Apprentice, Hero, and Legend) have completed costumes with an even higher quality of craftsmanship. Like the 501st, the 405th features a regional organizational structure: the Division is the entire worldwide group under which regiments (covering either entire countries like Canada, Mexico, and Singapore, or large regions like the US Midwest, South, and Southwest) operate, and under those groupings are battalions. Within their respective region, members will attend events or show up en masse at larger conventions like Dragon Con and Halo: Outpost Discovery.

The group's forums contain a wealth of information for aspiring costumers—everything from tutorials on how to use foam or fiberglass to make armor, visors, and weapons, to model files for 3D printers or Pepakura, decals, and electronics wiring. Moreover, the constant tinkering of the game's art and design (and the customization of player characters) means that there are hundreds of variations on the Master Chief and Mjolnir armor that cosplayers can produce and wear. And the 405th provides resources on not

---

27 "405th Costuming Club Mantle," 405th Infantry Division: Build Your Character (website), accessed December 4, 2021, https://www.405th.com/forums/pages/mantle.

only the wide range of side characters but the franchise's chief antagonists as well, such as the Elites and the hulking Hunters, which stand around twelve feet tall when completed.[28]

■ STARFLEET

The 501st Legion might be one of the biggest fan organizations in the world (in 2020, *Guinness World Records* listed it as the "Largest *Star Wars* costuming group," with 14,141 members[29]), but it's far from the only fan group dedicated to a large multimedia science-fiction franchise. Another major fixture in fandom is STARFLEET: The International Star Trek Fan Association, which had its start back in 1973 when John Bradbury and his fellow fans in Texas got together to found a club dedicated to Gene Roddenberry's TV series.[30] The club was for all things *Star Trek*, whether it be fundraisers, parties, or costumes. Like other groups, it is split into regional groups, which it calls Fleets. Unlike the 501st, membership in STARFLEET isn't dependent on owning or making a costume, although plenty of its members have them. Its objective is largely the same as those of the 501st and 405th: to spread appreciation of its favorite franchise to the world at large.

■ SCREEN ACCURACY

The screen accuracy movement comes largely out of groups like the Replica Prop Forum, and is carried along by groups like the 501st and Rebel Legions and companies like ANOVOS. These groups sought to replicate the experience of seeing characters on-screen, building up their own copies as ways to celebrate their fandom. They might have started out wanting to hold Han Solo's blaster, Indiana Jones's whip or hat, Darth Vader's helmet, or some other component of the worlds that they loved.

These groups put a heavy emphasis on research and development, tracking down the original, screen-used props for measurements, or figuring out what prop makers originally utilized for components.

---

28 Evan Narcisse, "The Biggest *Halo* Cosplay Yet," *Kotaku*, March 30, 2015, https://kotaku.com/the-biggest-halo-cosplay-yet-1694561617?.
29 "Largest *Star Wars* Costuming Group," *Guinness World Records*, November 18, 2020, https://www.guinnessworldrecords.com/world-records/420887-largest-star-wars-costuming-group.
30 "A Brief History of STARFLEET International," STARFLEET: The International *Star Trek* Fan Association (website), accessed December 4, 2021, https://sfi.org/history-of-starfleet.

The advantage of the group's variety of approvable costumes comes from set points of reference onscreen, so members are able to quantify what their costumes require.

While the 501st Legion was first developing, Johnson and his members decided that they wanted a uniform look among their ranks; if a member made their costume out of cardboard, for example, that would ruin some of the illusion. A formal organization could ensure a uniform standard of quality by imposing entry standards.

Each character has what is called a Costume Reference Library (CRL), a guide that comes out of the group's collective research and documentation. It lists each required component, codifying the costume to provide a minimum level of entry for potential members. This innovation allowed the group to do something unique: all of the group's members would look alike, furthering the illusion that they were part of a vast Imperial force. If you had ten, fifty, or one hundred stormtroopers in a room, they would all look roughly alike (accounting for differences in height, body type, and so forth).

The group also provided another type of subunit called a Detachment forum, which focused exclusively on one type of costume, such as a stormtrooper (First Imperial Stormtrooper Detachment, or FISD), a scout trooper (Pathfinders), Darth Vader (Sith Lord Detachment), and so forth. These specialized groups essentially acted as working groups for the larger body of the 501st Legion and cosplay community in general. Their members researched each costume exhaustively, studying the original props and costume pieces in the pursuit of building the most accurate costumes possible. Some, like the FISD and Path-

Bob Gouveia poses for a picture during Burlington Kids Day in Vermont in 2009. Boba Fett has remained a popular costume, not only because of the popularity of the character but because of the challenge of building a screen-accurate costume.

Courtesy of Andrew Liptak

finders, instituted tiered recognition for various costumes. In some instances, the base-level acceptance is a compromise between the costume seen onscreen and what was practically accessible for the general public. The groups added additional tiers to reward the effort that members put into their costumes to take them ever closer to acceptance, from minor details that didn't make it into their original kits, to hard-to-find or difficult-to-build details.

▬ COMMUNITY

These organizations—and many others, like The Royal Manticoran Navy (for fans of David Weber's Honorverse series) and Ghostbusters (for fans of the eponymous franchise)—offer fans a space through which they can find one another and share resources with the full group. They could be considered an outlier within the greater cosplay community, as there are plenty of cosplaying fans who aren't part of a formal organization. But these groups help that broader community by providing and preserving a platform for the institutional knowledge of their respective franchise's costumes, culture, and habits, allowing both new and existing fans to contribute to that bank of information.

For nearly a quarter century, the 501st has served as a definitive guide for anyone wanting to make a stormtrooper costume. This is made easier in part by its organization and structure, which allows the group to retain the collective knowledge and skills its members have gained, gathering it in one place so that it isn't lost in the noise of the internet. The same is true of the many other clubs out there.

The 501st Legion's New England Garrison and members of the Rebel Legion pose as a group before they march in the 2011 South Boston St. Patrick's Day/ Evacuation Day Parade.

Courtesy of Andrew Liptak

Structure is vitally important to fandom: it distributes the work needed to foster a community among all its members rather than just one or two individuals. These groups are open and responsive in their forums and lines of communication, and in helping out new members with their costumes and organizing in-person gatherings.

M Blackburn, a cosplayer who discovered costuming when they attended Dragon Con as a middle school student, noted that their membership in the 501st brought with it a sense of belonging. "The 501st is more connected," they told me. "I've found family there, where I can't say that with the [whole] cosplay community."[31]

The key, Blackburn says, is the structure of the group. The members of the Legion post regularly on message forums; see one another at various events; and meet up for after-troop meals, Garrison build days, or just social hangouts. "There's forums, there's message boards, there's group chats that simply don't exist in the cosplay community at large," Blackburn explained. Without that organization and shared identity, community-building is much more of a challenge. "It's hard to schedule with a group of random people on Instagram, even for something like, 'Let's sit down for dinner here.' "[32]

The most established cosplay groups—whether it's the 501st, Rebel Legion, 405th, or others—have that community structure in place that extends their activities beyond suiting up in costume: they're valuable social organizations, where members forge friendships, relationships, families, and bonds with their fellow fans. And their members put in the work to reinforce that community: attending a build day or convention does more than just help you build and wear your costume. It helps to strengthen the bonds within a group that could become your community for life.

Cosplayer M Blackburn poses at *Star Wars* Celebration in Chicago, Illinois, in 2019.

Courtesy of Andrew Liptak

---

31 M Blackburn in conversation with the author, February 2020.
32 M Blackburn in conversation with the author, February 2020.

8 THE RISE OF COMIC-CON

Every July, more than a hundred thousand people descend on downtown San Diego for Comic-Con International: San Diego (more commonly known as San Diego Comic-Con), an annual celebration of all things pop culture. Approaching the city's downtown core is an eye-opening experience: con-goers are decked out in shirts and costumes from every franchise imaginable, while advertisements for the latest superhero and genre films and TV shows hang from buildings and buses.

San Diego Comic-Con and its many imitators have become some of the largest institutions within fandom, now major gathering points for fans of all stripes to congregate and revel with their fellow nerds. Studios use the biggest conventions to launch trailers for their next major superhero and science-fiction films and bring out

The floor of San Diego Comic-Con in 2012. The event has seen enormous growth in the last two decades.
Image: Kevin Dooley

A-list actors to answer fan questions about their roles. Vendors set up shop in cavernous exhibition halls to sell anything a fan could want: film and television memorabilia, books, comics, action figures, toys, costumes, and more. Cosplayers bring out their best costumes to pose for pictures and meet up with their friends.

Today's events are a far cry from the smaller comic expos and meetups that began in the 1960s, a testament to the evolution that geek culture has undergone over the decades, transforming from a niche interest to one that dominates popular culture around the world.

▬ THE EARLY YEARS

In 1964, a group of comic book fans gathered in New York City to buy and sell comic books and meet some of the industry pros that they idolized. Guests at the event included artists Steve Ditko and Florence Steinberg, Stan Lee's assistant. Admission was $1.50, and among the attendees was an individual who would become one of the best-known figures in modern genre media: George R. R. Martin.[1] They didn't realize that they were party to something big: the birth of the comic book convention, Comic-Con.

The 1939 World Science Fiction Convention kicked off a string of major gatherings for science-fiction fandom, establishing some norms: panel discussions, face-to-face time with industry professionals, and, of course, costuming. After Myrtle Douglas and Forrest Ackerman dressed up in costume at that first convention, hundreds and eventually thousands of costumers followed their example.

Fandom was no longer limited to the literary world of genre fiction. The "Golden Age" of comics began in the 1930s and 1940s with pulp comic magazines printed on cheap paper and sold on newsstands, bringing us superheroes like Batman, Superman, and Wonder Woman. They became incredibly popular with readers, and, like science-fiction fandom, comic fans began to coalesce into organized groups in the 1940s. Fans "published crude fanzines. They mailed letters in the thousands to the publishers, offering story and character ideas and points of criticism," writes Reed Tucker in *Slugfest: Inside the Epic 50-Year Battle Between Marvel and DC.* "They were the founding fathers

---

[1] "Superheroes Decoded: Comic-Con | History," HISTORY, YouTube video, May 3, 2017, https://www.youtube.com/watch?v=3nAxyRlGHjA.

and mothers of the grassroots nerd culture that has become one of the most powerful forces in modern-day entertainment."[2] Comics fandom began to organize into a cohesive movement in the 1960s, and like the science-fiction fans before them, they began to organize regular meetups and conventions—at first low-key affairs at fans' homes or public spaces, then eventually larger affairs.[3]

A year later, fans gathered for the Detroit Triple Fan Fair, a convention that covered not only comics but science fiction and film as well. In 1967, conventions in St. Louis, Missouri, and Houston, Texas, popped up. In 1968, members of the growing war-gaming community, led by future *Dungeons & Dragons* cocreator Gary Gygax, established the Lake Geneva Wargames Convention in Lake Geneva, Wisconsin.[4]

Bigger things were on their way. In 1970, a small group of comic book fans plotted out a pair of small conventions: one held at the US Grant Hotel in San Diego in March, with a second event that followed in August. That first convention was held in the basement of the hotel, and it included comic book artist Jack Kirby and science-fiction writer Ray Bradbury. To everyone's surprise, more than three hundred people showed up, an auspicious start to an event that is now probably the most significant in the world of genre media.[5]

San Diego Comic-Con was set to transform with the times as this new genre media environment expanded fandom: in 1976, Lucasfilm brought an early look at *Star Wars* to the convention,[6] along with star Mark Hamill. An avid comics fan, he remembered the convention in the 1970s as "tiny."

"It was not mainstream at all," Hamill told the *Hollywood Reporter* in 2013. "If you wanted to attract girls, you kept the fact that you liked all this stuff to yourself. I remember ten or fifteen comic dealers in the basement of the Ambassador Hotel, with a 16 mm projector to show old *Flash Gordon* and *Captain Marvel* serials. I went one time

---

2   Reed Tucker, *Slugfest: Inside the Epic 50-Year Battle Between Marvel and DC* (New York: Da Capo Press, 2017), 83.
3   Tucker, *Slugfest*, 84.
4   Michael Witwer, *Empire of Imagination: Gary Gygax and the Birth of Dungeons & Dragons* (New York: Bloomsbury USA, 2015), 226.
5   Chris Chafin, "San Diego Comic-Con: The Untold History," *Rolling Stone*, July 19, 2017, https://www.rollingstone.com/culture/culture-features/san-diego-comic-con-the-untold-history-194401.
6   Star Wars (@StarWars), "Roy Thomas and Howard Chakin tell a less than packed audience about a film called Star Wars at @Comic_Con in 1976. #ThrowbackThursday #SDCC," Twitter, July 20, 2017, 11:30 a.m., https://twitter.com/starwars/status/888058442740625409.

to see the silent *Lost World*. There was a great sense of adventure and fun, much more underground. When San Diego Comic-Con got 5,000 people, we were amazed."[7]

In 1974, following the lead of traditional science-fiction conventions, San Diego Comic-Con instituted its own Masquerade Costume Competition. Initially held on Sundays, the convention's masquerade grew in popularity with each year, and eventually, costumes began to spill out from that one event.

In 1980, the convention moved to its current home: the San Diego Convention and Performing Arts Center, and that year's programming included screenings of *Star Wars* and a costume masquerade. Throughout the rest of the 1980s, the convention featured a mix of award ceremonies, comic book creators, film screenings, and masquerades, while also introducing the Artists' Alley and an events guide. In the 1990s, Hollywood began to take even greater notice of the convention as more actors and directors began to appear there for panels and presentations. By the late 1990s, some of the biggest film franchises got their start at the convention, such as *X-Men*, *The Lord of the Rings*, *Spider-Man*, *The Matrix*, and the *Star Wars* prequel trilogy.[8]

In 2000, attendance at Comic-Con began to grow—quickly, writes Rob Salkowitz. "Comic books and Comic-Con alone are not responsible for this; comics culture is." He describes "comics culture" as "the blend of superheroes, animation, movies, video games, television shows, art, fashion, toys, accessories, and personalities that has emerged as the result of a postmillennial convergence of media and the concurrent explosion of online channels for connecting fans with the objects of their fandom."[9] A record-breaking 48,500 people attended the convention that year,[10] but it was possible for someone to walk up to the event the day of and get a ticket. Five years later, that number ballooned to more than 100,000 attendees.[11] In 2008, the convention sold out

---

7   Tim Appelo, "Comic-Con: Mark Hamill Says 'I Can't Walk the Floor Anymore,' " *Hollywood Reporter*, July 18, 2013, https://www.hollywoodreporter.com/news/comic-con-mark-hamill-says-585633.
8   "A Pictorial History of Comic-Con: The 1980s, The Silver Age of Comic-Con," Comic-Con International: San Diego (website), accessed December 4, 2021, https://www.comic-con.org/sites/default/files/forms/cci19_sb03_1980s.pdf.
9   Rob Salkowitz, *Comic-Con and the Business of Pop Culture: What the World's Wildest Trade Show Can Tell Us About the Future of Entertainment* (New York: McGraw-Hill, 2012), 15.
10 CBR Staff, "Comic-Con International 2000 Breaks Attendance Records," *CBR* (website), August 10, 2000, https://www.cbr.com/comic-con-international-2000-breaks-attendance-records/.
11 Sarah Baisley, "Comic-Con International 2005 Report," *AWN*, https://www.awn.com/animationworld/comic-con-international-2005-report

The floor of FAN EXPO Boston in August 2021.

Photos courtesy of Andrew Liptak

Bystanders line up to take pictures of an assembled group of Spider-Man characters at Dragon Con 2019 in Atlanta, Georgia.

completely before the show, at least 125,000 attendees.[12] The most recent, fully in-person SDCC in 2019 pulled in at least 135,000 attendees,[13] and it's not uncommon for tickets to the con to sell out within hours or even minutes. Hotel rooms in the area are often booked a full year in advance for the convention weekend. New York Comic Con has experienced a similar growth over the years, pulling in 33,000 people in 2006,[14] more than 100,000 in 2011,[15] and more than 250,000 people in 2018.[16]

Those conventions are just two of many such events held each year as more and more

---

12 Calvin Reid, "San Diego Comic-Con 2008: Bigger and Better," *Publishers Weekly*, July 28, 2008, https://www.publishersweekly.com/pw/by-topic/new-titles/adult-announcements/article/15136-san-diego-comic-con-2008-bigger-and-better.html.
13 "Breaking Down Comic-Con 2019 by the Numbers," San Diego Convention Center (website), July 11, 2019, https://www.visitsandiego.com/component/content/article/10-news-stories-spotlights/scene/13-breaking-down-comic-con-2019-by-the-numbers?Itemid=101.
14 "New York Comic-Con Announces 2007 Dates," *ICv2: The Business of Geek Culture*, May 24, 2006, https://icv2.com/articles/comics/view/8738/new-york-comic-con-announces-2007-dates.
15 Heidi MacDonald, Beth Scorzato, and Calvin Reid, "Comics News Stands Out From the Crowds at New York Comic-Con 2011," *Publishers Weekly*, October 20, 2011, https://www.publishersweekly.com/pw/by-topic/industry-news/comics/article/49195-comics-news-stands-out-from-the-crowds-at-new-york-comic-con-2011.html.
16 Calvin Reid, "A Record 250,000 Fans Mob New York Comic Con 2018," *Publishers Weekly*, October 10, 2018, https://www.publishersweekly.com/pw/by-topic/industry-news/comics/article/78281-a-record-250-000-fans-mob-new-york-comic-con-2018.html.

regional and local conventions spring up all over the country. The success of the comic convention boils down to its catch-all model for all things "comic culture." Despite its name and branding, Comic-Con has become an event that acted as a massive bucket for all things associated with nerd culture. Fans of all stripes could find something at the convention that they like, and publishing and studio marketing departments have since learned to use it as a launching point for their next big releases by screening trailers or entire films and setting up immersive experiences like escape rooms to give fans a memorable experience.

Cosplay has become a natural fixture at these conventions. It's not hard to see why: it's a safe environment for someone to show off their costume, and it's an event at which many people will either at least recognize, if not have an affinity for, one's character in question. As with the earlier science-fiction conventions, these massive gatherings help to foster a larger community of like-minded individuals: they represent places where fans of all kinds can find one another and even reunite on an annual basis.

Furthermore, the proliferation of conventions across the country—from small, one-day events held in libraries, schools, and community spaces to the top-tier cons that pack multi-block city convention centers—expands that fandom and provides cosplayers plenty of opportunities to revel in the excitement of the weekend or show off their latest costume before an adoring audience.

9 COSTUME PLAY

While major science-fiction franchises like *Ghostbusters*, *Star Trek*, and *Star Wars* have found mainstream popularity with Western audiences, Japanese animation has risen to become a juggernaut in entertainment across the world in the past two decades. Its immense fandom has propelled it to the forefront of the cosplay scene, as cosplayers find an endless amount of inspiration in its thousands of shows and characters.

While fan costuming in the United States has existed for more than a century, the rise of anime cosplay got its start much later, when Japanese writer and studio founder Nobuyuki Takahashi traveled to the United States to attend L.A.con II, the 1984 World Science Fiction Convention.

▰ THE RISE OF ANIME

Japan has a long tradition of science-fiction and fantasy literature—the works of European authors like Jules Verne were translated for Japanese readers in the mid-1800s,[1] and local authors built their own science-fiction scene in the years prior to the Second World War. With the development of film and animation in the 1910s, Japanese artists

---

1 Andrew Liptak, "Narratives of Modernization: A History of Chinese Science Fiction," *Transfer Orbit* (newsletter), February 12, 2021, https://transfer-orbit.ghost.io/narratives-of-modernization.

like Oten Shimokawa, Junichi Kouchi, and Seitaro Kitayama began to create their own animated films—the foundation of what would become anime.

On August 6 and 9, 1945, the United States dropped a pair of atomic bombs on the cities of Hiroshima and Nagasaki before occupying the country. This moment changed humanity's relationship with science and technology forever. These bombings and the decades of rebuilding that followed had a profound impact on Japan's arts scene—movies like Ishirō Honda's 1954 *Godzilla* was a direct response to the nuclear holocaust.

And while manga had been published in Japan for centuries, the comic book industry had an enormous postwar boom. As the country had modernized in the nineteenth century, artists had begun printing their work in magazines and newspapers. Following the Second World War, newspapers and magazines resumed their operations. In his book *Pure Invention: How Japan's Pop Culture Conquered the World*, Matt Alt notes that the Japanese public's "ravenous hunger for escapist content" helped to fuel demand for the comics.[2] Creator, illustrator, and writer Osamu Tezuka turned his fascination with Disney cartoons and his own experiences with fire bombings into the inspiration for *Mighty Atom*, a manga series about a scientist named Dr. Tenma who creates a robotic boy named Astro after his son, Tobio, is killed in an accident.[3] The series, first published in 1951, follows an alien civilization that relocates to Earth after their planet is destroyed. Thanks to the popularity of the series, Tezuka became a prolific creator and pivotal member of the country's growing manga scene in the years that followed. As with any creative field, Japan's comics industry went through a definitive series of changes throughout the 1950s as creators explored new stories and characters and pushed the boundaries of what was acceptable to publish.

While animated video had also been around for decades in Japan, a handful of factors helped it explode in popularity in the post-WWII era. One major factor was imported cartoons from the United States; as the country rebuilt, the demand for such entertainment grew, prompting a number of local artists to launch studios to cater to audiences. Alt notes that Tezuka had set out to create his own independent studio and along the way began to explore producing animated films. He and his artists eventually decided to try their hand at adapting *Mighty Atom* as an animated series, with plenty

---

2   Matt Alt, *Pure Invention: How Japan's Pop Culture Conquered the World* (New York: Crown, 2020), 49.
3   Yuki Tanaka, "War and Peace in the Art of Tezuka Osamu: The Humanism of his Epic Manga," *The Asia-Pacific Journal*, vol. 8, issue 38, no. 1, September 20, 2010, https://apjjf.org/-Yuki-Tanaka/3412/article.html.

of artwork to draw on for inspiration.[4] Creating the show was an expensive challenge, leading the artists to cut costs wherever they could; but once the series did debut on Japanese television in 1959, it was a huge hit. It rose to even further popularity when NBC picked it up in 1963. The series is a touchpoint in the history of Japanese anime, Alt writes, not only helping to establish it in the US but also setting some of the medium's long-standing features and trends like the "striking of theatrical poses, the lingering freeze-frames, the limited range of motions" that would come to characterize this animation style.

In the decades that followed, anime television and films grew to astounding popularity within Japan as the country's economy rebuilt itself. By the 1980s, anime had become mainstream, and up-and-coming creators like Hayao Miyazaki, who founded Studio Ghibli, came to the forefront with films like *Castle in the Sky* and *My Neighbor Totoro*, while sci-fi anime shows like *Space Battleship Yamato* and *Mobile Suit Gundam* found huge audiences throughout the country and the rest of the world. Alt explains that anime's explosion in popularity over the decades was due to the fact that fans were not only growing up watching anime but remained staunchly loyal to their series and the medium even as they got older. "There was no precedent for this kind of behavior in the postwar era," Alt writes, "or Japanese history as a whole, or anywhere on the planet."[5] These superfans—referred to in Japan as *otaku*—collect manga, fanzines, and merchandise, and flock to fan-run conventions like Tokyo's Comic Market (known locally as Comiket), which was founded in 1975 and has grown to become one of the largest events in the entire world, with hundreds of thousands of attendees every year.

But while US-based fans had been dressing up for decades as their favorite characters at conventions, costuming was a niche activity for fans in Japan, writes Michael Bruno in his 2002 newsletter *Glitz and Glitter*.[6] It wasn't unheard of—Japanese fans had been attending conventions as their favorite anime characters since the 1970s, taking cues from the events that had been taking place at US conventions.[7] Alt notes that the first-known Japanese cosplayer was likely a woman named Mari Kotani, who appeared at the

---

4 Alt, *Pure Invention: How Japan's Pop Culture Conquered the World*, 50–51.
5 Alt, *Pure Invention*, 208.
6 Michael Bruno, "Cosplay: The Illegitimate Child of SF Masquerades," *Glitz and Glitter Newsletter*, Millennium Costume Guild, October 2002, https://millenniumcg.tripod.com/glitzglitter/1002articles.html.
7 Daisuke Okabe, "Cosplay, Learning, and Cultural Practice," in *Fandom Unbound, Otaku Culture in a Connected World*, ed. Mizuko Ito, Daisuke Okabe, and Izumi Tsuji (Danbury, CT: Yale University Press, 2012), 229.

1978 Japan Science Fiction Convention dressed as Ulysses Paxton, the lead character from Edgar Rice Burroughs's novel *A Fighting Man of Mars*.[8]

Everything began to change in the mid-1980s, when writer and anime producer Nobuyuki Takahashi came to Los Angeles for the 1984 Worldcon, known as L.A.con II, with plans to write about the event for publications back home. He was excited about what he encountered at the convention, particularly at the event's masquerade.[9] Nobuyuki was "amazed by what he saw," Bruno wrote. "Many people dressed as their favorite characters from *Star Trek*, *Star Wars* and even in their own costumed creations." From there, he set about sharing what he had encountered with his readers, hoping to bring the practice back with him.

Writing about the con for a Japanese outlet called *My Anime*, he had trouble describing exactly what he saw. "He struggled for a long time with what he could call this phenomenon," Bruno wrote. "He could use the word 'masquerade,' as the direct translation to Japanese is essentially the same as the original meaning in English, 'a costume party held by aristocrats.'" But "masquerade" didn't quite convey what the activity was: a sort of fan-driven costumed performance for fun.

He wanted something short and memorable, so he eventually settled on the portmanteau of "costume play," or "cosplay."

The phenomenon finally had a name.

JAPANESE COSPLAY EXPLODES

With its introduction and codification from Nobuyuki, cosplay grew in popularity within Japan, thanks in part to the resurgence of anime classics like *Mobile Suit Gundam* and *Urusei Yatsura*.[10] "Cosplay" as a term slowly trickled out, notes Brian Ashcraft and Luke Plunkett in their book *Cosplay World*, but came into widespread use within fan circles over the next couple of years.[11] Over the course of the 1990s, cosplay continued to grow in popularity, snowballing to become a major community that included costumes of manga comics, anime, and even costume-oriented rock bands.

---

8   Alt, *Pure Invention: How Japan's Pop Culture Conquered the* World, 205.
9   Theresa Winge, "Costuming the Imagination: Origins of Anime and Manga Cosplay," in *Mechademia 1: Emerging Worlds of Anime and Manga*, ed. Frenchy Lunning (Minneapolis: University of Minnesota Press, 2006), 66.
10 Okabe, "Cosplay, Learning, and Cultural Practice," 229.
11 Brian Ashcraft and Luke Plunkett, *Cosplay World* (Munich: Prestel, 2014), 20.

As cosplay has grown in popularity in Japan, it's taken on its own cultural characteristics and tendencies there, distinct from existing practices around the world. According to Bruno, there are some significant departures. Whereas cosplayers in US-based masquerades would often perform a short skit as the character at a convention masquerade and might appear in public in costume (even if they're just walking to and from a convention), Japanese cosplayers approach costuming and performance a little differently: "When they take the stage, they strike a pose, exactly as their character would," and then move on.[12]

The Japanese convention scene also has more restrictions for those in costume, dictating where and when they can dress up and appear, especially in public. Tokyo City University lecturer Daisuke Okabe writes that in its earlier days a handful of factors, ranging from convention neighbors' complaints to conflicts between costumed and non-costumed fans, led to strict new rules for attendees: Cosplayers are generally forbidden from wearing costumes in public spaces and are required to dress up on convention premises. And photographs from bystanders can be taken only in certain designated areas at a convention.[13] Indeed, cosplayers and fans looking to travel to Japan are generally encouraged to check with each event's specific guidelines and rules, so they can honor these significant cultural differences and practices when it comes to costuming.[14]

Despite these restrictions, cosplay has grown to become a mainstream activity within Japan, prompting the creation of an entire industry: Tokyo's Akihabara and Harajuku districts in particular are home to many dedicated cosplay stores, lounges, clubs, and restaurants. The industry has grown to such an extent that some have found they can make a comfortable living as professional cosplayers. In 2021 the Japanese government began to look into amending copyright laws to allow companies to charge fans for using their IP,[15] but it was forced to step back after cosplayers and fans voiced concerns about the detrimental effect it could have on the culture.[16]

---

12   Bruno, "Cosplay: The Illegitimate Child of SF Masquerades."
13   Okabe, "Cosplay, Learning, and Cultural Practice," 230.
14   R. Lowen, "What to Expect When Cosplaying In Japan," Around Akiba, https://aroundakiba.tv/stories/cosplaying-guide-japan.
15   Kelsey Endter, "Japan's New Copyright Law Proposal May Bring Changes For Cosplay," Cosplay Central (website), January 25, 2021, https://www.cosplaycentral.com/topics/cosplay/news/japans-new-copyright-law-proposal-may-bring-changes-for-cosplay.
16   Kelsey Endter, "New Cosplay Copyright Law in Japan Clarified by Government," Cosplay Central (website), https://www.cosplaycentral.com/topics/cosplay/news/new-cosplay-copyright-law-in-japan-clarified-by-government.

NORTH AMERICAN FANDOM

Doug Wilder, a member of AnimeCons.com's podcast staff, explained to me that the proliferation of anime conventions in the United States in the 1990s came out of the anime screening rooms that science-fiction and fantasy conventions had included in their programming over the years. "That's why you see many of the anime cons with heavy programming schedules with panels and discussions," Wilder says.[17] As anime fandom grew at these events, fans began to organize their own dedicated anime conventions. A-Kon, one of the first such conventions, began in Dallas, Texas, in 1990, while Washington, DC's Otakon first ran in 1994.

Anime began to grow in popularity in the United States during the 1990s as various networks brought over franchises like *Dragon Ball Z*, *Sailor Moon*, and *Pokémon*, which broadly appealed to US audiences.

As anime took off in the United States, Japanese studios began to license their shows more frequently to US distributors and networks. Turner Broadcasting launched Cartoon Network in 1992 as a standalone channel, and in 1997 developed a dedicated programming block for anime called Toonami. The Sci-Fi Channel had its own similar block in the mid-1990s called Saturday Anime. "Toonami brought anime into the mainstream with its cultural identity intact," says Kristian Williams in a video essay about Toonami,[18] explaining that the network understood what was most appealing about anime: not the action and adventure, but the fact that it told stories that didn't talk down to kids. In September 2001, Cartoon Network launched a block of adult-oriented animated shows, Adult Swim, which soon included anime. Williams said that "Adult Swim's biggest con-

Lin Han of Ottawa, Canada, poses as Ranka Lee from the anime series Macross Frontier.

Courtesy of Bryan Cruz

---

17   Doug Wilder in conversation with the author, February 2020.
18   kaptainkristian, "Toonami - A History of Broadcast Anime," YouTube video, January 19, 2017, https://www.youtube.com/watch?v=-Et4vu4lpPI.

tribution to television was its introduction to mature anime to an American audience, and it started with *Cowboy Bebop* in 2001."[19]

Across the country in Hawaii, cosplayer Dallas Nagata White noted that because of her Japanese ancestry and upbringing in the Pacific state, she was already keenly aware of the animation style growing up, from watching shows like *Dragon Ball Z* via fan-dubbed VHS tapes or on Toonami on television.

One reason for the rise in anime's popularity was its growing accessibility, says Wilder. In the mid-1990s, various shows were available to watch on VHS, but they were prohibitively expensive for casual fans: thirty to forty dollars for a single VHS tape with one or two episodes. The format led to some other problems as well, since the growing anime community was split between two big camps: those who watched their shows with an English dub and those who watched them in Japanese with English subtitles.

With the introduction of DVDs, studios could cram more data—meaning more episodes—onto each unit, as well as multiple audio tracks and options like subtitles. The broader availability of DVDs and their lower price meant that more people could begin watching. "That's why you see it really take off in the early 2000s," says Wilder. "And it's also when a lot more cons started popping up more and more. You saw more companies and fans going online to share information, and as a result, more people are finding out about more anime titles because it's just easier to get the information about them."[20]

Wilder explained that while it was the art style that initially drew people in, "suddenly we're hooked because we realize there's a deeper story going on, or a type of story that we're not used to seeing."

Nagata White concurred and chalked up anime's popularity to the fact that it provided an alternative to the cartoons available in the US: "I remember one of the early [shows] I got into because of the art style, *Fushigi Yûgi*, and there are a lot of mature themes. It was super taboo at the time, not like what we have now on HBO."[21]

Part of that, she notes, was simply due to different cultural norms. Shows like *Dragon Ball Z* or *Sailor Moon*, she says, were "the intro anime for people, and the versions we got here in America were more watered down than the original Japanese versions. One of my

---

19 kaptainkristian, "Adult Swim - The History of a Television Empire," YouTube video, April 11, 2016, https://www.youtube.com/watch?v=Pkup4zo97E0.
20 Doug Wilder interview.
21 Dallas Nagata White in conversation with the author, February 2020.

early memories of the original dub of *Dragon Ball Z* was an early episode when Vegeta shows up on Earth, they blow up a helicopter. You know people are dead, but in the dub, someone says 'Oh, they're fine, I see their parachutes,' and there are no parachutes."

The rise of anime in North America coincided with the introduction of the internet, which fostered a vibrant online community of anime fans. Also, streaming and downloading allowed fans to watch episodes immediately without having to wait for them to come to US networks months or years after airing on Japanese TV.

That intense anime fandom translated into an explosion of cosplay. There are not only quite a few long-running shows out there but a huge variety of them. Ottawa, Canada–based cosplayer Lin Han explained that anime as a medium is perfect for cosplayers: it allows for a range of interpretations, from super accurate to looser depictions of characters, to an endless number of different types of characters and costumes. It also tends to skew toward younger audiences, she observed, bringing new people into the scene. "It's always struck me that when you go to places like Dragon Con, you have people who have been there for a long time and tend to be older, because Western media has been around forever. Anime is geared and focused on a younger audience. You go to an anime con, and you have a much younger age group, and there's a different vibe to the cons."[22]

Wilder stressed that anime isn't a genre; it's a medium. "There's science fiction, there's comedy, there's martial arts, superhero stuff. There's all types out there, and sure, they might share a lot of similar tropes, but there's a whole bunch of different things."

Wilder also explained that the animated format leads to plenty of unique designs and characters. "These characters' designs are so vibrant and very brightly colored or very distinctive." He pointed to *Sailor Moon* as an example: the outfits worn by the characters in the show are fairly basic, but they stand out because of their colors. Other shows like *My Hero Academia* and *Naruto* follow a similar lead, providing plenty of variety and distinctive, eye-catching colors for cosplayers to use in their own outfits.

The tight-knit community of anime fans and the proliferation of anime conventions that followed are key factors in the development and growth of cosplay as a whole in the United States from the 2000s onward. While anime had yet to reach the mainstream status that it enjoys in the US today, it was the focal point of a rapidly growing movement of dedicated fans who would come together in gatherings small (local anime clubs at

---

22 Lin Han in conversation with the author, February 2020.

Anime transcends genre, and as a result, there's no shortage of characters for cosplayers to replicate or reinterpret.

Courtesy of Bryan Cruz

schools or other organizations) and large (conventions like Anime Expo), where they'd not only get to celebrate their fandom with others and find merchandise curated for them but also see others dressed up—sometimes elaborately—as their favorite characters.

After Takahashi witnessed cosplay in action at L.A.con II in 1984 and helped kick-start the movement's growth back home, the same factors that led to its rise in Japan launched it further into the mainstream in the United States. Accordingly, anime conventions sprang up across the country. The early 2000s were pivotal for both the anime industry in the US and the contemporary cosplay world. Major cosplay figures like Yaya Han would find their start by attending anime conventions and falling in love with the practice. It was also a period in which people were starting to connect with one another on internet forums and dedicated fan websites like Cosplay.com and American Cosplay Paradise (ACP). Cosplayers could find one another between conventions, further strengthening community bonds.

As a result, the broader cosplay field is anything but a singular vocation or activity: it's an amalgamation of fan traditions and movements that have come together. It's reminiscent of the older science-fiction fandom that had formed out of the 1920s–1930s publishing industry; of media fans who came to fandom through shows like *Star Trek* and movies like *Star Wars*; and of the dedicated clubs and conventions throughout the country in the mid-1980s. They all charted a path to the same goal: expressing their love and appreciation for the stories that inspired them.

10 MAINSTREAM ACCEPTANCE

For decades, science-fiction and fantasy film, literature, and television were looked down upon by their more mainstream genre counterparts and creators, a lingering result of their low-brow origins: cheaply printed paper, cardboard sets, and escapist themes.

In the mid-1990s, that began to change. Television creators like J. Michael Straczynski, Rick Berman, and Michael Piller began to experiment with the storytelling format on their shows *Babylon 5* and *Deep Space 9*, shifting away from standalone, episodic installments in favor of longer, serialized story lines. This set the groundwork for other ambitious projects that would follow, like Ronald D. Moore's reboot of the 1978 science-fiction series *Battlestar Galactica* on the Sci-Fi Channel. The series garnered widespread acclaim from critics, who pointed to its scientific realism and political relevance. This wasn't random escapism: it was a serious drama.

The 2000s was also when genre blockbusters took over movie theater box offices. Peter Jackson's *The Lord of the Rings* blew away audiences with its serious take on J. R. R. Tolkien's classic fantasy trilogy, while adaptations of J. K. Rowling's Harry Potter novels became just as popular as their source material. Superhero films like *X-Men* and *Spider-Man* kicked off the comic book adaptation bandwagon, setting the stage for the Marvel Cinematic Universe, which began in 2009 with *Iron Man*. J. J. Abrams revived *Star Trek* in theaters, while George Lucas finished out his *Star Wars* prequel trilogy and followed it up with an animated television series, *The Clone Wars*. Meanwhile, shows like *The Big Bang Theory* and *Community* helped to introduce and popularize traditional geek activities such as comic books, Comic-Con, *Dungeons & Dragons*, and cosplay for a much wider audience.

From that foundation, genre fans had plenty to choose from in the 2010s: on television, there was AMC's *The Walking Dead*; HBO's *Game of Thrones*, *Westworld*, and *True Detective*; The CW's *Arrow* (and its sister DC Universe shows); Netflix's *Stranger Things*, and the mini Marvel universe featuring *Daredevil*, *Jessica Jones*, *Luke Cage*, *Iron Fist*, and *The Punisher*; Amazon's *The Expanse*; Hulu's *The Handmaid's Tale*; and plenty more. Science fiction continued to take over as well: the Marvel Cinematic Universe played out over twenty-one installments; *Star Wars* returned to theaters with *The Force Awakens*; and Warner Bros. launched the DC Extended Universe. There were plenty of other high-concept genre projects as well, such as *Arrival, Annihilation, Blade Runner 2049, Ex Machina, Interstellar, Mad Max: Fury Road*, and *Gravity*. These projects have gone mainstream in ways that fans of yesteryear could have only dreamed of. Where stories about aliens, dragons, and zombies were once confined to a niche audience, the wider viewing public was now obsessed with them. Today, "fan," "nerd," and "geek" are no longer epithets: they're badges of honor.

Finally, the 2000s kicked off a new era of popularity for video games, with megagames like *Fallout, Gears of War, Half-Life, Halo, World of Warcraft*, and others exploding in popularity, due in part to the release of next-generation consoles (which allowed for better graphics) and internet access, which became only more universal as smartphones improved and hosted higher-quality games for hundreds of millions around the world.

Accompanying all this genre content was the proliferation of fan websites—the modern-day equivalent of the fanzines of old—which pulled together viewers to discuss the latest episodes, their favorite characters, theories on where the show/book/film would go next, and more. As the saying goes, "If you build it, they will come." With more genre content certainly came more fans in a long-running feedback loop that still shows no sign of slowing down.

As a result, the cosplay scene exploded. Fans had more characters than ever to choose from and more places to go in costume, and they could do so knowing that their fandom was no longer stigmatized.

Dana Gasser, cofounder of the since-closed costume company ANOVOS, explained that the company's founding in 2009 came right as cosplay and conventions were growing in popularity. "Look at that time frame," he told me. In 2009, "you could still get a ticket to Comic-Con at the door. There weren't a lot of conventions. Being a geek was a closet thing in the sense that you couldn't tell people you were going to Comic-Con without them looking at you funny."[1]

"It became a little more open in the sense where you started seeing television shows like *The Big Bang Theory* and competition shows," he explained. "Geek wasn't so nerdy at the time anymore. Nerds were in. This became more popular when people saw that these costumes were available, and that they were good quality. It took time for people to understand that, and because Comic-Con and anything geek became popular—that's when cosplay began to explode."

This incredible fan and media environment helped explode cosplay from a niche convention activity into mainstream acceptance. All those genre shows and movies and comics provided an endless stream of inspiration and reference material for dedicated cosplayers, who turned out to conventions and on Halloween in everything from DHARMA Initiative coveralls to Spider-Man suits; they dressed as zombies, Time Lords, Starfleet officers, and plenty more. Fans took their love of their books, comics, films, and shows from internet discussion forums to the convention floor.

Beyond the general rise in popularity of genre properties is another underlying factor: the costumes seen in games, movies, TV shows, and comics were well suited for cosplayer replication: there are more options than ever to make something that can stand out in a crowd.

Katie Henderson, a cosplayer from Vermont, appeared at Dragon Con in 2019 dressed as her own character from the Bungie video game *Destiny*. "Everybody does something different," she told me.

Henderson explained that she chose to design her armor based on her avatar in the game. She printed out reference images and templates based on the generic sets of armor that were available from other makers online and modified them to suit her body type and the look of her character. Henderson noted that the game allows players to customize everything about their armor, from the types of plates that they wear to the colors and

---

[1] Dana Gasser in conversation with the author, February 2020.

LEFT: Cosplayer Katie Henderson poses at Dragon Con 2019, in armor she designed to replicate her character from the video game *Destiny*.

RIGHT: Cosplayers suited up in armor from the video game *Destiny* pose for cameras at Dragon Con in 2019.

equipment and decorations, and that many of the people in attendance were dressing up as their own characters from the game.

As the *Destiny* cosplayers lined up for a massive group photo on a set of steps at the convention center that year, they walked around in suits of elaborate armor and massive weapons, much of which was crafted from foam. This degree of character individuality extends beyond *Destiny* to many video games, including *Gears of War*, *Titanfall*, and *Halo*, all of which allow for detailed customization in dress, build, and accessories. Accordingly, even the cosplayers who show up at conventions dressed as the same character will be wearing a wide range of interpretations on that character.

This level of customization means that foam is a crucial building material for these cosplayers. Unlike a trooper from *Star Wars*, for example, there is no one-size-fits-all solution for these types of characters: they're completely unique.

"I've met a couple of people who have one particular chest plate," she said, "but they all have a slightly different color on it, or something else that sets it apart. I have a bit of

Cosplayer Dallas Nagata White poses for a picture in her Spartan armor from the *Halo* video game franchise in Hawaii.

Courtesy of Dallas Nagata White & Ed White

a modified set of shaders and ornaments on my own guardian that I have then taken to my level."[2]

Dallas Nagata White notes that there is another reason video games are attractive source materials for cosplayers: they often demand a lot of time and emotional investment from players. They can not only spend days, weeks, or months working to beat a game, but as video games have incorporated vast open-world maps and multiplayer elements, they can sink an endless amount of time into the world and lore, forming an intimate relationship between gamer and game. Moreover, playing a video game puts players in a world in which they can affect their character's actions and decisions.

In many ways, cosplay is just a short hop away from that—a translation from digital

---

[2] Katie Henderson in conversation with the author, August 2019.

property into the real world that allows them to physically embody their character, right down to the preferences they use in the game.

The proliferation of anime alongside the rise in video games has also boosted cosplay's profile. As all these forms of genre entertainment have grown in popularity within mainstream audiences, cosplay has also appeared more often in the media and in public. News outlets run stories about cosplayers around major conventions either as a local interest piece or as part of national coverage.

Cosplay has appeared in mainstream productions and gone viral online. One notable example is violinist Lindsey Stirling, who released a video of herself dressed as Link from *The Legend of Zelda* franchise, playing a medley of music from the series.[3] She later followed it up with other medleys from stories like *Skyrim*,[4] *Game of Thrones*,[5] *Assassin's Creed III*,[6] *Halo*,[7] and more, using those videos and the associated coverage to gain an audience for her original music. The tactic worked, bringing in billions of views on YouTube since her first viral video in 2007. "I started doing original songs and would intersperse covers in between to try and get traction," she told Fandom.com in 2019. "I had this fun idea of doing electronic and dubstep and then I'd squeeze in *Legend of Zelda* and *Skyrim* to get the audience, and it worked!"[8]

Stirling's use of costumes was only one of many small instances in which cosplay went before a major audience.

Cosplay has appeared in other mainstream productions as well: it's a frequent element of the sitcom *The Big Bang Theory*, in which the main cast either appears in costume or talks about cosplay on the show. In an episode of the TV procedural *Castle*, one particularly meta moment is when the show's titular character (played

---

3   Lindsey Stirling, "Zelda Medley - Lindsey Stirling," YouTube video, November 26, 2011, https://www.youtube.com/watch?v=b3KUyPKbR7Q.
4   Peter Hollens feat. Lindsey Stirling, "Skyrim - Lindsey Stirling & Peter Hollens," YouTube video, April 3, 2012, https://www.youtube.com/watch?v=BSLPH9d-jsI.
5   Lindsey Stirling and Peter Hollens, "Game of Thrones - Lindsey Stirling," YouTube video, September 5, 2012, https://www.youtube.com/watch?v=_oNpmSAvpGQ.
6   Lindsey Stirling, "Lindsey Stirling - Assassin's Creed III (official video)," YouTube video, November 5, 2012, https://www.youtube.com/watch?v=MOg8Cz9yfWg.
7   Lindsey Stirling, "Halo Theme - Lindsey Stirling and William Joseph," YouTube video, May 23, 2013, https://www.youtube.com/watch?v=jLnL63cXmD8.
8   Tom Regan, "Lindsey Stirling Talks Using Fandoms for Good, Reinventing Violin & YouTube Fame," Fandom (website), December 19, 2019, https://www.fandom.com/articles/lindsey-stirling-interview.

by Nathan Fillion) not only dresses up in costume but cosplays as *his* character from *Firefly*, Malcolm Reynolds. Other shows, like *Brooklyn Nine-Nine*, *Community*, *CSI*, *Mythic Quest,* and *Supernatural,* and movies including *Fanboys* and *Galaxy Quest*, have all set scenes at conventions and depict cosplay in the background or as key plot points, further helping to highlight and normalize the hobby for audiences.

Cosplay has also been the focus of reality television. The Sci-Fi Channel, rebranded as Syfy in 2009, launched a reality series in 2011 about special effects makeup called *Face Off*, which ran for seven years and produced a spin-off, *Face Off: Game Face*, in 2017. The network also released *Heroes of Cosplay* in 2013 and 2014, featuring cosplayers such as Yaya Han, Chloe Dykstra, and Riki LeCotey; as well as *Cosplay Melee*, hosted by *Community*'s Yvette Nicole Brown. Both shows took viewers through the ins and outs of creating costumes each week and helped show off some of the cosplay world to a wider public. Frank Ippolito, a contestant on the first season of *Face Off*, explained to me that when he was a kid, "I saw *The Making of 'Thriller'* and it was the first time I ever saw someone glue rubber onto someone else's face to turn them into a zombie. I'm sure for the next generation, the first time they saw it was in the five or six years *Face Off* was on television."

Some cosplayers also break into mainstream attention with an eye-catching costume or outfit by going viral on social media. In 2009, cosplayer Jessica Nigri attended SDCC dressed as "Sexy Pikachu," a costume that consisted of a short yellow skirt, low-cut crop top, a tail, and ears. She quickly earned widespread attention from news outlets for her take on the character. In other instances, news outlets pick up stories about cosplayers like Alyson Tabbitha, who published a series of before and after photographs of her work,[9] or Mandy Pursley, who made a Cinderella costume with her prosthetic arm replacing the character's shoe,[10] further disseminating the scene to a mainstream audience.

All of these factors—the rise in genre entertainment; the increased connectiv-

---

9   Daniel Boan, "The Internet Is Obsessed with a Woman Who Can Transform Herself into Virtually Any Character," *Insider*, October 25, 2017, https://www.insider.com/cosplayer-transforms-into-characters-wonder-woman-photos-2017-10.
10 Priya Sridhar, "The Story of a Cinderella Costume With a Twist Goes Viral," with video by Matthew Bowler, *KPBS*, September 30, 2019, https://www.kpbs.org/news/2019/sep/30/oceanside-woman-inspires-others-cinderella-costume.

ity afforded by the internet; the ongoing DIY and maker movements; and the ease of access to supplies, materials, and tutorials—helped to propel cosplay into the pop culture zeitgeist. Whereas once cosplayers faced ridicule, or at the very least an odd look from family, coworkers, or strangers, they're now celebrated for their creativity and passion. The concept of cosplay is now familiar to most, and now that its genie is out of the bottle, someone only has to come up with a costume for it.

11 IDENTITY

Our racial and gender identities are often closely intertwined with the stories that we tell. We can relate to characters in narratives based on where they're from, their appearance, and how they interact with the world around them.

The majority of the books, comics, films, and television shows we consume in the United States are made by and intended for a white, cis male audience. This is a product of the structure that supports and produces these stories, and the product of our country's much deeper history of institutionalized racism and discrimination.

That being said, the fans of these stories have never only been white cis men. Women and people of color have been an integral part of science fiction from its inception, and have been in the ranks of its creators and fans for generations.

So, too, cosplayers represent a wealth of diversity, coming from all ethnic backgrounds, genders, and socioeconomic classes. The stories we love appeal to us on a universal level. As cosplay is a way to express one's fandom and appreciation for any given story, it's an opportunity to reimagine characters in new ways.

In one notable instance, writer and cosplayer Blair Imani attended San Diego Comic-Con for the first time in 2019. She had been invited to take part in a panel called "Super Salaam," about depictions of Muslims in comics. "I was trying to figure out, how do I fit into this conversation?" A lifelong *Star Trek* fan, she went down a rabbit hole on Wikipedia and discovered that the character Geordi La Forge (played by LeVar Burton in *Star Trek:*

The Next Generation) had been born in Mogadishu, Somalia, in 2335. "I thought, 'Oh, well, that's a majority-Muslim country, it's a Black country.' This feels very close to what, you know, who I am. I'm not Somali, but I'm a Black Muslim," she told me. "So I started to imagine what a woman Geordi La Forge would look like, a practicing Muslim, and I started to curate the outfit."

Imani noted that clothing was always a major part of her life. Her mother designed clothes for Neiman Marcus and a number of musicians throughout the 1980s, and as a result, "Dress as a form of self-expression was a part of my childhood."[1]

With inspirations such as Lady Gaga, Imani used how she dressed as a form of identity and to express herself. "I didn't go to school with a uniform, and so I would experiment with makeup looks, and I would wear tutus to school, and I was always very fashionable," she said. "I would start wearing clothes like on *Project Runway* instead of just school clothes.

"I think it really helped me articulate to the world this is who I am, before I could put words to it. I see it like dressing a cartoon character every day. Not a specific cartoon character, but like how some cartoon characters were wearing the same thing every day, and then others just dress like wacky, hyper-expressed versions of themselves. That's what I tried to do."

She bought a visor from a seller on Etsy. "I wanted to wear a hijab with it," she recounted. "Because that's how I'm most comfortable." When she told friends that she was attending the con in costume, they were excited. "People were like, 'Oh, wow, please keep it authentic to yourself!'"

Blair Imani posing as Geordi La Forge from *Star Trek: The Next Generation*.
Courtesy of Blair Imani
Photo by Kaelan Barowsky

---

1 Blair Imani in conversation with the author, August 2019.

Imani explains that she was nervous about wearing the costume to the convention. "I thought that I wouldn't get any acceptance for my outfit. I thought it would be very hostile. But that's because of how Muslims are treated in the media. I brought friends with me, in case I needed to change outfits or something. I brought a backup."

Imani's costume wasn't without detractors: she noted that people criticized it for being out of character for the world created by Roddenberry, who imagined a future without religion. "The biggest argument that I got from people was, 'Religion doesn't fit in!' It's so interesting that people look to secularism as progress when religion has existed for millennia and ebbs and flows with humanity."

Imani noted that she came up with the costume thinking about the world and the themes that Gene Roddenberry embedded in the world of *Star Trek*. "People who actually knew Gene came to my defense immediately," Imani said. "But it makes me think about the way that human bias is written into fandom, whether intentionally or accidentally. For some people, it might have been, 'Okay, I don't see Muslims as part of society, much less the future, so I'm going to imprint that onto someone else in a negative way,'" she said. "While other people were saying no, the future is infinite, it can be anything."

But primarily, "it turned out that there was a lot of acceptance," she explained. Pictures of her in costume went viral,[2] attracting the attention of Burton himself, who tweeted: "Best cosplay of Geordi, EVER . . . Thank you, little Sister, you honor not only me, but all the kids out there who saw LaForge as a hero."[3]

"A lot of people look to fandom and cosplay as an escape," Imani noted, "but for some of us, it's a way to look for hope. I think that as we look to escape from some of the harsher and difficult things in Western society, we can also look to cosplay as a way to make that path forward and open up that path for other people."

As we've established, the act of cosplaying encompasses degrees of accuracy, ranging from costumes that loosely approximate a character or moment to something that matches an originating character almost perfectly. As a result, there's wide latitude for cosplayers to take up their own interpretations of characters and the worlds that they inhabit, endlessly remixing and modifying them. And, like much of science fiction, *Star*

---

[2] Lindsay Lowe, "'Star Trek' fan at Comic-Con adds a hijab to her Starfleet costume," *Today*, July 24, 2019, https://www.today.com/style/star-trek-fan-comic-con-adds-hijab-costume-t159461.
[3] LeVar Burton (@levarburton), Twitter, July 20, 2019, 6:21 a.m., https://twitter.com/levarburton/status/1152523929346383872.

1. Dorasae Rosario's depiction of a Nargacuga monster from Capcom's video game *Monster Hunter World*.
2. Dorasae Rosario's depiction of a Faerie Dragon from *World of Warcraft*.
3. Dorasae Rosario posing as Shuri from *Black Panther* at Dragon Con 2019.
4. Dorasae Rosario (Akakioga) poses for a photo shoot at Katsucon 2019 as Argent Confessor Paletress from *World of Warcraft*.
5. Dorasae Rosario's interpretation of Sirfetch'd from *Pokémon: Sword and Shield*. In the game, this particular Pokémon is a large bird—Rosario has reimagined the character in human form.
6. Dorasae Rosario noted that she's faced discrimination and racist harassment from commentators for portraying characters of a different race.

Photos courtesy of Dorasae Rosario

Trek isn't apolitical, Imani points out. "It's very political. It had the first interracial kiss on TV—that's huge. And as much as we want to escape in sci-fi, we also have a duty to engage in reality, and be true to the original creator's vision of infinite diversity and infinite combinations and how that applies today."[4]

#28DAYSOFBLACKCOSPLAY

Dorasae Rosario, an African American cosplayer who goes by the username Akakioga, has similarly found inspiration in television shows and movies. "My first convention was

---

4   Blair Imani interview.

Anime Expo 2006 back in Anaheim, California," she says. "It was a spontaneous thing: my mom bought me tickets to go, and we went together. I didn't know what cosplay was when I walked through the doors of the convention, when I saw people dressed up from the shows I watched as a child."[5]

That encounter prompted her to begin cosplaying as she grew older. She started with costumes from outlets like Party City and later began making her own. As she entered the cosplay scene by attending conventions, she found a welcoming community that shared her passion for the same stories.

But she also faced discrimination and harassment from people online, an experience shared by many cosplayers of color. Online critics hammered them for dressing up as characters that didn't match their ethnicity, saying that they couldn't dress up as those characters because their skin was a different color.

Performing arts has a long and unfortunate history when it comes to race. Early minstrel shows utilized white performers in black makeup to play racist caricatures of African Americans, and while that practice has been relegated to the past, every year brings up some viral moment where a college student or overzealous costumer decides to color their face in a similar fashion. Even if it's an attempt to be accurate, the social

---

5   Dorasae Rosario in conversation with the author, February 2020.

IDENTITY

Fire_Forged_Cosplay poses at Dragon Con 2019 during the *Game of Thrones* photo shoot.

Photos courtesy of Andrew Liptak

A cosplayer poses during Dragon Con's *Game of Thrones* photo shoot in 2019.

impact and history of blackface outweigh that, and the action is rightly called out and condemned.

Cosplayers of color are often forced into an uncomfortable space, one where they are confined to either a limited number of characters who look like them who have appeared over the years, or stepping outside of their racial group and into a different one, tasked with reimagining the character at the same time. Rosario notes that she's been the subject of numerous racist attacks online because she cosplayed as characters who weren't Black. "At one point, I almost quit cosplaying," she says, "because I got so much racist hate. It was over a character that I really loved, Diva from *Overwatch*. People just got really mean, to the point where I asked if cosplay was even worth it. The voice actress who played the character in the game reached out to me online and defended me. That was the moment where I was like, 'There are people out there who need to see me do this, there are people who need to see other cosplayers being unapologetic about their skin color.' "

In recent years, Hollywood studios have come under fire for their lack of diversity in their films and in the crews that make them, with critics pointing out that actors and crew members from marginalized identities and backgrounds are not only underrepresented but face an ingrained culture of exclusion. Their productions included some of the biggest—and most cosplayable—franchises, like the Marvel Cinematic Universe and *Star Wars*. In response, studios have put out pledges that they are committing to doing better by hiring more diverse writers' rooms and crews and introducing more characters of color in their productions. There have been some notable changes: Marvel's *Black Panther* and Sony's *Spider-Man: Into the Spider-Verse,* each with Black actors prominently featured, hit theaters to box office and critical success, while Lucasfilm has introduced more women and characters of color into the *Star Wars* franchise in shows like *The Mandalorian* and *The Book of Boba Fett*. These successes have encouraged studios to invest more in diverse projects. But there's still a long way to go.

These efforts have a tangible impact on the fan community. South Carolina–based cosplayer Jenni Tyler explained to me that she got sucked into the world of cosplay when her fiancé began making her costumes. "The characters I have portrayed (thus far) were first approached because of how cool they made me look, but it sort of evolved from

Jenni Tyler poses as Raya from Disney's *Raya and the Last Dragon* at Dragon Con 2021.

Courtesy of Jenni Tyler

there into how I can grow my skills and into characters that I connect with," she explained. Tyler, who is Korean and African American, noted that she has yet to experience any racism while in costume, but says, "I'm about ninety-five percent sure it will happen at one point, as I have experienced it in almost every other facet of life."

As studios branch out and cast characters of color, fans and cosplayers find new role models that validate their identities. "When *Black Panther* came out, my cousins went to see it, and when they were told that there would be Black actors in the movie, they assumed that those would be the bad guys. And that assumption can't be the norm anymore," Tyler explained. "Representation isn't just important for people of color, I think it's great for everyone to grow up with an understanding that people with different skin tones and cultural backgrounds can and do exist in the same space. I think movies like *Raya and the Last Dragon*, *Luca*, *Moana*, and *Coco* are providing that space."

Within the cosplay community, there are efforts to highlight, champion, and celebrate cosplayers of color. Each February, cosplayers break out a hashtag called #28DaysofBlackCosplay, which they use to shine a light on their community. Rosario notes that the movement was founded by a cosplayer named Chaka Cumberbatch, who had cosplayed as a *Sailor Moon* character. "She is a Black girl, and she posted her Sailor Venus online, and of course, as racist white dudes do, they racist."

The moment coincided with Black History Month, and Cumberbatch started the hashtag to celebrate the Black cosplay community. The movement has been a success, bringing together cosplayers and forging new connections. "It's one of my favorite times of the year," says Rosario. "I not only get to share other Black cosplayers that I might have never heard about, but I get to celebrate with everybody. Do you realize how many cool Black cosplayers there are out there? Over the years, more and more people have not only started cosplaying, but because of this, have also taken the helm of getting the next generation of Black cosplayers into the community."[6]

IDENTIFYING GENDER

Dressing in costume—perhaps masks, hair dye, layers of cloth, or plates of armor—can obscure one's identity, transforming a fan into a favored character. Due to this, cos-

---

6   Dorasae Rosario in conversation with the author, February 2020.

Thorn Reilly, who identifies as nonbinary, posing in their Mandalorian costume at FAN EXPO Boston in 2019.

Photos courtesy of Andrew Liptak

play can act as a refuge: a way for an individual to not only change their appearance but possibly present as a different gender.

The LGBTQ+ community has made incredible strides toward achieving recognition and equality over the last couple of decades through high-profile legal victories, mainstream presence in television and film, and conversations in our day-to-day lives. Cosplay opens up a number of avenues for fans who are part of this community, because it inherently allows one to present themselves as they choose, regardless of the gender of that character. Cosplay doesn't require fans to adhere strictly to a character's depiction in canon: the final product is entirely up to the costumer. Cosplay can be a conduit for fans to explore their gender identity or operate under another name, and it provides a relatively safe environment for them to experiment with those depictions. This isn't to say that trans and nonbinary cosplayers are free from discrimination, hate, or other harassment from the community, but it is an environment in which changing one's appearance is the norm.

Thorn Reilly, a Vermont-based member of the Mandalorian Mercs Costume Club, noted that the group allowed them some incredible opportunities to experiment with how they were perceived by the world. "There's a bit in the Republic Commando series where

IDENTITY

author Karen Traviss specifically mentions that there are female Mandalorians," they explained, "and that you can't tell they're female because that's not important—they're all sort of 'Mando-shaped'—they're all made of metal, and in the lore of the book, they've got one pronoun: it's just 'Mando.' "

That particularly attracted Reilly, who first noted the warrior culture depicted in that particular piece of Mandalorian lore because of its lack of gender expression. "I was like, 'Oh, wow, I have permission now,' and I specifically made my chest plates flat, because why would I have boob plates, and a lot of people read me as male in-kit, because I have wide shoulders and all this stuff packed on me."[7]

M Blackburn, who goes by the online handle nonbinate, also noted that presentation is part of what makes cosplay wonderful for them. "As someone who doesn't really subscribe to the gender norms in my everyday life," they explained, "it makes it a lot easier for me to not really care about what characters I'm making to cosplay when it comes to gender. I can present myself as male, I can be female, I can present as an alien—and it tends to raise fewer eyebrows if people don't associate you with a gender, so you can do whatever you want, which I've enjoyed."[8]

As LGBTQ+ issues are recognized at the forefront of world culture and politics, studios and creators have worked to diversify their stories, introducing queer characters to audiences in shows, games, comics, and anime. Science fiction has explored these issues throughout the years, and there are notable examples of queer characters in *Babylon 5*, *Battlestar Galactica*, and *Star Trek*. Recently, Paramount made headlines when it cast the franchise's first nonbinary character, Adira (played by Blu del Barrio), and first transgender character, Gray (played by Ian Alexander), in the third season of *Star Trek: Discovery*.[9]

Blackburn noted that the cosplay community at large "tends to be pretty friendly and good at intersectionality to people of color and to LGBTQ cosplayers and people of different backgrounds. And in recent years, there have been more characters created without that sort of cis white male mindset: they've been for everyone."

---

[7] Thorn Reilly in conversation with the author, September 2019.
[8] M Blackburn in conversation with the author, February 2020.
[9] Startrek.com staff, "*Star Trek: Discovery* Introduces First Transgender and Non-Binary Characters," *Star Trek* (website), September 2, 2020, https://www.startrek.com/news/star-trek-discovery-introduces-first-trangender-and-non-binary-characters.

Stacie Dee Spencer, a trans cosplayer from New Hampshire, poses as Captain Marvel at Granite State Comic Con in 2019.

Courtesy of Andrew Liptak

Reilly notes that having those gender expressions represented in the source material matters quite a bit to queer cosplayers. "It's really, really important," they explained, but pointed out that there was still a long way to go. "You could tell that it was there, but that nobody committed to it full-force, and it was kind of like I was flying under the radar, but having that freedom of interpretation means that no one can tell me that I'm wrong."

"In the last ten years," Blackburn said, "there's been this skyrocketing amount of LGBTQ characters. A great example is Tracer—she was known as this sort of sexy, cute, look-at-her-butt little icon for *Overwatch*, and then they made her a lesbian. That was just hilarious and amazing, because for years, it was like, 'Here's this male fantasy.' I literally cried when I found out, because seeing representation was so important to me."

But, as writer and activist J. Skyler told *Vice* in 2015, the LGBTQ+ community still faces significant barriers and discrimination, even with transformative activities like cosplay.[10] Trans cosplayers can certainly find refuge in costumes, but cosplayers are harassed at conventions and online. I've seen derogatory comments made toward pictures that I've taken of trans cosplayers and have heard cosplayers deliberately misgender their trans counterparts or otherwise disparage their appearance. These are attitudes that can be changed in person and systematically: conventions and organizations can set expectations and rules for a member's conduct, and individual cosplayers can not only call out bad behavior but also support their fellow fans both in and out of costume.

Cosplay is an activity that caters heavily to identity and how people see themselves

---

10   J. A. Micheline, "Cosplaying While Trans: Exploring the Intersection Between Cosplay and Gender Identity," *Vice*, March 1, 2015, https://www.vice.com/en/article/wd4v5z/cosplaying-while-trans-569.

in the world. It allows cosplayers to alter their appearance to reflect the characters and identities that they identify with, and as the LGBTQ+ movement earns greater acceptance within the cosplay community and society at large, even more people will be able to comfortably explore their identity through the characters they love.

SEXISM IN COSPLAY

In 2012, comic book artist Tony Harris posted a brief rant to Facebook:

> I cant remember if Ive said this before, but Im gonna say it anyway. I dont give a crap.I appreciate a pretty Gal as much as the next Hetero Male. Sometimes I even go in for some racy type stuff (keeping the comments PG for my Ladies sake) but dammit, dammit, dammit I am so sick and tired of the whole COSPLAY-Chiks. I know a few who are actually pretty cool-and BIG Shocker, love and read Comics. So as in all things, they are the exception to the rule. Heres the statement I wanna make, based on THE RULE: "Hey! Quasi-Pretty-NOT-Hot-Girl, you are more pathetic than the REAL Nerds, who YOU secretly think are REALLY PATHETIC.[11]

His post underscored a sexist attitude that runs beneath fandom: that people who aren't straight white men aren't really fans, but only pretending to like nerd staples like comic books and *Star Wars* for the attention they get from other fans. It's an attitude that informs television shows like *The Big Bang Theory* and any joke that's ever been made about a woman who knows the ins and outs of any science-fiction franchise. Talk to any female-identifying fan, and they will more than likely have some experience of having their fandom questioned by a male fan. "I was like the 'party trick girl,'" cosplayer Dallas Nagata White explained, "where my guy friends would call me up and be like, 'Hey Dallas, what kind of ship is the *Millennium Falcon*?' and I'd be like, 'Oh, it's a YT-1300 Corellian freighter,' and whoever else was on the line was like, 'Oh, she's really fat and ugly, right?' "

Sometimes, the sexism isn't quite overt. A local comics-swap event that took place near me proudly proclaimed "More Comics, Less Cosplay!" and I've heard members of that

---

11   Valerie Gallaher, "Comic Artist Tony Harris Blasts Cosplay Girls: 'Yer Not Comics,'" *MTV News*, November 13, 2012, http://www.mtv.com/news/2627196/cosplay-controversy.

particular community say that they don't usually have issues with cosplayers, per se, but the cosplayers who treat it as a profession. Given that cosplay is largely a woman-dominated pastime and that most cosplay professionals out there are women, it's not hard to read between the lines and see the casual misogyny at play.

Harris's post highlighted an argument that has long been leveled against women who cosplay at conventions: that they're only there to show off their bodies and to somehow take advantage of the hapless nerds who are attending the cons. That their knowledge and understanding of comic books, *Star Wars*, *Star Trek*, *Battlestar Galactica*, *Pokémon*, or any other franchise or title out there is automatically inferior to theirs.

This argument of what constitutes a "true fan" is a type of gatekeeping that seeks to wall off those who love a franchise in a different way. One tweet that went viral in January 2020 is a good example of this: "Seeing the *Star Wars* movies does not make you a *Star Wars* fan." It went on to list qualifications, from reading the novelizations and comics to watching the animated shows and taking part in online discussions.[12] Notably missing are female-led disciplines such as cosplay or fan fiction. Intentional or not, these arguments seem to manifest somewhat in two distinct threads of cosplay.

On one hand, there are the makers and builders who came out of the prop replicas tradition who seek to re-create the costumes of the characters they love, ranging from painstakingly accurate and exacting reproductions to costumes that were simply as close as they could manage. On the other hand is the interpretive mindset, in which cosplayers seek not to copy a costume exactly, but reimagine it with a fresh lens. Both are valid approaches that demonstrate the range of expectations and ways in which people come to the hobby.

A cosplayer at FAN EXPO Boston poses as a sexified Predator from the *Predator* franchise.
Courtesy of Andrew Liptak

---

12 Ed Powell (@DrEdPowell), "Seeing the *Star Wars* movies does not make you a *Star Wars* fan. Actual *Star Wars* fans have done some of the following: * Read the novelizations * Read books in the EU * Read new canon books * Read some comics * Watched the animated shows * Participated in SW discussion groups," Twitter, January 2, 2020, 1:32 a.m., https://twitter.com/DrEdPowell/status/1212622645214273536.

GROUP DEMOGRAPHICS

Many of the largest cosplay groups, like the 501st or Rebel Legion, feature a set of membership standards that allows them to present a uniform look across the world. If you compare an approved 501st Legion stormtrooper in the United States and another in Russia, Canada, Colombia, or China, you'll find that they're fairly similar in appearance.

These groups with their screen-accurate approach don't have a monopoly on cosplay. Individual cosplayers will spend hours working to develop costumes that measure up to their screen-used counterparts, wanting to follow the same line of thinking: they're fans of the films, games, or television shows in which the costumes appear, and building those accurate costumes helps bring their fans and onlookers closer to the experience of meeting them in the real world.

A group of New England Garrison stormtroopers wait to step off for the 2010 Woburn Halloween Parade in Woburn, Massachusetts.

Courtesy of Andrew Liptak

The screen-accurate branch doesn't inherently discriminate based on sex or gender—thousands of women (and people who identify as women or nonbinary) are part of these groups—but it is a branch that has traditionally not been as open or accessible to a wider body of people, either due to the accessibility of resources, low-level or overt sexism, or cost, or because most of the characters that a particular group portrays aren't women.

Changing who appears in media has a direct impact on the cosplay community. Replica Props Forum owner Art Andrews noted that one particular turning point came in 2012 when cosplayer Jessica Nigri won a contest put on by Warner Media and IGN for a new video game, *Lollipop Chainsaw*.[13] The game follows a cheerleader named Juliet Starling, who fights through hordes of zombies with a chain-

---

13 Greg Miller, "Lollipop Chainsaw: The Search for Juliet," *IGN*, January 10, 2012, https://www.ign.com/articles/2012/01/10/lollipop-chainsaw-the-search-for-juliet.

saw. Nigri became the face of the character, touring conventions dressed in the character's cheerleading costume while wielding a prop chainsaw.

"Demographically," Andrews explained, "the RPF has always been extremely heavily male dominated, with girls being a very, very small minority of our membership. When she won that contest, I feel like it opened a new door where it suddenly didn't seem like a boys' club.

"I feel like she's the one who changed that narrative [for the site], and made it cool and made it interesting, and then so many girls jumped on it that it exploded across social media. You had a lot of women who were in costuming prior to that, like LeeAnna Vamp, but Jessica Nigri is the one from my perspective who opened the floodgates."[14]

▬ SEX APPEAL

Compared to the ranks of the 501st Legion and similar groups, the rest of the cosplay world is delightfully chaotic.

Cosplay doesn't require strict accuracy to be a relevant or valid experience for the cosplayer or bystander. In many cases, the costumes are a reflection of their own fandom for any particular property, and cosplayers might put their own spin on a character's appearance.

These types of costumes can manifest in a number of ways: a cosplayer like Jessica Nigri cosplaying as "Sexy Pikachu" is one way, while slapping a Deadpool mask onto any costume at all plays to the in-joke of the character's frequent fourth-wall breakage. These costumes can range from a fan's personal interpretation on a character to a take on a meme to some in-joke within the larger fan community.

Angelique Trouvere poses as Valeria, the Insect Queen, in 1974 at Discon II in Washington, DC.

Courtesy of Carol Resnick

Enterprising cosplayers have tapped into something that marketers and creators figured out long ago: sex sells. Comics, pulp magazines, book covers, and B-movies have long

---

14 Art Andrews in conversation with the author, January 2020.

IDENTITY   109

objectified women by putting their characters in revealing outfits to get audiences to pick something up off the shelf or pay to go see it—a trend that persists to the present with shows like *Game of Thrones* and *American Gods*. And there's a long history of comic artists and directors creating pornographic parodies with popular characters like Superman and Batman, taking sexuality beyond a mere implication with explicit films and comics.[15] Platforms like Pornhub have thousands of videos featuring familiar characters from popular films, TV shows, video games, and comics.

This phenomenon isn't limited to professional media: image-heavy social networks like Instagram have given rise to the "thirst trap," or the use of provocative pictures to lure in likes and comments.[16]

The economic reality of sex appeal is no different for cosplayers: leaning into a character's curves or skimpy costume hearkens back to the rationale behind their creation in the first place, and plenty of cosplayers have created sexier versions of their characters for that reason, building up huge followings as a result. Social media has made it easier than ever to practice this sort of cosplay, but it's hardly a new phenomenon: the first contestant to show up nude to a World Science Fiction Convention masquerade did so in 1952. In Mike Resnick's memoir, . . . *Always a Fan*, he writes that "all throughout the 1970s and early 1980s there were half a dozen or so nude costumes every year—and a lot of them were prize winners."[17] Some conventions ban nudity from their costume contests, but others take a more nuanced approach, like Balticon, which doesn't outright ban someone from showing up without clothing, but points out that "No costume is no costume and won't win any prizes," and that "if you feel that nudity is essential to your costume, please limit it to the Masquerade, and keep it covered in the public areas of the hotel."[18]

Sexy cosplayers might find that they can build up a considerable following for their work, but they also endure condescension, harassment, and criticism from the wider public or from fellow costumers who feel that what they're doing isn't appropriate or that it doesn't line up with what they define as cosplay—even though nudity has been part of the activity for decades.

---

15   Charlie Jane Anders, "The Bizarre History of Superhero Porn [NSFW]," *Gizmodo*, May 30, 2012, https://gizmodo.com/the-bizarre-history-of-superhero-porn-nsfw-5914178.
16   Dictionary.com, s.v. "thirst trap," accessed December 14, 2021, https://www.dictionary.com/e/slang/thirst-trap.
17   Resnick, ...*Always a Fan*, 69.
18   "Masquerade Rules for Balticon (Every Year)," Baltimore Science Fiction Society, accessed December 5, 2021, https://www.bsfs.org/masqrule.htm.

Most of those critics reveal their motivations by slut-shaming or sexually harassing their targets: an internalized misogyny that seeks to control women's behavior. "Ya know, if at least 50% of the women that 'cosplay' cosplayed like this, I wouldn't be so opposed to it," one Twitter user said online in response to a cosplayer in a medieval-style dress. "Instead they're all half dressed whores."[19]

Even setting this more outright misogyny aside, science-fiction and fantasy properties, comic books, and video games have spent decades objectifying women's bodies, putting female characters in outfits with plenty of exposed skin or giving them outlandishly proportioned figures. There's plenty of commentary on the implications of sex in genre media, but that is often followed by no small amount of hypocrisy in shaming women—especially consenting adult cosplayers!—for what they choose to do with their bodies, all while complaining that the actress playing Lara Croft doesn't have a big enough cup size[20] or that a cosplayer is the wrong size or shape for the character they're cosplaying as.

These attitudes can translate into real harm. Cosplayers have been approached, photographed, propositioned,[21] and touched inappropriately[22] at conventions and events. In

A poster outlining FAN EXPO Boston's code of conduct was displayed prominently on the convention's floor in August 2021.

Courtesy of Andrew Liptak

---

19   Status Queue (@Status_Queue), Twitter, March 5, 2020, 5:58 p.m., https://twitter.com/Status_Queue/status/1235701256984895489.
20   Amanda Kooser, "Fans Back Alicia Vikander after 'Tomb Raider' Breast Criticism," *CNET*, March 15, 2018, https://www.cnet.com/news/tomb-raider-alicia-vikander-lara-croft-bust-size-under-fire.
21   Lisa Granshaw, "Cosplayers Harassed by Camera Crew at Comic Con Fight Back Online," *Daily Dot*, October 14, 2013, updated June 1, 2021, https://www.dailydot.com/parsec/fandom/man-banter-new-york-comic-con-cosplay-harassment.
22   Ann Hoevel, "Popular Cosplayer Speaks Out about Being Groped outside of NYCC," *Daily Dot*, October 22, 2014, updated May 30, 2021, https://www.dailydot.com/parsec/cosplayer-harassment-nycc-yaya-han/?tw=dd.

2014, Bitch Media writer Janelle Asselin conducted a survey of fans in the comic world and found that "respondents were more likely to be photographed against their wishes" at conventions, and that "Thirteen percent reported having unwanted comments of a sexual nature made about them at conventions—and eight percent of all genders reported that they had been groped, assaulted, or raped at a comic convention."[23]

This widespread harassment of cosplayers has sparked backlash against conventions, which had up to that point failed to establish clear guidelines and anti-harassment policies to govern expectations, and to set up a mechanism with which to eject someone from the event. Groups like Geeks for CONsent and Cosplay Is Not Consent advocated for conventions to make major changes to protect con-goers from people acting inappropriately in the mid-2010s. Since then, conventions have slowly begun to come around to these arguments, changing their rules and policies to explicitly ban harassment and establish consequences for breaking those rules. One notable example that's seen at most conventions now is banners that read COSPLAY IS NOT CONSENT, with specific guidelines placed in prominent locations near entrances to make the rules clear to all attendees. There is still plenty of work to do on this front, but the community has made significant progress in labeling this type of harassment as a problem and taking steps to deal with it.

---

23 Janelle Asselin, "How Big of a Problem is Harassment at Comic Conventions? Very Big," *Bitch Media*, July 22, 2014, https://www.bitchmedia.org/post/how-big-a-problem-is-harassment-at-comic-conventions-very-big-survey-sdcc-emerald-city-cosplay-consent.

12 PROTEST COSPLAY

When President Donald Trump took office in 2017, women's rights activists worried that their worst fears were about to be realized. For decades, pro-life activists have fought over the legality of a woman's right to an abortion, which was granted by the landmark US Supreme Court case *Roe v. Wade* in 1973. Since that ruling, politicians and activists have sought to pick away at it by pushing to enact more restrictive laws on the state level.

While the Supreme Court has pushed back on some of these challenges and allowed others to pass into state law, it has been reluctant to undo the original ruling altogether. With Trump in office, his supporters saw a sympathetic figure who promised to do what they'd advocated for for decades: finally overturn *Roe v. Wade* by upending the political balance of the court.

As state-level politicians have put forth laws that undermine the ruling, they have also attracted intense protests across the country. In the aftermath of Trump's election, a group of protesters, inspired by Margaret Atwood's dystopian novel *The Handmaid's Tale*, decided to don the iconic scarlet-red robes worn by the book's characters to call attention to their plight.

Since its original 1985 publication, Atwood's novel has become widely discussed; and in her introduction for The Folio Society's 2017 edition of the novel, Atwood noted that it had become a "tag for those writing about shifts towards policies aimed at controlling

Models dressed as Handmaids from Hulu's *The Handmaid's Tale* appeared on a street in Chelsea Market, New York City, to promote the series in 2017.

Courtesy of Jodi Marmonti Anderson

women," and that "Revellers dress up as Handmaids on Hallowe'en and also for protest marches—these two uses of its costumes mirroring its doubleness. Is it entertainment or dire political prophecy? Can it be both?"[1]

The year 2017 was also when the streaming service Hulu launched its adaptation of Atwood's novel for subscribers. Trailers and ads teased its release, the story's Handmaids strikingly presented in their dramatic red robes. There was even an unsettling promotional stunt that saw costumed models walking around Austin, Texas's South by Southwest festival, seemingly bringing the novel's dystopian world to life.[2]

The event was inspiring to certain activists. Heather Busby, the executive director of NARAL Pro-Choice Texas, began organizing a protest against anti-abortion bills that were coming up in the Texas legislature aimed at restricting the procedure in the state.

---

1 Margaret Atwood, *The Handmaid's Tale* (London: The Folio Society, 2017), ix.
2 William Hughes, "Hulu Is Filling SXSW with Silent Handmaids," *A.V. Club*, March 11, 2017, https://www.avclub.com/hulu-is-filling-sxsw-with-silent-handmaids-1798259060.

Suffragette Inez Milholland Boissevain atop a white horse on March 3, 1913.

Images via Library of Congress

German actress Hedwiga Reicher dressed as Columbia during the March 3, 1913, Women's March in Washington, DC.

She explained to me at the time that they had used costumes in the past to drive their point home: "Back in 2015, we had folks in hospital gowns to protest another abortion restriction," and some within her organization suggested that they put together costumes to protest in once again.[3]

WOMEN'S RIGHTS

Activists have employed costumes for decades as a way to bring attention to their causes, drawing on the power of storytelling to reinforce their points and get people thinking about what they're trying to accomplish.

One notable early example of this was American suffragist Inez Milholland, a leading member of the movement in the early 1900s. Born in New York in 1886, she attended Vassar College and became an outspoken advocate for a woman's right to vote, holding meetings on campus and working to organize the movement. Following her graduation, she went on to obtain her law degree and began taking part in suffrage parades.

The movement grew, and on March 3, 1913, suffragettes held a massive parade in Washington, DC, that included many activists dressed up in costume, including

---

[3] Andrew, Liptak, "How *The Handmaid's Tale* Inspired a Protest Movement," *The Verge*, October 31, 2017, https://www.theverge.com/2017/10/31/15799882/handmaids-tale-costumes-cosplay-protest.

Milholland. Writing in the *Winterthur Portfolio*, Dr. Annelise K. Madsen explained that these parades were "a hybrid form of civic art," and that "the pageant raised the stakes of parading, framing the parade's claims in numbers, quality, and serious purpose through the lens of artistry and beauty."[4] Specifically, activists set up elaborate productions that helped to define their cause by drawing from established narratives throughout history. Examples of this include dressing up as or invoking the name of Joan of Arc, Columbia, or Lady Liberty, among others.

Milholland led the parade in a brilliant white outfit and cape, riding atop a white horse, while others dressed in flowing robes as Liberty and her attendants. They marched along Pennsylvania Avenue toward the Capitol through violent protesters, garnering national attention and sympathy for their cause. Costumes played a large role in the suffrage movement: in her book *These Truths: A History of the United States*, Jill Lepore notes that women used costumes for a number of protests: "Women who'd gone to prison for picketing took a train across the country in a Prison Special, wearing their prison uniforms. They dressed as statues; they wore red, white, and blue; they marched in chains."[5]

Activists dressed as Liberty and her attendants at the Women's March in Washington, DC, on March 3, 1913.

Image via Library of Congress

Activists have since picked up similar tactics over the years. At the height of the Tea Party protests in 2009 and 2010, conservative activists donned uniforms and costumes from the American Revolutionary War. One such protester, a reenactor named William

---

4   Annelise K. Madsen, "Columbia and Her Foot Soldiers: Civic Art and the Demand for Change at the 1913 Suffrage Pageant-Procession," *Winterthur Portfolio*, vol. 48, no. 4, accessed on JSTOR, Winter 2014, 285–286: https://www.jstor.org/stable/pdf/10.1086/679369.pdf?refreqid=excelsior%3Aa4a5cbebfeed02d3a3ee266fac0db918.
5   Jill Lepore, *These Truths: A History of the United States* (New York: W. W. Norton, 2019), 386.

Temple, told me in 2017 that they saw their use of costumes as a way to "remind folks of the first revolution and make the visual connection" to the events and actions that prompted the nation's founders to split from Britain in 1776.

■ INTERNATIONAL PROTESTS

Protest costumes aren't just limited to the United States, either: in June 2013, Turkish *Star Wars* fan Ates Cetin watched as anti-government protests erupted in his home country.

In an email to me, he explained that because Turkish media was heavily regulated by the government, people took to social media to spread word of the 2013 protests. Due to the nature of these platforms, photos and videos in particular carried weight. "I was very impressed by the creativity of the protesters," he said. "They were delivering their message not through violence, but through intellect. There was someone who just stood in the middle of the square and did nothing; there was another reading a book to the police; someone else was handing flowers to the police."

The images circulating online moved him to participate. "One weekend, I learned that there would be a gathering at a popular avenue near my house. I began to think: I disapproved of the police aggression, so I knew which side I was on," he explained. "I could either participate or do nothing. I could just get on the balcony of my house, hit on pots and pans like many others did, and become a member of the passive aggressive protestors. Against [my girlfriend] Gizem's wishes, I decided to go. Deep inside, there was a spark that was demanding me to do something extraordinary. And then it hit me: I was a *Star Wars* fan, why would I not participate in style? [Darth] Vader was a popular culture icon, and I could deliver a message which would say, 'Even the baddest character in film history supports this cause.' "[6]

He suited up and stepped outside. It was hot, he remembered, and as he approached the protesters, he began to worry. "What if people didn't understand [what I was doing]? What if I made a fool of myself? What if people didn't even recognize the character?" Those fears turned out to be unfounded. People flocked to him to take pictures, and bystanders stood up and cheered. "This feeling was beyond relief. I was not walking any more, I felt

---

6   Ates Cetin, email message to author, November 2019.

like I was floating," he said. When they reached the protest, they stood and watched the crowd. He decided to turn back because of the heat and stepped onto the road to cross the street. "There was thunderous applause, and one could say that they saw a red-colored Vader because of all the reflections of our nation's flags. I walked maybe fifty meters, Gizem was taking photos just a few steps ahead of me. I began hearing a weak humming of a familiar melody, then I saw a surprised look on Gizem's face. I looked back and saw that the crowd began to march behind me while humming 'The Imperial March.' It was Darth Vader who triggered them to march.

"We walked along the avenue, at another crossroads we stopped again. Now it was like a scene from *Braveheart*; I was touching my flag stick to the ones that were held by the front line of protestors. A few hundred meters more and then it was time for us to head back home."

Cetin's appearance in the parade went viral: videos of him in costume popped up on social media, as well as online media outlets like *BuzzFeed*. The response moved him to plan to attend another similar march a couple of days later, but he explained that violence was ramping up against Turkish protesters, and in the interest of personal safety, he opted to skip it. "However, the 2013 protests impacted the lives of many, and whenever people speak of those days, they mention how they participated. I know my participation was a unique one, and it always makes me smile when someone remembers how Vader influenced the crowds."

On March 20, 2017, Busby and the other members of her organization walked into the Texas State Capitol dressed in the iconic red robes and white bonnets worn by the Handmaids and sat quietly in the balcony as the state legislature debated the bills in question. Weeks later, women's rights activists in Missouri followed suit, dressing up in costume and sitting in the public viewing area of the legislature to protest a budget proposal that would strip away money for family planning.[7]

These instances caught the attention of news outlets, which reported on the groups' actions and messaging. In 2017, New Hampshire–based activist Emily Morgan saw the possibility of a national costumed protest. She set up a website called The Handmaid

---

[7] Sarah Fenske, "Protesters Channel a *Handmaid's Tale* at Missouri Capitol, With Attire Straight out of Dystopia," *Riverfront Times*, May 3, 2017, https://www.riverfronttimes.com/newsblog/2017/05/03/protesters-channel-a-handmaids-tale-at-missouri-capitol-with-attire-straight-out-of-dystopia.

Coalition, which had the tagline: "Fighting to keep fiction from becoming reality."[8] The group provided resources for protesters, including a guidebook that offered directions on how to make the costumes as well as information about their rights. Chapters of the coalition began to spring up all over the United States, and in October 2017, the organization set up a nationwide protest that saw handmaids appear in all of the country's state capitols.

The Handmaid Coalition as an organization lasted for more than a year. Though it seems to have dissolved, it has since been replaced by other groups, like the Boston Red Cloaks and the Handmaids Army DC, which have continued to organize costumed protests.

CRITICISMS AND COMPLICATED HISTORIES

Wearing costumes to protests can be controversial. In 2021, ahead of a planned Rally for Abortion Justice march in Washington, DC (planned by the Women's March), organizers specifically banned Handmaid costumes inspired by the show, claiming that "the use of *Handmaid's Tale* imagery to characterize the controlling of women's reproduction has proliferated, primarily by white women across the country, since the show has gained popularity," and noting that it's caused problems with allies over concerns of erasure, among other issues.[9] The Handmaids Army DC said that its members wouldn't bring their costumes, stating that "we acknowledge that our demonstrations elicit valid mixed responses from observers," but also defending the use of the costumes as a whole: "We use the *Handmaid's Tale* uniforms to demonstrate the erasure of identity that occurs when reproductive freedoms are limited," the group wrote. "We believe in the power of visual imagery to influence change."[10]

Criticisms of Handmaid costumes aren't without merit: while they might be effective, there are valid critiques of Atwood's book and the protesters who don her costumes. Part of the claim here is that white women in the feminist movement are ignoring equally important systemic issues that intersect with it, and that the use of these costumes is an

---

8 "Fight to Keep Fiction from Becoming Reality," Handmaid Coalition (website), accessed December 5, 2021, https://web.archive.org/web/20190604001051/https://handmaidcoalition.org.
9 "Rally for Abortion Justice: What to Bring," Women's March (website), accessed December 5, 2021, https://womensmarch.com/oct-2021-march#what-to-bring.
10 HADC Admin, "About the Women's March Ban on Handmaids," Handmaid's Army DC (website), September 26, 2021, https://www.handmaidsdc.com/post/about-the-women-s-march-ban-on-handmaids.

expression of those inherent biases. There likely isn't an answer to these criticisms that will satisfy everyone; it's a complicated issue, and one that people will raise well into the future.

If a protester is looking to tap into a real-life issue with a costume from a fictional world, they must contend with the fact that there are complicated and nuanced histories at play—and that not everyone perceives a story the same way.

A good example of this is the classic Imperial stormtrooper and the other representatives of the Galactic Empire from the various *Star Wars* movies. I fell in love with the look and feel of the stormtrooper costume the moment I saw it, and still admire the look of the various troopers out there. But there's no denying that those troopers represent a horrific regime that regularly commits genocide and other monstrous acts within the *Star Wars* universe. The design of those costumes isn't an accident: director George Lucas and costume designer John Mollo specifically wanted to evoke the imagery of Germany's Nazi party to convey these connotations.[11] The stormtrooper is the most common costume within the ranks of the 501st Legion, and we're out in public quite a bit, which has brought about the argument that we're normalizing fascism.[12] In some instances, trooper costumes have been banned from parties or locations because of the aforementioned connotations.[13]

Real-world politics can complicate a costume for cosplayers. In 2021, Lucasfilm dropped *Mandalorian* actress Gina Carano from the franchise following a series of anti-COVID-vaccine and anti-lockdown posts on social media. Plenty of cosplayers had flocked to the costume when she had appeared in the show's first season, noting that they saw her as a good role model, a tough and fearless female character that was underutilized in the franchise. Upon seeing Carano's posts, many of them were disappointed and frustrated. Some gave up the costume, while others noted that they were working to separate the character from the actress portraying her.[14]

---

11 Cole Horton, "From World War to *Star Wars*: Imperial Officers," *Star Wars* (website), August 20, 2014, https://www.starwars.com/news/from-world-war-to-star-wars-imperial-officers.
12 Dave Lartigue, " 'When Fascism Comes to America It Will Be Wrapped in White Plastic Armor and Carrying a BlasTech E-11 Blaster Rifle'—Sinclair Lucas,' " Dave Ex Machina, the website of Dave Lartigue, July 11, 2008, https://web.archive.org/web/20080803081615/http://www.daveexmachina.com/wordpress/?p=2321.
13 Douglas Ernst, "Stormtrooper Costumes Banned from '*Star Wars*'-themed College Reunion over Alleged Nazi Inspiration," *Washington Times*, March 1, 2017, https://www.washingtontimes.com/news/2017/mar/1/stormtrooper-costumes-banned-from-star-wars-themed.
14 Andrew Liptak, "Cara Dune Cosplayers React to Gina Carano's Firing from *The Mandalorian*," Cosplay Central (website), February 22, 2021, https://www.cosplaycentral.com/topics/cosplay/feature/cara-dune-cosplayers-react-to-gina-caranos-firing-from-the-mandalorian.

There are also bad actors who look to reappropriate historical imagery for their own purposes. In 2017, a Denver-based convention called Rocky Mountain Fur Con ended up canceling because of security issues that loomed with the growth of an alt-right/neo-Nazi movement within the Furry community, in which certain members wore Nazi-like armbands as part of their costumes, a source of much concern.[15] That movement dates back to the mid-2000s, with some Furries reporting that they were called slurs by these members at conventions.[16]

Bad actors can and will work to exploit such historical connections, and it's up to the rest of the community to ensure that the space remains safe, through their own actions and efforts to put systems in place within their costuming organizations, conventions, and social circles to prevent such activity.

Those who dress in costume rarely see themselves as the flag bearer for an oppressive political theory, and a common saying within the 501st Legion is that we're "bad guys doing good," pointing to the group's emphasis on charitable giving and community service while in costume. Indeed, there are plenty of villains throughout the entertainment world who get a lot of attention from cosplayers, such as the Borg from *Star Trek*, the Covenant (and depending on who you talk to, the UNSC) from *Halo*, the Punisher from Marvel comics, and plenty of others. Reenactors also have to deal with this issue: Civil War and World War II reenactors wishing to portray the Confederacy or German forces walk a fine line in conveying ideology against genuine historical interest and accuracy.

Everyone has their own reason for coming to a costume, and it's worth noting that stories are nuanced: it's hard to take a moral absolutist take on any particular character. For example, the decision of most members of the 501st to wear an Imperial costume begins and ends with their appreciation of *Star Wars* and the costume design, rather than as an endorsement of the moral underpinning of the Galactic Empire. We like the costumes because they look cool, because they're recognizable fixtures of the universe, and because people like seeing them. But it's certainly a question that's always worth taking into consideration and examining, as not every-

---

15 Eric Killelea, "Does the Furry Community Have a Nazi Problem?" *Rolling Stone*, April 14, 2017, https://www.rollingstone.com/culture/culture-features/does-the-furry-community-have-a-nazi-problem-194282.
16 Jim Groat, "Nazi Furs," *From the demented mind* (blog), Live Journal, February 8, 2007, https://krag-carbine.livejournal.com/301570.html.

one shares the same point of view and appreciation that we might have for the characters.

POLITICS AND COSPLAY

Even outside of protest in the political sphere, activists don costumes in service of their causes. They have long been used in equality marches and other activities, and just as protesters have found, a costume can call attention to a cause from bystanders, journalists, and other activists.

A couple of years ago, my local chapter of the 501st Legion, the New England Garrison and Green Mountain Squad, took part in a handful of local pride marches in Boston and Burlington, Vermont, dressing in costume augmented with custom decorations to fit with the theme. We wanted to support our group's LGBTQ+ members and turn the uniforms of the oppressive Galactic Empire on their heads, undermining the in-universe connotations that they carry.

We weren't the only participants in costume at the marches. Members of Tir Asleen, a local chapter of an immersive fantasy experience community called Hearthlight, showed up in bright costumes that spanned every color of the rainbow. Cosplayers from several other franchises have put their skills as craftspeople toward supporting the wider community at parades and events. The global cosplay community is made up of people from a wide swath of different backgrounds, and fandom in many ways transcends geography, ideology, and identity. Costuming can not only highlight what cosplayers care about but also provide a bridge to those who don't have the same set of experiences and beliefs they do.

Green Mountain Squad member Eeka Thaxton poses as Princess Leia at the Burlington, Vermont, Pride Parade in September 2019.

Courtesy of Andrew Liptak

13 CHARITY

In February 2020, a post appeared in the forums for the 501st's New England Garrison: The Vermont chapter of Make-A-Wish had requested a handful of troopers to perform a send-off for a child who was heading to Disney World for the week. We were to show up and greet the family in the branch's offices in Burlington, before they got into a limo and headed off to the local airport with a police escort.[1] As a member of the group, there's no hesitation when it comes to participating in such an event: we sign up, ask for time off from work, and commit to driving hundreds of miles across state lines to take part.

Since the formation of the 501st, charitable troops and a sense of community service have been an integral part of the organization, seen as a way to give back to the community and people who might appreciate a visit from their favorite characters. "Charity is sort of a happy accident," Albin Johnson explained. "We would tend to go to these events that needed people or some level of production value or excitement and those tended to be charity events." Those types of events took places at schools, Toys for Tots fundraisers, and others: "A means to an end," says Johnson, who wanted to get the word out about the group, especially when conventions were nowhere near as popular as they are today.

Johnson's own experiences with charity-style events hit close to home. In 2004, his daughter Katie had begun to exhibit some worrying health signs: she fell down a lot,

---

1 Make-A-Wish Vermont, Facebook post, February 21, 2020, https://www.facebook.com/makeawishvermont/posts/10156584251557504.

and after a visit to a doctor, they were horrified to learn that she had an inoperable brain tumor and likely had only months to live.

The legion that Johnson had created rallied to Katie's cause, providing emotional support from around the world. The R2-D2 Builders Club took it upon themselves to construct a pink R2 unit—Katie's favorite character—to keep her company in her final days.[2] That movement has translated into a major part of the 501st Legion and other similar groups. Take a survey of 501st members, and one of the first reasons that they might give for joining is the chance to give back to the community in the form of charitable support. They undertake thousands of events to raise awareness for autism, breast cancer, MS, and childhood literacy; and visit the hospital rooms of kids (and some adults) who are in dire need of cheering up.

In September 2016, the 501st Legion partnered with Make-A-Wish to establish an endowment fund. Their goal was to raise $150,000 by September 2021. The organization surpassed that in mere months.

Charity is a "huge dynamic," Adam Baker-Siroty told me, noting that the group is indirectly responsible for generating $8–10 million a year for charitable causes around the world. "I think that does give us some level of respect and protection, because it makes for good PR."

Jamie Hathaway, the CEO of the Vermont branch of the Make-A-Wish Foundation of America, notes that they've worked closely with groups like the 501st to bring about wish events for children. "It's no secret that for a lot of kids, *Star Wars* is their favorite movie," he explained to me in an interview. "They become obsessed with it because they find a lot of comfort with it, when they watch the movies in the hospital, for example. It's a diversion, so it's not uncommon for us to get a lot of *Star Wars* wishes, whether that's to go to Disney World or to meet Chewbacca."

Cosplay, Hathaway says, is the ideal way to fulfill some of those wishes. "It affords us the ability to create a magical moment for a child that we couldn't have done without it. It's not easy to go out and get authentic costumes. So the people who engage in cosplay with that attention to detail and attention to the integrity of the character; that's not something we can do easily. Cosplay groups play an important role in granting those

---

2   Andrew Liptak, "The Heartwarming Story Behind R2-KT, and How She Joined *Star Wars* Canon," *io9*, November 28, 2015, https://io9.gizmodo.com/the-heartwarming-story-behind-r2-kt-and-how-she-joined-1744986951.

LEFT: Jamie Hathaway, President and CEO of Make-A-Wish Vermont, speaks to a family at an event held at the organization's headquarters in January 2020.

ABOVE: Members of the 501st Legion's Green Mountain Squad taking part in a Make-A-Wish event in Burlington, Vermont, in January 2020. *Photos courtesy of Andrew Liptak*

wishes for children who have used the movie and characters as an escape from the hospital or illness."[3]

These interactions play out in a handful of ways, ranging from donation boxes that groups like the 501st put out at conventions (we solicit suggested donations in exchange for pictures), to hospital visits in which cosplayers suit up as their characters to hang out with children—something certain film actors have done as well—to massive, citywide events like the one held in San Francisco for "Batkid" in 2013.[4] That day, in the largest-ever event staged by Make-A-Wish, tens of thousands of people showed up to carry out a wish for five-year-old Miles Scott, who wanted to be Batman. The organization put together a massive event, coordinating various city offices to take part in it. Scott found himself part of an elaborate program in which he and his brother teamed up with Batman to save the city from the Joker. A local news station played an "appeal" to Batman and Batkid from the city's police chief to stop a handful of villains from destroying the

---

3 Jamie Hathaway in conversation with the author, February 2020.
4 John Crane Films, "Official Batkid Video," Make-A-Wish Greater Bay Area, YouTube video, January 15, 2014, https://www.youtube.com/watch?v=Gw3aWPxtpfE.

CHARITY

city, while the public—many dressed in costume for the occasion!—cheered the two on as they moved across town.

In other instances, cosplayers have stepped in to help provide emotional support or to combat the stigma of bullying. In 2010, writer Carrie Goldman learned that children at her daughter Katie's school had been teasing her for loving *Star Wars*, telling her it was only for boys.[5] After learning that Katie wanted to be a stormtrooper for Halloween, members of the 501st Legion pooled their resources to build her a suit of stormtrooper armor, a demonstration that not only was *Star Wars* for girls but she could be a stormtrooper herself.[6] That suit of armor was then passed along to another girl, and then another a couple of years later.[7]

This attitude isn't just for *Star Wars* costumers either. In 2019, a mother realized that her daughter was being bullied at day care and vented about it on social media. One cosplayer, Jack, who goes by "The Batman of Spring Hill," reached out to her and offered to walk her to day care in costume, even giving her a costume of her own: Supergirl.[8] Other organizations, like the Ghostbusters, 405th Infantry Division, or Justice League of WNY, include charitable work as a core component of their mission; while some groups, like Guardians of Justice or Cosplay4Charity, exist with the sole purpose of giving back to the community.

At the event in Burlington in February 2020, a couple of other troopers and I suited up in our armor and waited for our own Make-A-Wish kid to arrive. They did, and the excitement in the room was infectious as they went from character to character, astonished at what was before them: a handful of stormtroopers, Rey, and Chewbacca. Troopers who participate in these troops often say that the full-faced helmets are useful in these situations; there wasn't a dry eye in the place.

"This child," Hathaway says, "was able to have a moment where all of her friends came to life, and she won't forget that, her family won't forget that, and the people that watched it won't forget that. Cosplay is able to make make-believe real, and for the sake of the child, it's real."

---

5   Carrie Goldman, "Anti-Bullying Starts in First Grade," *ChicagoNow* (blog), November 15, 2010, http://www.chicagonow.com/portrait-of-an-adoption/2010/11/anti-bullying-starts-in-first-grade/#ixzz17eZDPpm3.
6   Carrie Goldman, "Aren't You a Little Short for a Stormtrooper? *Star Wars* Fans Worldwide Join to Build a Halloween Costume for One Lucky Little Girl," *ChicagoNow* (blog), October 29, 2012, http://www.chicagonow.com/portrait-of-an-adoption/2012/10/aren%E2%80%99t-you-a-little-short-for-a-stormtrooper-star-wars-fans-worldwide-join-to-build-a-halloween-costume-for-one-lucky-little-girl.
7   Andrew Liptak, "A Girl Was Bullied for Liking *Star Wars*, and Was Helped in the Best Way," *io9*, August 22, 2015, https://io9.gizmodo.com/a-girl-was-bullied-for-liking-star-wars-and-was-helped-1725893704.
8   Andrew Liptak, "In Florida, Another Instance of Cosplayers Helping to Combat Bullying," *Tor*, September 6, 2019, https://www.tor.com/2019/09/06/in-florida-another-instance-of-cosplayers-helping-to-combat-bullying.

part two

Traditions

14 STREET THEATRICS

The early history of costuming stems from religious ceremonies and early theatrical performances, but the use of costumes is also central to a number of traditional folk rituals and street performances. Despite the differences in context, costumes have always maintained the same role: they help performers convey a story to their audience.

▬ STREET PERFORMANCE

While early theater would coalesce into permanent facilities from which actors could stage performances, many other such acts took place in public spaces. In *The Seven Ages of the Theatre*, Richard Southern points to a series of European traditions that utilized costumes and didn't rely on stages, such as the Bavarian Wild Men, the mummers play, and Italian masquerade carnivals, while others, like fantasticals, emerged on the streets of American cities.

The Bavarian Wild Men, Southern writes, is a pagan folk tradition that emerged from the German region of Bavaria and spread to other parts of Europe, coinciding with St. Nicholas Day in December. Other descriptions say that village members would dress up in elaborate, animal-inspired costumes, which would "allow them to cross the line between human and animal, real and spiritual, civilization and wilderness, death and rebirth."[1] This

---

1 Rachel Hartigan Shea and Charles Fréger, "Europe's Wild Men," *National Geographic*, April 2013, https://www.nationalgeographic.com/magazine/2013/04/europe-wild-men.

A woodcut from 1566 by Pieter Bruegel the Elder depicting *The Masquerade of Ourson and Valentin*.

Via the Metropolitan Museum of Art

An engraving of Christmas mummers from 1847.

My Own Treasury, 1847

ritual persists to the modern day throughout Europe, with innumerable variations from village to village, serving as a rite of passage for young men, or as a way to ward off evil.

This costumed practice appears to have sprouted numerous successor rituals and activities. The mumming tradition emerged in Europe and took root in England: according to the Library of Congress, "In traditional European cultures, 'mumming' involves disguising oneself, going door to door, and performing songs, dances, and plays in neighbors' homes and in public places."[2] Southern says the tradition tells the story of Saint George and typically depicts the fight between a hero and villain, accompanied by a death-and-resurrection theme.[3]

The practice eventually made its way to the United States, becoming particularly prominent in Philadelphia, which still holds an annual Mummers Parade today. Mumming first arrived in the city in the seventeenth century "as a continuation of the Old World customs of ushering in the New Year," writes Philly Mummers, the organization that supports the parade. "Mummery in America is as unique to Philadelphia as Mardi Gras is to New Orleans." Those early parades included noisemakers and guns, with participants going from door to door singing songs and performing dances. The event evolved with time, organizing into two major groups of performers—"The Fancy Dress

---

2   Steven Winick, "Mumming at the American Folklife Center," Library of Congress, December 24, 2013, https://blogs.loc.gov/folklife/2013/12/mumming-at-the-american-folklife-center.
3   Richard Southern, *The Seven Ages of the Theatre* (New York: Hill and Wang, 1961), 45.

ABOVE: Mummers take part in the 2011 Mummers Parade in Philadelphia, Pennsylvania.

RIGHT: A mummer takes part in the 2011 Mummers Parade in Philadelphia, Pennsylvania.

Images: Carol M. Highsmith

Clubs" and "The Comic Clubs"—and in 1901, the city organized an official parade. Today, the parade includes more than ten thousand marchers in both modern and historically inspired costumes, which now include "four distinct divisions: Comic, Fancy, Fancy Brigade, Wench Brigade and String Band."[4]

Masks and masqueraders appeared in carnivals as well. In the thirteenth century, masks became associated with the Carnival of Venice, which coincided with Lent and gave rise to a wide variety of styles and costume types over the centuries. The masks told stories in their many forms, including the grotesque Bauta, feathered Colombina, the beaked Plague Doctor, the mouthless Moretta/Servetta muta, full-faced Volto, and others. While masks were later banned in the 1700s, the Italian government eventually resurrected the festival in 1979 as a way to promote the country's cultural heritage. Similar carnivals spread around the world to celebrate Lent, such as Brazil's Carnival in Rio de Janeiro.

Other festivals, such as Mardi Gras, developed in the United States. First arriving in French-American colonies in the seventeenth century, the event got its start in La Mobile (now Le Moyne, Alabama), and evolved into a parade and street festival that is still celebrated today, incorporating dramatic sculptures, masks, and costumes.

---

4 "Who and What Are Mummers," PhillyMummers.com, https://web.archive.org/web/20211030205959/https://phillymummers.com/extended-history/.

STREET THEATRICS

▰ FANTASTICALS

Also within the United States, another type of costumed performance appeared in the 1800s: troupes of amateur actors known as fantasticals, who took to the streets as a form of political protest. This movement had deeper roots within early American political culture, wrote Susan G. Davis, who noted that the streets were home to a vibrant mix of traditions, including "mock election, charivari, and costumed burlesque," designed to attack and satirize the local politicians. Focusing on Philadelphia's folk traditions, Davis notes that "Burlesques, parodies, and maskings were probably known in Philadelphia and its surrounding countryside from the earliest period of European settlement" in North America. "The best known eighteenth-century uses of street theater were the stylized and ritualized actions of revolutionary crowds and mobs," she wrote. "Philadelphians and other colonial urbanites relied on dramatized action to voice disaffection, defend popular prerogatives, or threaten justice to wrong-doers."[5]

Davis points to the economic gap between the rich and poor that galvanized the popularity of folk traditions, Mummer performances, and dramatic theater in the city. "While elites withdrew their tolerance for the old customs," she writes, "the new, commercial theatre and popular press reinvigorated folk dramas," and "Burlesque, the humorous or mocking exaggeration of traits, burgeoned in Philadelphia's popular theater and street literature."[6] This led to the rise of organized parades that mocked local militia requirements and systems, a product of existing class inequality.

In 1825, Philadelphia residents elected a laborer named John Pluck as the colonel of the 84th Foot Regiment: "A poor, ignorant, stupid fellow . . . As a laborer who cleaned stalls for a living, the new colonel ranked among the lowest of the low, especially compared to the other officers, who were usually lawyers, merchants, and bankers. As a manual laborer, Pluck was often filthy, and since he owned no tools and part of his pay was in lodging, his work placed him in the condition of a servant or retainer."[7]

On May 18, 1825, Pluck led the men of the 84th in an official militia parade, in which they furthered the parody by mocking the readiness and uniform of the system.

---

5   Susan G. Davis, "The Career of Colonel Pluck: Folk Drama and Popular Protest in Early Nineteenth-Century Philadelphia," *The Pennsylvania Magazine of History and Biography*, vol. 109, no. 2, April 1985, 180.
6   Davis, "The Career of Colonel Puck," 183.
7   Davis, "The Career of Colonel Puck," 186.

An etching depicting the Grand Fantastical Parade in New York City on December 2, 1833.

Art: David Claypoole Johnston

"The Colonel made an outrageous officer," Davis wrote, "mounted on a spavined white nag and be-hatted with a huge *chapeau-de-bras*, a shoulder-covering woman's bonnet, the bow knotted under his chin. His baggy burlap pants were cinched up with a belt and enormous buckle; spurs half a yard long with murderous rowels and a giant sword parodied ceremonial military dress and made Pluck appear still shorter."[8]

The men of the unit carried their mockery further, carrying brooms and cornstalks—something Davis notes was common practice, given that they were often too poor to carry real weapons—and marching in a disorderly fashion. The parade became a sensation as newspapers covered the news widely across the East Coast. In the following years, Pluck would make repeat performances in New York City and Albany before being court-martialed for incompetence.[9]

Pluck's notoriety sparked imitators throughout the region, conveying a widespread sense of unease with the political systems of the day. "Albany, New York, and then New

---

8   Davis, "The Career of Colonel Puck," 188.
9   Davis, "The Career of Colonel Puck," 190.

STREET THEATRICS

133

York City witnessed large fantastical processions in 1831 and again in 1833. In Albany, 'fusiliers' and 'invincibles' protested the state law dressed in wild costumes, women's curls, and enormous whiskers." Cartoonist David Claypoole Johnston preserved one event that took place on December 2, 1833, in New York City, depicting the "Grand Fantastical Parade," in which a number of men on horseback wear a variety of outlandish costumes, hats, blackface, and weapons, and carry banners reading: "OUR GENERAL!! May he soon meet his reward in heaven for his everlasting services on earth, DEATH to the MILITIA SYSTEM, and SOLDIERS in peace. CITIZENS in war."

By the 1850s and 1860s, fantasticals were becoming a well-established concept with groups such as the Irishtown Rangers,[10] the Magnetizers,[11] the Santa Anna Light Foot Cavalry,[12] the Santa Anna Guard,[13] and the Scrusendyike Artillery and Bungtown Battalion[14] appearing at parades throughout the region.

Descriptions of the troupes stated that "outlandish costumes . . . of all nations were worn in fragments to suit the fancy of the wearers . . . The longest of swords were worn by the shortest of men, oddly coupled companions, and platoons of the most incongruous make up, formed together a most laughable exhibition."[15] The *Lancaster Intelligencer* described the fantastical companies as wearing "ludicrous costumes,"[16] while the *Pittston Gazette* noted in 1856 that a local group was "arrayed in every imaginable burlesque costume, and wore tiles apparently manufactured from damaged hardware, and discarded hats reduced to a shocking bad state. The captain wielded with herculean grasp a long wooden scimitar, and maneuvered his men with military skill to the music of a well soaked fife and drum, operated by well soaked performers."[17]

With time, the purpose of these groups appears to have turned from targeted mockery and satire to a more theatrical comedic purpose. The fantasticals marched for laughs, staging humorous speeches, skits, and pranks for crowds.

Sometimes, the jokes went too far, as demonstrated in an instance in 1868 in Phil-

---

10 "Two Corrections," from City News and Gossip section, *Brooklyn Daily Eagle*, October 6, 1852.
11 "Fantasticals," from New York City section, *New York Times*, October 8, 1852, 8.
12 "Incidents on the 4th," *Lancaster Examiner and Herald*, July 6, 1853.
13 "The Fourth at Safe Harbor," *Lancaster Examiner and Herald*, July 1, 1855.
14 *Sunbury American*, July 11, 1857.
15 "Fantasticals," 8.
16 *Lancaster Intelligencer*, January 9, 1855.
17 "Fantastical Parade," *Pittston Gazette*, January 4, 1856.

adelphia. A group of fantasticals marched through the city, giving comical speeches at each stop, when tragedy ensued. The leader of the party, George W. Rumel, was giving a comedic speech before a house in the city. "After Rumel had concluded his humorous address, George W. Mayberry, of the party, walked up behind Rumel and discharged a pistol at a tall hat he wore. The pistol, it is said, had no ball or shot in it, but the wad passed through the hat and into the brain, causing death in a very short time."[18]

Fantastical marches also tended to be noisy and disruptive, which attracted the ire of the public and local officials. One report in 1858 notes that an entire company called the Wabash Club was arrested. "Sixteen of their number, who were dressed and painted as Indians and clowns, were fined $5 each [about $150 in 2020]."[19] The troupe left, and the fines were dropped, and a citizen helped pay some other costs. "The freedom of manners of some of the individuals belonging to these clubs does not seem to take well in some of the 'rural districts,'" the paper noted.

Another newspaper editorial, published in June 1858, noted with pleasure that in the lead-up to the Fourth of July celebrations in Pennsylvania, "the Anniversary of our National Liberty was celebrated in a becoming and patriotic manner—and that too without the exercises of the day being interspersed with 'the firing of squibs,' 'the fizzing of spit devils,' . . . 'scratched faces,' 'blackened eyes,' 'torn coats, [etc.] . . . no 'fantastical' demonstrations to burlesque and desecrate a day that should ever be kept sacred by all who appreciate the rights and privileges of American citizens."[20]

The Fantasticals movement died away by the onset of the twentieth century, although their parades seem to have been inspiration for the costumed affairs in New York City that emerged around the same time: the Thanksgiving ragamuffin parades that coalesced out of the early trick-or-treating practice that the city's children undertook while their parents were making Thanksgiving dinners at home.

But the movement left behind a legacy of costuming as a means of street-level storytelling, mixed with the political commentary of the day. This legacy demonstrates that the early concept of costuming wasn't limited just to the dramatic arts or onstage at a theater, but for a wide range of purposes both serious and comedic.

---

18 *Pittsburgh Daily Commercial*, January 4, 1868.
19 "Philadelphia 'Fantasticals' Arrested in Wilmington DL," *Public Ledger*, July 7, 1858.
20 "From Our Own Contributors & Correspondents," *Altoona Tribune*, July 15, 1858.

15 BRINGING THE PAST TO LIFE

Dramatic theater and onscreen entertainment are not the only places in which people use costumes to tell a story. For centuries, people have turned to period garb as a way of bringing the past back to life, whether as professional historians in living history exhibits, reenactors who want to experience what the past might have been like, or simply enthusiasts who appreciate historical garments.

Reenactments and living history exhibits aren't cosplay—but they're adjacent to it and fit under the same broader umbrella: costumes in the service of storytelling.

FORT TICONDEROGA

If you drive north from New York City, you'll arrive at Fort Ticonderoga in about four and a half hours. Nestled along the shores of Lake Champlain and sequestered behind acres of lush northern forests, the site is a reconstruction of a military fortress with a long and storied history.

Members of the local Iroquois tribe originally used the area to cross the lake, but as French and English colonial settlers soon claimed the region, the site became one of strategic importance. The English erected a small wooden fort there in 1691, and decades later in 1755, the French built a larger stone structure named Fort Carillon. It played a pivotal role in the eventual French and Indian War and the campaigns in the St. Lawrence River Valley in 1757. The British later captured the fort in 1759, renaming it Fort Ticonderoga, and it continued to play a role in various conflicts in the region in the decades that followed.

After the American Revolution, the British eventually abandoned the fort. It fell into disrepair as local farmers scavenged its stone for walls, fences, and buildings, and in the early 1800s, a local family purchased the ruins and surrounding lands and turned it into a tourist attraction, eventually restoring it to its former glory. It's now a museum that uses historical immersion and costumes to educate the public about the role the fort played in the country's history.

Walking into Fort Ticonderoga on a blisteringly hot day in July 2019, I was greeted by a fascinating sight: museum staff entirely dressed in period garments. Led by Stuart Lilie, the museum's vice president of public history, they represent part of the museum's living history efforts, giving visitors a visceral glimpse into what life might have been like for the fort's prior inhabitants. Since Lilie joined the museum in 2011, it has become a well-known destination to see history come alive through demonstrations, workshops, and period-accurate garments, which are hand-stitched by the museum's staff.

Cannons protect the walls of Fort Ticonderoga in Ticonderoga, NY.
Courtesy of Andrew Liptak

Stuart Lilie, assembling a British uniform.
Courtesy of Andrew Liptak

Lilie is a tall, thin man, and while I sat in his workshop to chat with him, he hunched over a large drafting table with a pattern to which he pinned a bolt of scarlet red fabric. As he worked, he explained that he was re-creating a British officer's uniform.

BRINGING THE PAST TO LIFE

Living history, he explains, is an old method of historical interpretation, one that fills "the interpretive void between a visitor and the history of a site that surrounds them."

In 1957, writer Freeman Tilden published a book that codified historical interpretation: *Interpreting Our Heritage*, defining how historians, park officials, and educators can convey the past. He defines the field as "an educational activity which aims to reveal meanings and relationships through the use of original objects, by firsthand experience, and by illustrative media, rather than simply to communicate factual information."[1] Tilden lays out six fundamental principles for the practice: Interpretation that isn't related to the subject isn't useful; interpretation in and of itself isn't information; interpretation is an art form; its chief goal is to provoke the audience; it must present the entirety of a subject; and interpreters shouldn't oversimplify their work for children.[2]

Essentially, historic interpretation needs to bring the past to life. It should be more than the recitation of fact—it's multidisciplinary and thought-provoking. These principles have helped to guide educators and reenactors alike, providing a model through which they can bring the past to life for the general public.

"Period costume, or really living history, inflicts that interpretation with more of the pieces of what one might have to imagine otherwise," Lilie explained while he cut his fabric. "It's sort of like illustrating a book relative to a non-illustrated book, and how we illustrate that in living fashion, it's of more use for the education and inspiration of our guests—if done with greater fidelity."

Simply put, living history is a way to bring the distant past into the present based on the extensive research that historians conduct. The desire to reenact the past for educational purposes goes back centuries—Lilie points to early reenactments of the Battle of Fort Carillon, an iconic battle that took place in 1758 right at the site where we were sitting, as one example.

In his book *Living History: Effective Costumed Interpretation and Enactment at Museums and Historic Sites*, David B. Allison points out that museum education and living history reenactments are inherently linked to a nation's larger story: early examples in Scandinavia "set out to represent the past as it actually was and also to preserve the his-

---

1   Freeman Tilden, *Interpreting our Heritage* (Chapel Hill: The University of North Carolina Press, 2009), 8.
2   "The History of Meaning Making," National Parks Service, accessed December 15, 2021, https://mylearning.nps.gov/library-resources/tildens-six-principles-ace.

torical skills and trades of earlier times. In addition, these nascent museums often had political motivations.[3]

By the 1960s and 1970s, museums across the United States were beginning to develop their own living history programs, particularly in the lead-up to the nation's bicentennial. Allison notes that the period was one of "profound disillusionment with government and the idea that America was essentially a righteous nation," and that the "rise in popularity of living history museums was one offshoot" of the challenges that the nation faced at the time.[4] Living history put a tangible spin on history, something that pulled costumes from displays and textual explanations out into the real world for audiences.

Indeed, entertainment mogul Walt Disney's visits to the Henry Ford Museum and Greenfield Village helped to inspire his immersive theme parks in California and Florida. Allison explained that Disney "was drawn to the nostalgia-laced and sanitized vision of America as presented at Greenfield Village and sought to reinvent amusement parks by creating one that provided the fun of fair rides, food, and a main street without the dirtiness and consumer excess that he saw at places like Coney Island."[5] The postwar period was one of profound change for Americans, who found comfort in Disney's entertainment offerings, from his cartoons to his eventual theme parks.

From the time that living history museums peaked, institutions have worked to further refine their interpretations of the past, depicting it yet more accurately. It's an educational method that's put into practice each year at Fort Ticonderoga.

Lilie explains that the museum employs around twenty-five people each summer, and it's his department that supplies them with a set of garments to wear while on station, re-creating the uniforms and garments of a particular year in the fort's history. During my visit, the museum's interpreters were clad in the blue and red uniforms that the fort's French soldiers wore in 1758.

An incredible amount of work goes into the creation of each individual garment. "We start out," Lilie explains, "at a very basic level, [with] design, which comes from looking at original images, studying extant garments, which are the most applicable to what we're trying to re-create. It's fairly rare in clothing that we have exactly *so-and-so*'s

---

3   David B. Allison, *Living History: Effective Costumed Interpretation and Enactment at Museums and Historic Sites* (Lanham, MD: Rowman & Littlefield, 2016), 14.
4   Allison, *Living History*, 17.
5   Allison, *Living History*, 11–12.

uniform, so an awful lot of what we do is finding original objects that are close and interpreting from there the other details associated with it."

Once they complete their research on any given piece of clothing, the team moves on to designing the patterns and crafting their own versions, utilizing period fabrics that they order from the original mills in Europe. "We then go ahead and apply those patterns to whatever we're making, doing alterations such that the garments in turn fit the people who they're made for in the manner of eighteenth-century clothing," Lilie said. "We do those alterations such that you get not just the details of the original but also the silhouette of it, how it would drape upon a person."

The goal, he says, is to "stir the imagination," which he hopes will "lead to a deeper conversation and foster a dialogue with the past." There's a power that resonates with audiences and historians in putting a literal voice to that past, he says.

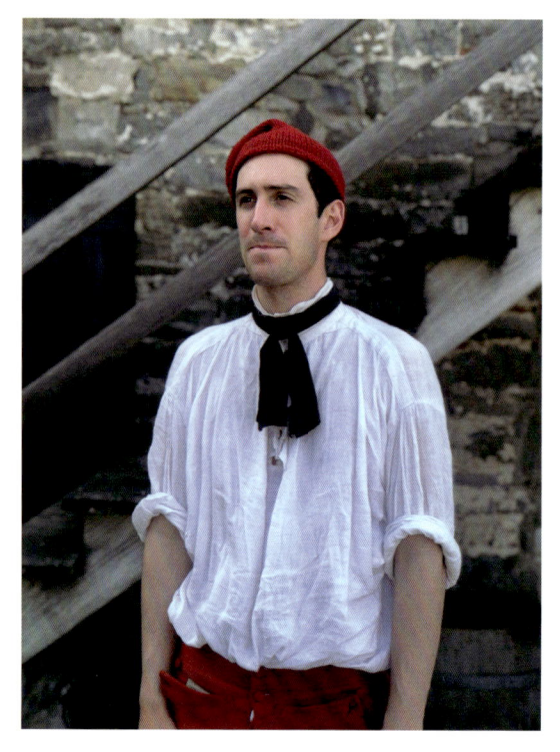

Matt Schlicksup, a cobbler, at Fort Ticonderoga in July 2019.

Courtesy of Andrew Liptak

He notes that while costumes and period garments are sometimes used for commemoration or celebration, living history has a different goal: to educate. "I feel like a lot of our goal with living history and my underlying construct is a functionalist one. My goal is not in any way or inadvertently to denigrate the past, but to show how it worked."

By re-creating period garments, historians gain some insight into the lives of the people who inhabited those clothes. Lilie pointed to a practical example: the seams of the clothes, they discovered, were designed to provide extra room as needed, tucking in excess to let a garment in or out depending on the wearer. "It tells you that the tailor was building in wiggle room," Lilie said, "so the garment could be fit to whomever it was going to, even if it was a custom garment."

That practicality was on display when I walked downstairs to where the fort's cobblers

LEFT: Fort Ticonderoga employees demonstrate the steps taken to fire a cannon, in July 2019.

ABOVE: Fort Ticonderoga employees line up to march in the fort, in July 2019.

Photos courtesy of Andrew Liptak

were set up. Dressed in light white work shirts, red pants, and red caps, museum employee Matt Schlicksup and his companion were working to assemble shoes for the museum. They ran me through the process: they took measurements of their coworker's feet and cut an insole out of thick leather. From there, they cut out the various panels that would make up the sole, then tacked them together with small pegs of wood and some glue.

Like the uniforms, they set their process by working backward from existing shoes. In this case, Schlicksup explained that they were basing their work off a set that archaeologists had discovered in a shipwreck. Centuries underwater had left them in pristine condition, some even bearing their maker's marks. They don't quite know *all* the details, Schlicksup said, like how those original cobblers pierced the leather to make holes, or precisely how they drew the threads through the various parts, but by looking closely at existing examples, they were able to roughly re-create the process.

The museum's efforts are spectacular in person. Looking out over the fort's courtyard, I watched as its fife and drum corps assembled and began to play. Their uniforms were grubby from a summer's worth of use, and the scene does give me a good idea of what life might have been like in the 1700s. It's one thing to read about a battle in a history book and another to feel the concussive blast of a cannon or see a member of the museum staff sweating in the summer heat.

BRINGING THE PAST TO LIFE

While Lilie and his fellow staff members dressing in costume isn't exactly what you'd call cosplay, it's something adjacent to fan costuming and reenactments. Lilie draws a line between his work and others': living history is about the experience of the guest, who will hopefully take away an educational component from their visit, learning from the past. In contrast, he says, reenacting is more about the experience for those who *participate* in the practice.

Ultimately, Lilie cautions that the work they're doing shouldn't be interpreted as the be-all and end-all of the story. Our knowledge of the past is constantly changing as historians make new discoveries through their research. The clothing reproduced at the museum is their best educated guess, based on meticulous work. As they learn new facts about process and design, they incorporate those changes into their uniforms. Their costumes, he says, are a tool to interpret the past, and the better the tools at their disposal, the better the experience for the guests who visit their historic fort.

16 LIVING IN THE PAST

Costumes have long been an element of storytelling, and as actors and historians have both realized, they can effectively immerse audiences in the story they're presenting, whether that be a fictional drama or the historical past.

Whereas living history is an educational venture, costumes and reenactments can also serve deeply nostalgic purposes. Participation in Renaissance fairs allows enthusiasts to use costumes to re-create the past with no single distinct purpose: reenactors may seek to relive the glory days of old through rose-tinted glasses, engage in an activity that requires camaraderie, or inspire one another to look deeper into the past by living it.

THE EGLINTON TOURNAMENT

While scholars and enthusiasts have sought to re-create the past throughout history, there's one event that stands out for its influence on modern-day reenacting: the Eglinton Tournament, held in Scotland in 1839. On August 29–30, crowds descended on Eglinton Castle in Ayrshire for a weekend of activities designed to remind people of the nation's glory days.

The early 1800s marked a new social era in Europe, a response to an increasingly rational society that was undergoing rapid modernization and industrialization. "The outburst against abstract reason and the search for order made up one continuous effort, which has acquired the historical name of Romanticism,"[1] writes Jacques Barzun in *From Dawn to Decadence: 1500 to the Present, 500 Years of Western Cultural Life*. The movement linked together like-minded artists, musicians, sculptors, and philosophers of the day, who placed an emphasis on individualism, nature, and an affinity for the past.

Within the period came subjects like romances (think Sir Walter Scott's *Ivanhoe*) and Gothic literature (such as Mary Shelley's *Frankenstein: The Modern Prometheus*), novels that emphasized the individual and grappled with the rapidly changing world.

Outside of the arts, people were working to understand the bucking of tradition. One such instance was the coronation of Queen Victoria in 1837, which departed from the traditions of her predecessors. "The state banquet in Westminster Hall, the romantic challenge by the Royal Champion and all the other picturesque ceremonies were done away with," writes Ian Anstruther in *The Knight and the Umbrella: An Account of the Eglinton Tournament 1839*. Traditionalists like the Earl of Eglinton—Archibald William Montgomerie—were furious. His stepfather, Sir Charles Lamb, would have been the Marshal for the Royal Champion, and Anstruther notes that "he was highly irritated at being denied the fun of watching his step-father, clad in a scarlet dress slashed with blue and a scarlet cloak and blue stockings, clear the floor of Westminster Hall for the Champion."[2]

An avid horse racer, Montgomerie and a friend had an idea: at an upcoming race, they would introduce certain medieval challenges, a revival of the tournaments that kings put on centuries ago, and which had brought together the bravest knights to prove their valor. The idea caught on, and word spread throughout England that he would soon hold an entire medieval tournament, a throwback to the romantic ideals of England's glory days. Montgomerie liked the idea of a traditional tournament and, encouraged by his family, he announced that he would hold such an event, with a feast to follow.

The tournament would prove an expensive undertaking. "The organization of all the participants—all of whom had to be enlisted," writes Anstruther, the "armour, lances, costumes, and tents—all of which had to be made—required a staff of hundreds, while the cost of mounting and equipping even one single combatant proved to be astronomical."[3]

---

1 Jacques Barzun, *From Dawn to Decadence: 1500 to the Present, 500 Years of Western Cultural Life* (New York: HarperCollins, 2000), 465.
2 Ian Anstruther, *The Knight and the Umbrella: An Account of the Eglinton Tournament 1839* (Birkenhead United Kingdom: Geoffrey Bles Ltd., 1963), 9–10.
3 Anstruther, *The Knight and the Umbrella*, 12.

A piece of art depicting the fight that took place at the Eglinton Tournament in 1839.

Art: James Henry Nixon

That fall, Montgomerie went to an arms dealer in London, where he began to recruit his prospective knights and purchase or commission armor for them to wear. One hundred fifty would-be contestants showed up,[4] but after realizing the cost, only about forty remained.[5] In June 1839, the knights held a rehearsal near Regent's Park, where they practiced moving around in armor, as well as riding and jousting. Their second dress rehearsal in July for an audience of 2,690 people "went off perfectly. All the knights were bright with armour, all their steeds were gay with caparisons, all their tents were adorned with banners, all the heralds were tricked in tabards, while men at arms in appropriate costumes kept the crowds at bay with gleaming halberds."[6]

By the time the date of the tournament arrived in August, public interest had been sparked. Eglinton had planned for around four thousand attendees, but the response was overwhelming: an estimated 100,000 people arrived from all over the country. Prince Louis-Napoléon Bonaparte of France was the official guest of honor.

Fourteen knights in all participated in the tournament, arriving with their own companies. Lord Viscount Glenlyon, "Knight of the Gael," arrived with seventy-three men: "four

---

[4] Anstruther, *The Knight and the Umbrella*, 122.
[5] Anstruther, *The Knight and the Umbrella*, 144.
[6] Anstruther, *The Knight and the Umbrella*, 162.

officers, three sergeants, four corporals, four pipers, two orderlies, and fifty-six privates," each "equipped in a new and specially made uniform of a blue jacket with short tails without facings, green kilt and plaid of hard Athole tartan, red and white diced stockings, black brogues and blue Glengarry bonnet with a silver badge, and each carried his kit with a knapsack lettered ATHOLE and each defended himself with a light target and a broadsword."[7]

On the day of the event, the opening parade was late, but it was apparently a sight to behold. "The Eglinton Herald in a massive tabard, the Judge of Peace in crimson velvet, the Knight Marshal in steel and surcoat on an armed, plumed, caparisoned horse, the Ladies Visitors in minivered jackets, the Ballochmyle Archeresses 'a band of nymphs in Lincoln green,' the King of the Tournament in cape and coronet, Lord Eglinton himself in a suit of gold, and all the knights complete in armour, with pages, esquires, retainers, musicians, more than a hundred of whom were mountained and more than a hundred of whom were armed—the procession was half a mile in length and more than three hours late."[8]

The tournament was about to kick off when the worst-case scenario struck: a torrential downpour. Rain drenched the assembled crowds, who were all but unable to make out the knights assembled on the field. The guests soon fled, walking back along muddy roads, "jostled together like cattle at a fair and behaved with as little civility."[9]

Eglinton attempted to salvage the event and rescheduled for Friday, August 30. The weather had improved, and the reassembled knights held a joust before the remaining crowd, who stayed that evening for the banquet and dance. But despite the success of the makeup date, it was a far cry from what had been planned. Poor weather returned over the weekend, and by early the following week, the guests began leaving for home. Before they parted, the knights held one final ceremony, presenting Eglinton with banners of their house colors, which remained hanging in the castle until the 1920s.[10]

Failure though it was, the Eglinton Tournament represents an interesting moment in time, which Debra N. Mancoff sums up in her book *The Return of King Arthur: The Legend through Victorian Eyes* as providing "chivalric idealism its much-needed anchor in reality" during a time of considerable political change in England.[11]

---

7 Anstruther, *The Knight and the Umbrella*, 184.
8 Anstruther, *The Knight and the Umbrella*, 195.
9 Anstruther, *The Knight and the Umbrella*, 213.
10 Anstruther, *The Knight and the Umbrella*, 225.
11 Debra N. Mancoff, *The Return of King Arthur: The Legend through Victorian Eyes* (New York: Harry N. Abrams, Inc., 1995), 35.

Eglinton had tapped into a deep-seated desire on the part of the English public to relive some of the stories at the heart of the country's mythology. Mancoff points to other instances where this pops up in British history: Prince Albert attended a costume party in 1842 dressed as Edward III, and later posed for a portrait in armor with Queen Victoria.[12]

Taken out of their historical context, these instances boil down to a simple activity: playing a small part in the stories that matter to us the most. While not the first examples of reenacting or cosplay as we know them, they show that this desire existed centuries before the advent of their expression in modern popular culture.

REENACTING

History enthusiasts aren't limited to depictions by museums or educational institutions. Reenacting is another major avenue through which individuals don period costumes to try to place themselves in the past.

Military reenactments in the United States date back to the mid-1800s, when groups of mock militias would gather to perform "sham battles" from the Revolutionary War, according to R. Lee Hadden in *Reliving the Civil War: A Reenactor's Handbook*. Hadden notes that reenactments for the Civil War began almost as soon as the war itself was over, as veterans' organizations "recreated camp life to show their children and others how they lived" during the war.[13]

While enthusiasts performed sham battles in the decades that followed, the American reenacting scene exploded in popularity with the coming of the Civil War Centennial in 1961 and the United States Bicentennial in 1976. Hadden notes that reenacting as it's known today grew out of the black-powder competitive shooting scene, for which members began to don imitation period wear.

Following the United States Bicentennial, reenactors began to focus on accuracy. "Research began on uniforms and equipment, and manufacturing of good reproductions was started," Hadden writes. They wanted to better understand what life was like for the

---

12 *Queen Victoria and Prince Albert at the Bal Costumé of 12 May 1842*, Royal Collection Trust, accessed December 15, 2021, https://www.rct.uk/collection/404540/queen-victoria-and-prince-albert-at-the-bal-costume-of-12-may-1842.
13 R. Lee Hadden, *Reliving the Civil War: A Reenactor's Handbook* (Mechanicsburg, PA: Stackpole Books, 1999), 4.

A cavalry squadron takes part in a reenactment at the Daniel Lady Farm in Gettysburg, Pennsylvania, on July 3, 2021.

Courtesy of Andrew Liptak

soldiers on the battlefield and conducted closer research into the equipment, clothing, and lifestyles of the people they were emulating.

By the 1980s, Hadden notes that a "split began during this period between professional historians and the reenactors," driven in part by the growing popularity of reenacting.[14] Historians were concerned that reenactors were too fixated on individual historical events, and that the events they brought to life weren't, strictly speaking, historically accurate. Reenactors shot back that "historians did not have a monopoly on [historical] interpretation."[15]

This split underpins a foundational difference in motivation between the two camps. While both are deeply interested in researching the events of the past, one group is interested in the educational components of the activity, while the other is concerned with performance. Daniel Celik, a member of the Champlain Rifles, a Civil War group that represented the 14th Vermont and 123rd New York Regiments, explained that "the relationship between history and reenacting is very closely intertwined. To tell the authentic story of the Civil War, one must 'live' it and believe that in earnest." He explains that he was predisposed to the hobby: his father had been a member of the group, and he himself studied history and education in college.[16]

---

14 Hadden, *Reliving the Civil War*, 6.
15 Hadden, *Reliving the Civil War*, 6.
16 Daniel Celik email with the author, February 2020.

Celik notes that accuracy is incredibly important to the hobby, as reenactors and living historians research period-accurate fabrics, patterns, and equipment. "I prefer to have uniforms that are period-authentic," he says. "It even comes down to hand-sewn buttonholes rather than ones that are machine-sewn." Focusing on medical scenes, Celik explained that he drew on primary-source material to inform his appearance and has traveled to Civil War battlefields such as Appomattox, Antietam, and Gettysburg to get a better sense of what the environments were like.

In particular, Celik explained that he portrays certain specific historical figures, ensuring that he learns as much about the individual in order to honor their memory, even making the effort to visit one man's gravestone on an annual basis to clean it up, and remaining in touch with his family to let them know what he is doing.

Celik doesn't just limit himself to historical reenacting. He's also a member of the 501st and Rebel Legion *Star Wars* costuming groups. He explained that while the two hobbies draw from different sources, they're linked, noting that members of both communities have an affinity for collecting uniforms and conducting close research on the characters they're most interested in. "Cosplay is just another step into the world of fiction. It gives me a better idea, and in some ways puts me in sync with the character, the time, and the world in which things are set."

TOP: Reenactor Dan Celik portraying Surgeon M. J. Hyde.
BOTTOM: Dan Celik during a Civil War reenactment.
Courtesy of Daniel Celik

History is a powerful story in and of itself. Walking through a Gettysburg reenactment at the Daniel Lady Farm in the summer of 2021, I overheard an attendee say that

LIVING IN THE PAST

LEFT: Reenactor Jason Miller takes part in World War II Weekend at Reading, Pennsylvania's Mid-Atlantic Air Museum as a member of the 3rd Infantry Division in June 2021.

CENTER: A team of 101st Airborne reenactors prepare to jump out of a perfectly good airplane during Mid-Atlantic Air Museum's World War II Weekend in Reading, Pennsylvania, in June 2021.

RIGHT: John W. McCaskill takes part in the Mid-Atlantic Air Museum's World War II Weekend in June 2021, dressed as a Tuskegee Airman. He noted that every year, he comes across someone who's never heard of the Tuskegee Airmen, and uses the opportunity to educate them about the unit and its legacy.

Photos courtesy of Andrew Liptak

one of his ancestors had fought at the battle, 158 years to that day, and that the personal relationship and desire to connect with his past had moved him years earlier to take up reenacting as a hobby.

Reenacting isn't limited to portraying only soldiers. That Gettysburg event had reenactors depicting dressmakers, Associated Press reporters, mapmakers, chaplains, surgeons, surveyors, and other individuals who played a role in the story of the battle.

Reenacting goes beyond the American Civil War as well. The Mid-Atlantic Air Museum in Reading, Pennsylvania, hosts an annual gathering of World War II reenactors who depict service members from America, Britain, Russia, Germany, and other countries; and bring along plenty of vehicles to boot, giving visitors an idea of what a wartime experience might have looked or sounded like. It's an educational experience for all involved. One reenactor, John W. McCaskill, took part in the event as a Tuskegee Airman, the first African American aviators in the US military. He explained that he was drawn to the personal story of the airmen, and that by depicting one of its members, he could bring them to life for attendees. In many cases, he explained, he would meet guests who had never heard of the airmen, and by interacting with them, he could provide a bit more insight into the conflict.

17 HALLOWEEN

If you've ever worn a costume, there's a good chance that it's been on or around October 31. Despite its origins as an agricultural celebration, it has become a time of all things popular culture, with children and adults dressing up as their favorite characters as they trick-or-treat or attend parties. In most cases, it's one's introduction to costuming—a night on which one is allowed to pretend to be someone else for a short while, opening the road to more costumes in years to come.

Children try to catch pennies during Thanksgiving masking sometime between 1910 and 1915.
Image via Library of Congress

How did Halloween become synonymous with costumes? Its origins stretch back centuries, and it has since pulled together folk traditions, superstitions, and popular culture. The *New York Times* observed that "Halloween was, in many ways, one of the earliest manifestations of what we now call fandom,"[1] pushed along in part by the efforts of costuming companies to cash in on licenses for

---

1 Jennifer Harlan, "Your Halloween Costume Expires Sooner Than You Think," *New York Times*, October 24, 2019, https://www.nytimes.com/2019/10/24/us/pop-culture-halloween-costumes.html.

popular characters from films and television shows. In doing so, they helped inspire generations to look beyond the night of October 31 to dress up as their favorite characters.

ORIGINS

Like most holidays, Halloween has a complicated origin story. In her book *Trick or Treat: A History of Halloween*, Lisa Morton says that it's "undoubtedly the most misunderstood of festivals."[2] The holiday comes from ancient Celts, who celebrated a holiday called Samhain between summer and winter. "A Celtic day began when the sun went down, and so Samhain started with the onset of darkness on 31 October," she writes, "with a feast celebrating the recent harvest and temporary abundance of food."[3] While experts argue about the influence of the holiday on its modern-day successor, "it seems likely that the Celtic festival's peculiar mix of harvest, rowdy celebration and fearful supernatural beliefs gave Halloween much of its character."[4]

The holiday is believed to have emerged from pagan times, when worshippers believed that the day marked a point in the year where the veil between our world and the supernatural otherworld was thinnest and easily traversed by spirits. To ensure a favorable winter, people would leave out food and drink, while others believed that spirits would try to visit their homes. As part of the festivities, people would go from door to door dressed in disguises or costumes, which was eventually altered by the Roman Catholic Church in an attempt to overwrite the local traditions, transforming the day into All Hallows' Eve, All Souls' Day, and All Saints' Day.[5]

After the colonization of the British Isles, the traditions of Samhain were absorbed into other local practices. The holiday became associated with religious fears as the Black Death swept over Europe; and later as Europe descended into a frenzy of witch trials, with some of the victims specifically accused of consorting with the Devil on Halloween. Morton cites a myriad of other events, from the annual tradition of burning effigies of Guy Fawkes to the rituals of bonfires in Scotland and Ireland, which ranged from simply getting rid of leftover

---

2   Lisa Morton, *Trick or Treat: A History of Halloween* (London: Reaktion Books, 2019), 11.
3   Morton, *Trick or Treat*, 14.
4   Morton, *Trick or Treat*, 16.
5   "How the Tradition of Trick or Treating Got Started," Today I Found Out (website), October 17, 2012, http://www.todayifoundout.com/index.php/2012/10/how-the-tradition-of-trick-or-treating-got-started.

litter to warding off fairies and witches. What emerged was a tradition of mischief with supernatural overtones. In 1780, Scottish poet John Mayne described the festival's pranks and ghostly leanings in a poem called "Hallo'ween," while fellow Scotsman Robert Burns's 1785 poem "Halloween" carried on the theme by describing the holiday in practice.

As such, the holiday became associated with several divergent elements. First, there were the lingering agricultural components, holdovers from the Celts. Second, there was an element of supernatural intrigue, which came from the Celts' practices, but also parts from European history. Third, mischief entered into the holiday's traditions—it became an outlet for pranks and troublemaking.

As Europe expanded its reach across the world in the sixteenth and seventeenth centuries, its traditions followed; and when migrants arrived in the United States, they brought their holidays and traditions with them, including Halloween.

By the late 1800s, publications such as the *Ladies' Home Journal* described the holiday as a pagan one with supernatural overtones: "In modern times Halloween has always been enjoyable because of the popular superstitions attaching to it as a night when any supernatural story might be believed, any charm tested, any frolic permitted—a night when imagination might run riot, and any ceremony, however extravagant, be indulged in."

The holiday's propensity for mischief also made its way to the United States. Across the country, numerous towns and cities had to contend with an increasing level of property damage and larceny; petty pranks grew more serious. In some instances, this prompted cities to crack down on Halloween activities, instituting curfews for children to prevent them from causing problems, while communities worked to figure out ways to divert the youthful, destructive energy into something less costly.

One solution was to establish some alternatives that would appeal to children and young adults and keep them under some sort of supervision. The Halloween party was one such solution, in which families decorated their homes and set out games to play with friends and families. *Ladies' Home Journal* described a number of games that attendees could partake in, noting that "Any innocent joke, perpetrated in a spirit of friendly mischief, will befit the night."[6] Games included fortune-telling games, bobbing for apples, searching for a ring in flour, and others.

---

6   Anna Margaret Price, "Halloween Romps and Frolics: Merry Halloween Games," *Ladies' Home Journal*, October 1897, 25: https://babel.hathitrust.org/cgi/pt?id=mdp.39015012341627&view=2up&seq=404.

RAGAMUFFIN DAYS

The early practices of the holiday largely didn't include costuming, but another annual holiday did: America's Thanksgiving.

The Thanksgiving holiday has existed since the beginning of the United States. George Washington first declared the holiday in 1789, though it was only occasionally celebrated. In 1863, President Abraham Lincoln issued a proclamation that established November 26 as a national Thanksgiving Day, after which President Ulysses S. Grant signed a law that established the day as a federal holiday.[7]

Along with the holiday came an interesting tradition in New England, according to the *New York Times* in 1893: "This is really a relic of an old New-England custom, forgotten there, but living still in its queer travesty in the city streets. In an old book descriptive of New-England characters and customs one reads that on Thanksgiving Eve it was the custom for the poorer people, servants, and dependents to go to the houses of the rich to ask for substantials to help celebrate the coming feast day. And the richer people felt it incumbent on their dignity and hospitality not to allow any one to go away from their doors empty handed."[8]

That tradition died out in New England but appears to have migrated to the region's larger cities, where children began to dress up during the holiday. It eventually became known as Ragamuffin Day or Thanksgiving Masking, during which children dressed up as the homeless or as vagrants and went from door to door begging for treats or money. "Basically," Carmen Nigro, the managing research librarian for the New York Public Library, told the *New York Times*, "kids would go around, probably while their parents were creating the holiday meal, knocking on their neighbors' doors and saying, 'Anything for Thanksgiving?'"[9]

Nigro explained that for their efforts, ragamuffins would typically get a small reward—

---

7 Roy P. Basler, ed., "Proclamation of Thanksgiving," Abraham Lincoln Online, accessed December 10, 2021, http://www.abrahamlincolnonline.org/lincoln/speeches/thanks.htm.
8 "Thanksgiving Is At Hand; Some Studies of the Holiday, Past and Present," *New York Times*, November 26, 1893, https://www.nytimes.com/1893/11/26/archives/thanksgiving-is-at-hand-some-studies-of-the-holiday-past-and.html?searchResultPosition=1.
9 Tammy La Gorce, "What Door-to-Door Tradition Came Before Trick-or-Treating?" *New York Times*, October 21, 2016, https://www.nytimes.com/2016/10/23/nyregion/what-door-to-door-tradition-came-before-trick-or-treating.html.

Before it became a Halloween tradition, children would dress up and "trick-or-treat" on Thanksgiving.

Images via Library of Congress

pennies, an apple, or candy.[10] She mentions a 1909 *New York Tribune* article that said the tradition appears to have started around the 1870s. Children initially dressed up as "ragamuffins," but the scope of the costumes eventually expanded to include costumes of all types and varieties. In his book *Death Makes a Holiday: A Cultural History of Halloween*, David J. Skal notes that the practice was well established by the 1880s and that children had begun to move on from dressing up as vagrants and the impoverished. He cites Thanksgiving historian Diana Karter Appelbaum's description of the scene:

"As early as 1881, Thanksgiving in New York was attended by streets full of 'robbers, pirates, fiends, devils, imps, fairies, priests, bishops, gypsies, flower girls, kings, clowns, princes, jesters—all in variegated and bewildering attire.' "[11] The practice was popular, and lucrative for those who made costumes: according to Carlisle, Pennsylvania's *The Sentinel* in 1902, the holiday was "the biggest time of the year for the manufacturers of and deals in masks and false faces."[12] Companies sold "enormous" quantities of masks during the season and made it a point to release new types every year, ranging from "brownies, 'yaller kids,' parrot visages," to masks depicting "prominent men and foremost political leaders."[13]

---

10 Carmen Nigro, "Thanksgiving Ragamuffin Parade," New York Public Library (blog), November 23, 2010, https://www.nypl.org/blog/2010/11/23/thanksgiving-ragamuffin-parade.
11 David J. Skal, *Death Makes a Holiday: A Cultural History of Halloween* (New York: Bloomsbury USA, 2002), 45–46.
12 "False Faces," *The Sentinel*, November 24, 1902, https://www.newspapers.com/newspage/344417362.
13 "False Faces."

HALLOWEEN

The scene would have been vibrant, chaotic, and loud. The *Brooklyn Daily Eagle* wrote in 1883 that "the city gave itself up to rejoicing and gratitude with fervor. Bands of fantasticals and ragamuffins paraded the avenues, clad in grotesque and at times bewildering habiliments, and headed by musicians who had little regard for time or measure in their frantic efforts to create and prolong a distracting and discordant uproar."[14]

In 1891, the *Times Union* described the parades of children as including "harlequins, clowns, cowboys, Indians, colored men, and women, and in fact, every phase of human character was portrayed."[15] The *Standard Union* of Brooklyn also described the scene as "deafening." There might have been parade costumes more painful to the artistic eye, but the ragamuffins and others made themselves as outlandish as the means at their command would permit, and they served their purpose by delighting the children, enjoying themselves, and amusing a goodly portion of the citizens of this town."[16]

In 1893, the *New York Times* described the children as "dressed in all sorts of ragged and ill-fitting garments, or gay with fantastic costumes that savor of the circus ring, every child masked, they make grotesque and (to themselves) delightful processions in the streets. They march in groups and singly, tooting their horns, shouting, and racing, and then go from door to door, begging for dainties to put in their baskets. In spite of the scanty handfuls of nuts and cakes, and now and then a poor orange or withered apple, which crusty elders generally bestow on them, the children have a merry time and plenty of fun with one another, and come in flushed and bright-eyed for the dinner that awaits them."[17]

The annual spectacle was a chaotic one, with children playing pranks—hitting doors or people who didn't give out money or treats with socks full of chalk or flour—and with fights and even gunfire erupting in the streets.[18]

While the ragamuffins and fantasticals initially shared the streets with one another, the ragamuffins appear to have won out, according to Skal, and by the 1920s, the chaotic mess of children begging for treats gave way to parades marching down city streets and avenues.

With the onset of the Great Depression, Skal notes, the ragamuffins' days were

---

14   "The Fall Feast: How Thanksgiving Was Observed in the City," *The Brooklyn Daily Eagle*, November 29, 1883.
15   "Long Island News: The Day on Long Island: Thanksgiving Day in the Towns and Villages," *Times Union*, November 27, 1891.
16   *The Standard Union*, November 27, 1891.
17   "Thanksgiving Is At Hand," *New York Times*.
18   Tom Deignan, "The Thanksgiving Tradition of Ragamuffin Day in Irish Neighborhoods," October 16, 2021, https://www.irishcentral.com/opinion/others/irish-americas-halloween-ragamuffins-thanksgiving.

numbered. "By 1932, New York schools were doing their part to officially discourage Thanksgiving begging, and the press lent its editorial support."[19] The noise and chaos of the crowds appears to have turned the public against the practice—helped by the state of the economy, where households could scarcely afford to give away money or treats to the community at large.

There were other factors as well: the launch of Macy's elaborate annual Thanksgiving Day Parade in New York City provided an alternative spectacle for families to observe. By 1930, the *New York Times* noted that the tradition was on its way out, quoting a policeman who observed that "all I've seen is just about six kids dressed up like we used to dress in the old days. Things ain't the way they used to be."[20] The paper said that while the practice had begun to fade, it still persisted in the city's outer limits, and worried that the tradition would die out completely. "In Flatbush, the Bronx, Greenpoint, and other places where the subway lines end . . . the ragamuffin is vanishing."[21]

But while the ragamuffins found other things to do, they didn't vanish completely. The practice lingered on for another couple of decades, and Nigro says that the last documented ragamuffin parade of the era appears to have been in 1956 in the Bronx.[22] In the following decades it saw some resurgences: the *New York Times* reported in 1972 that the Bay Ridge neighborhood had organized a ragamuffin parade for the last six years, featuring "pirates, sea monsters, marching kettledrums, twirlers, tramps, caged animals, a well-clad Lady Godiva, clowns and athletes."[23]

The parade is still running today, described as a "pre-Halloween activity," while other parades in places like Park Ridge, New Jersey, and Pleasantville and Briarcliff Manor in upstate New York have also kept the tradition alive.[24]

But while the widespread ragamuffin tradition largely died out in New York City,

---

19 Skal, *Death Makes a Holiday: A Cultural History of Halloween*, 46.
20 "Parading Thanksgiving Ragamuffins Scarce, Except Out Where City's Subway Lines End," *New York Times*, November 28, 1930, https://www.nytimes.com/1930/11/28/archives/parading-thanksgiving-ragamuffins-scarce-except-out-where-citys.html.
21 "Parading Thanksgiving Ragamuffins Scarce, Except Out Where City's Subway Lines End."
22 "Thanksgiving Ragamuffin Parade," New York Public Library (blog), November 23, 2010, https://www.nypl.org/blog/2010/11/23/thanksgiving-ragamuffin-parade.
23 "35,000 Watch 6,000 Children March in Bay Ridge Ragamuffin Parade," *New York Times*, October 16, 1972, https://www.nytimes.com/1972/10/16/archives/35000-watch-6000-children-march-in-bay-ridge-ragamuffin-parade.html.
24 La Gorce, "What Door-to-Door Tradition Came Before Trick-or-Treating?"

Skal notes that the practice of dressing up and begging for treats didn't go anywhere, but simply transferred itself over to another holiday: Halloween.

HOLIDAY INDUSTRIAL COMPLEX

In the midst of the Great Depression, Halloween began to undergo a transformation. From its origins as a pagan holiday that morphed into an annual night of property damage, it's since become the second largest holiday, one that's characterized by costumes, trick-or-treating, and parties.

In the 1930s and 1940s, the practice of dressing up for Thanksgiving transferred itself over to Halloween, finding a welcome home with the long tradition of masking and pranks celebrated throughout the holiday. Towns and cities had had enough of the holiday's costly pranks during the season, and in 1939, Doris Hudson Moss came up with a solution for *American Home* magazine: bribe the neighborhood children with a party. "If the decorations are spooky enough," she wrote, "and if you provide food and a hearty welcome, you can be sure that the little rowdies from the other side of town will join in the party spirit and leave your front gate intact."[25]

What likely happened was a patchwork effort on the parts of communities to try to stem the tide of property destruction and violence. "It does seem clear that the American custom of trick-or-treating," Skal wrote, "whatever its specific sources, inspirations, or influences, became widely known and adopted as a distinct property-protection strategy during the late Depression."[26]

The commercialization of various holidays by manufacturing and selling costumes was something that companies had latched onto decades earlier.

In the mid-1800s, the Dennison Manufacturing Company of Framingham, Massachusetts, started out by manufacturing and selling jewelry boxes and quickly morphed into manufacturing jewelry tags, gummed paper (stickers), and crepe paper. In 1901, it began selling tags and wrapping paper for the Christmas holiday season, and in 1911 added Halloween decorations to its lineup.

According to the Framingham History Center, Halloween had seen a decline in the

---

25 Skal, *Death Makes a Holiday: A Cultural History of Halloween*, 53.
26 Skal, *Death Makes a Holiday*, 54.

preceding years, and "many credited Dennison products as the driving force that made the holiday popular again with the public."[27] Among its offerings was its Bogie Books, which outlined how to create decorations for the holiday, ideas for parties, ghost stories to recount for guests, and suggestions for costumes.

The company's 1920 book noted that "weird designs and bright orange in contrast with black make it possible to create very striking costumes for the Hallowe'en party with very little work," and that partygoers could easily make costumes using crepe paper glued or sewn onto a cloth foundation, which could be made to slip over one's clothes.[28] "The foundation of a slip-over costume is a full width of crepe paper cut out for the neck and of sufficient length to reach from the shoulders to the bottom of the skirt, front and back. To this foundation are attached ruffles, streamers or cut out designs."[29]

The book shows a party scene in which attendees wear vibrant orange, white, and black costumes decorated with pumpkins, black cats, witches, and other holiday iconography, which appear to be the first such mass-produced costumes offered to the general public.

The company didn't limit its costume suggestions to Halloween. Other catalogs, such as its 1922 Gala book, offered suggestions and products for holidays such as St. Valentine's Day, St. Patrick's Day, and the Fourth of July. "A tiny child or a grown-up will be equally attractive dressed in a slip-over topped with a huge ruffled heart," the catalog trumpets. "'Baby Valentine' is very sweet in her dainty pink and white dress. The valentine itself can be made elaborate or simple as occasion requires, and even a big girl can wear a costume made in just the same style."[30]

The early 1900s marked a pivotal time for the practice of Halloween in America, as companies began to capitalize on the fiscal return of the evening. Today, the practices of dressing up in costume and trick-or-treating are synonymous, but it was around that time that the two practices began to merge. The tradition of trick-or-treating migrated to earlier in the calendar year as companies made a concerted effort to raise the profile of the holiday to boost candy and costume sales.

---

27 "The Dennison Mfg. Company: 1844–1990," Framingham History Center: News and Events, March 27, 2015, https://framinghamhistory.org/dennison-mfg-co-1844-1990.
28 "Dennison's Bogie Book," The Library of Congress, 1920, https://archive.org/details/dennisonsbogiebo00denn/page/24, 24.
29 "Dennison's Bogie Book."
30 "Dennison's Gala Book," The Library of Congress, 1922, https://archive.org/details/dennisonsgalaboo00denn/page/n25, 25.

Companies like the Dennison Manufacturing Company helped to create the market for Halloween costumes, but for decades, Thanksgiving and Halloween costuming was a low-effort occasion for families. "In the past, costumes had been relatively simple homemade affairs," writes Morton, "and had often utilized the image of the outsider: costumes for gypsies, hobos, bandits, and pirates were all easy to produce, requiring little more than old castoff clothing and a few accessories."[31]

The necessity to expand and adapt one's business in the midst of the Great Depression prompted companies to recognize the potential that Halloween held for their bottom lines. A number of companies used the opportunity to begin producing cheap, mass-produced costumes for would-be trick-or-treaters, which would become synonymous with the holiday itself.

In Brooklyn, brothers Ben and Nat Cooper ran a company that catered to New York City's vaudeville scene and provided costumes and sets for school productions. As economic woes put pressure on the theater industry in the 1930s, the Coopers began producing costumes for Halloween.

One of the company's early successes was the acquisition of a license from Walt Disney Enterprises, allowing them to produce costumes based on the company's already popular characters such as Snow White and the Seven Dwarfs, Donald Duck, Mickey and Minnie Mouse, and the Big Bad Wolf.[32] Later, the company also acquired the rights to produce costumes of Davy Crockett, Superman, and Zorro.[33] Those existing properties helped transform the company into a Halloween institution.

Disney also recognized that people would want to dress up as their characters. In 1930, a seamstress created a pattern for people to sew their own Mickey and Minnie Mouse dolls, which in turn inspired Walt Disney Enterprises and the McCall Pattern Company to team up and offer an official pattern for parents to sew their own Mickey and Minnie costumes in 1933.[34]

---

31 Morton, *Trick or Treat: A History of Halloween*, 83.
32 Phyllis Galembo, "Halloween Costume," in *Encyclopedia of Clothing and Fashion Volume 2*, ed. Valerie Steele (New York: Charles Scribner's Sons, 2004), 167.
33 Harriet Shapiro, "Trick and Treat! Ben Cooper Bags Millions as the Halston of Halloween," *People*, October 29, 1979, https://people.com/archive/trick-and-treat-ben-cooper-bags-millions-as-the-halston-of-halloween-vol-12-no-18.
34 "Disney Halloween: A Look Back at Early Disney Costumes," The Walt Disney Company (website), October 30, 2012, https://www.thewaltdisneycompany.com/disney-halloween-a-look-back-at-early-disney-costumes.

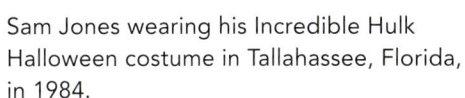

Sam Jones wearing his Incredible Hulk Halloween costume in Tallahassee, Florida, in 1984.

Image: State Library and Archives of Florida

A girl dresses up as Minnie Mouse during the Children's Halloween Parade in Lowell, Massachusetts, in 1987.

Image: Douglas DeNatale

Other companies took similar approaches, like the Pennsylvania-based Collegeville Flag and Manufacturing Company, which got its start manufacturing flags in the 1910s before moving into costumes, and the H. Halpern Company (known as Halco). These three companies would become synonymous with Halloween, each producing extremely cheap, mass-produced costumes that included a thin plastic mask and a plastic outfit that were sold in major retailers such as J. C. Penney, Sears, F. W. Woolworth, and W. T. Grant, as well as smaller five-and-dime stores.[35]

When the Second World War ended in 1945, the US economy went into overdrive, and trick-or-treating came into its own. The mandated wartime rationing of items like rubber and sugar meant that those resources were now freed up for a civilian marketplace, something that companies took advantage of. "Major candy companies like Curtiss and Brach, no longer constrained by sugar rationing, launched national advertising campaigns specifically aimed at Halloween. If trick-or-treating had previously been a localized, hit-or-miss phenomenon, it was now a national duty."[36]

Costume companies were also able to take advantage of new manufacturing techniques that allowed them to bring a new level of sophistication to Halloween costumes.

---

35 Helaine Fendelman, "Vintage Halloween Costumes," *Country Living*, October 1, 2007, 63.
36 Skal, *Death Makes a Holiday: A Cultural History of Halloween*, 55.

HALLOWEEN

"As manufacturing techniques changed in the 1950s and facilitated silkscreening on cheap rayon or vinyl," Morton writes, "and as plastic production allowed the creation of inexpensive, colourful masks, shop-bought costumes began to replace the traditional homemade outfits."[37]

The aftermath of WWII brought additional changes to the US. The country's industrial infrastructure had remained untouched during the war, allowing companies to shift their production from a wartime footing to serve a civilian marketplace that was increasingly enjoying all the benefits of a middle-class lifestyle. Millions of soldiers who returned home from war were able to take advantage of massive government programs like the GI Bill and home loans, allowing them to buy houses, get a college education, and start families. The country instituted major infrastructure programs in the postwar era, constructing the interstate highway system and massive suburbs for middle-class families. That added income and infrastructure aided the popularity and growth of the modern form of Halloween festivities—the newly constructed suburbs proved to be the perfect setting for trick-or-treating.

In this environment, the Halloween industrial complex exploded. Ben Cooper, Inc., Halco, and the newly rebranded Collegeville Costumes were all well positioned to deliver an array of costumes to eager children, allowing them to dress up as everything from animals, pirates, and witches to a whole range of licensed characters from popular films and television shows.

By the 1960s, companies were increasingly looking toward films and television shows for inspiration and characters to license. "Licensing was the key to our success," former Ben Cooper president Bob Cooper said in a documentary called *Halloween in a Box*. Kids were excited to dress up as their favorite characters from movies and TV—characters that studios had designed to appeal to children—and they happened to be the right age to go out trick-or-treating. Ben Cooper, Inc. found early success when it licensed characters from Disney and Superman, and the 1960s brought a wealth of new characters for them to utilize.

Other companies took slightly different approaches to their costumes, such as Don Post Studios. The company's namesake founder initially began making rubber masks as a hobby and soon built a business supplying theaters in Chicago in the mid-1930s, while

---

37   Morton, *Trick or Treat: A History of Halloween*, 83.

also stocking novelty stores with masks of clowns, old ladies, devils, and hobos, as well as ones depicting individuals like Adolf Hitler, Joseph Stalin, and Benito Mussolini.[38]

When World War II brought about mandatory rationing of supplies like rubber, Post relocated at the end of the war to Los Angeles, where he began to make masks for movie productions, starting with *Invasion of the Body Snatchers* in 1956.[39] Post recognized that his skills could be turned to the commercial Halloween market, and in 1948 he "approached Universal Studios and obtained the licensing rights to produce the world's first licensed mask of the Frankenstein Monster."[40]

In the late 1970s, *Star Wars* became a massive merchandising juggernaut, and companies like Ben Cooper, Inc. and Don Post Studios acquired licenses to produce costumes, masks, and helmets for the holiday season. The companies were lucky: George Lucas's science-fiction film was far from a sure hit when it debuted in theaters in 1977, and its popularity caught toy retailers like Kenner off-guard, leaving its stores with not nearly enough merchandise for that year's Christmas season.

A year later, another film would have an enormous impact on the holiday: John Carpenter's *Halloween*, which helped draw adults into the festivities, turning Halloween into something more than just a night of fun for kids. "Halloween had been spooky and eerie but not gory or scary until that movie," Halloween historian Lesley Bannatyne told the

After finishing his stormtrooper, David Rhea moved on to Darth Vader. He ended up wearing it around town and to the local movie theater.

Courtesy of Cheryl Rhea

---

[38] Lee Lambert, *The Illustrated History of Don Post Studios* (Blacksparrow, Inc., 2014), 13–14.
[39] Lambert, *The Illustrated History*, 10.
[40] Lambert, *The Illustrated History*, 35.

New York Times.[41] Carpenter's film brought plenty of that, and it helped draw teenagers and adults into the holiday, transforming it from purely a children's activity into something more pop-culture oriented.

However, a real-world horror in 1982 slammed the brakes on the holiday. Seven people in Chicago died after they ingested Tylenol laced with potassium cyanide. The resulting panic hit the Halloween industry hard as rumors spread that Halloween candy could be poisoned, or that people were hiding razor blades in candy or apples. Parents held their kids back from trick-or-treating, and when they did allow their children to go out, they were extra cautious. However, while there's never been an actual instance of poisoning or deliberate sabotage of Halloween candy, those concerns have persisted to the present day, with some communities holding "safe" events or offering to X-ray candies to allay parents' concerns.[42]

There were silver linings for certain Halloween-focused companies. Howie Beige, the vice president of Rubie's Costume Company, told me a couple of years ago that they had been in the midst of an upgrade: they had started selling costumes that were a step above Collegeville's or Ben Cooper's, with better fabrics and masks, and even as the industry constricted due to concerns, not everybody abandoned trick-or-treating or costuming. They simply changed locations. "As [the hoaxes] happened, more people were doing a lot more parties in their schools or churches or homes," he explained, "which led to costume contests and everything else."[43]

According to Beige, the hoaxes and parental concern pushed Halloween to become a more supervised, family-friendly activity, and parents were willing to spend more on better costumes for their children. The masks and costumes sold by Ben Cooper, Collegeville, and Halco were made of cheap plastic—the outfits themselves were typically inexpensive vinyl smocks with the name of their character or film branded on the front. They weren't necessarily designed to replicate the characters they depicted. Rubie's introduced better fabrics and masks that were slightly more expensive than those of their competitors but looked much better.

---

41 Jennifer Harlan, "Your Halloween Costume Expires Sooner Than You Think."
42 Jonathan M. Pitts, "Halloween Activities Address Adult Fears, Too," *Baltimore Sun*, October 30, 2015, https://www.baltimoresun.com/maryland/bs-md-halloween-safety-20151030-story.html.
43 Andrew Liptak, "Why Have Children's Halloween Costumes Gotten So Much Better?" *The Verge*, October 31, 2017, https://www.theverge.com/2017/10/31/16513936/halloween-costumes-quality-rubies-hasbro.

Faced with costumes that were more sophisticated, the industry stalwarts began to fall away. Rubie's acquired Ben Cooper, Inc. in the early 1990s, swallowing up its licenses as it did so. In the years since, those Halloween costumes have grown even more elaborate. Beige pointed to advances in manufacturing that helped make their costumes more appealing to discerning families: new fabrics, shaped foam to create armor or muscle definition, and more—all designed to help kids turn into their favorite characters.[44]

HALLOWEEN TODAY

Today, Halloween is a far cry from the traditions our ancient ancestors honored: it's become a celebration of all things pop culture, often with a bit of spookiness and horror layered in. Its amalgamation of various folk traditions and use of costumes throughout generations primed children and adults in the twentieth century to appreciate the idea of costuming; and with the advent of mass media and entertainment franchises, costuming exploded beyond the confines of Halloween night and into the rest of the year.

In his TED Talk, Adam Savage explained that while he loved his childhood *Jaws* costume, it's appalling compared to the quality of costumes kids can get today.[45] He pointed to advances in technology as a factor in these improvements. "It's become a lot cheaper to print directly onto four-way stretchy fabric," said Savage. "This started in the movies, where they were printing muscle patterns into Spider-Man's suit. You could have the most worked-out guy in Hollywood, but if you put Lycra on him, it flattens the muscles out."[46]

Furthermore, toy and costume companies have recognized that consumers are far more discerning now than in years past when it comes to the quality of costumes, and that not all costumes are destined for only a night of trick-or-treating. Companies like Hasbro have released high-quality wearables like its Black Series stormtrooper and Resistance pilot helmets, which feature injection-molded plastics and sound effects, and look almost like the ones seen in the films. These can serve as either a decoration in one's home or a vital component of one's costume.[47]

---

44   Liptak, "Why Have Children's Halloween Costumes Gotten So Much Better?"
45   Adam Savage, "My Love Letter to Cosplay."
46   Liptak, "Why Have Children's Halloween Costumes Gotten So Much Better?"
47   Liptak, "Why Have Children's Halloween Costumes Gotten So Much Better?"

Other companies, like Trick or Treat Studios, recognized the opportunity that a more discerning customer base offers, betting that a higher-quality costume or mask would stand out among the vibrant culture of fan-made masks. Founder Christopher Zephro explained to me that he had set out to launch his company because "everything at the time, in our opinion, was of terrible quality, lacked in innovation, and looked the same. I knew that there would be a demand for a high-end mask company." The company now sells high-quality masks to adult costumers around the world.

PIPELINE TO COSPLAY

Talk to any cosplayer, and you'll likely find that they enjoyed dressing up for Halloween as a kid. "I definitely bought costumes," Dorasae Rosario told me. "I was really big into going trick-or-treating with my family and dressing up, and I went from buying costumes at Party City to asking my mom to buy me costumes at Halloween."

"Halloween was always big," Bob Gouveia explained to me. The founder of Wretched Hive Creations and a member of the 501st Legion who's suited up as everything from a stormtrooper to Boba Fett to Darth Vader, he explained that he had fond memories of Halloween as a kid. "I always wanted new costumes. Back in the day, I wore the old Ben Cooper things with their plastic mask and suits." He said that the holiday ignited a real interest in costumes—first around Halloween, but later expanding beyond to other festivities. "I remember as a kid, I loved the original TV series *V*, and we had a Halloween party. My birthday was November 3, so Halloween and my birthday were always in tandem. I remember my mom throwing me a birthday party, and instead of wearing the old Ben Coopers, or sheet ghosts, I made a *V* costume. I used a ridiculous red blazer with padded shoulders, and with one of those little Halloween makeup kits, I made myself a half-lizard face with a ping-pong ball for an eye."[48]

Others found the holiday useful for inspiration. Lin Han explained to me that she began dressing up as her favorite characters for Halloween contests put on by her local anime club. "I was like, oh, that would be fun to dress up as an anime character," she said. "That's really where I started, kind of small in that way, and when I went to my first con, I learned that people dressed up there too."

---

48 Bob Gouveia in conversation with the author, January 2020.

The holiday also prompted people like Thorn Reilly to improve their costume-making skills. "It was a litany of increasingly complicated costumes that my mother was tired of sewing," they explained. "When I was in sixth grade, she was like, 'Okay, here's some fabric, here's how you work the sewing machine, have at it, you're old enough to sew.'" They later translated that skill set into practical uses, making their own "ridiculous" clothes that fit them well and came in handy when they later joined the Mandalorian Mercs and Society for Creative Anachronism.

Halloween has served as an accessible entry point to costuming for huge numbers of people in the cosplay community. In the days when science fiction, comic books, and genre pop culture were largely stigmatized by society, Halloween was the one night of the year they could get away with dressing as a fantastical character. For those who truly enjoyed it, it was a first stop on the road to future costumes: a time to plan out an elaborate costume for the next year or that upcoming party, which in turn might prompt one to look for *other* opportunities to dress up.

Given the ongoing rise in popularity of franchises like *Star Wars* or the Marvel Cinematic Universe (at least, at the time of this writing), and the growing access to high-quality costumes, the holiday will continue to evolve and introduce new generations of children and adults to costumes and cosplay for decades to come.

part three

Production

18 INSTRUMENTS OF STORYTELLING

▬ CLOTHING AS A STORYTELLING DEVICE

In order to understand where costuming came from, we have to examine its broader purpose: storytelling.

In his book *On the Origin of Stories: Evolution, Cognition, and Fiction*, Dr. Brian Boyd highlights the argument that humanity's ability to create art is a product of our evolutionary upbringing. He points out that art comes with a cost: energy and effort that might be better spent gathering food, finding shelter, or avoiding being eaten by an apex predator. If art was useless, societies without art would thrive. That art has remained an integral part of human society suggests that there is an advantage to it. Boyd suggests that art is a type of "cognitive play, the set of activities designed to engage human attention through their appeal to our preference for inferentially rich and therefore patterned information."[1] Art and storytelling stimulate creative thinking, allowing people to comprehend and overcome problems and relay information from generation to generation.

According to Phyllis G. Tortora and Keith Eubank in their book *Survey of Historic Costume*, the first depictions of clothing date back to cave paintings from 30,000 years ago, and archaeologists have found evidence of textiles dating back to 27,000 years ago in the form of needles and imprints on ceramic pots. From antiquity, archaeologists,

---

1 Dr. Brian Boyd, *On the Origin of Stories: Evolution, Cognition, and Fiction* (Cambridge, MA: Belknap Press of Harvard University Press, 2009), 95.

An image of ancient Syrians from an 1896 text, *Struggle of the Nations: Egypt, Syria, and Assyria*, as depicted in monuments.

Image via the Internet Archive

My friend Marc Halsey and me, in Wyoming, 2014. My shirt imagines H. P. Lovecraft as a spokesperson for canned octopus.

Courtesy of Andrew Liptak

academics, and historians have plenty of examples of how people throughout history have dressed based on paintings, statues, and remnants of period clothing.

Middlebury College costume designer Mira Veikley says that humans didn't begin to wear clothes just as a form of protection against the elements. "The primary reason people wear clothes is actually ornamentation," she explained to me when I visited her office in 2019. "You'll find people would wear ornaments even in climates where they wouldn't need protection from the elements. It's societal communication—communication with an *other*, like a spiritual plane or something. When you dress up in a way that is fancy or which obliterates your human form, that is a way of communicating with the spirits to literally be outside of yourself."

Tortora and Eubank echo this in their book, noting that people have plenty of reasons for wearing clothes, especially where it wasn't strictly required for survival, such as for decoration, modesty, protection, or signaling social status. "Of these four reasons, that of decoration is generally acknowledged to be primary," they write.[2]

---

2   Phyllis G. Tortora and Keith Eubank, *Survey of Historic Costume*, 5th Edition (New York: Fairchild Books and Visuals, 2010), 1.

Costuming is in many ways a form of play or communication that allows the wearer to enhance or immerse themselves and their audience in a fictional construct, whether that's reenacting a story or trying to commune with a deity. Our earliest ancestors might have grabbed some sort of prop to aid in telling a story over the flickering light of a fire, or adorned themselves with something to better convey the particular traits of a character or creature.

Think about the clothing you have on right now: the various items you're wearing (provided you're not reading this book naked) each have a purpose. Perhaps you liked the design and color of your shirt. You might have a favorite pair of pants or a bra that is particularly comfortable. The jacket hanging by the door might convey a certain message in addition to protecting you from the cold: its numerous pockets say that you're prepared for anything. Many of the shirts I own feature logos or icons from my favorite films, companies, and interests; and seeing similar shirts on the street signals to me that *this* person is *also* a fan of the things that I like—or it shows me their other interests, from sports teams to colleges to favorite beers, or perhaps something about their attitude. What you wear tells its own particular story about who you are and what habits and interests you have.

Costumes serve much of the same purpose. Just as the clothing people wear signals something about their interests and personality, the costumes that actors wear in a production help to cue the audience in on something about the characters that they're portraying. Look at Han Solo from *Star Wars*: his outfit includes a loose white shirt, vest, pants with a military-style stripe, holstered blaster pistol, equipment belt, and high boots. All these elements support the type of character that Harrison Ford portrays—a smuggler ready for action. Ellen Ripley in *Alien* casually wears a crewman's uniform on the *Nostromo*, one that's loaded with patches that identify her standing within the crew, as well as pockets that show off a level of practical functionality.

The crew uniforms of the USS *Enterprise* are color-coded to signify where someone works within Starfleet Command: officers wear yellow or gold; blue means science or medical; red means security. This is similar to the color-coded uniforms on an aircraft carrier's flight deck, designed to quickly identify someone's role—a blue uniform signifies that they're an aircraft handler or tractor driver; yellow is a plane director; green means air wing maintenance or catapult/arrest crew; white is a landing signal operator; purple is fuel; and red means ordnance or explosive ordnance disposal.

Clothing can tell a story all by itself.

FROM LEFT:

1. Sailors set up an emergency crash barricade during a flight deck drill on the US Navy's only forward-deployed aircraft carrier, the USS *Ronald Reagan*.

2. A cosplayer poses as a Starfleet science officer at Dragon Con in Atlanta, Georgia, in August 2019.

3. A cosplayer poses as a Starfleet command officer at Dragon Con in Atlanta, Georgia, in August 2019.

4. Boatswain's Mate 3rd Class Marick Lombard, from San Jose, California, signals the pilots of an MH-60R Seahawk, assigned to the "Wolf Pack" of Helicopter Maritime Strike Squadron (HSM) 75, on the flight deck of the USS *Bunker Hill* (CG 52).

1. US Navy photo by Mass Communication Specialist 3rd Class Gabriel A. Martinez; 2 & 3. Courtesy of Andrew Liptak; 4. US Navy photo by Mass Communication Specialist 2nd Class Brandie Nuzzi

▬ THE ORIGINS OF COSTUMES

How people have worn costumes in professional environments has changed to accommodate their circumstances or audience. Thus, to get a good idea of how costuming was first utilized in the service of entertainment, we must look at the history of theater and drama.

The very first instance of a person donning a costume to enact a character is lost to the annals of history, but the practice has evolved over millennia around the world. In *The Seven Ages of the Theatre*, theater designer Richard Southern outlines the history of the scene by breaking it down into a series of concrete advances, starting with "the costumed player." He explains that a mask is probably one of the earliest innovations of this form of storytelling, noting the obvious advantages for an actor: "It takes away the person we know (it can even take away humanity). And it invests the wearer with something we do not know, but which is awful and non-human, a god or devil."[3]

"Take now an 'extension' of his mask, and with it let the hands be gloved, the feet shod, the arms and legs clad, and the body invested, and you have a complete concealment of the world and a complete revelation of the supernatural," Southern wrote. "And you have the origin (and can appreciate the significance) of theatrical costume."[4] Southern further outlines that there is an evolution to how people conducted performances, starting with religious rituals in which performers embodied characters in traditional ceremonies such as St. Nicholas Day in the Bavarian mountains.[5]

The modern world of dramatic theater in the West descends from the performances put on by cults in Ancient Greece. Followers of Dionysus enacted dramatic performances that built on the god's mythology in ways that differed significantly from traditional religious rituals. In *The History of the Greek and Roman Theatre*, Margarete Bieber writes that Dionysus's story was far more dramatic than that of his fellow gods, and that the "Dionysian religion was from the beginning inclined to disguise individual personality in favor of a transformation into a higher being. There is no better aid in representing somebody else than to take his costume."[6]

---

[3] Richard Southern, *The Seven Ages of the Theatre* (New York: Hill and Wang, 1961), 29.
[4] Southern, *The Seven Ages of the Theatre*, 30.
[5] Southern, *The Seven Ages of the Theatre*, 37.
[6] Margarete Bieber, *The History of the Greek and Roman Theater* (Princeton: Princeton University Press, 1939), 1–2.

Greek actors used a number of tools to aid their performances. Masks with highly exaggerated features allowed audience members to recognize various characters even if they were seated at the back of the amphitheater, while costumes helped to depict the fantastical and otherworldly characters that they embodied. Greek theater eventually utilized sets that depicted locations and buildings, helping to further immerse the audience in a story. Rome would eventually co-opt Greek theatrical traditions and conventions and build upon them.

The plays of Greece and Rome went on to influence artists and writers of the Middle Ages in Europe. Bieber notes that performance continued throughout the period through the work of jesters and mimes. "Such lower-class performances are always more conservative and more persistent than those of literary drama. In Europe the actors of the mime gave their third-rate entertainments in the small cities and villages, in inns and in castles."[7] Renaissance writers found a renewed interest in the Greek and Roman works.

The evolution of theater and costume wasn't limited to Europe. People throughout the world engaged in costumed performance as part of religious rituals, public festivals, and more, employing elaborate costumes and performances to convey all manner of stories. In *The Oxford Illustrated History of the Theatre*, Farley Richmond points to performances dating back to 200 BCE in India,[8] while Colin Mackerras notes that the theatrical traditions

An illustration of Greek muses from *Handbook of Archaeology: Egyptian, Greek, Etruscan, Roman* by Hodder M. Westropp (1867).
Image via Internet Archive

---

7   Bieber, *The History of Greek and Roman Theatre*, 254.
8   Farley Richmond, "South Asian Theatres," in *The Oxford Illustrated History of Theatre*, ed. John Russell Brown (Oxford: Oxford University Press, 1995), 448.

in China, Japan, and Korea brought about extremely complex performances that involved complicated puppets and costumes.[9]

As Europe entered the Renaissance in the 1500s, the theater continued to evolve, with practitioners developing new written forms, costumes, sets, and trends that pushed the medium to new boundaries.[10] Dedicated permanent theater spaces began to appear, Louise George Clubb writes in *The Oxford Illustrated History of Theatre*, as "professional actors needed places to which they could charge admission, and the charitable brotherhoods who ran hospitals for the poor found from the 1560s onwards that they could hire out their own yards or others for the purpose."

Performers began to adopt even more elaborate costumes and properties (props) to further immerse themselves and their audience in the roles that they played onstage. "Costume identified his role and liberated him to perform its function before auditors who pressed in on him from below and above," Peter Thomson notes in the *The Oxford Illustrated History of Theatre*.[11] It was also used to help audiences differentiate characters in complicated stories.[12]

By the time the 1700s and 1800s arrived, theater designers and playwrights were growing increasingly sophisticated, going beyond simple visual cues for the audience to enhance a performance. "For his performance as Hamlet [actor David Garrick] had a wig-maker produce a trick wig whose hair he could make literally stand on end in his confrontation with his father's ghost."[13]

Other actors adopted realistic garments for costuming: "Such authenticity in costume reached a turning-point when in 1789 Talma, who significantly had begun his theatrical career in London, sought advice from the artist David and appeared in Voltaire's *Brutus* wearing a Roman toga. After recovering from the shock of seeing bare arms and legs on stage, the public were soon won over to this new style of presenta-

---

9   Colin Mackerras, "East Asian Theatres," in *The Oxford Illustrated History of Theatre*, ed. John Russell Brown (Oxford: Oxford University Press, 1995), 465.
10   Louise George Clubb, "Italian Renaissance Theatre," in *The Oxford Illustrated History of Theatre*, ed. John Russell Brown (Oxford: Oxford University Press, 1995), 108.
11   Peter Thomson, "English Renaissance and Restoration Theatre," in *The Oxford Illustrated History of Theatre*, ed. John Russell Brown (Oxford: Oxford University Press, 1995), 180.
12   Thomson, "English Renaissance and Restoration Theatre," 186.
13   Peter Holland and Michael Patterson, "Eighteenth-Century Theatre," in *The Oxford Illustrated History of Theatre*, ed. John Russell Brown (Oxford: Oxford University Press, 1995), 263.

tion, so much so that when two years later Talma wore a Roman hair-style for the role of Titus, he inaugurated a fashion which was to become the rage for modish French revolutionaries."[14]

Some critics lambasted the trend toward elaborate costumes, scenery, and other supporting technologies, such as lighting. They complained that these elements overshadowed the actors and their lines. "The fact that it was the complaint of a minority of critics rather than a majority of the audience, who greeted this style enthusiastically, ensured the continuance of such production methods into the twentieth century," wrote Michael Booth in *The Oxford Illustrated History of Theatre*.[15] But costumes, sets, and props were here to stay.

---

[14] Holland and Patterson, "Eighteenth-Century Theatre," 273.
[15] Michael R. Booth, "Nineteenth-Century Theatre," in *The Oxford Illustrated History of Theatre*, ed. John Russell Brown (Oxford: Oxford University Press, 1995), 336.

19 DO IT YOURSELF

In the aftermath of the Second World War, the United States underwent a massive economic expansion that lasted for decades. Following the Great Depression and wartime restrictions, millions of families entered the middle class, fueling the economic boom. Their growing income allowed them to buy new consumer goods, cars, and houses, and go on vacations and trips to the movie theater.

In part, it was new manufacturing innovations and efficiencies that sped the economy along by making all of these cheaper. Making one item at a time by hand could yield a high-end product, but if you could manufacture far more items with assembly lines or automation, you could make even more in the same amount of time.

Despite the conveniences that consumer culture brought to the US and the rest of the world, many people still found appeal in making things with their own hands. Toys like the Erector Set, model cars and train sets, LEGO, and Tinker Toys allowed children to build things on their own, allowing their imagination to run wild as they created fantastic machines and cities. In the 1970s, enthusiasts got together to form clubs to make their own computers. Automobile enthusiasts rebuilt car engines and restored antiques, while books like Reader's Digest's *Back to Basics: How to Learn and Enjoy Traditional American Skills* and the *Complete Do-It-Yourself Manual* taught people how to construct their own homes, plant gardens, build furniture, or fix anything around the house that might break. And of course, enthusiastic fans were already going out of their way to construct their own costumes, from simple replicas constructed out of spare army helmets, papier-mâché, or cardboard to vacuum form plastic and molded resin.

These separate tendencies—all linked by the desire to make something for oneself—coalesced into what's now known as the Maker Movement, a free-ranging, countercultural artistic movement that encourages people to build, make, and learn, utilizing a wide range of technologies, techniques, and social networks in a community-driven fashion.

The formalization of the Maker Movement is largely attributed to the launch of *Make Magazine*. First released in January 2005, the magazine focused on a number of DIY topics ranging from computers to woodworking. Writing in his book *Free to Make: How the Maker Movement Is Changing Our Schools, Our Jobs, and Our Minds*, Doug Dougherty described the movement as "a platform for creative expression that goes beyond traditional art forms and business models." Dougherty explains that making is an activity that people are inherently "wired to do," and that it allows for a creative, innovative economy and society, allowing for new inventions, and new ways to approach and solve problems.[1] It's a collaborative form of problem-solving, from the practical to the hypothetical, leading to new products, new ways of learning, and new ways of doing science."[2]

ANOVOS produced a number of high-quality wearables aimed at cosplayers for several years, including some of the first official costumes from the *Star Wars* sequel trilogy.

Courtesy of Andrew Liptak

He pointed to a long tradition of this mindset, starting with publications such as *Popular Science* and *Popular Mechanics* (I'd also cite Hugo Gernsback as a good representative example, for he started up not only the first dedicated genre magazine, *Amazing Stories* but also other enthusiast publications such as *The Electrical Experimenter* and *Modern Electrics*), which ultimately demonstrated that people had the capability to be self-reliant and capable of designing and building things that might improve their lives. The economic expansion that the US experienced, he argues, is the "golden age of

---

1   Doug Dougherty, *Free to Make: How the Maker Movement Is Changing Our Schools, Our Jobs, and Our Minds* (Berkeley: North Atlantic Books, 2016), xvi.
2   Dougherty, *Free to Make*, xv.

tinkering in America. It was a middle-class virtue that enabled the people to have things and do things that they needed or wanted but couldn't afford, like expanding the house for a new family member, sewing clothes, or repairing the car because they couldn't afford a new one."[3]

Over the course of the latter half of the twentieth century, the country became a nation of consumers, pushed on by advertising and a consumer mindset. "We became detached from the questions of how our food, cars, electronics, toys, shampoo, and so on were made, where they came from, and who produced them."[4] Making, Dougherty says, went "underground and over the next fifty years, emerged mostly in subcultures."[5] That expressed itself in numerous ways, from independently produced music, crafting, home-built computers, to model railroads, fashion, prop replicas, and more.

The internet and the companies that rely on it are probably some of the biggest success stories to come out of this broader Maker Movement. Silicon Valley is full of stories about companies founded by innovative inventors who assembled computers in their garages or homes, eventually building their passions into multimillion-, billion-, and trillion-dollar businesses. The internet itself spawned an avid open-source movement on the idea that this massive network should be open and free for everyone to use—that a rising tide lifts all boats.

In his book *Every Tool's a Hammer: Life Is What You Make It*, Adam Savage writes that the explosion of tools like 3D printers, open-source software, and the internet helped bring about a more cohesive DIY movement because of the ability to quickly spread

A cosplayer on the floor of FAN EXPO Boston in August 2021. This is a fantastic costume, made from all sorts of different objects, like foam and piping. It might not be screen accurate, but you can see the passion in the build.

Courtesy of Andrew Liptak

---

3 Dougherty, *Free to Make*, 7.
4 Dougherty, *Free to Make*, 8.
5 Dougherty, *Free to Make*, 9.

ideas, tutorials, and projects throughout the larger community.[6] This landscape proved to be the perfect breeding ground for cosplayers, who tapped into the DIY mindset to share techniques and ideas. Build threads, video tutorials, and step-by-step guides appeared on forums for groups like the 501st and Rebel Legions, websites like Instructables, and more, allowing for people to quickly learn how to do things on their own. Meanwhile, sites like Thingiverse provided quick, easy access to existing designs for the growing number who owned 3D printers.

In New Jersey in 2019, the North Bergen High School drama department went viral with their production of *Alien*, which utilized an impressive array of costumes and sets, all of which the students had constructed from found materials. The school's art teacher, Steven Defendini, explained that in many instances, he saw his students going out and making their own costumes after they had worked on projects at school. "We had [a] student, Danny, who made a Flash costume," Defendini explained, "because the year before, he made Power Ranger costumes. The thing that we strive for is, 'Are they ever going to do this stuff again? Maybe not.' But they know how to use a drill now, and they know how to use drill bits, and they know what different adhesives do."[7]

One major appeal of cosplay is the technical and artistic challenges that the hobby presents. Bringing a character to life by reconstructing their visual appearance is often a multidisciplinary effort. As costumes become more complex, they can require a wide range of skills, such as sewing, foam or plastic fabrication, 3D printing, painting, design, electronics, and performance.

All of these elements bring us back to the central nature of the Maker Movement, which encourages individuals to experiment and build things for themselves, whether it's something practical (like fixing something in your house or designing a tool that makes your life easier) or more aesthetically oriented, like a costume.

Ultimately, what the Maker Movement supported was not technological innovation or a new explosion of devices designed to cater to budding and experienced makers but instilling the simple love of creation, of making something with their own hands and providing a much larger community to cheer on their compatriots as they tackled their next project.

---

6   Adam Savage, *Every Tool's a Hammer: Life Is What You Make It* (New York: Atria Books, 2019), 3.
7   "Adam Savage Tours North Bergen High School's *Alien: The Play* Artifacts!" Adam Savage's Tested, filmed and edited by Joey Fameli, produced by Kristen Lomasney, YouTube video, November 6, 2019, https://www.youtube.com/watch?v=giSvH_EYWCo.

20 THE ACT OF COSPLAYING

As we've seen, costumes are omnipresent throughout history: in theatrical and cinematic performances, on "traditional" holidays like Halloween (and before that, Thanksgiving), at theme parties, protests, charitable events, conventions, and more. So what exactly is "cosplay"?

Merriam-Webster's definition of "cosplay" is "the activity or practice of dressing up as a character from a work of fiction (such as a comic book, video game, or television show)."[1] To highlight the focal point of this book—the evolution of "cosplay"—we must explore the differences in intention between the use of each costume: How is costuming used in a given situation?

PERFORMANCE

After you've completed your costume? It's showtime—meaning time to debut the costume for all to see. Cosplay is more than just the act of wearing the costume—it's a performative act.

In his TED Talk, Adam Savage observed that cosplayers try to replicate not only the

---

1 *Merriam-Webster.com Dictionary*, s.v. "cosplay," accessed December 7, 2021, https://www.merriam-webster.com/dictionary/cosplay.

A trio of stormtroopers (Andrew Liptak, Nicholas Scott, and Michael Anton) of the Green Mountain Squad at a Free Comic Book Day event in Burlington, Vermont, in 2015. Stormtroopers are incredibly popular costumes within the 501st Legion.

Courtesy of Andrew Liptak

look of the character but how they act. "They rehearse their costumes. At Comic-Con or any other con, you don't just take pictures of people walking around, you actually go up and say, 'Hey, I like your costume, can I take your picture?' And then you give them time to get into their pose."[2]

Characters are more than just the clothing that they wear: they're individuals with specific lines, voices, personalities, movements, and habits. A cosplayer stepping out onto the floor of a convention or any other event is working to invoke a specific feel, as though they're bringing a character to life before an audience. A cosplayer might memorize a character's catchphrase or some other familiar line of dialogue for their audience. Over the years, most members of the 501st Legion will decide on a routine to play when encountering someone at an event. We watch the films endlessly and study the characters we're portraying. Troopers have a number of memorable lines that they can use for the benefit of an audience:

"Someone was in the pod. The tracks go off in this direction."

"Look sir, droids!"

"How long have you had these droids?"

"Let me see your identification."

"You can go about your business."

"Move along, move along."

---

2 Adam Savage, "My Love Letter to Cosplay."

"TK-421, why aren't you at your post?"

"Give me a regular report, please."

"Do you know what's going on?" / "Maybe it's another drill."

"Have you seen the new VT-16?"

"What's all this? Let's see some scan docs."

"Stop right there!"

Fitted with a microphone and amplifier, troopers can perform a back-and-forth with the audience, which enhances the moment from a passive viewing to an interactive experience. Other characters obviously have additional memorable lines, and it's not hard to come up with dialogue on your own that suits your character to engage with an audience.

At Walt Disney World's Galaxy's Edge theme park, visitors will encounter stormtroopers who excel at this back-and-forth, interrogating guests with scripted routines that bring the park just a bit more to life.

"If there's one Jedi left, it's not you."

"Thank you for your service."

"I see your lightsaber. I'm assuming you're a collector. Only a collector."[3]

A cosplayer's performance goes beyond just memorized or improvised dialogue. Body language is the third major component to their performance. If you watch the hangar scene in *Captain America: Civil War* (which begins at the 1:28:00-minute mark), you'll see a handful of superheroes gathered alongside one another: Iron Man, War Machine, Captain America, Black Panther, Black Widow, Spider-Man, Ant-Man, Falcon, Hawkeye, Wanda Maximoff, Vision, and Winter Soldier. Each has a different way of moving. Spider-Man is a hyperactive teenager; Iron Man and Captain America move with purpose; War Machine exudes raw power; Black Panther and Black Widow are flexible and graceful.

Any character that's depicted stands or poses in some way that is recognizable to audiences. Cosplayers will pick up on how they hold themselves and work to replicate it. Sometimes it's as simple as marching in formation with other stormtroopers. Other

---

[3] "Galaxy's Edge Stormtroopers | *Star Wars*," SAGAtoday, YouTube video, June 10, 2019, https://www.youtube.com/watch?v=lheRhb0Ou70.

I pose with a young fan at Burlington, Vermont's Church Street Marketplace during Free Comic Book Day in 2015.

Photos courtesy of Andrew Liptak

Mark Poutenis as Chewbacca at FAN EXPO Boston in 2019. He's a particularly good Chewbacca, and puts a lot of effort into getting the performance of the character right.

times it's Spider-Man crouching in an acrobatic pose. These moments further bring the character to life for audiences.

From its inception, the 501st Legion has attended a wide range of events, primarily outside of the conventions or movie openings where one might typically see cosplayers. The Legion attends thousands of events around the world every year, everything from college sports matches to Free Comic Book Day to hospital visits. Albin Johnson noted that after he started dressing up as a stormtrooper for the special edition releases in theaters, the 501st Legion began attending a range of events, not just at the movie theater. He recalled one early event in which a gaming store held a *Star Wars* collectible card tournament. The attendees were amused by the sight of a couple of stormtroopers, but quickly turned their attention back to the game that they were there to play. Johnson realized that they'd have to not only show up as the character but that being *in* character enriched the experience.

One of the first times I suited up in public in armor was for the midnight release of *Star Wars: Revenge of the Sith* in 2005, and the reactions to my armor were the same as that of Johnson's experiences: the shock value wore off once you stood around with the same group of people for a little while. There was another attendee in line dressed in costume: as Legolas from *The Lord of the Rings*, who explained that he didn't have a *Star Wars* costume but wanted to take part in the excitement that comes with an opening-night line. We had some fun with it, making the entire line laugh when I "escorted" him at gunpoint to the back of the line, and again when he chased me forward.

Performance is central to what cosplayers do, explained Mark Poutenis, a member of the Rebel Legion's Alderaan Base. A lifelong fan of *Star Wars*, he was particularly fond of Chewbacca, Han Solo's loyal Wookiee first mate. He joined the group after coming across them through a friend, initially dressing up as Han Solo. "I frickin' loved Chewbacca," he explained to me. "When I got into the group, I thought 'Well, it sucks that we don't have a Chewbacca, but I don't know how you can do a Chewbacca.'" But then he discovered people had re-created the character, extensively modifying the off-the-shelf costume produced by Rubie's. He began to look into the logistics and ended up building his own, using a mesh suit that he'd woven fur into.

Poutenis's eye for detail led him to build a superb Chewbacca suit, but it isn't the costume alone that sells it. "The mission statement [of the 501st/Rebel Legions] wasn't simply to make screen-accurate costumes, because if that was [all it was], we would just do costume contests and stand there to have people look at us," he says. The appeal of the group is to bring the characters of the franchise to life. "If you're going to be Chewbacca, you'd better try and be Chewbacca.

"My whole thing is that I'm a hyper guy, and while I wouldn't say I studied him, I would watch him, and that's probably why I fell in love with him in the first place. Peter Mayhew would do these things, like cocking his head or opening his mouth a little to breathe, like he was a real thing," Poutenis explained. "They're not hard to do—you can watch him and figure it out in five seconds, but you have to be a bit of an extrovert, to be very animated, very flamboyant." He notes that it doesn't matter how good a suit is: if you aren't selling the role, you're not really Chewbacca. "I think that's why a lot of people trick themselves subconsciously into thinking that my suit is better than it is—because I sell it and try to sell it."[4]

---

[4] Mark Poutenis in conversation with the author, January 2020.

He pointed to a time when at a convention he and a Han Solo cosplayer were joined by a new cosplayer dressed as Princess Leia. "Joy will be the first person to tell you that she looks nothing like Carrie Fisher, and I can't tell you how many times I've overheard grown adults walking away after taking a picture, saying, 'Oh my god! That Princess Leia looks just like Carrie Fisher! She's so funny; it was so great when she bossed them around!'" Poutenis recalled. "It took it to the next level."

COSPLAY VS. PROFESSIONALS

The above definition implies a level of amateur performance, as opposed to professional performance. Robert Downey Jr. dressing up on the set of *Avengers: Endgame* as Tony Stark isn't cosplay: he's acting as the character for a movie production. The fans who go out and make their own armored Iron Man suit, grow and shape a beard to match, or otherwise replicate Tony Stark are the cosplayers. Indeed, one could consider the moments when Ryan Reynolds, Gal Gadot, or Ron Perlman suit up as Deadpool,[5] Wonder Woman,[6] or Hellboy[7] as cosplay, when they're not necessarily performing the role in a professional capacity.

Those differences extend beyond just the performance. The costumes constructed for films typically differ greatly from those used by cosplayers on convention floors: they're designed for the production for specific scenes, not necessarily to be used or even seen outside of the moments that they're captured on film.

Film productions will often use a number of copies of each costume throughout production: they'll be weathered or damaged for certain scenes, or will be constructed with a higher level of detail for close-up shots (generally referred to as "hero" costumes).

In some instances, they can be fantastically expensive because of the labor hours and materials that go into them. Armored suits and space suits, like the ones seen in *Iron Man*, *The Expanse*, or *Star Trek: Discovery*, can run productions hundreds of thousands of dollars each.

---

[5] Lindsey Robertson, "Ryan Reynolds Dressed up as Deadpool to Visit a Little Boy with Cancer," *Mashable*, May 22, 2015, https://mashable.com/2015/05/22/ryan-reynolds-deadpool-cancer-visit.

[6] Chelsea Cirruzzo and Stephanie Ramirez, "*Wonder Woman* Star Gal Gadot Visits Sick Kids at Virginia Hospital," *USA Today*, July 10, 2018, https://www.usatoday.com/story/life/people/2018/07/09/wonder-woman-star-gal-gadot-visits-sick-kids-virginia-hospital/768746002.

[7] Seth Abramovitch, "Ron Perlman Visits Child in Full Hellboy Makeup for Make-A-Wish," *Hollywood Reporter*, July 6, 2012, https://www.hollywoodreporter.com/heat-vision/ron-perlman-make-wish-hellboy-346196.

Cosplayers don't appear to impact the professional costume design world, Art Andrews explains. "I think ninety-nine percent of the time, they're trying to do their own thing. I can tell you for a fact like with Marvel, the process and materials they use are so incredibly complex and complicated that it is virtually impossible for costumers to make them at the level that they're made there." Dedicated prop-production companies like Ironhead Studio, which produced costumes for films including *The Amazing Spider-Man 2*, *Oblivion*, *Tron: Legacy*, and others, use advanced, often expensive techniques to put them together. Andrews noted that he didn't believe that studios give any thought to how people might replicate their costumes after the fact. "They're trying to make the best story that they can."

Over the years, certain costumes have been famously difficult for the actors wearing them, from Leonard Nimoy enduring hours in a makeup trailer to get his ears put on[8] to Michael Keaton being unable to move in his original Batman suit.[9] When I asked Frankie Adams about wearing her Martian marine suit in *The Expanse*, she expressed relief at not having to wear it in the then-upcoming fourth season of the series: it was uncomfortable and constricting. While costumes are designed to be worn by an actor, they're designed primarily to look good onscreen, while the actor's comfort is usually a secondary consideration.

For an example of how costumes have changed over the years, one doesn't have to look much further than the two different styles of stormtroopers seen in *A New Hope* and *The Force Awakens*. The costumes in the first were vacuum formed plastic in the 1970s, worn over the actor in a fairly practical fashion. The latter's costume is much more complicated: while they're an evolution of the design language, they're more complicated to don, with extra details at the elbows, shoulders, and knees, and are worn a bit differently than their older counterparts. "In no practical sense does that thing do anything," Andrews observed. "You can't even sit easily, you can't do anything easily."

Andrews explained that Lucasfilm and Marvel have begun to design their costumes to be worn in layers. "They're so complicated with so many layers, but they're built that way so that actors have a full range of motion." He pointed to Kylo Ren from *Star Wars:*

---

[8] William Shatner, *Leonard: My Fifty-Year Friendship with a Remarkable Man* (New York: Thomas Dunne Books, 2016), 70.
[9] "Michael Keaton Explains How Ripping His Costume Helped Him Play Batman," *Syfy Wire*, https://www.syfy.com/syfywire/michael-keaton-explains-how-ripping-his-costume-helped-him-play-batman.

The Force Awakens as an example. "He wears a shirt, which is the bottom layer, but it's almost like a mesh. There's nothing there in the center. The arms are the only thing with details. Then he has a vest over that. When it's together, it looks like a complete shirt. That's so there's complete mobility there with that. Almost every single piece for Marvel has that same idea."

Costumers don't face those same requirements, and more often than not, don't have access to the resources available in a professional studio. They're free to take shortcuts—and as much time as they need—to replicate a costume. Unless they're shooting a fan film or taking part in a particularly ambitious photo shoot, their costume may not need to be worn for hours at a time under hot lights on a film set, nor do they need to be subjected to stunts or extreme movement. At a convention, they may only need to stand in one place for a period of time, posing for pictures with bystanders.

REPLICATION

Cosplayers might not always have access to a professional workshop, but a full load-out of tools isn't necessarily a requirement to make a good costume. A creative individual can make use of almost anything to make a convincing costume, whether that's a pile of cardboard boxes, scrap plastic, foam, cloth, or other materials that they have access to.

What goes into a fan-made costume will vary depending on the design of whatever they're trying to replicate. Like Stuart Lilie at Fort Ticonderoga, cosplayers are interpreting what they see onscreen and building something based on that.

The first step for any cosplayer or builder is generally research. To replicate a costume, you need to first know exactly which one you're choosing and what it looks like in detail. The starting point for any such project is the source material, whether that's a comic book panel, film, television show, action figure, screen-used prop, or simply your imagination.

This phase has evolved with time. Early costumers like Morojo and Forrest Ackerman designed their costumes based on the subjective concept of what a character from the pulp magazine stories they were reading might have looked like. Later cosplayers like David Rhea or Sean Schoenke would be able to rely on actual garments and pictures from films, working off of numerous visits to theaters and limited pictures of costumes in magazines.

But there are other minute technological changes that, while not part of the fabrication process, help to push forward prop making all the same. A prime example of this is video cassette—in the 1960s and 1970s, fans found limited resources when it came to providing visual reference for projects like *Star Trek* or *Star Wars*. With its release in 1976 (in Japan) and 1977 (in the United States), the Video Home System (VHS) and Betamax provided a game-changing moment for movie fans: they could own a copy of the film or television show and watch it whenever they wanted. This on-demand ability allowed viewers to pause while looking for a specific detail or moment.

VHS had its limitations: the resolution was low, something that improved with the release of the Digital Versatile Disc (DVD), which came with a higher storage capacity, in turn meaning better resolution for consumers. A viewer could pause a film at the right moment without having to worry about static in the image and take a closer look at a specific frame.

But the biggest advances came with the successor of the DVD: the Blu-Ray disc. "You could see details far better or clearer," Bob Gouveia explained. A longtime member of the Boba Fett costuming scene, he noted that up until that point, fans had a good idea of what props looked like onscreen, but because the resolution was lower for earlier film formats, they still had to make some educated guesses. "Once things started coming out on Blu-Ray, everyone paid more attention to detail, and were able to pick up on things that you never would have seen before, which upped the ante on the costumes."

One example that Gouveia cited was some of the tiny, found pieces that prop makers used to make the original Boba Fett suit. "People were finding things like a dental expander on the gauntlet. On the other gauntlet, there's an actual Eveready flashlight, and there's a calculator pad that's from a Casio calculator."[10] There are other examples as well: fans of stormtroopers realized how bad the original trooper costumes looked in *A New Hope*, noticing parts that didn't close correctly, or the tape that held some of the costumes together.

In most cases, this leads to improved costumes. My first set of stormtrooper armor was the FX kit, worn by a huge percentage of 501st stormtroopers. It came in a big brown box, and I assembled it in a day and wore it for over a decade.

---

10   Bob Gouveia in conversation with the author, January 2020.

By the end of that decade, the standards for a stormtrooper had shifted, in part because fans had access to better reference materials. The FX kit had been sculpted by a fan working off of images, rather than a direct viewing of the suit itself. The proportions of the chest plate and helmet were off, while the abs plate featured details that only approximated what was seen onscreen. While anyone remotely familiar with *Star Wars* would be able to identify it as a stormtrooper uniform, those who had spent a lot of time looking closely at the costumes and comparing them to their onscreen counterparts noted significant differences.

Sharp-eyed fans with access to better images—or even the screen-used suits—developed their own kits, which were far more accurate than the old FX kit. Kits bearing names such as ATA (Accurate Trooper Armor), TM (Troopermaster), RS (RS Props), MTK (Mike TK), T/MC (Tray/MonCal), CAP/W, RT-MOD, and others arrived on the general stormtrooper marketplace, each with its own advantages. Some are better for tall or large-bodied individuals. Others are expensive but super accurate, versus those that are fairly accurate but reasonably priced. And if you live in the UK, you can buy a stormtrooper from Shepperton Design Studios based on the original molds used in *A New Hope*—the closest you can get to the original suit.

As a result, the FX kit that so many suited up in during the early days of the 501st is no longer acceptable for membership: it's considered too inaccurate for approval, and although you will sometimes still see those suits in the ranks at events, they have slowly left the ranks as members retire or upgrade their costumes or leave the group.

This series of iterations and collective upgrading is entirely due to the flow of information between fans who are able to share their measurements and observations with one another. The forums help to build and support an environment where people who have a high bar for attention to detail and presentation are able to convey those tendencies. Absent such a group, the scattered fans who wanted to be a stormtrooper would likely still be stuck with the existing FX kit, one of the "deluxe" stormtrooper costumes offered by Rubie's—a costume that almost never clears the high bar for acceptance within the 501st Legion due to its vinyl construction and inaccuracies—or be forced to do all the research, sculpting, and building on their own without a road map.

Internet forums and chat rooms allow costumers to chat back and forth, share their research, and help one another out as they work toward their own costumes. Museum exhibits or costume displays at conventions, events, or movie theaters also provide fans with access to the original garments, providing the opportunity to study them from every angle. In rare cases, museum or studio archives or even collectors will allow makers to take measurements and pictures firsthand. And costumers are sometimes able to find the original components that designers used to make the costume.

As fans have greater access to their source materials, the quality of prop replicas and costumes will continue to improve. The advances in video resolution technology haven't stopped either: 4K video is quickly growing, on its way to becoming a new standard, with 8K resolution expected to follow. ANOVOS cofounder Dana Gasser explained that he was able to preview the 4K remaster of *Star Wars*. "It's beautifully done," he explained. "My god, the detail you can see now."[11]

THE BUILD

Once a prospective costumer has completed their research, they plan out their design, then take those images and figure out how to craft it. That process might involve developing a body form tailored to one's measurements or repurposing a garment that looks close enough to the costume. It might involve sculpting pieces of armor by making a mold out of clay and plaster, or mapping out a part in a 3D modeling program. After their initial design, makers identify the materials that they need to bring those plans to life, which could include fabric, metal, rubber, plastic, resin, wood, foam, or something else.

Once a costumer's got their plans and materials squared away, the fun begins: the build. They'll construct their costume piece by piece, cutting out the individual parts, then sewing, gluing, welding, screwing or otherwise attaching them to one another in a form that's wearable. Once that's done, they put on the finishing touches: cleanup, paint, weathering, and testing it to figure out where they need to make improvements or changes.

It's impossible to say how long this will take any given costumer. When it comes to building a costume, it can take weeks, months, or years in a cosplayer's life to cross the finish line. They might spend a sporadic hour or two or full days in a row working on a project. Sometimes, they might finish their costume in a hotel room minutes before the convention doors open to guests.

---

11   Dana Gasser in conversation with the author, February 2020.

SCALING UP

Enterprising costumers can extend this sense of immersion beyond the individual level. Groups like the 501st Legion, Ghostbusters, 405th Infantry Division, and others scale up those interactions by bringing numbers to their events. Cosplayers at major conventions will sometimes collaborate with one another, forming their own real-world supergroups. As a group, they can interact as those characters might with one another—Peter Parker wisecracking at Captain America, Batman fighting the Joker, or stormtroopers chasing after Rebel Fleet troopers. These interactions aren't always planned, either: sometimes, all it takes is the right cosplayers encountering one another to bring about an entertaining moment captured on camera by lucky bystanders.

Those organizations have an advantage here: they can easily plan out these encounters. Ahead of big events, members will deliberate which costumes to wear, sorting out who will suit up as Darth Vader or another recognizable "face character." (Outside of conventions, you don't typically want duplicates of such characters, because it breaks the illusion.) By pooling resources, they can figure out what costumes to wear depending on what others are able to bring. A handful of stormtroopers might encourage others to bring out their kits, or a particular theme for an event might call for certain costume types over others.

And these groups can do more than just costumes. Their members will sometimes build elaborate sets, vehicles, and props to further the illusion of a scene or character cast by bringing more of the original story to life. These are projects that typically go beyond individual efforts, depending on the scale and size of what you're constructing. At *Star Wars* Celebration in 2019, visitors were greeted with a handful of life-size sets that they could pose next to: an X-wing and TIE Fighter stood in one corner of the exhibition hall, along with a replica of a *Tantive IV* hallway, while across the vast hall sat a near-complete interior of the *Millennium Falcon* next to a TX-225A "Occupier" ground assault tank. At another convention in Rhode Island later that year, members of my home garrison constructed the interior of the Death Star's hangar bay and the bunker entrance on Endor. The build team used a garage door opener to control the doors, furthering the illusion.

The tank was built by Don West, which he began in 2017, right after he saw *Rogue One*. A member of the 501st who suited up as a sandtrooper, he had formerly served in the United States Army as a tanker.

Don West, the builder behind the Occupier tank project. He built the replica vehicle on top of a Mercury Grand Marquis, and used steel, plywood, foam, and plastic to bring it to life.

Courtesy of Andrew Liptak

West explained that he and his team "found the actual vehicle that it was built off of, an Alvis Shielder [British armored vehicle], and from that, I got the dimensions, and was able to go from there. I transferred that onto Tinker CAD, and that's how I was able to get a digital reference. It took me about four months to build it on a computer."

From there, they started looking for a vehicle to work off of, and eventually settled on a Mercury Grand Marquis. He and his team cut the vehicle down and welded it onto a steel frame, over which they added plywood, foam, and plastic. "The guns, everything that's on the sides of the main compartment is all modular," he told me, pointing out details as we talked from the side of the vehicle. "You can basically just lift it up five inches on the sides, and it just disconnects from the vehicle itself."[12]

West brought the tank out to parades and conventions like Celebration and allowed visitors to climb onto the back of the tank. To further the illusion, they invited 501st members to help out with the display. Suited up as a shoretrooper from *Rogue One*, I

---

12   Don West interview with the author, April 2019.

THE ACT OF COSPLAYING

took part. My costume wasn't the exact match for the characters seen operating the vehicle in the film, but once I stood up on the prop, it was a short jump of the imagination to see one of the troopers operating one. Visitors climbed up on top in twos and threes, posing for pictures next to the main gun.

Because visitors weren't always sure where to look, the other troopers and I took charge. "We're a man down," I'd tell them. "I need you to man the turret and to take out that Rebel placement." The visitors would oblige and pose behind the gun, and I'd point downrange. Once I saw the tank staff member in position with the visitor's camera, I'd point him out. "Rebel sighted!" I'd call out. "Weapons free; fire at will!" Once we got the thumbs-up from the cameraman, the guest would climb down and retrieve their camera, and the act would start over again.

Over the years, we've put together other similar big props. For parades, my local garrison has constructed a life-size Jabba the Hutt puppet; a Dewback; Luke's Landspeeder; speeder bikes; Rey's Speeder; the *Millennium Falcon*'s cockpit and lounge area; and a corner of the Death Star's hangar bay, complete with a set of doors that slid open and closed, operated by a repurposed garage door opener. At other times, we've printed up large vinyl backdrops that depict scenes like the *Tantive IV* hallway, the forests of Endor, and other notable locations that people can pose in front of.

This sort of immersion isn't necessarily limited to massive props and sets. An individual cosplayer can bring out a bit of immersion on their own with a prop or two. In recent years, I've taken to building additional props for my costumes: a set of macrobinoculars for my clone trooper and a set of the Death Star plans for my shoretrooper. Other troopers carry similar accessories or the guns that their characters are known for. While posing for a picture, I'll hand my prop off to the fan next to me (first making a judgment call as to whether they might drop, break, or run off with it) and tell them strike a pose with it.

Each of these items brings another world to life for a brief moment, allowing someone to close their eyes and imagine that they're in George Lucas's galaxy far, far away. Engaging with stormtroopers or Princess Leia or an Ewok in a brief performance goes beyond mere optics: it engages your other senses and your imagination. You might get a picture of yourself on top of an Imperial Occupier tank, but you come away with the experience of blasting rebels alongside Imperial troopers. It's a form of play and a fun escape from the real world, if only for a few moments.

A cosplay medic rolls up his sleeves in the middle of a crowd at Dragon Con in Atlanta, Georgia, in August 2019.

Photos courtesy of Andrew Liptak

Cosplay medic Paige Robbins poses for a picture on the floor of the 2019 Dragon Con in Atlanta, Georgia. She's equipped with everything one might need for on-the-spot repairs at the con: glue, thread, tape, and more.

COSPLAY REPAIR

If you attend a major convention, there's a good chance that you'll run into someone like Paige Robbins walking around the event floor. When I met her in 2019 at Dragon Con, she was surrounded by a handful of costumers but wasn't in costume. She was a cosplay medic. Volunteers like her have become a fixture at conventions as cosplay has risen in popularity, filling a vital role for the legions of cosplayers who jam convention halls.

Loaded down with a heavy backpack and equipment vest, Robbins is easy to spot in the crowd halls of the convention center, thanks to a canvas flag mounted on her pack emblazoned with a red cross symbol bracketed by the words COSPLAY REPAIR.

THE ACT OF COSPLAYING

Costumes are complicated projects, held together with screws, rivets, glue, Velcro, thread, and tape, all of which can come completely undone without warning.

"I've always kind of been the 'mom friend' of the people I hang out with," she explained to me. "When I was in high school doing tech for our theater, I had a small box of fix-it repair stuff for show night that I call the 'Techie Repair Kit.'" After discovering the convention scene in college, she started attending in costume, bringing along an emergency costume kit. While backstage at a contest at Tekko anime con in Pittsburgh, Pennsylvania, one contestant's armor ripped. The judge sent her to Robbins, remembering that she had a kit. "We were able to fix them before going onstage, and it was like the light just came on, this is what I wanted to do at cons. Since then, Tekko has actually started a repair room and brought me on staff to be the mobile unit."[13]

The Boy Scouts of America has a motto: Be Prepared. This is advice that I've found to be useful on more than one occasion. As a stormtrooper in the 501st, it's become habit for me to carry along some extra supplies when I go out on a troop: I'll throw a roll of white duct tape into my case before I leave, and for major events, I'll bring along a tool bag with extra glue, hand warmers, tape, razor blades, extra Velcro, zip ties, and whatever else I think I might need. The kit isn't just for me; it's for anyone who could use assistance.

This is something that is born out of experience. While I was trooping at a museum as a clone trooper, someone bumped into me a bit too roughly while we crowded into an elevator. There was an audible crack as the costume's plastic belt snapped into two pieces. This belt was an integral part of the costume: it held together the ab plate and backplate, and when it went, the other two did as well. Cosplayers put a lot of time and effort into their costumes, and when something goes wrong it's embarrassing, not just because part of the garment that's covering you suddenly gives way, but because of the fear that immediately plows through your mind that all your hard work will go to naught.

This is where individuals like Paige Robbins and Caitlin Brown (who goes by the name Sgt. Swift Stitch while on duty) and groups like the International Cosplay Corps come in. The group was founded by a cosplayer going by the name Captain Patch-It, who initially started it as an accident: in 2014, he had been planning to attend a local convention in Melbourne, Australia. "Usually I would have had a costume prepared

---

13 Paige Robbins in conversation with the author, February 2020.

well in advance," he explained to me in a Facebook chat. This time around, however, he wasn't sure what he wanted to be, and there were only a couple of weeks left. As some friends were preparing their costumes for an upcoming convention, he thought, "I could just turn up carrying some gear to assist them with repairing any of their costume malfunctions." He picked up a costume police vest and various repair items, and showed up at the convention. "Turns out my services were in way more demand than I ever imagined." When someone posted a picture online of him in action, people began to reach out, asking if they could do something similar.[14]

That sparked the start of a larger movement as he set up a page called the International Cosplay Corps, "a small group of Cosplay enthusiasts around the world, united in offering assistance and a helping hand to Cosplayers at conventions and events worldwide!"[15] The group isn't a formal organization, but it helps point people in the right direction by providing suggestions for how to put together something similar and what to carry in their packs. Caitlin Brown explained that they got into the activity after falling out of cosplay. "I had a lot of body image issues, and every time I tried to cosplay early on, I found a very strong derogatory community at the time. If you didn't do it perfect, they wanted nothing to do with you."

But then they came across an article about Captain Patch-It. "I thought, hot shit, that's awesome. That's what I want to do." Brown explained that they had always been interested in sewing and painting and realized that this was one way they could contribute to the community. "I've jokingly said that I have a fetish for being helpful." They reached out to Captain Patch-It and asked for permission to copy the idea, then began to attend conventions, handing out their phone number for cosplayers to use if they needed help.

Captain Patch-It notes that there is a wide range of things that he fixes at cons. "The most common thing? Shoes. For some reason, I keep finding that they seem to have an extremely high rate of failure while at conventions, be it high heels breaking, soles falling off, or just the entire piece giving up the ghost." The most common things he uses in repairs? Safety pins and zip ties. "Safety pins for quite a lot of fabric-related issues, while we end up finding more and more uses for zip ties, so they've definitely become one of the more popular pieces of kit over the last few years!"

---

14 Captain Patch-It Facebook conversation with the author, January 2020.
15 "About," The International Cosplay Corps Facebook Page, accessed December 7, 2021, https://www.facebook.com/pg/InternationalCosplayCorps/about/?ref=page_internal.

Captain Patch-It doesn't limit his services to cosplayers, either. "We get quite a few civilians who turn up with broken shoes that we'll help stitch together, tape up, and send back out onto the convention floor."

Changes in materials and technology have also made the work more challenging, he says. While it varies from convention to convention, "I've definitely seen a noticeable shift to more complicated outfits! Eight to ten years ago, someone sticking some LED lights into a costume was a pretty cool thing at the time. Nowadays, you're seeing swords with LED strips and microcontrollers that allow the colors to change and can be programmed to react to various inputs!" That has "definitely pushed us repairers to become more prepared for covering all possible issues that may arise—for instance, I regularly carry a portable soldering iron now (which isn't something I would have bothered with back in 2014)."

Medics give their services to the community, and while they fund some of their supplies out of their own pocket, they also earn tips, which go into a supply fund, or solicit donations through Patreon accounts or Amazon Wish Lists.

Cosplay repair isn't limited just to volunteers wearing a repair shop on their bodies. Some will get a booth space or room at a convention, setting it up as a workshop to per-

Paige Robbins repairs a cosplayer's broken blaster with a bit of superglue.

Photos courtesy of Andrew Liptak

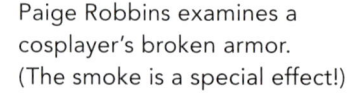

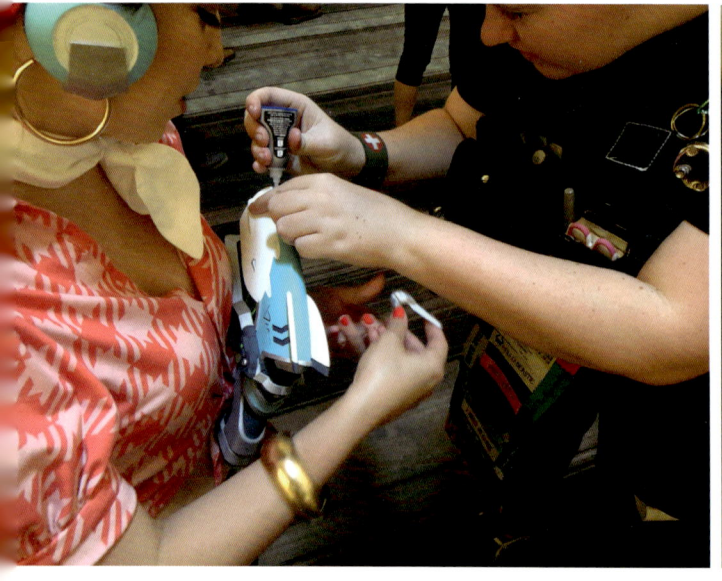

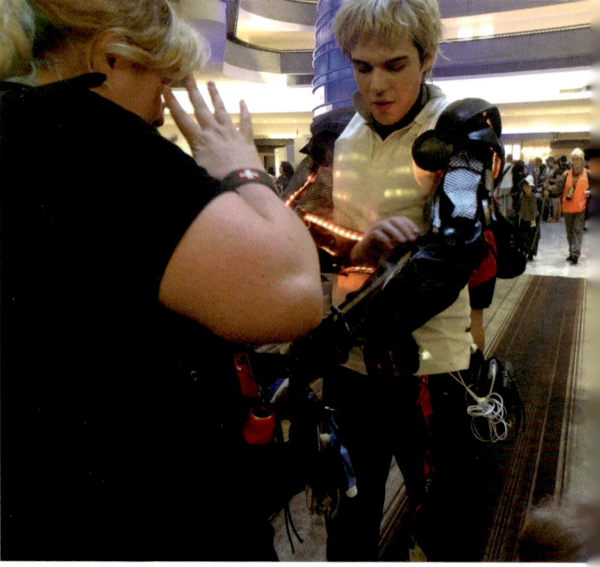

Paige Robbins examines a cosplayer's broken armor. (The smoke is a special effect!)

form repairs on the spot for those in need. Captain Patch-It notes that the scene has changed a bit, and that conventions have begun to introduce their own versions. "Back then, I was turning up to conventions paying my own ticket to get in and hauling my gear around by hand," he explained. "Nowadays, a lot of con-goers somewhat expect there to be some kind of repair service, and so conventions may cater to this by allocating an area for a local repairer to set up shop!" Companies and brands have also jumped on the idea, sponsoring areas as a service while also showing off their products.

Medics say that it's an extremely rewarding way to participate in a convention. "I found it amazing that I was able to help out others," Captain Patch-It says. "Making myself useful as well as being able to keep other people happy by helping them continue on with their day, instead of packing it in early due to a minor malfunction. Nowadays, it definitely makes me happy to see how far this whole movement has spread. I've made friends around the world who have been inspired to go out and help strangers at conventions, because they want to."

Robbins agrees. "There have been times people find me and they are just so done with everything, something isn't working right and they just want to go home. I always just sit down with them, and even if that repair takes an hour or takes us from plan A to plan Q, we work together to find a way to fix it. I've disassembled someone's boot to fix a zipper, I've sewn a girl from hip to neck into her dress so she could make her photo shoot." Robbins says that each year at Dragon Con, she serves nearly two hundred people. Ultimately, medics say that it's an extremely rewarding role to play at conventions. "It's helping people. I know that's really sappy, but it really is what I love the most. I've had people come up to me and tell me that I saved their con, and it's enough to make your heart want to melt."

21 SELLING STUFF ONLINE

When I first decided that I wanted to dress up as a stormtrooper, the options for making one's own suit of armor were limited. I thought about approaching my high school shop teacher with the idea that I could fashion one out of metal, but talked myself out of it when I couldn't figure out how to make the required dome for the helmet. Internet searches generated some resources, such as Studio Creations, a prop-making website that provides a comprehensive set of directions for building a stormtrooper suit from scratch. It explains how to make your own body cast, sculpt and create plastic molds, build a vacuum forming table, form the armor, and put it all together. The site also features sets of directions for a scout trooper, Rebel Fleet trooper, and a *Ghostbusters* Proton Pack.

If you wanted to buy a suit of stormtrooper armor in the 1990s or 2000s, you would have had to spend a considerable amount of time searching the web, looking through forum posts and personal blogs to track down someone who might have a connection to a maker. The costuming world was one of secrecy: manufacturers were cagey about what they were doing. After all, they were reproducing trademarked intellectual property (IP) for a small profit, an activity that could send unwanted legal attention in their direction.

Organized fan groups like the 501st provided some guidance, acting as well-trod paths from people who had gone through the purchasing process and were able to walk others through it. These transactions were handled through private forums and direct email, with a significant level of faith that makers would follow through with the purchase. When I purchased my own suit of armor in 2003, I mailed a check to my contact, who acquired the armor, presumably with some markup, and sent it to me via UPS.

The online world of 2022 is a far cry from that of 2003, thanks in part to a variety of new platforms that provide a direct pipeline from maker to prospective cosplayer. Sites like eBay, Etsy, and even Amazon now allow fans to purchase a costume with just a few clicks of a button.

MAJOR RETAILERS: eBAY AND AMAZON

In the summer of 2019, Sony's *Spider-Man: Into the Spider-Verse* left a considerable impression on my son, who wanted to dress up as Spider-Man. A quick search on Amazon led me to a listing for a Lycra and spandex Miles Morales Spider-Man in a variety of sizes. Within days, the costume arrived at my home. This development is still unfathomable to me. Growing up, making a costume like this would take considerable skill with a sewing machine (which I lacked), access to the right materials, and a good eye for detail to make sure the end result looked good. In 2003, that would have taken hours and hours, plus a good chunk of money. In 2019, all it took was a quick search and fifty dollars.

This retail environment didn't appear overnight. While early tech innovators had conceptualized ways to buy products online as early as 1972, the National Science Foundation—the body responsible for developing and rolling out the internet to universities and scientists—prioritized internet access to institutions.[1] By 1991, they had begun to expand the infrastructure around the world and finally lifted restrictions on how private companies could hook into the National Science Foundation Network (NSFNET). In 1995, the NSF rolled out a new, commercialized version of the system that allowed private companies to hook into it. This change paved the way for the entire online marketplace. Companies like Amazon and eBay (originally named AuctionWeb) appeared, allowing those with internet access to buy items online.

eBay in particular was an extremely useful site for prop builders and cosplayers. Where they were once limited to selling items via message board (if they had access to one), or in

---

1 "A Brief History of NSF and the Internet," National Science Foundation (website), August 13, 2003, https://www.nsf.gov/news/news_summ.jsp?cntn_id=103050.

My son, Bram, wanted to dress up as Spider-Man, so I went on Amazon and ordered a very realistic-looking costume, then received it within a couple of days. This sort of speed for a costume so precise was unheard of just a decade ago.

Courtesy of Andrew Liptak

person at conventions and other events, they now had access to the full internet public. Makers could put their items up for sale on eBay and sell them anywhere in the world.

The new retail environment wasn't without its faults. Studios soon recognized that prop makers were selling knockoffs of their IP and would compel eBay to remove sales listings or ban people from the site. In other cases, disreputable makers would sell their products at wildly inflated prices or misrepresent the quality of their goods to unsuspecting buyers. Members of cosplay forums took to calling eBay "FleaBay" and warned newcomers to avoid buying suits of armor or other props, telling them to go through internet forums instead, where buyers were at least known by reputation and could be trusted.

This model largely remained the same for the next decade or so: people looking to buy costumes and props could make their own, buy components from makers via existing networks of cosplayers, or take a risk on eBay. When I joined the cosplay scene in 2003, I was warned against going to eBay for stormtrooper armor because of the price inflation and probability that what I was getting was probably recast (a pirated copy of work). In 2008, I ended up buying a suit of clone trooper armor from eBay—which indeed turned out to be recast from another maker.

The retail environment began to change in the 2000s, however, when Amazon launched its third-party marketplace. A slew of other sites then popped up in the 2010s that allowed for more variety and options for online consumers. These companies allowed makers to set up their own shops online and sell directly to cosplayers, or to otherwise generate some income from the work they did as costumers. The result has helped push cosplay from a casual hobby into a full-time vocation for makers and cosplayers alike.

ETSY

Regular, persistent demand for items also helps drive access as makers realize that they can service a large pool of fans directly. Founded in 2005, the website Etsy was designed as a platform through which makers could sell their homemade goods directly to consumers. Within four years, the site quickly grew, tapping into the larger DIY entrepreneurial spirit that its makers exhibited.[2] The platform became an ideal match for prop and costume makers. Historian Glenn Adamson wrote that homemade and handcrafted items were becoming big in this environment: "The new crafter wave is fueled by an intriguing alliance of the oldest and newest of social technologies, the sewing circle and the blog."[3] The site's purpose came out of the online crafting community and was a reaction to the larger societal wave of mass production. The global recession also helped matters: the site allowed people to generate their own income in their own homes.

Jeff Rodriquez II, who runs an Etsy store called DH-P/FX, explained that prop making was something he initially started for fun. He became known for creating a handful of frequently requested items, including components for X-wing pilots like helmets, chest boxes, and rank cylinders.

Rodriquez explained that he got into cosplay around 2000, making his own components. As friends and other cosplayers saw what he was making, he ended up taking commissions for the same pieces. "People ask where you get something, and you say, 'I made it!' and they're like, 'Wow! Can you make me one?' and the next thing you know, you're making a mold of a piece that you kitbashed. Business just takes off from there."

---

2   Max Chafkin, "Can Rob Kalin Scale Etsy?" *Inc.*, April 2011, https://www.inc.com/magazine/20110401/can-rob-kalin-scale-etsy.html.
3   Kaitlyn Tiffany, "Was Etsy Too Good to Be True?" *Vox*, September 4, 2019, https://www.vox.com/the-goods/2019/9/4/20841475/etsy-free-shipping-amazon-handmade-josh-silverman.

A builder by trade, Rodriquez explained that the 2007 housing crisis and recession was the impetus for the start of his business. "We would drive an hour and a half to two hours to go make eighty bucks for the week. And then I would come home and pack a bunch of orders I was selling on eBay and make a lot more than I was making hanging drywall." As the economy began to recover, he realized that he didn't want to go back into the construction business and turned his attention to making prop replicas and costume components.

"When I got on Etsy," Rodriquez said, "it was more for crafts people." He had been looking for a change in selling venue: eBay had raised its fees, reducing the amount of money he could earn from the site. "I would sell something for a hundred dollars and have to pay out almost twenty dollars in fees. I was getting murdered."[4] Etsy allowed him to open up a dedicated storefront, rather than relying on forums and word of mouth. Other makers like Rhode Island–based cosplayer Maya Gagne, who operated an Etsy storefront called MCosplaySupplies, utilized the store as a full-time source of income for a couple of years. She specialized in creating foam Spartan armor from *Halo* that she could easily create based on templates, which cosplayers would then finish into a final costume. "Etsy has given artists a way to directly advertise their work and make a living," she explained in a message. It has allowed them to access "a huge base of people they wouldn't have usually been able to access. It also helped a lot of cosplayers expand their accessibility to cosplay items they might not have the skill or time to make."[5]

When I decided to build an X-wing pilot costume, I went to Jeff Rodriquez, who runs an Etsy store called DH-P/FX. He promptly shipped me a kit with all the necessary components, which I then turned into a finished helmet.

Courtesy of Andrew Liptak

---

4   Jeff Rodriquez in conversation with the author, September 2019.
5   Maya Gagne in conversation with the author, February 2020.

Predominantly, these online storefronts provide an avenue for cosplayers to purchase costumes or parts. This sweeping access is one reason that the cosplay scene has grown so quickly in the last decade: drop the barriers to entry (such as forums, unwieldy person-to-person transactions, and makers wary of corporate IP owners cracking down on unlicensed products), and more people will simply have the means to access it.

Furthermore, as more people join in on the hobby, the new demand for costumes and related components encourages new makers to begin selling their wares. Theoretically, a higher manufacturing capacity leads to lower prices and higher quality for everyone, and that's largely what's taken place. It's relatively simple to find a stormtrooper costume for sale these days, and almost certainly for less money than you might have found it for two decades ago.

■ COSPLAY COMPANIES

The growing cosplay market has meant that some businesses now recognize what fan prop makers knew all along: not all cosplayers are interested in making their own outfits; many are happy to outsource at least some of the work to others.

In the mid-2000s, dedicated companies like CosplaySky popped up, offering up complete costumes to buyers. Based in China and utilizing retail outlets like eBay to move their products, they began producing lines of costumes for cosplayers looking to get a quick jump on the convention season. According to its website, CosplaySky had a number of tailors on staff who would produce custom-made costumes designed to one's measurements. "This is the main difference between our costumes and other fancy dress and cheap mass products," the company said.[6] The company—and its successors, TrendsinCosplay and CosSky, as well as others like Xcoser—produced a wide range of costumes for some of the biggest franchises, including the Marvel Cinematic Universe, *Star Wars*, and others.

Adam Savage noted that while companies like Xcoser don't always provide the highest-quality costumes, it does make it easier for cosplayers to get what they need. "It lowers the threshold to entry for someone to put on a reasonably accurate costume. And when they put on a reasonable one, and they see what they like and what they don't

---

6 "About Us," CosplaySky (website), accessed December 3, 2021, https://cossky.com/pages/about-us.

like—most of our early costumes would be embarrassing to us today. I'm not embarrassed because it's a learning process."[7]

ANOVOS AND DENUO NOVO

Other companies have gone the official route by licensing their products directly from studios.

Founded in 2009 by two former 501st members, Joe Salcedo and Dana Gasser, ANOVOS was one of the first companies to go beyond mass-producing costumes for events like Halloween and cater directly to people who wanted a more accurate costume. Their goal was to take the detail-oriented approach common in the prop replica world to the wider market of cosplayers and pop culture enthusiasts.

Gasser explained that he and Salcedo had decided to undertake a new costuming project: the Viper pilot costumes from the Sci-Fi Channel reboot of *Battlestar Galactica*. "We really dove in and tried to get as much research as possible without the means of the studios to re-create those." They worked in a group and were able to come up with their costumes. "We went down to finding the exact buckles, snaps, and fabrics, and to offset some of the costs, made extras to sell within the larger costuming community.

"We were really successful through word of mouth, and we thought, 'Wow, you know, there's a market for this.'" Because of their work, they were asked to help with a series of *Battlestar Galactica* auctions, allowing them to meet some of the people involved with the show's production and costumes. "The thought was, even though we could never afford an auction piece that was screen-used, there's a market for those screen-used parts," Gasser said. "These are people who don't care if it was worn by an actor in the show—it's a much bigger market."

From there, they started to work out what it would take to officially license a costume, utilizing the same workshops that created the components from the original show. They reached out to the studios and made a business plan for their idea and hit a brick wall. "At first, it was just a no," Gasser says. The studios didn't understand what the market was for high-end costumes, and "it took meeting after meeting after meeting" to convince Hollywood that they had a viable idea. Soon, the studios began to understand what

---

[7] Adam Savage in conversation with the author, December 2019.

they were looking to do. In 2009, CBS signed a licensing agreement with them to produce *Star Trek* costumes, and NBC came through and licensed the costumes from *Battlestar Galactica*. In 2014, the company picked up a license to produce stormtrooper, Han Solo, Darth Vader, and Luke Skywalker costumes,[8] later expanding their offerings to include First Order stormtroopers.[9] The company also offered various replica helmets and accessories, as well as costumes and parts from the Marvel Cinematic Universe and *Ghostbusters*.

Gasser noted that, as a company offering officially licensed merchandise, they could do a couple of things that the larger cosplay community couldn't. He recounted a moment when a customer commented on the price of a uniform at a convention. "What I explained to the guy was, 'Yeah, you could probably make this yourself at a fraction of the cost, but you'll wear it once and want to upgrade it as you find more information and details,' and that they might go through several iterations and upgrades, and you'll likely spend the same amount of money in the long run."

By contrast, ANOVOS had access to the original parts, fabrics, and designs, rather than working off images on a screen. "We take [care of] that research so you don't have to worry about it. We do it for you." Included in the price is the hours of research that Gasser and his companions had sunk into the costume's development, meaning that a prospective cosplayer didn't have to hunt down the right buttons or fabrics. "We have the fabric made by the same company that milled the fabric [for the show] cut and sewed for them. We got the same buttons, same patches, and everything was from the same place

My ANOVOS Stormtrooper helmet, which I frequently wear for troops. It's made of light-weight ABS plastic, and is extremely comfortable to wear.

Courtesy of Andrew Liptak

---

8   Bonnie Burton, "Channel Han, Luke, and Darth with official *Star Wars* costumes," *CNET*, April 25, 2014, https://www.cnet.com/news/channel-han-luke-and-darth-vader-with-star-wars-costume-replicas-from-anovos.
9   Andrew Liptak, "You Will Soon Be Able to Suit Up as a *Force Awakens* Stormtrooper," *io9*, May 27, 2016, https://io9.gizmodo.com/you-will-soon-be-able-to-suit-up-as-a-force-awakens-sto-1779114540.

the production used, so it's no different than what you saw onscreen. It just wasn't worn by an actor."

While that official license means that the costumes that ANOVOS makes are accurate and of good quality, there are some drawbacks. Whereas a cosplayer can whip up a costume themselves and wear it, Gasser explained that his company had to go through safety and packaging testing, with the IP holder signing off every step along the way, which means that the company might not be able to churn out a costume for a consumer audience as quickly, especially for costumes made with a number of different materials, like plastics, leathers, or fabrics. Halloween costumes, by contrast, aren't nearly as complicated to produce—and are usually less detailed and cheaper as a result.

The company may also have to coexist with other licensees for any given franchise. One example Gasser pointed to was Columbia's *Rogue One* Captain Cassian Andor Rebel Parka. "We could make that exact same jacket, but theirs can't look like a prop replica. There are these rules, boundary lines that they can only make it this way, and we can only make it that way. The categories are similar to one another, but there are contractual guidelines to keep them separated. Our products need to fit within a certain price point, and away from other licensees to make sure there's no overlap. The point of a license is to not have competition."

Unfortunately, ANOVOS ran into some significant problems: because of the approval processes it had to go through, it became known for delaying its products, and its customers began to complain about the company and its practices—loudly. In some instances, customers waited for years for products that they had paid for, and complained not only to the company but to the Better Business Bureau, which gave the company an "F" rating. In 2019, a customer filed a lawsuit against the company. As of 2021, ANOVOS appears to have lost the license for its *Star Wars* products and vanished, while another company, Denuo Novo (founded by Rubie's and the National Entertainment Collectibles Association, or NECA), has promised to fill its long-overdue backorders, while restarting sales of the former company's product line.[10]

---

10 Andrew Liptak, "Squandered Legacy," *Transfer Orbit* (newsletter), https://transfer-orbit.ghost.io/star-wars-anovos-deuno-novo-cosplay.

COSPLAY SUPPLIES

Other companies elected to sell not the costumes themselves but the raw materials that cosplayers needed. While hardware stores have long been a good source of materials and tools, they don't always have the right supplies. As the internet became a major platform for retailers, new companies popped up, catering directly to cosplayers by stocking items that they needed.

One such website is Cosplay Supplies, which first came online in 2004. According to the company, it saw a niche because there were so few options for cosplayers—particularly for specialty items like shoes and wigs. The company has grown organically over the years, adding products as cosplayers request them and as other businesses reach out to have their items sold through the site.

"One of our biggest pushes was for thermoplastics," a company spokesperson explained to me in an email. "We were the first to bring Wonderflex to the cosplay market and did a lot of education and outreach back in the mid 2000s." In 2013, the site began selling Worbla, a thermoplastic that is easy to manipulate and has accordingly become widely used by cosplayers. The company has since added foam and LED lighting products to its roster. "A lot of the time," the company said in a statement, "the additions to our store are a reflection of the community, and sometimes, we bring something to the community that they maybe haven't had access to before."

In other instances, major retailers have picked up on the market potential that cosplayers represent: fabric retailers JOANN Fabric and Craft Stores and Michaels are two companies that have begun to cater to cosplayers.

In 2016, cosplayer Yaya Han partnered with CosplayFabrics.com to develop a line of four-way stretch fabrics in a variety of colors and textures (ribbed, hex-patterned, scaled, netted, and others) specifically intended for the activity. While some of the patterns remained exclusive to the site, the two also partnered with JOANN to sell the collection in its stores across the country.[11] Speaking with *Forbes* in 2016, Han explained that she "really approached this line with the mindset of, 'What would I wear? What would I use?'

---

11   "Calling All Cosplayers: The Yaya Han Cosplay Fabric Collection Exclusively Available at Jo-Ann Stores and Joann.com," *Business Wire*, March 16, 2016, https://www.businesswire.com/news/home/20160316006011/en/Calling-Cosplayers-Yaya-Han-Cosplay-Fabric-Collection.

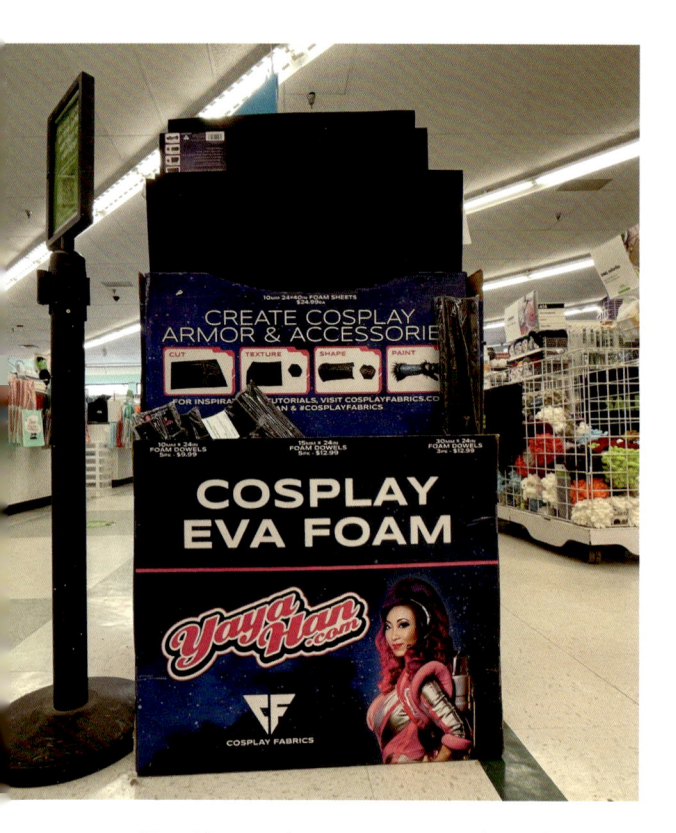

Yaya Han got her start as a cosplayer, but she's since branched out into licensing and selling materials that cosplayers use. Here, a display box holds EVA foam of various thicknesses, specifically advertised to cosplayers.

Courtesy of Andrew Liptak

I want cosplayers to be able to get that kind of quality even at their local store."[12]

The year before, Han partnered with the McCall Pattern Company to develop a line of costume patterns aimed at cosplayers. Her first two in the set—Yaya Han's Ultimate Bodysuit Pattern and Yaya's Original Peacock Costume—debuted in April 2015. She described her bodysuit pattern as something that was "sorely missing in the cosplay world—I know from having to alter and draft my own bodysuit patterns for many years. This pattern will make it easy for cosplayers (and everyone else) to tailor a bodysuit that will fit them like a glove, and use it as a base for thousands of costume ideas."[13] In the years since, McCall's has released dozens of additional patterns for cosplayers to use.

In JOANN's initial press release, vice president and general merchandise manager of fabric and sewing Lynne Schron explained that the company had noticed a surge in interest from cosplayers looking for different types of fabrics, and that they hoped to bring together a number of items to help save cosplayers time and energy when sourcing their materials. The company has since begun selling Yaya Han's line of EVA foam and other similar materials. In 2019, the store began selling 3D

---

[12]   Lauren Orsini, "How The Internet's Most Famous Cosplayer Is Democratizing Costume Fabric," *Forbes*, March 17, 2016, https://www.forbes.com/sites/laurenorsini/2016/03/17/how-the-internets-most-famous-cosplayer-is-democratizing-costume-fabric/.

[13]   Yaya Han, "Today is an incredibly exciting day!!! I feel incredibly lucky that on my birthday, I can finally reveal a long-awaited dream come true with all of you. . . . ," Facebook, April 10, 2015, https://www.facebook.com/yayacosplay/posts/10152807770756608.

printers, adding to its existing offerings of Cricut machines and Glowforge 3D laser printers.[14]

Together, these outlets provided much greater access to people looking to get into cosplay or another maker field, whether they needed the pattern for a commonly used garment or a tool to fabricate a required component for their outfit. The importance of this access can't be overstated: designing one's own pattern is a big endeavor, and established blueprints take out some of the guesswork. Ready access to needed materials is also revolutionary: previously, cosplayers would have to make their way to specialized garment districts in places like New York City or custom order them from retailers. Being able to order online or inspect them in person at a local store eliminates much of that work. It's this very access that has helped cosplay transform from a niche activity to one in the mainstream.

ETHICS

This isn't to say that the process is without bumps. Some makers find their own work pirated—known as "recasting" within the cosplay community. For something like a suit of stormtrooper armor, that means reverse-engineering a vacuum-forming buck to make a direct copy, allowing someone to bypass the sculpting phase and start making their own armor. With the introduction of digital manufacturing, all someone needs to do now is take STL files for a 3D printer and upload them to a website to pass them off as their own or begin selling them themselves.

Anyone with a 3D printer or skill with resin casting can turn their basement into a factory. Some makers are good at what they do: they turn out high-quality props that they've created themselves (or with permission from another maker), provide a clean print or resin model, and turn around orders in a timely manner.

Some are not. Longtime costumers note that in the 1990s–2000s, it wasn't uncommon for makers to take money from a prospective cosplayer and wait months—even years—to provide them with what they'd purchased, either a prop or a prop turned over for a paint job. People would be forced to wait: sometimes, these makers were known for their craft and simply worked on their own time, while others were

---

14 "JOANN Launches Exclusive 3D Printers, Enhances Shopping Experience to Encourage Handmade Holidays for All," *Business Wire*, November 4, 2019, https://www.businesswire.com/news/home/20191104005450/en/%C2%A0JOANN-Launches-Exclusive-3D-Printers-Enhances-Shopping.

unscrupulous, creating a sort of pyramid scheme in which they paid off one set of orders with another.

Quality can be a crapshoot as well. Members of the 501st have frequently warned prospective members against picking up costumes on eBay, citing numerous issues with quality and the ease with which people could be fooled by recasters or scammers.

It's easy for makers to set up a storefront, but it's also easy for someone to get in over their head. In early 2017, a group of my friends pooled their money and ordered several sets of First Order stormtrooper armor, with the intention of assembling the suits for the premiere of *Star Wars: The Last Jedi*. The maker unfortunately pushed back their delivery timeline by months, citing a myriad of excuses: they were sick, they had supply and time problems, and so forth. My friends eventually canceled their order and went with another maker, who also didn't deliver. It wasn't until the fall of 2019 that they finally received their armor, only for some of them to realize that they'd simply lost enthusiasm for the build in the first place, deciding to sell it off and move on to other things.

This is a risk with relying on a market that's served largely by enthusiastic amateurs who make costumes or parts as a side hustle. They might be skilled, but they aren't always bound by the same pressures and guarantees that companies abide by. The somewhat obscure nature of prop makers also means that there's less of a safety net for buyers: they might send off their money to a maker only to have them vanish off the face of the earth, sometimes for perfectly reasonable reasons like one's health or livelihood, or other times for more nefarious ones, like someone working a scam or not realizing that they've bitten off far more than they can chew. With the rise of platforms like PayPal or Etsy, buyers can sometimes claw their money back, but that's not always the case.

In some ways, the modern e-commerce marketplace, with one-click ordering, quick shipping, and high-quality merchandise, has primed consumers to have a high level of expectation when it comes to ordering products online. Individual reputations can suffer if makers fall out of favor. Builders and cosplayers will spread the word if they've been stiffed for purchases or been provided with subpar items. After bad reviews and word of mouth, some makers might drift out of the marketplace or rebrand themselves under a new name.

But problems aren't always limited to amateur builders. With the growth of the adult cosplay marketplace, legitimate companies have begun to step into the space, and they aren't immune to the complexities of manufacturing. As mentioned, ANOVOS, one of the first players in the space, continually delayed the delivery date for its First Order stormtrooper armor, angering fans.

The growth of the cosplay market brings other questions to consider as well: What is the impact on the people making costumes?

The last decade has brought about new opportunities for people looking to make a living. Apps like Airbnb, Upwork, Fiverr, TaskRabbit, and Uber have created workplaces through which people can operate as independent contractors, providing their goods or services on demand. Platforms like Etsy or Patreon are well-tailored for this style of work, as cosplayers and makers can sell their wares directly to consumers.

But while this type of platform touts flexibility as a major perk for people looking to make a little extra income on the side, it can also be harrowing for workers, who depend on their respective apps for work and have little in the way of financial stability. Classified as independent contractors, these workers aren't provided with health insurance, 401(k) retirement plans, or withheld taxes as salaried workers are. Thingergy Inc. studio founder Frank Ippolito noted his bewilderment at this type of work, wondering about the long-term feasibility for people making YouTube videos or building props full-time. One maker that I follow on Facebook runs regular sales so they can afford to buy the resin and other materials that they need to keep going, and when they get sick or fall behind, that's income that doesn't appear to be coming in. Others seem completely unprepared for the pace of work required to produce merchandise on a regular basis: what works as a hobby doesn't necessarily translate well to a factory in one's basement. It's not uncommon to see a builder pop up online, operate for a few months or years, and then shut down.

If they don't properly prepare, makers might find that a relentless production grind to fill orders has ruined what was previously a fun and exciting hobby. This doesn't apply to just makers either: the push for new costumes, the demand from Instagram or Patreon followers for an ever-constant stream of content, complaints or unreasonable demands from customers, or the need for a new YouTube video every week can burn creators out, ejecting them from the field completely. "I see people making costumes every month, and that just looks exhausting," Bill Doran of Punished Props explained to me. "I can't keep up with that."

Which isn't to say that people can't be successful in this line of work. But it's no easy task to keep up with a demanding and rapidly changing costume market, especially if makers overcommit and find themselves unable to make customers happy.

22 TECHNOLOGIES

Technology has always been at the center of cosplay. Cosplayers have utilized skills like sewing, welding, carpentry, design, and engineering; and materials such as metal, plastic, foam, cloth, glue, and rivets; and tools ranging from shears to 3D printers to bring their characters to life.

▬ EARLY COSPLAY TECHNOLOGIES

Early cosplayers turned to whatever they might have had on hand to create their costumes, but over the course of the twentieth century, they were able to take advantage of a number of new technologies that allowed them to make their own fantastic costumes, replicating the methods used by artists, film studios, and prop makers to create their own parts.

At the heart of prop making and costuming is the art of sculpture, which dates back thousands of years. Ancient sculptors created durable objects out of molten metal, first by developing a clay master, and then building a plaster jacket around it, from which they could make a two-part mold.[1]

One of the major methods for making costumes, particularly within the *Star Wars*

---

1 "A Short History of Plaster Casts," Cornell University Library, accessed December 7, 2021, https://antiquities.library.cornell.edu/casts/a-short-history.

community, is vacuum forming or thermoforming. Engineers originated the process in the 1930s while trying to make canopies for airplanes, and developed it throughout the 1950s and 1960s.[2] A number of significant objects in your life are likely made with this process, including bathtubs, car dashboards, signs, equipment enclosures, and toys. The process also made its way over to the film industry. In 1976, when George Lucas needed dozens of sets of stormtrooper armor for *Star Wars*, the film's costume designers turned to Andrew Ainsworth, who produced the film's stormtrooper costumes through his plastics company, which utilized a vacuum forming machine.[3]

Most plastic armor seen in the ranks of the 501st Legion has been molded with a vacuformer: a machine that heats plastic and sucks it against a buck with a vacuum. The armor worn by these two clone troopers (Bob Gouveia, left; me, right) went through this process to obtain its shape.

Courtesy of Andrew Liptak

Vacuum forming allows a manufacturer to mold a sheet of a material, such as plastic or fiberglass, into a certain shape. The process is fairly simple, involving a heating element, a mold, and a vacuum source. A sheet of plastic is placed in the machine and heated, making it pliable. Once it's ready, the machine's operator removes the heat source and pulls the plastic over the mold, then activates the vacuum. As the air is sucked out from under the plastic, it's pulled against the mold and into the desired shape. Once the plastic cools and is removed from the mold, it holds its shape, allowing the operators to trim the excess off.

Unlike manufacturing techniques like injection molding—a process that's largely outside of the price range for amateur and at-home makers—vacuum forming is rela-

---

2   Stanley R. Rosen, "A History of the Growth of the Thermoforming Industry, Chapter 1: Thermoforming Pioneers 1930–1950," SPE Thermoforming (website), accessed December 7, 2021, https://thermoformingdivision.com/wp-content/uploads/History_of_thermoforming_chap1.pdf.
3   "Our Story," Shepperton Design Studios + originalstormtrooper.com (website), accessed December 7, 2021, https://www.originalstormtrooper.com/our-story-19-w.asp.

tively simple: a setup can be made out of an old stove and a vacuum cleaner. The ease with which a handy costumer can put one together makes it a useful tool to construct uncomplicated costume parts, like individual pieces of armor, helmets, or props.

Ainsworth's method for producing stormtrooper armor proved to be extremely useful for the cosplayers that would follow. Once makers understood how the armor was constructed, they were able to re-create the process. In the late 1990s, Jeff Allen outlined the process on his website, showing aspiring costumers how to start from scratch by sculpting the armor molds,[4] building one's own vacuum forming machine,[5] and finally actually making the armor.[6]

PEPAKURA

In some instances, cosplayers found that the costumes that they wanted to make were too complicated for vacuum forming, such as the armor worn by Master Chief and other characters in the *Halo* franchise. This armor is more complicated than that of a stormtrooper, with lots of edges, undercuts, and detailing. As a result, aspiring cosplayers had to find alternatives. One early method was a piece of software called Pepakura.

Pepakura is a method of modeling a two-dimensional surface (paper) into a complicated 3D sculpture. Designers put together a 3D model on a computer, which calculates how one would cut up a sheet of paper or cardstock and fold it into the proper shape. With it, cosplayers can put together helmets and the various pieces of armor that make up the costume.

Once a cosplayer has folded and glued their components into shape, they then must go about turning it into a durable, wearable object using an automotive filler like Bondo or fiberglass to strengthen each part and fill in gaps and seams. From there, they sand and paint the surface to their preference.

Pepakura brought two advantages: the ability to model complicated 3D shapes and realize them as costume pieces, and a high degree of flexibility for cosplayers while in cos-

---

4 "Sculpting the Armor," StudioCreations (website), accessed December 7, 2021, https://www.studiocreations.com/howto/stormtrooper/sculpting/index.html.
5 "Vacuumforming: An Introduction," StudioCreations (website), accessed January 20, 2022, https://www.studiocreations.com/howto/vacuumforming/index.html.
6 "Vacuumforming: Preparing the Plastic and Heating Unit," StudioCreations (website), accessed December 7, 2021, https://www.studiocreations.com/howto/vacuumforming/preparing.html.

tume. Any standardized armor that is easy to replicate with a set of molds and a vacuum forming machine (like the uniform of a stormtrooper or Cylon) tends to come with a one-size-fits-all approach. If you're too tall, too short, too heavy, too thin, or otherwise divergent from the original model, you'll have to make extensive modifications to get it to fit just right. Pepakura allows makers to scale their builds up or down to suit them better, meaning that they can customize the costume as much as they wish.

This method, though, is also quite complicated: it requires significant time and expertise to not only generate and appropriately scale the models but also to painstakingly assemble and finish each set of armor. It's a labor-intensive process, but not without its rewards.

▬ EVA FOAM

Ethylene-vinyl acetate (EVA) is a type of closed-cell elastomeric polymer that is both tough and flexible, and is used in everything from plastic wrap, packaging, shoes, and craft foam to floor mats and yoga mats. It's also a particularly useful material when it comes to costuming.

Movie designers have utilized foam as a building material for decades. It's cheap and easy to shape, and as such, it provides a useful base for everything from building facades to movie monsters. Eventually, cosplayers began to realize that it was a useful tool for costume making as well.

An early pivotal moment came in 2003 when a cosplayer by the username Penwiper published an online tutorial for constructing a costume out of foam. "I was searching for a cheap, light, but nice-looking material to make armor out of, and I discovered one—craft foam!"[7] The material, they noted, was readily available at craft stores and was cheap, flexible, and comfortable. As one cosplayer noted on Twitter, "Every cosplayer should say thank you to this 2003 tutorial because we literally wouldn't make armor the way we do today without it . . ."[8] They also pointed out that "17 years later, it's still not a bad tutorial at all. We have better access to upgraded materials but the base of it is SO SOLID that

---

7   Penwiper, "Craft Foam Armor Tutorial," Entropyhouse (website), 2003, http://entropyhouse.com/penwiper/costumes/helmsdeep.html.
8   Arkady (@ArkadyKoshka), Twitter, November 20, 2019, 11:35 p.m., https://twitter.com/arkadycosplay/status/1197373060690497541.

TECHNOLOGIES

it still works and has been a launching point for almost all innovations in cosplay armor."⁹

In a post on Tumblr, Penwiper noted the reason their tutorial resonated with cosplayers: existing costumers had spent years perfecting their craft but weren't exactly open about their techniques. "Some of them came from professional backgrounds where this knowledge literally was a trade secret, others just wanted to decrease the chances of their rivals in competitions, but for whatever reason, it was like getting a door slammed in your face."¹⁰

Moreover, the cost of investing in equipment like a vacuum forming table or leatherworking tools placed the hobby outside of the budgets of aspiring cosplayers. The gatekeeping that cosplayers had experienced, they noted, led aspiring makers to "materials that 'serious' costumers would never have considered," like EVA foam.¹¹

The introduction of EVA as a building material "changed the face of costuming," writes Penwiper. "People who had been intimidated by the sci-fi competition circuit suddenly found the confidence to try it themselves, and brought in their own ideas and discoveries."¹²

A cosplayer suited up in armor from the video game Destiny *poses at Dragon Con in Atlanta, Georgia, in August 2019. The armor is made completely from EVA foam, which is easy to cut and manipulate into the right shapes for armor.*

Courtesy of Andrew Liptak

"The last ten or more years, people started gluing together floor mats," Bill Doran of the YouTube channel Punished Props explained to me in February 2020. "Eva Carpenter was the first person I saw making massive armor formats with it, and that's where I got started." He noted that the type of material that cosplayers began settling on was different from what major Hollywood studios were using. "It's got different properties and it reacts differently,"

---

9   Arkady (@ArkadyKoshka), Twitter, November 20, 2019, 11:49 p.m., https://twitter.com/arkadycosplay/status/1197373988030177280.
10 Penwiper, "Rain Makes Applesauce," tumblr (blog), accessed December 7, 2021, https://penwiper.tumblr.com/post/189251630312/so-a-couple-days-ago-some-folks-braved-my.
11 Penwiper, "Rain Makes Applesauce."
12 Penwiper, "Rain Makes Applesauce."

EVA foam is an ideal material for cosplayers. It's cheap and flexible, and can be molded into any number of shapes before being sealed and painted. Here, Jack Durnin and Jenni Tyler pose as Martian marines from *The Expanse* at Dragon Con 2019. Durnin 3D-printed the helmets but made the rest of the armor out of EVA foam.

Courtesy of Andrew Liptak

he says. "Cosplayers *love* it. It's cheap, you don't need a vacuum former, you don't need power tools other than a rotary tool, some knives, and glue. The barrier to entry is very low."

Lightweight and easy to cut and mold into different shapes, EVA foam has two other advantages: First, it's reasonably cheap and easy to acquire—all you need to do is go to your local Walmart, Home Depot, or other major retailer. A six-pack of 24" x 24" foam interlocking floor mats runs about twenty-six dollars at Home Depot, and retailers like JOANN and others sell a range of cosplay-specific foam products, allowing costumers to acquire the needed materials for a costume at a far lower rate than a comparable sheet of ABS or HIPS plastic. Second, plastics like ABS and HIPS are tough and moldable but require significant effort to get into the right shape: you need a heat source and a mold. For something like a stormtrooper uniform, it's an ideal material, because the costume was originally designed to be assembled in parts that could easily be vacuum formed. As the costumes in movies, television shows, and video games be-

TECHNOLOGIES

came more sophisticated and elaborate, such forming methods became less useful.

The fact that EVA foam is flexible and reasonably durable means that cosplayers can utilize it in a number of different ways. With the right preparation and effort, cosplayers could finally trace and cut patterns from foam, which they could then shape into the right forms. Even better, EVA foam comes in a variety of sizes and thicknesses, meaning that once a maker assembles a base form, say a breastplate or gauntlets, they can then carve out thinner sheets of foam to add additional detail. "I think the execution of foam building has become so much more sophisticated," Adam Savage told me in December 2019. "The foam really allows for compound curves on a much easier scale."

The result is that the material allowed for new vibrant cosplay groups to form, unhindered by the difficulty that other methods and materials might pose. EVA foam allowed cosplayers on a budget to construct even more elaborate costumes, keeping up with the complex new characters popping up on screens.

Destiny cosplayer Katie Henderson noted that while the use of EVA floor mats was a big initial step early on, the cosplay community has become far more sophisticated over the years. "It used to be all EVA floor mats," she explained at DragonCon in 2019, "but they're really difficult to work with: they're thick, not very bendy, and bulky."[13]

EVA foam's availability and attributes are a major reason that cosplay has flourished. "If you can't afford to buy a set of stormtrooper armor for $500," Savage said, "you can go get some craft foam and a PET bottle that you've heated in your oven, [and] you can cobble together a very reasonable-looking set of stormtrooper armor. The barrier is your labor, not the cost of materials."[14]

Cosplayer Katie Henderson at Dragon Con 2019. Her costume is made entirely of EVA foam.

Courtesy of Andrew Liptak

---

13   Katie Henderson in conversation with the author, August 2019.
14   Adam Savage in conversation with the author, December 2019.

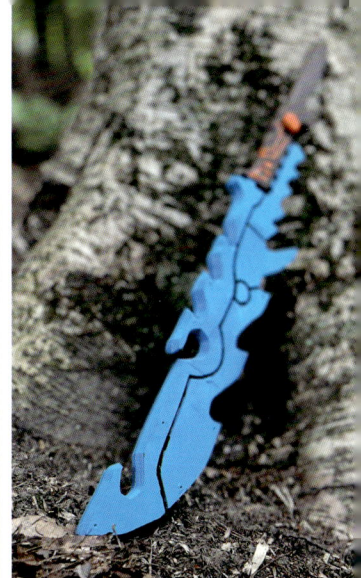

LEFT: A Sheikah Slate that I printed at a local library. Not all costumes need to be entirely made of 3D-printed parts: sometimes all you need are a couple of accessories.

CENTER: Not all costumes are made of high-end materials. For Halloween 2017, I made my son, Bram, a costume from *The Legend of Zelda: Breath of the Wild*. My mother sewed together the shirt and hood, and I painted on the details, constructed the faux leather components, used craft foam for the bracers, and had a local library 3D-print the Sheikah Slate.

RIGHT: A 3D-printed Guardian Sword++ from *The Legend of Zelda: Breath of the Wild*.

Photos courtesy of Andrew Liptak

3D PRINTING

In the summer of 2017, I picked up a Nintendo Switch and began playing the latest installment of Nintendo's The Legend of Zelda series, *Breath of the Wild*. My son, Bram, and I hacked and slashed our way through Hyrule. Featuring a massive open world, the game is full of fascinating costumes, objects, and weapons, and, without question, we settled on a Halloween costume for that year: one of the main character Link's colorful outfits, to be accompanied by a handful of cool-looking items: a sword, shield, bow with quiver of arrows, and a magical tablet called a Sheikah Slate (a magical data pad).

My local library had just installed a 3D printer, and after a bit of poking around online, I found the files for the Sheikah Slate, then sent them a file to print. A day or so later, I had the white tablet in hand. After a little sanding, some paint, and a ribbon, I had a serviceable replica. When I came across another set of plans for a lightsaber-like

TECHNOLOGIES

Guardian Sword++,[15] I had a friend with a 3D printer of his own print me one. Before I knew it, I had two of my items for the character.

The process of 3D printing also goes by "additive manufacturing," "computer automated manufacturing," "layered manufacturing," or "rapid prototyping."[16] The process starts with a designer-developed 3D object known as a Computer Aided Design (CAD), which the software converts to a file that can be read by a printer (usually a Standard Tessellation Language file, or STL). This STL file guides the computer to lay down plastic in a series of fine layers. As the machine lays down each successive layer, one can slowly build up a three-dimensional object like a part for a costume. While slow, the process allows makers to print extremely detailed objects that you might not be able to create with traditional manufacturing methods.

My personal 3D printer: a Snapmaker, which I've used to print a variety of parts for costumes. The expiration of 3D-printing patents has helped the home-printer market explode.

Courtesy of Andrew Liptak

There are three main 3D-printing methods makers can use. The most common is fused filament fabrication (FFF), in which a spool of thermoplastic (like ABS or PLA) is melted in a heated nozzle and extruded onto a build surface to form the object. The next method is stereolithography (SLA), in which a printer beams a laser into a vat of resin, bonding the material into a solid object, layer by layer, as it slowly works its way from bottom to top (or top to bottom). The third method is called selective laser sintering (SLS), in which a machine puts down a layer of powdered material like fine resin or metal. When the layer is in place, the machine uses a laser to trace the desired pattern, fusing the layer into the right shape. Once one layer is complete, the machine lays down another layer of powdered material, and the process repeats itself.

---

15 "3D Printing Zelda: *Breath of the Wild* – Guardian Sword++," Adafruit Industries, YouTube video, May 10, 2017, https://www.youtube.com/watch?v=BNUuwJpeilM&feature=emb_title.
16 "Rapid Prototyping," eFunda (website), accessed December 7, 2021, http://www.efunda.com/processes/rapid_prototyping/intro.cfm.

Each of these methods can be used in a variety of ways. Chemist David E. H. Jones had initially proposed the process in his *New Scientist* magazine column in 1974, observing that "many liquid monomers can be polymerised to solid by ultraviolet light, or even visible light. Accordingly, a laser-beam shone through a tank of monomer should leave an optically straight fibre in its path," he wrote. "A laser beam aimed in the right direction zig-zags all around the tank to create an interlaced web of fibres. By proper settings of the mirrors anything from a Brillo-pad to a vest can be made: and with no moving parts at all!"[17]

From here, engineers and scientists began to devise systems to realize his theory. In 1981, Japanese scientist Hideo Kodama wrote a paper for the *Review of Scientific Instruments*—"Automatic method for fabricating a three-dimensional plastic model with photo-hardening polymer"—in which he described the method for printing up an object,[18] which several companies and entrepreneurs followed a couple of years later before registering a series of patents for specific systems. Thus, 3D printing was born.

The automated process initially found a home as a manufacturing technique. It allowed companies to construct new types of models, but also became an easy way to create a prototype of an object: one merely needed to develop a computer model and print it up, without having to manufacture a new set of molds or a machine part. But the process didn't immediately become widespread, thanks in part to the patents that individuals and companies held on these techniques. That began to change in the mid-2010s as those patents expired, causing a boom in the availability of 3D printers. As Filemon Schöffer wrote in *TechCrunch*, "When the Fused Deposition Modeling (FDM) printing

A cosplayer poses as Tony Stark/Iron Man at FAN EXPO Boston in 2019. His armor was entirely 3D-printed.

Courtesy of Andrew Liptak

---

17   David Jones, "Ariadne," *New Scientist*, vol. 64, no. 917, October 3, 1974, 80.
18   Hideo Kodama, "Automatic method for fabricating a three-dimensional plastic model with photo-hardening polymer," *AIP Review of Scientific Instruments*, vol. 52, issue 11, 1981.

process patent expired in 2009, prices for FDM printers dropped from over $10,000 to less than $1,000, and a new crop of consumer-friendly 3D printer manufacturers, like MakerBot and Ultimaker, paved the way for accessible 3D printing."[19]

Prop-making studios in Hollywood have used the technology for years to create costumes, but the newfound availability of home devices has been a boon for cosplayers, allowing them to create individual props or entire costumes.[20]

Before the widespread availability of 3D printers, sculptors had to rely on a variety of techniques to replicate costume parts: carving out EVA foam, making resin molds, machining metal parts, sculpting bucks for vacuum formers, and other techniques—a lot of effort if you're looking to build only one item or a limited run of items. Now, a cosplayer can print up an entire preset suit of armor with a 3D printer.

Ahead of Dragon Con 2019, Jack Durnin of Charleston, South Carolina, decided to build a Martian marine from Syfy's science-fiction series *The Expanse*. "I saw the promo for season two," he told me at the convention, "and I saw the Martian marines in the teaser, and was like, 'What is this show?'" and ended up binging the entire series.

Durnin was already an experienced hand when it came to costuming. In high school and college, he made short films, for which he built many of the sets, costumes, and props himself. As he got into cosplay, he built Commander Shepard's N7 armor from *Mass Effect*. When he watched *The Expanse*, he realized that he could put together his own set of the Martian marine power armor.

While some of the show's fans had tracked down the real-world helmets and components that the studio's makers had used to create the onscreen costumes, the Martian marine costume was different. It was entirely original to the series, and if he wanted his own version, he'd have to make it himself, from the ground up. "I started with the helmet," he explained, "because I knew that would be the hardest and would take the most time. I started with screenshots and then the initial shape, trading the three dimensions of the helmet, and then started sculpting it." From there, he went to work on sculpting the forearms and armor, using the same EVA foam that he had used for his *Mass Effect*

---

19 Filemon Schöffer, "How Expiring Patents are Ushering In the Next Generation of 3D Printing," *TechCrunch*, May 15, 2016, https://techcrunch.com/2016/05/15/how-expiring-patents-are-ushering-in-the-next-generation-of-3d-printing.

20 This technology isn't limited to building pieces for costumes. Using free software, I designed a handle to replace the one that broke on my freezer door, and had a friend print it up. I've also used my own small printer to print up little toys and gizmos for my son and nephews.

armor. Durnin and his then-girlfriend (now wife), Jenni Tyler, debuted their costumes at that year's convention. Their work was rewarded by astonished onlookers and even garnered praise from the cast and crew of the show.

Access to a printer has another effect on the costuming community: it democratizes the field in a completely unprecedented way. In earlier days, a skilled modeler could produce a detailed model to sell to or share with the community at large. But this method inherently came with a bottleneck: said maker could produce their products only one by one. By creating a file and sharing it with others, ten or more makers could put together the piece at the same time. Hundreds of identical costumes could materialize worldwide almost simultaneously.

In the lead-up to *Rogue One: A Star Wars Story*, interested cosplayers started a number of groups to create costumes for one of the film's new trooper classes: the shoretrooper. While some makers decided to go the traditional route of sculpting and vacuum forming their own versions, one maker decided to model up his own printable version.

In 2016, Sean Fields launched a website featuring a Dropbox link that contained all the files required to put the costume together. Best of all, he released the files at no cost for anyone to download on their own. As a result, hundreds across the world built their costumes from his design. Fans from the US, Europe, Asia, and elsewhere constructed the costume, turning out at events clad in it. Others followed: a maker named Paul Prentice developed his own set of highly accurate shoretrooper armor, which he gave to interested makers in exchange for a charitable donation.

This technology had another, unexpected side effect: it helped to shorten the amount

Brian Anderson sits in the *Millennium Falcon*'s lounge booth at FAN EXPO Boston in 2019. He's spent decades building costumes of all types, and has focused extensively on 3D printing, making everything from droids to costumes to the game figures sitting on the table before him.

Courtesy of Andrew Liptak

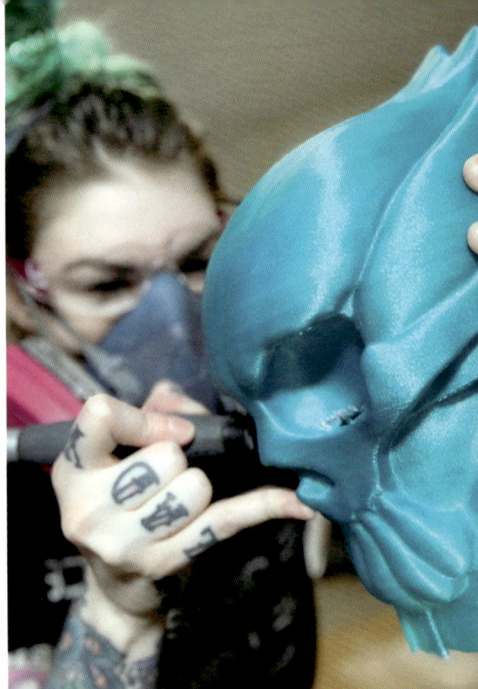

LEFT: Cosplayer Amie Dansby uses 3D printing extensively in her costumes. This is her take on Vanellope von Schweetz from the Disney film *Wreck-It Ralph*, and much of the costume features parts that have been separately printed.

RIGHT: Cosplayer Amie Dansby works on a helmet that she's 3D-printed. Printed parts typically require a considerable amount of work to produce a finished version.

Photos courtesy of Amie Dansby

of time it would take someone to develop and build a costume. "When I was first becoming a prop maker," Brian Anderson explained to me at FAN EXPO Boston in 2019, "there was an enormous investment in being able to produce something."

When Lucasfilm released the television series *The Clone Wars* in 2008, Anderson, a long-time member of the 501st Legion, wanted to build a set of clone trooper armor from the series. "It took me over a year to sculpt and produce the molds for that suit, and an investment of several thousand dollars and materials just to get to that very first set." Making armor in that fashion, he explained, wasn't something one could do on impulse: it required a lot of planning and investment to complete. But once that money was spent, "subsequent suits were easy to make, because I could then vacuum form the armor [onto the existing molds]."

But with those molds already formed, he couldn't easily improve them, especially as new details came to light. "Now, with 3D printing, the risk is so much lower." At the time we spoke in August 2019, the final *Star Wars* film, *The Rise of Skywalker*, had yet to hit theaters, but he had already printed up a helmet that would appear in the film. "They were just shown in publicity photos for the first time a couple of weeks ago," he said, but if there was a significant change, the original developer could simply take the model, tweak it, and rerelease it online for builders to print out again. "That happened to me with the helmet from *The Mandalorian*; I've already made that helmet from the file that Sean Fields produced. He said from the beginning, 'This file probably isn't accurate, and as I find new details, I'm going to iterate on the model, and anyone who buys the file now will get every free iteration through completion.' When I first started working on that, a bunch of people asked why I was wasting my time on it if I knew it wasn't going to be accurate. It's twelve dollars' worth of filament to print one. If I have to print a new one, it's no big deal. And so, it lets people jump on trends very early and not have to worry so much about getting it right on the first try."

But while 3D printing has proved to be useful to cosplayers, it's not the be-all and end-all technique that will replace the methods that preceded it. Processes like traditional sculpting, molding, and others remain in use throughout the world, and printing an object doesn't mean that one can simply pull it off a printing bed and step into a convention with it in hand. These objects often require postproduction work, usually sanding down the lines left by the printer to a smooth surface (itself a labor-intensive process), filling in cracks and seams made when joining two parts together, and priming and painting the object.

Even once complete, a prop might not be very durable. A maker might opt to print out a hollow version of their desired prop, with a honeycomb-like interior structure, to save printing time and weight. A couple of years ago, I bought a replica gun from Neill Blomkamp's 2013 film *Elysium*. The parts were beautifully designed and printed and were extremely light. I built the prop, but when it fell (twice!), it broke along a couple of weak points, requiring fixes. When a friend printed up Link's Guardian Sword for me, I had him do it as a solid part, realizing that it would be much sturdier.

Given that 3D printing often relies on melting plastic to extrude, props can also be extremely susceptible to heat: more than one cosplayer has noted that they've had a prop or costume part that's melted on them in extreme heat, like in a hot car in the sun or if left next to a heater. This isn't to say that other manufacturing methods are inherently better: objects cast in resin can melt, deform, or shatter; fiberglass and plastic can crack with age or strain; and fabrics can tear.

But despite those drawbacks, 3D printing is a game-changing technology, allowing cosplayers to work up entire outfits and costume components quickly and cheaply, opening the field to new costumers who might not have been able to take part previously.

LASER CUTTING AND CNC

Another technological advance that cosplayers have put to use is laser cutting, an industrial process in which a computer-guided machine uses a laser to cut out precision parts from a variety of materials such as foam, leather, metal, plastic, or wood.

Lasers are a long-term standby of science-fiction books and movies, and have their real-world origins in some of Albert Einstein's theories from 1917. In the years that followed, physicists chipped away at the theory, and in 1960, Theodore H. Maiman, working at the Hughes Research Laboratories in California, developed the first laser device. Because lasers concentrate energy on a precise point, they can be used in industrial processes, cutting through a vast array of materials.

Because lasers are so precise, engineers began using lasers to cut out parts in the aerospace industry, which improved efficiency.[21] Since then, the technology has become more widespread. The cost of a laser cutting machine has dropped, though they aren't as cheap as 3D printers. They can range anywhere from thousands to tens of thousands per unit—not necessarily affordable, but still within reach of a dedicated builder or makerspace.

Cosplayers have turned to laser cutting for the same reasons that Boeing did in the 1960s and 1970s: precision and duplication. The device allows makers to cut out parts to very exact specifications, and they can share their files so that others can reproduce their work on another machine.

One mainstay of fantasy and medieval armor is chain mail: a sheet of interlocking rings that forms a flexible set of protection for the wearer. Because creating it was a time-intensive process, early costume designers turned to a type of knitting to replicate the look for movie productions. For *The Lord of the Rings*, Wētā Workshop utilized PVC piping and injection-molded plastic rings to achieve a lightweight alternative that looked more authentic.[22] In 2020, maker Ben Eadie devised a new method for creating replica chain mail:

21 "The History of Laser Cutting Technology," Precision Waterjet & Laser, August 30, 2016, https://web.archive.org/web/20191031040033/http://www.h2ojet.com/news/the-history-of-laser-cutting-technology.
22 "Adam Savage Geeks Out Over EVA Foam Chain Mail!" Adam Savage's Tested, filmed and edited by Gunther Kirsch, YouTube video, January 29, 2020, https://www.youtube.com/watch?v=x8KmARIgCdY.

after using a laser cutter to cut a pattern of continuous loops on a 1 mm sheet of EVA craft foam, the maker weaves together the loops and blasts them with a heat gun, which forms a chain mail–like sheet that weighs a fraction of what traditional chain mail might weigh.

Cosplayers have found other uses for laser cutters as well. Mike Iverson, the maker behind Blind Squirrel Props, detailed how he utilized one to create replica pistols, noting that he had created the templates in Adobe Illustrator, and "planned out the parts so they could be built using layers of laser-cut MDF. This would allow for maximum accuracy as well as the engraving on the barrels."[23] Svetlana Quindt of Kamui Cosplay showed off a similar technique when building the laser rifle for Master Skin Nova from *Heroes of the Storm*: she used a laser cutter to carve out individual pieces of foam.[24]

ELECTRONICS AND MOTORS

Fiction allows creators enormous creativity when it comes to the outfits and accessories that characters wear. Iron Man wears an advanced suit of armor with plenty of abilities: panels that flip up and down, electronics, weapons, and more. Some characters feature lights in certain places or screens that display information for them to read. These types of special effects present a unique challenge to cosplayers striving to make their costume the most accurate, or at least wanting to make it a showstopper.

Increasingly, cosplayers are adding special effects elements to their costumes. Though such systems may be complex to incorporate, they unquestionably bring another level of reality to the costume.

As with other technologies, incorporating these elements into a costume seems to be driven by affordability and ease of use, aided by the prevalence of online tutorials. One major source of these electronics is a company called Adafruit Industries. Founded in 2005 by MIT hacker and engineer Limor Fried, the company has made a name for itself by providing a range of easy-to-use electronics products and kits for hobbyists and makers, as well as tutorials for their construction.

In an email in March 2020, Fried explained to me that "the stuff we sell at Adafruit

---

23 Blind Squirrel Props, "Laser Cut MDF Cosplay Pistols," Instructables (website), accessed December 7, 2021, https://www.instructables.com/id/Laser-Cut-MDF-Cosplay-Pistols.
24 "Nova – A Cosplay That Took Me Two Years," Kamui Cosplay (website), October 17, 2017, https://www.kamuicosplay.com/2017/10/17/nova.

are the things we used to make on the weekends as students." They started out small, producing and selling electronics kits; and now, a decade and a half since they started, they offer more than four thousand different products.

A major reason for that growth, Fried says, is the proliferation of cell phones, which has led to cheaper wiring, LEDs, and sensors. "The processor in the Raspberry Pi was originally designed for mobile devices as a video assist," she said. The "sensors we use for motion detection, temperature, and environment came from [the aerospace industry] and were eventually incorporated into cell phones. That made prices plummet due to competition and scale."[25]

That drop in price made those components ideal for cosplayers' use—something Fried noted from the company's earliest days. "We've been making props and wearable projects since we first started Adafruit, so we've always tried to show off the way LEDs and sensors can make cosplay fun!" Fried says that as they've simplified the kits and their instructions, their sales have grown.

The company has continued to cater to the cosplayer market. In 2019, it introduced the Adafruit Prop-Maker FeatherWing, a microcontroller that they designed after looking at "hundreds of prop builds."[26] The device allows cosplayers to control lights and sound, and detect motion. "We're seeing folks use it to make a lot of handheld props: wands, swords, staves, ray guns," Fried says. She notes another advance that has improved ease of use for cosplayers: "From doing a lot of projects for events like Maker Faire and Burning Man, we know that field repair is really important, so we love CircuitPython because the boards show up as a USB key. Sound and image files can be dragged and dropped onto the drive to change effects without needing a programming setup or development environment. You can edit the code anywhere, even on a mobile device!"

Sometimes, electronic components are simply there for the comfort of the wearer. Some cosplayers have devised water-cooling systems to help wick away heat on hot days[27] or installed tiny fans within helmets to keep the air around their face circulating, allowing them to remain in costume longer.

---

25   Limor Fried in an email to the author, March 2020.
26   "Adafruit Prop-Maker FeatherWing," Adafruit (website), accessed December 7, 2021, https://www.adafruit.com/product/3988.
27   Sgtpearce, "Odst Cooling System," 405th Infantry Division (website), March 14, 2014, https://www.405th.com/forums/threads/odst-cooling-system.36349.

▰ MAKEUP

Cosplay isn't only about re-creating the garments or armor that a character wears: it's about re-creating both the appearance *and* experience of their character for others within the context of that character's original medium. Body art and makeup have long been part of theatrical, cinematic, and cosplay costuming. Alongside staple items like wigs, clothing, and accessories, makeup can become a special effect in and of itself, allowing cosplayers to re-create not only the characters that they're emulating, but the media format from which they originate.

In 2009, Karin Dodge, a MAC Cosmetics artist who was based in Chicago at the time, decided to take part in the company's annual Halloween makeup challenge. She had grown up in Iowa and worked at MAC since 2005, and was attracted to its emphasis on artistry and creativity. That year, she explained to me on a phone call in September 2021, there were four categories, one of which was comic art. "The comic book look was the one I struggled with the most," she said. "Because I never really read comic books, and I wasn't really interested in comic book characters; it wasn't a thing for me."

Despite that, the prompt represented a challenge, and Dodge began to look through comics for inspiration. "I was typing into Google 'comic book,' 'makeup,' 'comic girl,' and all sorts of things, and I really didn't find anybody who had created that look." As she continued digging, she came across artist Roy Lichtenstein, who is probably best known for his comic-book-influenced pop art, with works such as "Drowning Girl," "Oh Jeff . . . I Love You,

In 2009, Karin Dodge entered a MAC Cosmetics company contest. Inspired by the art of Roy Lichtenstein, she turned a model into a living comic book character. The look has since become extremely popular among cosplayers.

Courtesy of Karin Dodge

TECHNOLOGIES

Too . . . But . . . ," "In the Car," and "Sleeping Girl," which utilized the Benday process and vivid colors to re-create the look and feel of older comic art.

"I felt an immediate connection," she recalled, and began reading up on the artist and his particular style of pop art. "His art was something I could really connect with in terms of the color palette—mostly primary colors and a lot of black and white, and the style of art being with comic books, [there was] a lot of thick lines and a lot of contrast. And then there was the use of Benday dots, which was really fascinating to me."[28]

With Lichtenstein's art to guide her, she set about preparing for the contest. "I was quick to jump in and try and get something done, and I decided to use a painting called 'Girl with the Hair Ribbon.'" She asked her boyfriend to take pictures and another friend to act as her model and set about applying the makeup. "I tend to just sort of jump into things without necessarily doing all my research first," she says, "and didn't understand the Benday dots had to be aligned in a certain way—they can't be just random dots everywhere. I didn't like the first attempt at it, and we scrapped it."

But the idea stuck with her, and she brought in a different friend for another attempt. "This time," she says, "I felt a little bit more confident knowing what I was going to do and how I was going to achieve the look." Dodge set about replicating Lichtenstein's art by placing bright-red Benday dots on her model's face, along with thick, black contours to highlight her eyes, lips, and nose, and topped it off with a bright yellow wig and oversize earrings, transforming her into a living embodiment of a comic book character.[29]

She and her team went out to a local mural, where they took pictures, and turned them in. It wasn't until MAC Cosmetics released a video featuring her style that she learned that the company had chosen her look. But the images that would end up going viral weren't actually her own: MAC took the look and directions that she'd sent in and brought in an in-house artist to replicate it. Dodge noted that there were some legal and rights issues at play behind the scenes, but was a little disappointed that the pictures that went viral weren't actually her own. Still, she's happy with how popular her idea has become. "Many, many people have created that look and have done it beautifully," she said. "There's so much talent out there, and it's wonderful to think that I could have taken inspiration from somebody like Roy Lichtenstein, who took his inspiration from comic

---

28   Karin Dodge in conversation with the author, September 2021.
29   Tashamarie, "It's the Most Wonderful Time of the Year," *Charmed: Documenting Life* (blog), October 9, 2009, https://charmedtasha.blogspot.com/2009/10/its-most-wonderul-time-of-year.html.

book artists, and now other people are taking inspiration from the makeup looks. I think that's really the beauty of art and the cycle of how our influences progress with time."

Since Dodge's idea went viral, it's become a popular look that's been emulated by other makeup artists, who've posted their own tutorials on YouTube, teaching others how to replicate it themselves.[30]

Where YouTube has provided a platform for cosplay makers and personalities, it's done the same for makeup artists. The site is home to thousands of tutorial-driven influencers who make a living on the platform, posting regular videos with routines for millions to try at home. Unsurprisingly, there's overlap here with the cosplay community, as makeup can be an integral part of replicating a character—look no further than characters like Ahsoka Tano, Darth Maul, or Princess Amidala, all of which require extensive work to re-create their facial features.

Following Dodge's work with her comic girl, cosplayers began to utilize similar pop art techniques to better realize their characters, supported by the vast network of YouTube tutorials. Cel-shading has become popular for cosplayers looking to emulate animated characters, like those in FX's animated series *Archer*, which employs a distinctive style that hearkens back to comics of the 1960s and 1970s.[31] Fans looking to re-create the characters don't have to work too hard to assemble a costume: the title character's ensemble is a gray suit with a black tie and a glass of whiskey. Cosplayers go further, applying dark contours to accent the features on their faces, and the result is incredible: they transform from a person in a suit to a fully realized, recognizable character.

The same is true for Gearbox's video game series *Borderlands*, which employs a distinctive art style that resembles cel-shading—a method designed to make 3D objects look flat—which, as in the show *Archer*, employs contours and bold colors. Cosplayers are able to replicate the effect with makeup and by painting their props and costumes,[32] effectively turning the cosplayer into not only the character but the character in the 2D style that they were initially designed in.

---

30 "Watch a Pop Art Character Come to Life: Roy Lichtenstein's," POPSUGAR Beauty, YouTube video, October 28, 2011, https://www.youtube.com/watch?v=VMOM1vwbeAg.
31 Scott Timberg, "The Art of *Archer*: 'The Arc of the Character of Archer Is Really Interesting,'" *Salon*, December 6, 2016, https://www.salon.com/2016/12/06/the-art-of-archer-the-arc-of-the-character-of-archer-is-really-interesting.
32 Jody Macgregor, "Cosplayers Are Bringing Cel-Shaded Characters to Life," *PC Gamer*, October 14, 2018, https://www.pcgamer.com/cosplayers-are-bringing-cel-shaded-characters-to-life.

The result is a creative added effect that brings the fictional character into the real world in an eye-catching fashion. Dodge notes that the experience hasn't turned her into a comic book fan (it's just not her thing, she admits), but it has given her a new appreciation for Lichtenstein's art and his influences.

▰ DIRECT INCOME PLATFORMS

As some cosplayers have worked to turn their hobby into a full-time vocation, they've been able to take advantage of a handful of platforms that allow them to generate income directly from fans and audience members. These direct-income platforms include the likes of Patreon, OnlyFans, Ko-fi, and others, each of which works in slightly different ways.

Patreon is probably the biggest such direct-support platform used by cosplayers. Founded in 2013 by musician Jack Conte and developer Sam Yam, the site allows individuals to sign up for an account and support a creator on any number of membership tiers. Each month, the site charges their credit card, keeps a percentage for itself, and sends the rest on to the person they're supporting. In return, creators provide a reward proportional to the amount that they have received. Lower-tier backers might get access to blog posts or a thank-you note, while those who pledge ten, fifty, or even one hundred dollars a month get more rewards: access to the creator in question, exclusive photo shoots, and so forth.

Numerous cosplayers have launched Patreon pages of their own, encouraged by their friends, fellow cosplayers, or fans. Cosplayer Dorasae Rosario (Akakioga Cosplay) explained that for her, it's not something that will pay the rent or many of her living expenses, but she uses it to fund some of the projects that she's been working on. "It definitely helps with buying materials for costumes," and sometimes, she feeds the money that she makes back to her supporters by sending them physical rewards.

She explained that she primarily focuses on the work that goes into her costumes, providing her followers with tutorials and how-tos, which her backers then get access to.[33]

M Blackburn explained that there's another, simpler motivation for setting up a Patreon: it's a way to showcase something that a cosplayer might already be doing, especially

---

33 Dorasae Rosario in conversation with the author, February 2020.

if they're frequently making new costumes or projects, or hitting the con floor frequently. "I think a lot of us do it because it's a great way, even if it's not income-worthy, to fund your hobby. If I can break even, then that is well enough for me." Some cosplayers will set up a specific goal for a project, appealing to their followers to help them fund it.[34]

The platform helps bring about an element of community, Rosario notes. She explains that there are some backers who simply want to show their appreciation to a cosplayer: the impulse of "I want to feel like I'm helping you continue to make a costume, or feel like I'm part of this costume" is one such motivation. In her case, she provides her backers with access to a Discord server where they can hang out and chat with her online.

One's success on the platform can vary wildly, Blackburn notes. "People can make thousands of dollars a month," they say, "or they can make a hundred." An element of that comes down to what cosplayers offer up to fans each month. This level of success goes far beyond just setting up an account and waiting for people to come to you with their money. Backers expect certain rewards, whether they're physical products like signed prints, stickers, or other merchandise, or digital rewards like exclusive image galleries or access to a closed chat room for backers. There are also the logistics that go into setting up exclusive photo shoots, and the construction of new costumes. This can put considerable pressure on creators, who find that they need to continuously provide content for their backers.

Patreon isn't the only payment platform that cosplayers use to generate income. Some cosplayers use Ko-fi, a sort of virtual tip jar that allows fans to pay creators directly with a one-time or monthly payment—usually three dollars, or the price of a cup of coffee.

In recent years, some cosplay professionals and models have turned to another platform, OnlyFans. Founded in 2016, the British website allows individuals to create accounts and post content privately for paying subscribers, like Patreon.

The company has highlighted the growing number of cosplayers on the platform, noting that they fall into a weird niche that's somewhat outside of mainstream influencers, and that they can run into copyright issues. "Cosplay creators are turning to OnlyFans to generate income by providing exclusive content, like behind-the-scenes

---

34   M Blackburn in conversation with the author, February 2020.

footage, character videos, and direct message content for their loyal fans who are willing to subscribe to see more."[35]

Compared to other social media sites like Instagram, Facebook, or Twitter, the site is far more permissive of adult content, which has made it popular with adult film stars and models.[36] Given the performative nature of cosplay, some cosplayers have found that modeling, boudoir photo shoots, and explicit content can be a reliable source of income. With the tiered structure offered up by these platforms, cosplayers can provide segmented offerings for backers, ranging from relatively tame content to galleries of more risqué photos or videos.

Despite its reputation as a platform for pornography, OnlyFans is part of a much larger online movement: it allows content creators to offer the feeling of a one-on-one relationship with their followers, turning massive fan bases into a revenue stream. Twitter introduced "Super Followers" in 2021, while newsletter platforms Substack, Revue, Ghost, and others have allowed writers (myself included) to build their own followings, one subscription at a time. A sexual element isn't required for this to work, either: some cosplayers have set up accounts on Patreon and OnlyFans, offering up perks like behind-the-scenes looks at their builds, or merch like stickers or signed photographs.

These sites do what was previously unheard of: provide the ability to cosplay for a living, rather than treating it as a hobby or side hustle. While cosplaying full-time isn't the norm, more individuals are finding that they can forge their own career within the community. As that community grows, there will be more demand for such content, and a larger audience willing to pay to support cosplayers for their work on a sustainable basis.

---

35   Julia Mascetti, "Cosplay Creators on OnlyFans," OnlyFans (blog), August 21, 2019, https://blog.onlyfans.com/cosplay-creators-on-onlyfans.
36   Jacob Bernstein, "How OnlyFans Changed Sex Work Forever," *New York Times*, February 9, 2019, https://www.nytimes.com/2019/02/09/style/onlyfans-porn-stars.html.

23 CYCLES OF COSTUMING

Within the original cosplay circuit at science-fiction conventions, costumes have always been a way to express one's fandom in a social setting. Worldcon and others continue to hold masquerade balls that involve prizes and spectators. These were initially casual affairs with con-goers assembling a costume to take part, and while the activity largely hasn't changed, these costumers were once more limited in the number of places they could wear their outfits: Worldcon is held only once a year, and a participant might be near a regional con or two. But with the recent proliferation of conventions all over the world, costumers have plenty of opportunities to make use of their creations.

Art Andrews of the Replica Prop Forum noted that as cosplay has grown, a new pattern of behavior has emerged on the scene: costumes rotate in and out of use. Within the prop replica community and groups like the 501st and Rebel Legions, it's not uncommon to see a cosplayer spend months or even years working on their costume, taking the time to identify and install components to ensure that their work is as screen accurate as possible.

For groups like the 501st and Rebel Legions, building a replica costume is part of their mission, and entry requirements are such that potential members must ensure that their costumes adhere to the group's standards, which are based on the costumes seen onscreen. Similarly, fan groups for franchises such as *Ghostbusters* or *Star Trek* also look closely to the screen as a guide for creating costumes.

When a cosplayer puts this much effort into one costume, it likely means that they'll wear it more than once. (I'm one of those costumers—I used my first stormtrooper for more than a decade before upgrading to a more accurate version, and as I've added suits of armor to my repertoire, I've used them frequently, repairing and upgrading them to keep them in wearable condition.) A costume like a set of stormtrooper armor is perennially popular at cons, and you'll likely see a handful of these at any given one you attend.

With greater access to expertise, materials, and tools, the cosplay and costuming scene has dramatically transformed since it started in the 1930s, thanks in part to the shared distribution of knowledge and labor. As it becomes easier to make and build costumes, more people partake in the hobby. Moreover, this ease of access to materials and expertise allows people who build costumes to follow the trends of the moment, creating a cyclical parade of popular costumes that are put aside when the next hit character makes their debut.

"This is one of the huge changes that I've seen from costuming to cosplay," Andrews explained. "The first time we saw that was *The Dark Knight* and [Heath Ledger's] Joker. People went *insane* for that costume. But it was a big deal for one season, then nobody cared. And nobody cares today."

Andrews suspects that there is a generational element at play. Fans who saw *Alien*, *Ghostbusters*, *Star Wars*, or *Terminator* in theaters as kids became quite attached to those stories in part because they were part of a limited selection of science-fiction or fantasy films hitting theaters at the time. Those costumers made up a bulk of the replica props community: now grown up, they have the ability, resources, and free time to build the costumes and props that they fell in love with as kids. "We've started to see that more as a trend,

Members of the 501st Legion's Green Mountain Squad gather in Burlington, Vermont, for a build day ahead of the release of *The Force Awakens* in 2015.
Courtesy of Andrew Liptak

A cosplayer poses with a ghost trap at Granite State Comic Con in Manchester, New Hampshire, in May 2011.

Courtesy of Andrew Liptak

Han, of Ottawa, Canada, poses as ka Lee from the anime series *Macross ntier*.

rtesy of Bryan Cruz

where before you have people making stuff for thirty years, from movies from thirty years ago, but they still love those movies," Andrews says.

Fast-forward a couple of decades, and the media landscape has completely changed. Genre films are no longer an oddity in theaters; it seems as though films that appeal to science-fiction or fantasy fans debut every other week, along with the flood of genre television shows and video games that have saturated the market. More content simply means more inspiration for cosplayers, and with new conventions out there, there are more places to wear costumes. Lin Han, a cosplayer from Ottawa, Canada, explained that one side effect of this is that cosplayers face an ever-increasing pressure to build and debut specific costumes at conventions. "You see series within anime or video games that become incredibly popular, and then people do costumes from them during that season, and then they move on very quickly."

In some ways, it's a trend that's almost like fast fashion—an industrial production model that allows companies to quickly respond to the latest trends and release hot-ticket items to the public as soon as possible. "The turnaround time has become much faster," Han says. "There's a lot of popularity in there, where people are going to try and do the newest thing, whatever the newest costume is."

She pointed to one example from 2019: *Fire Emblem: Three Houses*. "Everybody is doing it, but before that there was something else that was very popular, so people moved on very quickly." Han echoed Andrews's sentiment about generational factors: "That's also part of this new generation, where everything just happens very quickly, and there are a lot of new properties coming and something exciting is happening all the time."

The result is that if you walk into a convention hall

CYCLES OF COSTUMING

241

Members of the 501st Legion's New England Garrison at the 2010 Woburn Halloween Parade in Woburn, Massachusetts. The stormtrooper costume hasn't gone out of style and is consistently popular with fans and builders.

Courtesy of Andrew Liptak

on any given year, you'll likely see before you a good representation of what's popular at the moment in entertainment. But there's a downside to this: costumes simply don't get the same attention to detail that they used to. "When you look at something like the Praetorian Guard from *The Last Jedi*," Andrews says, "how long will people be making those? Maybe one or two people. It doesn't last the way it used to."

Those costumes might still pop up at conventions or within dedicated communities like the 501st and Rebel Legions, but they simply don't have the staying power of the original iconic stormtrooper. "Those characters are hot and those communities pop up, but do they last as a community, and are you creating long-term relationships there?" Andrews pondered. "Some of the people from the [Replica Props Forum] I have known for over twenty years, and we have a lot of mileage behind us. These are lifelong friendships, and we've learned from each other. I'm not sure you can quite get that from these smaller groups."[1]

Bill Doran of Punished Props explained that he's observed a similar phenomenon: whereas he might make a single new costume a year, he's seen people making a new costume every month. "This is just me guessing, but I think early on in the RPF, their focus was on quality," he noted. "They wanted it to be one-to-one; the goal was to use your craft to perfectly replicate this thing as closely as possible."

That seems to have changed a bit in recent years: the modern cosplay scene seems to prize speed and relevance over the screen accuracy that earlier cosplayers prized. "There

---

1 Art Andrews in conversation with the author, January 2020.

LEFT: Bill Doran poses in a suit of "impact armor" that he custom made from EVA foam, at Dragon Con in August 2019. *Courtesy of Bill Doran*

RIGHT: A cosplayer poses at FAN EXPO Boston in August 2021. Catwoman is one example of a character that remains popular with cosplayers, whether it's because there are new versions, it's easy to put together, or it's just plain iconic. *Courtesy of Andrew Liptak*

are two different sets of values and goals," Doran said. "I think that it's also having techniques and better materials that are very quick to work with. I think we can satisfy that goal of building your costume quickly and wearing it to one or two conventions. That's what they want to do—they want to just be that character, go to that convention with their friends, and have a good time."

Certainly, some costumes are perennial: you'll easily find superhero staples like Spider-Man, Superman, Wolverine, variations of The Doctor, stormtroopers, and others year after year. But cosplayers will react to the projects that have recently come out in theaters and on streaming services. In 2016, Harley Quinn was one of the hottest costumes at San Diego Comic-Con, due in part to the impending release of *Suicide Squad* later that summer—as well as her appearance in the New 52 comic series and the Arkham video games.[2] At SDCC in 2017, there were still plenty of Harley Quinns running around, but she had been overtaken by another DC superheroine, Wonder Woman, due in part to the release of Patty Jenkins's film earlier that summer.[3] Since then, other popular costumes have included

---

2 Jacob Kastrenakes, "Harley Quinn Cosplayers Are Taking Over Comic-Con," *The Verge*, July 23, 2016, https://www.theverge.com/2016/7/23/12263556/harley-quinn-cosplay-sdcc-2016-harleypalooza.
3 Andrew Liptak, "The Popularity of Wonder Woman Cosplay at Comic-Con Is a Message to Hollywood,"

Cosplayers pose as two different versions of DC's Wonder Woman at FAN EXPO Boston. Following the release of Patty Jenkins's 2017 film, *Wonder Woman*, there's been a resurgence of depictions of the character.

Photos courtesy of Andrew Liptak

Some characters are easy to replicate, and thus become extremely popular with cosplayers—this Bean from Netflix's *Disenchantment* nailed not only the look but also the attitude of the character at FAN EXPO Boston in 2019.

variations of Spider-Man from *Into the Spider-Verse*, Deadpool, Hela from *Thor: Ragnarok*, Black Panther, Link or Zelda from *Breath of the Wild*, Bean from Netflix's *Disenchantment*, Rey from *The Force Awakens*, and Joaquin Phoenix's Joker.

    This type of character churn happens for a couple of reasons. These costumes are more widely available, meaning that it's far easier for a cosplayer to assemble one for a convention before moving on to the next thing. Some still require work—foam for Wonder Woman's armor; or resin, 3D printing, or papier-mâché for *Thor: Ragnarok*'s Hela—while others are extremely simple: one can easily go to Amazon or Etsy to find any variation of Spider-Man. I was able to assemble the broken-down Peter Parker from *Into the Spider-Verse* with a green jacket, sneaker, hiking boot, gray sweatpants, and a Spider-Man–themed compression shirt I found on eBay—but I wasn't the only one who showed up in similar garb.

    There's also a sense of one-upmanship that takes place at conventions. Cosplayers are

---

The Verge, July 28, 2017, https://www.theverge.com/2017/7/28/16034094/wonder-woman-cosplay-san-diego-comic-con-message-hollywood-sdcc-2017.

Cosplayer Zlecky poses at Florida Supercon in Miami in 2019, showing off a literal moment in *Spider-Man: Into the Spider-Verse*. It's an excellent example of how cosplay can go beyond not just replicating costumes, but also notable scenes.

Courtesy of Lyle Peele

a community of skilled builders and makers, and cosplay is performative not just in terms of the characters but for the craftsmanship that goes into costumes as well. The primary objective of a cosplayer working on an ambitious build might be to show off their skills to their friends and rivals, and then they move on to the next challenge for the *next* convention or *next* season of costuming. In this way, the cosplay scene seems to take a page from the fashion world: people want to stay up-to-date in the season's latest outfit.

Accordingly, costumes that might have wowed a convention floor two decades ago, such as a stormtrooper costume, will barely turn heads nowadays, whereas an updated character like a well-constructed Captain Rex from *The Clone Wars* or Sith trooper from *The Rise of Skywalker* will garner attention and views on social media.

This cyclical behavior goes beyond the costumes themselves: some cosplayers capture topical character moments from popular films. One of the best examples that I saw of this was from *Into the Spider-Verse*. One cosplayer didn't dress up as Spider-Man, but as one of the anonymous scientists in the background. In one of the movie's scenes, Peter B. Parker steals a bagel from the cafeteria of a scientific facility. As he and Miles Morales escape, Miles throws the bagel at their pursuers, hitting one on the head. Instead of a sound effect like "*Pow!*" or "*Bam!*" the onscreen caption read "*BAGEL!*"[4] It's a genuinely funny bit in the film, and this particular cosplayer captured the moment by re-creating the word bubble over her head. Other cosplayers have used costumes to replicate the internet memes that flood social media—the Distracted Boyfriend, in which a man in the picture ogles a woman in front of his very irritated girlfriend,[5] is perfect for

---

[4] creepy knees, @creepyknees, "someone cosplayed the bagel sound effect from spiderverse and gave me a sticker im losing my MIND," Twitter, July 6, 2019, 11:19 a.m., https://twitter.com/creepyknees/status/1147525599310811136.

[5] "Distracted Boyfriend," Know Your Meme (website), accessed December 7, 2021, https://knowyourmeme.com/memes/distracted-boyfriend.

impromptu photo shoots at conventions, as cosplayers call attention to the tendency to always look for the next cool costume or hot character.[6]

Andrews notes that something gets lost when cosplayers churn through costumes quickly: costumers don't seem to pay heed to the same level of detail that they used to, identifying individual components on Boba Fett's armor. If there is one driving reason behind this, it's that by the time someone finishes their research on a costume months or years later, the costuming scene will likely already have shifted to the next hot character. This isn't to say that one mode is necessarily better or worse than the other, but there's value in that intense focus on a single costume, as a community, as a way to document costumes or apply new approaches to building them.

There are a few bulwarks to this: for example, Facebook groups like Shoretrooper Fam have created a durable community around one character, helping to keep that enthusiasm and research going for a figure that first briefly appeared in *Rogue One* in 2016, and later in the live-action shows *The Mandalorian* and *Andor*. Despite this limited number of appearances, the costume remains popular with fans, not only because of its appearance, but because it's been incubated by the community that's sprung up around it. These dedicated cosplayers devote lots of time to getting the details right, and they show up at events kitted out in the armor.

Popularity also isn't distributed evenly: it's probably safe to say that Christopher Nolan's *The Dark Knight* is remembered more clearly than Zack Snyder's *Batman v Superman* or David Ayer's *Suicide Squad*, and, accordingly, you'll still see people dressing up as Christian Bale's Batman in addition to Ben Affleck's, soon to be joined by Robert Patterson's version of the character in this year's release of *The Batman*. Similarly, Netflix's cyberpunk series

Cosplayers bought Columbia's replica *Empire Strikes Back* crew snow suits, and staged a moment replicating the filming of a film at Star Wars Celebration 2019.

Courtesy of Andrew Liptak

---

6   @jujukitty2323, "Oh my! This lil pic has blown up all over the place!!! Thank you @socalcostumes and @grifincostumes for the fantastic meme idea and letting me be a part of it!! And of course, thank you @wasted_fett for capturing it so perfectly!!" Instagram photo, July 2018, https://www.instagram.com/p/BllPoVagJZo.

Shoretroopers initially appeared for only a couple of brief moments in *Rogue One: A Star Wars Story*, but a devoted group of builders ensures that the costume remains a popular one. It's since popped up in *The Mandalorian, Andor,* and *Star Wars: Battlefront II*. A group of troopers pose at *Star Wars* Celebration in Chicago, Illinois, in 2019.

Courtesy of Andrew Liptak

Altered Carbon was largely critically acclaimed, but was only talked about for a couple of weeks after it was released: it simply didn't make as strong an impression on the cultural zeitgeist as another, ongoing series on Netflix, *Stranger Things*. As a result, you will see far more people dressing up as the characters from the latter than the former at a convention.

Some cosplayers lament the churn that occurs, especially in environments where uniformity and familiarity are useful. As Rebel Legion member Mark Poutenis explained to me, "I wish that people would self-police themselves and think about the greater issue," pointing to instances of 501st events that might have one or two stormtroopers outnumbered by more obscure characters. "People complain that they wanted to troop as a character from this one *Star Wars* video game, that only a small, small portion of fandom even knows about, let alone the general public," he explains. "Know your audience. Cons? That's the time to do something obscure and weird, because people geek out over the fact that you did something so unknown. You don't go to Fenway Park and do that, because people are like, 'What are you supposed to be?' People get upset about this! You go to a hospital troop, people want to see Princess Leia rather than Galen Marek, [a.k.a.] Starkiller."[7]

■ REPLENISHMENT

While at Dragon Con 2019, I watched as members of the *Battlestar Galactica* community came together to take a group picture. As they waited to assemble, attendees chat-

---

7   Mark Poutenis in conversation with the author, January 2020.

ted in groups, comparing costumes and reminiscing about the show that brought them all together. It was an impressive showing for a television show that had been off the air for a decade: dozens of officers, soldiers, and cylons from the series (mostly from Ronald D. Moore's reboot, but some from the original series) lined up on a staircase.

In the coming decade, we will certainly be inundated with new anime, books, comics, films, TV shows, video games, and more. We'll have plenty of new installments of established franchises from the likes of DC, Lucasfilm, and Marvel, as well as any number of new projects that will hit theaters or streaming services and gain a massive following. These will inspire an endless parade of new costumes and lead to more fan groups and followings.

A photographer directs a group of *Battlestar Galactica* cosplayers at Dragon Con 2019 in Atlanta, Georgia.

Courtesy of Andrew Liptak

The high turnout of the *Battlestar Galactica* group speaks to the quality and lasting appeal of the series during its original run; it still pops up as a highly recommended show for genre fans. But members have noted that the group doesn't have the same presence as other franchises. You might see a cosplayer or two dress up as Lee Adama or Starbuck at any given convention, but over the course of that Dragon Con weekend, group pictures for projects like *Game of Thrones* dwarfed their numbers by a considerable margin. That could change: as of 2022, NBC is planning a relaunch of the franchise with a new film and streaming show, which could bring an influx of fans into future group pictures once it's released.

The lack of new material or content from IP holders can have a detrimental effect on cosplay groups. Costuming communities certainly don't need to be juggernauts like the 501st or Rebel Legions, but people lose interest, drift off, or find other projects. Without new endeavors, cosplayer groups will eventually disintegrate. With regular original installments, fan groups for franchises like *Star Wars* and *Star Trek* will continue to live on, bolstered not only by their enduring popularity but also the infusion of additional costumes on a roughly annual basis.

24 FROM FAN TO PRO

As cosplay has grown in popularity, it has greatly evolved in range, providing practitioners with ample opportunity to dress up as their favorite characters, and even to take that passion a step further.

Cosplayers have found that the skills they learn in their hobby can transfer over to other avenues of their lives, prompting some to find work in the costuming or props industries that support major studio productions. For others, the growing cosplay world means that there is plenty of demand for people to purchase costumes and props from them. Still others have found that their massive social media followings can help support them full-time as cosplay personalities, utilizing new platforms to generate income from fans around the world.

Adam Savage explained that sites like the Replica Prop Forum attracted a number of like-minded people, becoming a sort of incubator for talent. "The brain trusts that became the foundation of HDC Fabrication and Master Replicas, Props Summit, the GBFans Forum, and The R2 Builders Club—all of those guys came out of the Replica Prop Forum."

That confluence of talent that began on the RPF helped form the foundation of the modern cosplay movement, by developing a generation of amateur makers whose skills underpinned the eventual development of large-scale groups.

More than that, the RPF helped a number of talented individuals to not only hone

An R2-D2 replica constructed by Bob Gouveia poses for a picture at FAN EXPO Boston in 2021. Members of the R2-D2 Builders Club have built sophisticated robots to display and use at events: they're often equipped with electronics and motors that allow them to be controlled from a distance, giving bystanders the illusion that they're operating independently.

Courtesy of Andrew Liptak

their own making skills but be part of a community that provided an opportunity to launch businesses of their own. "Look at Marc Kitter from the Adventurebilt Hat Company," Savage explains. Kitter wanted a replica of the hat that Harrison Ford wore in *Indiana Jones and the Raiders of the Lost Ark*, but couldn't find a company that would make one to the original specifications. "So he teaches himself millinery, forms the Adventurebilt Hat Company, they make about forty to fifty hats a year, and when the [request for proposals] goes out for the fourth film, he gets the contract to make the canon *Raiders* hats. There are a lot of those stories."[1]

Art Andrews notes that he's seen many examples of fans who were able to break into the professional prop-making world due to skills they gained in the forums. "A great example is Harrison Krix of Volpin Props. He was literally a kid when he came to the RPF. That kid, growing his talent, going into business for himself, growing that business into something impressionable, and finding his niche in the gaming world, building trophies and displays for gaming companies.

"We have seen that over and over. What's really interesting is not to say that the RPF 'made' all these people that way, but it has played a part in the role of almost every major and minor player. When you look at Hollywood and Burbank and all the special effects shops from the generation that we idolized, they're now full of our kids making this stuff," Andrews says. "So much stuff for *The Mandalorian* was made by RPF guys! So much of the stuff in *The Rise of Skywalker*, even to the point of the models that were made for Solo of the *Millennium Falcon*—that was a guy who used to make Falcon models on the RPF!"[2]

---

1 Adam Savage in conversation with the author, December 2019.
2 Art Andrews in conversation with the author, January 2020.

COSTUME DESIGN

A modern Hollywood film is a complicated beast, and genre films, with their elaborate costumes, props, sets, and visual effects, are the products of the work of literally thousands of individuals who work to provide the producers, actors, and directors with the components they need to bring a fictional world to temporary life.

That necessity has given rise to numerous studios and shops that build the costumes, creatures, and props that appear in the finished film—even if it's only for a fleeting moment.

Cheralyn Lambeth explained to me that it was a love of costumes and Halloween that steered her in the direction of costuming as a profession. Her mother taught her to sew so that she could make the costumes on her own, and when she went to school, she "realized that you could actually make a career out of this."[3]

She ended up studying Dramatic Art at the University of North Carolina at Chapel Hill and went on to study at The Juilliard School in New York City. She worked on a number of Off-Broadway shows and school productions before finding work with several studios, including Jim Henson Productions, where she created Muppet costumes, and Paramount, where she was a production supervisor for Star Trek: The Experience and other projects. At the same time, she designed and produced her own costumes and worked on *Star Trek* fan films.

Lambeth noted that the rise of cosplay has been useful to some extent within the film industry. "Cosplay has made it a lot easier to create for the industry, as it now caters to the cosplayers who contribute to it," she explains. "I think it's easier to get a hold of certain materials and supplies much more so than it used to be because of that."

One example that she notes: "In *Star Trek: The Next Generation*, the original uniforms were closed with invisible zippers." The company that produced the components for the invisible zipper, she says, was about to phase it out, only to be persuaded to keep them in production after the show released, because there was a greater demand for them from cosplayers.

While cosplay as a larger movement existed when she was starting out in the 1990s, Lambeth explains that it wasn't a particularly popular thing, especially within the professional costuming world. "Industry professionals really looked down on cosplayers,"

---

[3] Cheralyn Lambeth in conversation with the author, January 2020.

she said. "The term wasn't popular at that time, and myself, I had to be careful to tell people in the industry that I did this kind of thing, because they considered it amateur."

That attitude has begun to change a bit, she notes. "It's not looked down on as it used to be, although it's interesting to know—and a lot of cosplayers are excellent and as good as professionals—that the process is a little different. A lot of cosplayers can go into the industry, but as cosplayers, they have months to work on things and to get the materials that they need, whereas in the industry, you might only have two or three days [to make something.]"

Frank Ippolito, the founder of prop studio Thingergy Inc., concurred. Speaking with me by phone in February 2020, he explained that he'd moved to Los Angeles in 2000, where he worked in makeup effects for a decade on projects like *Pirates of the Caribbean* and *The Chronicles of Riddick*. In 2010, he started picking up prop-making jobs and was able to start his own business making props for films. He noted he's had clients tell him that he should avoid using cosplayers to make things for his shop, and he's had bad experiences bringing them on, because the world of fan-building is enormously different from costume-building for movies. "Building something for a cosplayer or a hobbyist is totally different than building something for the film industry. If you need to build a costume that stands up on set, it has to be durable, adjustable, cleanable, and we have to build that costume in four weeks. That, verses a cosplayer who spends six months with only a self-imposed deadline and only has to fit them or their friends and is held together with hot glue or double-stick tape."[4]

Ippolito isn't dunking on cosplayers—he notes that many "make these things that really photograph well, but they just don't hold up in the same way for the abuse of filming." The professional-hobbyist divide essentially comes down to the fundamental difference between cosplay as a hobby and the professional props and costumes that they imitate: intention. Both costumes might look similar or even identical, but their construction differs in that they have very different roles to fulfill. But Ippolito notes that "they raise the bar for me because they do such a good job that I have to be that much better. It's tough sometimes, because some of these people are so talented!"

The environment that cosplay provides can be a useful one for those who discover that

---

[4] Frank Ippolito in conversation with the author, February 2020.

costume production and creation is what they want to do with their lives: it's an excellent way to hone one's skills working with everything from foam to plastic to resin. Speaking on the *Star Wars* costuming podcast *Armor Party* in 2021, costumer designer and 501st member Drew Hart explained that he had been a fan of the franchise for as long as he could remember, and after learning about the Mandalorian Mercs, he began building a costume to join the group. He ended up getting a job at a professional theater in New Hampshire before making the leap to pursue a career in Los Angeles. "It was just one freelance gig to the next to the next," he says. He picked up jobs as a costume assistant on film and TV productions, working on movies like *Little Women* and *Free Guy* before landing at Ironhead Studio, where he worked on projects like *The Mandalorian*, *WandaVision*, *Thunder Force*, and more.[5]

501st member Drew Hart poses for a picture at *Star Wars* Celebration in Chicago, Illinois, in 2019.

Courtesy of Andrew Liptak

▮ PROP SHOPS

Most cosplayers aren't interested in jumping from the ranks of fans to the ranks of Hollywood professionals; they simply want to express their fandom. But some are interested in turning that fandom into a full-time job, and by catering to the larger cosplay community, a few have been able to make that jump. Users on forums like the RPF have a long history of taking commissions for the items that they're equipped to make, building a name and reputation for themselves as the place to go if you want to get some particular part for your Boba Fett costume or an accurately machined lightsaber.

This pool of potential buyers has only grown as the price of equipment such as

---

5 "Armor Party with Drew 'The Costumer' Hart," June 29, 2021, in *Armor Party*, podcast, https://anchor.fm/armorparty/episodes/Armor-Party-with-Drew-The-Costumer-Hart-e13kqnq.

FROM FAN TO PRO 253

3D printers has dropped and it becomes easier to reach other cosplayers through social media. A maker working on their own could build a prop for themselves—but with a little extra effort based on what they've learned, they can now produce copies. Someone with a handful of 3D printers could turn their basement into a faux weapons factory, turning out blasters for other cosplayers looking for that one particular item.

Jeff Rodriquez II of DH-P/FX is one example: he sells a variety of components for cosplayers that were in persistent high demand through his Etsy storefront such as X-wing pilot helmets, comm pads, Mandalorian armor, blasters, stands, and more. Bob Gouveia set up Wretched Hive Creations, where he specializes in sculpting masks for *Star Wars* cosplayers, like Bith heads and hands or Ahsoka Tano headpieces.

Gouveia studied art and graphic design at the University of Massachusetts Lowell, where he had picked up techniques for sculpting and painting, and eventually joined the 501st Legion in New England. When he was laid off from his regular graphic design job, he began looking for other work, eventually landing as a freelancer for Timberland. As a side project, he pitched the company some ideas for new displays: clear boots cast in resin to look like ice, or boots floating on champagne fountains. He sculpted and executed the designs, which ended up in stores across the country.

When his daughter wanted to dress up as Ahsoka Tano from *The Clone Wars*, he began to learn how to make a rubber headdress of his own for her. When other fans started asking if he'd make them one too, he started Wretched Hive Creations in a makerspace in Lowell, Massachusetts, in 2017. There, he began sculpting his own molds, layering in fine details and texture to make the parts look lifelike. Since establishing the shop, he's moved into other masks as well: masks for Emperor Palpatine, Maz Kanata, and Bith musicians. His head-

In 2017, Bob Gouveia set up Wretched Hive Creations in Lowell, Massachusetts, where he started making his own replica masks for the *Star Wars* costuming community.

Courtesy of Andrew Liptak

dresses are in high demand: he noted that he's had a monthslong waiting list, and as long as these characters continue to return as part of the franchise, it's likely to stay that way.[6]

IMPERIAL BOOTS

On the other side of the world, cosplayer and 501st member Vincent Rondia opened up a storefront of his own in 2015. Originally from Belgium but based in Shanghai, China, he was frustrated with the difficulty he'd experienced trying to find a handful of items, particularly the boots worn by stormtroopers. Working with his existing contacts in China's manufacturing sector, he was able to prototype and begin selling replica stormtrooper boots to the legions who were likewise coming up empty in their searches. Upon launching his website, Imperial Boots, he was quickly inundated. "Three days later, I had to shut it down because there were too many orders. We weren't ready, we could not make that many boots, and there was no way we could ship all of them."[7]

Rondia explained that he and his team closely researched the boots to figure out the right patterns and materials, then worked with a network of small shops in the region. "I don't think we could do what we're doing if we weren't in a country [with resources] similar to what China has to offer," he said. "When we make a shoe, we look at all the reference materials to try and figure out what the sole looks like. If you take a [First Order stormtrooper] shoe, we never found a real-world one, unlike the shoretroopers, which used Orca Bay shoes. So we had to look carefully at the sole, and found something that was a ninety-five percent match to the one that they had. And then, we're limited in size and so forth."

From boots, he slowly drifted into other costume parts, and his offerings exploded. Soon, he was selling the soft (i.e., non-armor) components for scout troopers, Boba Fett, royal guards, TIE pilots, stormtroopers, AT-ST drivers, Rebel pilots, and more. What's more, he began to bundle the various components into costume packages.

When I decided that I wanted to suit up as one of the X-wing pilots (General Antoc Merrick) from *Rogue One: A Star Wars Story* in the summer of 2019, Rondia's store proved to be a nearly one-stop shop. For around $800, I was able to pick up a flight suit, the flak vest, white gloves, ejection harness, belt, boots, and ammunition bandolier. Just weeks

---

6   Bob Gouveia in conversation with the author, January 2020.
7   Vincent Rondia in conversation with the author, July 2019.

When I ordered my costume from Imperial Boots in the fall of 2019, I got what looked like a professionally produced outfit within a couple of weeks.

Courtesy of Andrew Liptak

after placing my order, it arrived in a large box, direct from China. Another order to DH-P/FX's Etsy store got me the required comm pad, chest box, and X-wing pilot helmet kit that I needed to complete the ensemble.

This is a transaction that would've been inconceivable even a couple of years ago. The craftsmanship on the suit is comparable to any garment that you might purchase from a regular store—and it very well might have been made in one of the same factories.

China offered Rondia some advantages. "If you go to the right places, you'll find fifty or a hundred manufacturers making soles. Look at their catalogs, and you're okay to buy from them, provided you're able to buy a bunch in advance. Then you can make [the boot]," he explains. "China has been the heartland of production for such a long time, all of these manufacturers are still around. We talk to them and find the materials." He notes that they buy from a number of different factories because every costume is different. "I'm in with probably three factories for different fabrics, I have two for glove leather, three for shoe leather (because of different colors), and I have a supplier who does all our aluminum parts for us." He says it can be a "total nightmare," because prices fluctuate wildly, and products may be discontinued without warning. "It's a lot of work."

Rondia acknowledged that his business exists on the whim of corporate inattention and urgency. While Halloween is a multibillion-dollar industry, the market for high-quality movie replicas remains infinitesimally small: it's not large enough for major companies to crack down with cease and desists, and the benefit that this type of community provides the franchise owners likely outweighs the negatives.

part four

Legality/
Franchise
Support

25 FAN WORKS

If there was one thing that made *Star Wars* fans sit up and realize that they could possess their very own suit of stormtrooper armor, it was a ten-minute short film called *Troops*, which premiered at San Diego Comic-Con in 1997 and was later hosted on *Star Wars* fan website TheForce.net. The film was a mockumentary that imagined the stormtroopers of Tatooine in the form of the TV show *Cops*. Its release set off a flood of imitators and other projects from budding filmmakers who realized that they, too, could tell their own stories in a galaxy far, far away.

Fan films are what they sound like: unofficial productions put together by fans of a particular existing property, part of a much larger movement of fan-generated work that includes fields like fan art, fan fiction, fanzines, and even cosplay.

Fandom contains multitudes, and while some people are simply content to just take in the stories that they read or watch, others want to engage with their favorite properties directly. It's a movement that goes back as far as fandom itself, as aspiring science-fiction writers and fans penned their own short stories in fanzines. The field has ebbed and flowed over the decades, but got its biggest shot in the arm with the premiere of *Star Trek* in 1966. These new fans were hungry for new material, and turned their efforts to writing their own stories, fan fiction, which became a major fixture within the franchise's fan community.

The movement of fan writers allowed not only for aspiring professionals to fine-tune their craft but for fans to put their own interpretation out there for others to read, canon or no. Many professional authors got their start writing fanfic, with some even able to publish their own novels after they sufficiently altered the texts to avoid infringing on the original property.

Fan films are another facet of that world. As franchises like *Star Wars* and *Star Trek* established themselves in theaters, and as Marvel and DC later expanded their comic book universes, fans naturally made their own works based on those worlds with Super 8 cameras and other emerging technologies. These works didn't travel far, if at all.

In the late 1990s, Kevin Rubio began planning out his own story, imagining what the life of a stormtrooper out on patrol might be. In 2008, he told The Force.net that he and his crew were just were fooling around: "All any of us was trying to do was carve a place for ourselves in the industry . . . *Troops* was initially an attempt to ride the current 'wave/trend' in Hollywood that was getting people noticed."[1]

He recruited five people—Eric Hilleary, David Max, Caleb Skinner, and Kohar and Kenar Yegyayan[2]—to play the troopers on patrol as they work to track down a missing droid. Rubio explained that the costumes ended up being the hardest part of the project. "You can't just walk into a costume rental place and get an SW outfit. Every costume shop thought I meant 'Nazi' stormtrooper. Fortunately, I was able to hook up with five very talented artists from the ArtCenter College of Design in Pasadena. Each person made their own outfit from scratch."[3]

Troops' impact after its release was twofold. First, it kick-started an entire microindustry within fandom: the *Star Wars* fan film. It showed that such a format was possible with high-quality costumes, and its distribution on sites like TheForce.net helped to popularize that notion. Secondly, it demonstrated to fans that armor could be more than just an expensive Halloween costume: you really could put yourself in the *Star Wars* universe.

Fan filmmakers weren't limited to just *Star Wars* projects. Fans of *Doctor Who* and *Star Trek* helmed their own short films, with the latter developing an impressive follow-

---

1 Dustin, "TROOPS: Ten Years Later," TheForce.net, accessed January 20, 2022, https://www.theforce.net/fanfilms/story/TROOPS_Ten_Years_Later_112870.asp.
2 Kevin Rubio, "A Word from Kevin Rubio: Director of *Troops*," TheForce.net, accessed December 7, 2021, http://www.theforce.net/fanfilms/shortfilms/troops/director_index.asp.
3 Chris Gore, "*Troops*: C.O.P.S. Meets Stormtroopers in a Galaxy Far, Far Away . . . ," TheForce.net, accessed December 7, 2021, http://www.theforce.net/troops.olde/troops.shtml.

The main bridge of the starship Enterprise, *re-created in Ticonderoga, New York, as part of* Star Trek *Tours, a walkable, fan-made museum to the franchise.*

Courtesy of Andrew Liptak

ing. Fans like James Cawley went to great lengths to produce their own *Star Trek* fan films; he built an exact replica of the original *Enterprise* sets in Ticonderoga, New York, which he used for fan films and as a licensed *Star Trek* attraction. (As of 2021, he is hard at work building a replica of the *Enterprise* from *The Next Generation*.)[4] Other *Star Trek* fan filmmakers utilized top-of-the-line special effects and brought on some of the show's original actors to reprise their roles.

These projects relied heavily on cosplayers and the techniques they had developed to replicate the costumes and accessories that brought the worlds back to life. Throughout the 1990s, Jack Durnin made his own costumes and sets while in high school and college, and he went on to shoot his own short films, eventually putting together an unofficial sequel to Peter Jackson's *The Lord of the Rings*. "I made tons of costumes and props for that," he explained at Dragon Con in 2019. "I like telling stories, but I'm also an engineer and like figuring out how to make things." For that project, he ended up building interior sets, designing a medieval village, and outfitting an entire army. The experience brought him to cosplay as he figured out how to design and construct his own costumes and armor.

---

4   Cat Viglienzoni, "Sneak Peek at *Star Trek: The Next Generation* Set Under Construction in Northern NY," WCAX, September 29, 2021, https://www.wcax.com/2021/09/29/sneak-peek-star-trek-next-generation-set-under-construction-northern-ny.

Jack Durnin filming a battle in his *The Lord of the Rings* fan film.

Courtesy of Jack Durnin

In another notable instance, the drama students of North Bergen High School in New Jersey staged an ambitious remake of Ridley Scott's science-fiction horror film *Alien* in 2019.[5] Students constructed the sets and costumes from whatever they could find; in prior years they had also constructed a replica of the Iron Throne from *Game of Thrones* with cardboard dowels, paint cups, cardboard, and metallic paint. For their Space Jockey set for the *Alien* play, they used EVA foam, tubing, and a recycled desk.[6] While not entirely accurate to the screen, the result blew away audiences both in the theater and online, because they had adapted the story so thoughtfully for the stage.

Cosplay and fan films essentially fall under the same massive umbrella: the creative expression of one's passion for a story. Pulling from the same sources of inspiration, fan films are a step beyond cosplay; where the latter puts an individual in the shoes of a character, the fan film re-creates an entire world and extends the story for a new adventure.

---

5 "Adam Savage Checks in With North Bergen Student Cosplayers," Adam Savage's Tested, filmed and edited by Joey Fameli, produced by Kristen Lomasney, YouTube video, November 6, 2019, https://www.youtube.com/watch?v=Bu1y4m7Y738.

6 "Adam Savage Tours North Bergen High School's *Alien: The Play* Artifacts!" Adam Savage's Tested, filmed and edited by Joey Fameli, produced by Kristen Lomasney, YouTube video, November 6, 2019, https://www.youtube.com/watch?v=giSvH_EYWCo.

26 WALKING, TALKING COPYRIGHT VIOLATION: INTELLECTUAL PROPERTY

Throughout the mid-1990s, the replica props and costuming world operated out of sight and under the radar in order to avoid attracting the potential ire of one of the major studios' legal teams. If you wanted to buy a suit of stormtrooper armor, you had to know a guy who knew a guy; there were very few places that openly sold the costume to consumers.

While you can easily find costumes online through outlets like Etsy, most small prop shops manufacturing costume parts won't provide listings for you to simply add to a shopping cart and purchase like you might on Amazon (though there are some exceptions to this). In most cases, you'll have to contact the maker directly, get a quote, and send payment along via PayPal or another online payment service.

There's a reason for that: makers don't want to be sued into oblivion by a studio with enormous legal resources.

LEGAL THREATS

While the development of the Replica Prop Forum and other communities provided a safe environment for prop makers to operate in the mid-1990s, cosplayers and makers still faced significant hurdles. "At the time, it was very scary," Art Andrews recounted, noting that studios at the time were extremely litigious, and that a number of makers had been slapped with lawsuits for creating and selling their own replicas. Andrews hired a lawyer on retainer for The Dented Helmet to provide assistance to makers who had been approached by studio lawyers.

They had reason to be worried: as *Star Wars* costuming grew in prominence following the release of the special editions and prequel trilogy in the 1990s, fans flocked to the internet to set up their own websites, and some makers decided to capitalize on the surge in interest. The rise of makers producing and selling their own unlicensed costumes raised red flags at Lucasfilm.

"[Gerardo] Follano was the one that got the multimillion-dollar lawsuit from Lucasfilm in 2001," Jeff Allen recounted.[1] Follano was selling stormtrooper armor on his website in Canada and attracted the attention of Lucasfilm's lawyers. "They sent him a cease and desist, and he did not cease and desist." The studio asked for $100,000 per instance of infringement and an additional $50,000 in punitive damages.[2] Both sides eventually reached a settlement: Follano destroyed his original molds and stopped selling his suits online.

Studios had an obligation to protect their intellectual property, and Lucasfilm wasn't the only one exercising its rights. In October 2001, *STARFLEET Communiqué*, the official publication of the international *Star Trek* fan club, wrote about the Follano lawsuit, and noted that while Lucasfilm had been lenient, other studios were not, "especially Viacom—who owns Paramount/*Trek*, and Warner Brothers, who own *Babylon 5, Batman*, and quite a few others . . . crushing auctions on eBay, issuing not just cease and desist orders, but also demanding that the offending prop be turned over to them immediately."[3]

Rather than pursue smaller makers, Lucasfilm opted to go after larger targets. In 2004, Andrew Ainsworth, the original developer of the *Star Wars* stormtrooper suit, began to manufacture and sell costumes using the original molds from *A New Hope*, noting that "the movie memorabilia market had really grown in popularity," and that "there

---

1 Jeff Allen in conversation with the author, January 2020.
2 "Russell Crowe to Trip the Light Fantastic, Plus: Lucas Gets Litigious; Catherine Zeta-Jones Back in *Zorro*; Hitchhikers Guide to the Galaxy film on the Way – Maybe," The Guardian, July 20, 2001, https://www.theguardian.com/film/2001/jul/20/news.russellcrowe.
3 Ken Waid, "Prop Collecting: Days of Glory, Days of Darkness," *STARFLEET Communiqué*, October/November 2001, https://db.sfi.org/com/docs/CQ107.pdf.

was a great deal of interest in my authentic replicas."[4] Lucasfilm sued the maker, saying that his work infringed on their property, and in 2006, a US court awarded Lucasfilm $20 million in damages.

"The court found that Shepperton Design Studios had been marketing unlicensed copies of stormtrooper helmets and costumes, and TIE fighter pilot helmets from the *Star Wars* films, as well as making misleading claims about the authenticity and origins of these items," Lucasfilm wrote in a press release after the ruling, quoting Lucas Licensing president Howard Roffman as saying, "Infringers like Shepperton need to understand that we will pursue them anywhere in the world to shut them down and seek restitution."[5]

Ainsworth didn't back down: while he stopped selling the costume in the US, he took his suit to the UK court system, and it eventually made its way to the UK Supreme Court in 2011.[6] That court handed him a victory, ruling that he had the right to sell the costume in the UK.[7] Costumers based outside the US can still go to Shepperton Design Studio's website and purchase a costume directly from Ainsworth.

That threat of legal action had a chilling effect on the prop-making community: many feared that their interests and hobbies were under attack, and that makers might be legally obligated to pay millions for making and selling parts within their community. From a legal perspective, studios do have a compelling argument: fans producing their own costumes and selling them to others could eat into revenue that they might otherwise earn because those makers haven't bought a license to use the likeness of the costumes and props from the worlds that they adore.

But the fan-driven prop and costume community initially arose precisely *because* the studios weren't creating detailed replicas of those objects and garments at the time. Certainly there were plenty of toy blasters, phasers, helmets, and Halloween costumes

---

[4] "Our Story," Shepperton Design Studios + originalstormtrooper.com (website), accessed December 8, 2021, https://www.originalstormtrooper.com/our-story-19-w.asp.

[5] "Lucasfilm Ltd. Wins Major Copyright Infringement Lawsuit Against *Star Wars* Stormtrooper Pirate," Lucasfilm Ltd. Pressroom, October 11, 2006, https://web.archive.org/web/20110910135838/http://www.lucasfilm.com/press/news/news20061011.html.

[6] Stuart Kemp, "George Lucas' Lawsuit Over Stormtrooper Costumes Goes to U.K. Supreme Court," *Hollywood Reporter*, March 8, 2011, https://www.hollywoodreporter.com/thr-esq/george-lucas-lawsuit-stormtrooper-costumes-165318.

[7] Susan Krashinsky, "The Lucasfilm Empire Strikes Out," *Globe and Mail*, July 27, 2011, https://web.archive.org/web/20110728011544/https://www.theglobeandmail.com/report-on-business/international-news/european/the-lucasfilm-empire-strikes-out/article2112181.

on the marketplace, but these were aimed at a younger age bracket. The replica props community had other things in mind: producing high-quality fixtures from movies and television shows for either display or for serious costuming.

Andrews explained that each studio approached the community differently, but makers were commonly issued a cease and desist notice. "Considering what we do," he says, "studios have been incredibly lenient. But they used to be a lot harsher than they are today." He recognized that the legal system was daunting for both sides of the fence: prop makers could find themselves up against a formidable wall of lawyers from a major studio, while the studio's lawyers didn't know any of the makers or their intentions: they were just out to enforce the company's intellectual property rights.

Andrews, living in Las Vegas, began to attend the major licensing shows that took place annually there. "Almost all of the IP lawyers who are with the major stories attended," he explained, "and I've gotten to know them on a very personal level. Go out and drink and party with them, and once they know who you are, that changes the narrative a little bit."

That effort helped soften the approach a bit. Before, where a builder on the forum might get an official cease and desist from a law firm, they might now get an emailed warning. "We eventually developed a relationship where they understood that we weren't trying to screw them: we love their properties, and they're trying to promote it. That changed the way they dealt with us."

Andrews points to Lucasfilm as being one of the first studios to recognize that the existence of a fan community building prop replicas outweighed the effort that it took to send a cease and desist to each and every person potentially infringing on their IP. Following the lawsuit against Follano, Jeff Allen noted that Lucasfilm worked to allay some of the concerns of fan prop makers. "They see that the stormtroopers out there are free publicity. As long as you keep it hush-hush and under the radar and don't look like you're a gigantic company [of your own], they're not

Albin Johnson poses with two other troopers during a screening of *Star Wars: The Phantom Menace* in 1999.

Courtesy of Albin Johnson

going to send a cease and desist." Armor makers could continue what they were doing but had to keep it at a grassroots level.

Adam Savage explained that studios like Lucasfilm recognized the differences between a professional company and amateur builders, recounting a conversation that he'd had with the company's lead counsel over a poker game. "He said 'Oh, we know everything that's going on out there. We're not interested in shutting anyone down unless we see someone trying to turn a real profit. When someone sells stormtrooper armor for under a grand, we know that no one's making any money in that transaction. But as soon as you're selling twenty or thirty suits a year for more than that, that's when we want to come in and stop them.'"

Other studios eventually relaxed their stances, recognizing the benefits of an energetic and creative fan base. That acceptance on the part of major studios proved to be a key reason why the prop- and costume-making community began to take off. Without the constant threat of a legal takedown notice, prop makers could develop and sell their wares, provided they didn't do so too openly or attract too much notice. A fan constructing and selling a handful of highly accurate replicas of Han Solo's DL-44 blaster is catering to an extremely small market and would be allowed. But mass-producing something for a much bigger audience would likely result in a stern warning to cut it out.

While the threat of legal action isn't quite as pressing as it was in the 1990s and early 2000s, major studios will still act to enforce their rights. Following the release of *The Mandalorian* on Disney+, Disney issued hundreds of takedown notices for makers on Etsy who were manufacturing Baby Yoda merchandise, a flood of which arrived on the internet in the absence of official products.[8] Other makers have been handed takedown notices for Etsy listings for costume parts from properties like *Firefly* in 2013[9] and *The Elder Scrolls* in 2014.[10] In some cases, the takedown notices came when the studios sold costume licenses to other companies, meaning that there was potential competition between rights holders and unlicensed makers.

---

8   Chaim Gartenberg, "Disney Is Hunting Down the Most Popular Baby Yoda Toys on Etsy," *The Verge*, January 17, 2020, https://www.theverge.com/2020/1/17/21069124/baby-yoda-dolls-etsy-disney-mandalorian-copyright-takedown-enforcement.
9   Jill Pantozzi, "Are You a *Firefly* Fan Who Makes Jayne Hats? Watch Out, Fox Is Coming For You," *The Mary Sue*, April 9, 2013, https://www.themarysue.com/jayne-hats-fox.
10 Tarchinoko, "Zenimax Takedown Notice," The Replica Prop Forum (website), June 18, 2014, https://www.therpf.com/forums/threads/zenimax-takedown-notice.216090.

Some makers and *Star Wars* fans worried that the entry of license-holding companies like Rubie's and ANOVOS in the adult costuming field might spell the end of the fan-made stormtrooper scene. Indeed, ANOVOS's entry brought with it a flood of new members to the 501st, who could now easily buy and assemble their own armor.

STUDIO CONTROL AND CONTACT

The 501st Legion is an anomaly in its relationship with Lucasfilm—because it has so many willing, well-suited volunteers who work with and for the company, it has an unprecedented level of access to Lucasfilm, as well as its acceptance and approval.

This is no small thing: a group like the 501st Legion is utilizing a major corporation's intellectual property, largely with homemade or fan-created kits. Strictly speaking, this is an activity that a major company's legal team would likely want to crack down on in the name of preventing the unauthorized use of their IP. But by working with the 501st Legion, Lucasfilm was able to figure out how to make the situation work in just about everyone's favor. They could encourage the fan group to put into place certain rules and expectations: they wouldn't hire themselves out or appear with politicians, nor would they be allowed to appear in places like strip clubs or bars. In return, they would continue to exist, providing their services in a variety of ways, and would even be boosted in the public's eye by Lucas himself.

Steve Sansweet, the former head of fan relations for Lucasfilm, explained that in the late 1990s, shortly after the group was formed, he and his colleagues began to hear about fans dressing up in stormtrooper armor and working under the banner of the 501st Legion. "Lucasfilm became aware of the fact that there were a bunch of people out there wearing stormtrooper costumes and became a little concerned about it, and wasn't quite sure what to do."[11]

Sansweet says that he encountered the group at Dragon Con in 1997. "There was a 501st member who had set up a booth and was selling things," he recounted. "That was my first encounter, and I thought, 'This is going to raise hackles.' It was a very public demonstration." He began to investigate the 501st and came in contact with the group's

---

11   Steve Sansweet in conversation with the author, January 2020.

Members of the New England Garrison dressed as Delta Squad prepare to march in Woburn's Halloween Parade in Woburn, Massachusetts, in 2010. Together, they interact and play the part of the squad as seen in the video game from which they're inspired, *Republic Commando*.

Courtesy of Andrew Liptak

founder, Albin Johnson. "I had some initial conversations with Albin, to explain what Lucasfilm's view was, and the fact that Lucasfilm wasn't trying to shut it down. In my point of view, we welcomed it, because here we were in an era where we were releasing the movies, and we wanted to encourage fandom."

Lucasfilm opted to lay down some basic rules. Members of the 501st could make and sell their own merchandise like patches and coins internally, but not to the general public or for a profit. They also had to be careful where they appeared in public. "These rules evolved over some years," Sansweet says. "We didn't want someone in the 501st or Rebel Legion to go to a used car lot on a Saturday and be promoted as [official] characters. People needed to understand that these were fans dressing as *Star Wars* characters, [not] actual actors from the films or anything official."

LEGALITY

There have been instances where studios have cracked down hard on fan works. In 2014, a team of *Star Trek* fans produced a short fan film called *Prelude to Axanar,* a project with high production value and a number of professional actors in its cast, such as Gary Graham (*Star Trek: Enterprise*), Richard Hatch (*Battlestar Galactica*), Tony Todd (*The Flash*), and Kate Vernon (*Battlestar Galactica*). The team used the fan film as a stepping-stone for a larger fan film, *Axanar,* which they financed by launching a pair of crowdfunding campaigns. Together, they pulled in more than $1 million in fan pledges and began work. But in 2015, Paramount issued a lawsuit in federal court against Axanar Productions, saying that it went beyond that of a typical fan film and infringed on Paramount's property "by using innumerable copyrighted elements of *Star Trek*, including its settings, characters, species, and themes."[12] Although filmmakers J. J. Abrams (who directed *Star Trek* and *Star Trek Into Darkness*) and Justin Lin (*Star Trek Beyond*) urged Paramount executives to drop the lawsuit,[13] the company proceeded, and in 2017 a judge threw out the Axanar team's arguments that what they were doing fell under fair use.[14]

The lawsuit and verdict left a chilled effect on the *Star Trek* fan community, as well as the larger cosplay and fandom community. Paramount issued a ten-point list of guidelines for future fan films:[15] It limited the running time of each production to no more than fifteen minutes per standalone story or thirty for a two-part arc. They were not allowed to use the phrase "Star Trek" in the title, or clips from existing *Star Trek* productions, or any unlicensed merchandise or costumes. They could not pay their actors (or use actors from prior *Star Trek* productions), could not raise more than $50,000 from pledges, had to be family-friendly, had to use a disclaimer that it was a fan production, could not register a copyright, and could not imply that CBS or Paramount had endorsed the project.[16]

Axanar Productions eventually settled with Paramount,[17] announcing in 2019 that

The exterior of the *Star Trek* Original Series Set Tour in Ticonderoga, New York. The tour is a re-creation of the sets from the original iconic series, allowing visitors to walk through the halls of the Starship *Enterprise*.

Courtesy of Andrew Liptak

---

12   Eriq Gardner, "Crowdfunded *Star Trek* Movie Draws Lawsuit from Paramount, CBS," *Hollywood Reporter*, December 30, 2015, https://www.hollywoodreporter.com/thr-esq/crowdfunded-star-trek-movie-draws-851474.
13   Andrew Liptak, "Paramount's Lawsuit Against Axanar Productions *Star Trek* Fan Film is 'Going Away' (Updated), *io9*, May 21, 2016, https://io9.gizmodo.com/paramounts-lawsuit-against-axanar-productions-star-trek-1777959978.
14   Andrew Liptak, "*Star Trek* Fan Film Isn't Protected by Fair Use, Rules US Judge," *The Verge*, January 5, 2017, https://www.theverge.com/2017/1/5/14181534/star-trek-fan-film-copyright-lawsuit-paramount.
15   CBS & Paramount, "*Star Trek* Fan Film Guidelines Announced," *Star Trek* (website), June 22, 2016, https://www.startrek.com/article/star-trek-fan-film-guidelines-announced.
16   "Fan Films," *Star Trek* (website), accessed December 8, 2021, https://www.startrek.com/fan-films.
17   Andrew Liptak, "Axanar Has Settled Its Lawsuit with Paramount over Its *Star Trek* Fan Film," *The Verge*, January 20, 2017, https://www.theverge.com/2017/1/20/14340666/axanar-productions-settled-lawsuit-paramount-star-trek-fanfilm.

it would move forward under the new guidelines,[18] but other productions were left dead in the water. Jim Bray, a longtime *Star Trek* fan filmmaker, had planned a three-episode series called *Star Trek Anthology*, only to completely change his plans when Paramount issued its rules. Forced to abandon the uniforms that they had ordered from a Las Vegas costume designer, they started over with a new project, *The Outer Rim*, featuring new sets and costumes, launching their first installment in 2019.[19]

Is cosplay itself a *legal* activity? Certainly, makers walk a fine line when they manufacture and sell their own replicas without a studio license. And organized groups of cosplayers and fans can run into the ire of studios if it becomes clear that they're making a profit or otherwise acting in a way that impacts the studio's branding.

But how about the *act* of cosplay—dressing up and appearing as a character?

It's not entirely clear where the matter lies, but most proponents will point to the Fair Use doctrine within US copyright law. The US government describes it as the "legal doctrine that promotes freedom of expression by permitting the unlicensed use of copyright-protected works in certain circumstances."[20]

"Section 107, Limitations on exclusive rights: Fair use" states the following:

> The fair use of a copyrighted work, including such use by reproduction in copies or phonorecords or by any other means specified by that section, for purposes such as criticism, comment, news reporting, teaching (including multiple copies for classroom use), scholarship, or research, is not an infringement of copyright. In determining whether the use made of a work in any particular case is a fair use the factors to be considered shall include—
>
> (1) the purpose and character of the use, including whether such use is of a commercial nature or is for nonprofit educational purposes;
>
> (2) the nature of the copyrighted work;
>
> (3) the amount and substantiality of the portion used in relation to the copyrighted work as a whole; and

---

18 Jamie Lovett, "Star Trek Popular Fan Film 'Axanar' Resumes Production," ComicBook.com, February 28, 2019, https://comicbook.com/startrek/news/star-trek-axanar-resumes-production.
19 Ken Picard, "Vermont Trekkies Transport Original Film to New Universe," *Seven Days*, March 8, 2017, https://www.sevendaysvt.com/vermont/vermont-trekkies-transport-original-film-to-new-universe/Content?oid=4488020.
20 "More Information on Fair Use," US Copyright Office, last updated May 2021, accessed December 8, 2021, https://www.copyright.gov/fair-use/more-info.html.

(4) the effect of the use upon the potential market for or value of the copyrighted work.[21]

In essence, an individual is free to use a copyrighted character in certain situations, like teaching, research, and other instances as determined by the three criteria: Is it being used for commercial purposes? Is it being used in whole or in part? And will using it in a fair way impact the market or value of the work?

Creating a copy of a prop seen in a film and selling it (even not at a profit) violates this law, because that activity is a commercial one, and could damage the potential market for such an object. Advertising yourself as a costumed character and hiring yourself out for birthday parties as Superman or Spider-Man also isn't protected by that fair use doctrine. Indeed, Disney and other studios have sued companies using their characters, although said party companies have found ways around that by simply listing their characters as "Princess" or "Hairy Guy."[22]

In other instances, making and selling costumes for a profit without a licensing agreement will certainly lead makers afoul of studio legal departments, as in the case of Gerardo Follano in 2001, or the time a company from Shenzhen, China, promised to manufacture a high-quality Mark III Iron Man suit in 2013. Marvel put a stop to the project shortly after it was announced.[23] As more studios begin to recognize the potential market in prop replicas or costumes, makers have wondered if licensees will ask the studios to clamp down on fan-made productions to reduce the competition. That doesn't appear to have happened yet.

In some ways, the close relationships that studios like Lucasfilm have formed with groups like the 501st and Rebel Legions, or Microsoft with the 405th Infantry Division, help ensure that cosplayers stay within the fair use lines. Those groups are allowed to appear at events—although some require approval from the studio, which restricts certain

---

21 "Copyright Law of the United States (Title 17) and Related Laws Contained in Title 17 of the United States Code," US Copyright Office, updated May 2021, accessed December 8, 2021, https://www.copyright.gov/title17.
22 Eriq Gardner, "Disney Finds It's Not So Easy to Sue Over Knockoff Characters at Birthday Parties," *Hollywood Reporter*, August 13, 2018, https://www.hollywoodreporter.com/thr-esq/disney-finds-not-easy-sue-knock-characters-at-birthday-parties-1134235.
23 Darrell Etherington, "Crowdfunded Iron Man Suit Project Seeking 5K Pre-Orders for Production Run," *TechCrunch*, December 17, 2013, https://techcrunch.com/2013/12/17/iron-man-suit-pre-orders.

activities, like store appearances and concerts—but aren't permitted to charge for their services or say that they're officially part of the studio or franchise.

COSPLAY PROS

As cosplay has taken off and reached the mainstream, some entrepreneurial-minded cosplayers have realized that they can not only sustain their hobby but transform it into their full-time work, attending conventions and providing content for their followers. The rise of social media has led to a new model of advertising: the influencer, who is embedded enough in a particular scene or culture to be deemed credible by advertisers, and who can levy their reputation to pitch products, companies, or individuals to their followers.

In 2009, Jessica Nigri decided to attend San Diego Comic-Con in her "sexy Pikachu" costume. She was inundated by photographers at the convention, prompting her to go viral and catapulting her to a level of fame never seen before in the cosplay community. In the years since, she's built up an impressive following: more than a million followers on both Twitter and YouTube, four million on Instagram, and six million on Facebook, which she uses to show off her latest costumes. She has also worked as a spokesperson and model for a handful of games.

Other prominent cosplayers have found that they can make a full-time living as cosplayers through other avenues. Kamui Cosplay, made up of Svetlana and Benni Quindt, have been cosplaying since 2003, and have written a number of books designed to guide cosplayers in their own builds—*The Book of Foam Armor: Comfy & Affordable*, *The Book of Foam Props: Lightweight & Affordable*, and *The Book of Cosplay Armor Making: With Worbla and Wonderflex*—and have created downloadable patterns for everything from armor to helmets to props. They've partnered with companies like EA to produce costumes and tutorials based on their video games, including *Star Wars Battlefront II*[24] and *Anthem*.[25] Bill Doran of Punished Props has also produced a line

---

24   Kamui Cosplay, "Finished my Iden Versio cosplay from the single player campaign of EA Star Wars Battlefront 2. Get the game here: http://x.ea.com/46251 . . . ," Facebook, accessed December 8, 2021, // https://www.facebook.com/155539481141240/posts/finished-my-iden-versio-cosplay-from-the-single-player-campaign-of-ea-star-wars-/2109227382439097.
25   "Hammerhead Rifle Replica - Anthem," KamuiCosplay, YouTube video, March 11, 2019, https://www.youtube.com/watch?v=t9taaMg6YmU.

of books, called the *Foamsmith Trilogy*, designed to help cosplayers work with foam to make props and armor.[26]

In other instances, cosplayers don't necessarily need to make a full-time living with cosplay. Online influencers with a significant following might partner with any number of companies for useful sponsorships, devoting a post or two on Instagram or TikTok to highlight a product or service that they've been paid to promote. It could be an article of clothing, an electronic device, or a household good, and will sometimes come with an exclusive discount code that encourages the cosplayer's followers to check out said product. One example is a Los Angeles–based cosplayer who goes by the username bekahsoka, who has built up a significant following on Instagram and other platforms, and now serves as a brand ambassador for pop culture brands Her Universe and Heroes & Villains, which cater extensively to the dedicated fan community.

Some cosplayers also find that they can put their skills to work as a side gig, by producing armor, hard-to-find components, or sewn cloth garments and selling them directly to other cosplayers; or by taking on commissions for things like finished helmets, paint jobs, or entire costumes.

Others have built up other types of careers. Born in China in 1980, Yaya Han grew up watching anime from an early age. Following her parents' divorce, she went with her mother to Germany. Alone in a new country, as she explained in her 2020 book, *Yaya Han's World of Cosplay: A Guide to Fandom Costume Culture*, she found an escape in those animated worlds, and went on to study art. In 1998, she packed up and moved to the United States with the goal of becoming an animator for Disney. The transition in those early years was rough, but she discovered others with similar interests in anime and manga through clubs devoted to watching and drawing anime. "For the first time ever, I felt that I belonged to a community where people genuinely appreciated my artistic abilities and passion for Japanese animation," she wrote. "No matter how hard everyday life was, I had a little sanctuary where I could retreat to be myself, and that was worth staying for."[27]

Soon thereafter, Han discovered conventions. She attended Anime Expo in 1999 and was enamored of the idea that people could—and would!—dress up as their favorite

---

26 "Print books," Punished Props Academy, accessed December 8, 2021, https://www.punishedprops.com/product-category/print-books.
27 Yaya Han, *Yaya Han's World of Cosplay: A Guide to Fandom Costume Culture* (New York: Sterling, 2020), 15.

characters. The moment was a life-changing one for her that she says gave her direction. With help from friends, she dressed up as Kurama from Yoshihiro Togashi's manga series *YuYu Hakusho*. "In the end, my Kurama cosplay was unrecognizable, but I will never forget the feeling of putting it on for the first time," she wrote.[28] She began to focus on making more costumes and was soon invited to conventions around the world as an official guest and panelist, eventually accepting commissions from other cosplayers to make costumes and quitting her office job. Along with her partner, Brian Boling, she went freelance, turning what had previously been a side gig into a full-time vocation. As they stopped accepting commissions and focused on accessories and supplies, they began selling their products at conventions. In 2013, she appeared as a judge on Syfy's reality series *Heroes of Cosplay*—an experience she criticized in her book for being overly dramatic, deceptive, and unfaithful to the community she was part of. But it did serve as an introduction for many aspiring cosplayers, and she says that while it presented its difficulties and challenges, "I don't regret participating because the project did what I hoped it would: It brought new people into the world of cosplay."[29] The show opened up new opportunities for her: she partnered with the McCall Pattern Company to design patterns to sell to fabric and craft stores like JOANN, which led to other partnerships. She later released a line of cosplay fabrics with fabric manufacturer Wyla,[30] and then her own line of EVA foam. Most recently, she partnered with rotary tool manufacturer Dremel to market a new version of the tool, Dremel Lite.[31]

PRO ACTING

The skill set that cosplay imparts can also occasionally lead its practitioners into the entertainment industry.

Lucasfilm's close relationship with its costumed fan groups in particular has led to

---

28 Han, *Yaya Han's World of Cosplay*, 26.
29 Han, *Yaya Han's World of Cosplay*, 185.
30 "Calling All Cosplayers: The Yaya Han Cosplay Fabric Collection Exclusively Available at Jo-Ann Stores and Joann.com," *Business Wire*, March 16, 2016, https://www.businesswire.com/news/home/20160316006011/en/Calling-Cosplayers-Yaya-Han-Cosplay-Fabric-Collection.
31 "Dremel Partners with Yaya Han to Debut Dremel Lite to Cosplay," Dremel Newsroom, February 3, 2020, https://us.dremel.com/en_US/dremel-press-releases/-/asset_publisher/rSeHpKK9sJI4/content/dremel-partners-with-yaya-han-to-debut-dremel-lite-to-cospl-1?inheritRedirect=false.

unique opportunities for some cosplayers. Verona Bule, who had joined the 501st Legion in 1999 as Boushh, a Tusken Raider, and an Imperial officer,[32] began appearing in *CSI*, *Shameless*, and other TV shows and online videos in 2010, before eventually making her way over to serve as a voice actor in a number of *Star Wars* projects, like *The Force Awakens* (the Resistance's PA announcer), *Rogue One* (the voice of the Scarif Antenna Computer), and video games like *Vader Immortal: A Star Wars VR Series* and *Star Wars Battlefront II*.[33] When the crew of *Ted 2* came to New York Comic Con to film a scene that was set at a convention, 20th Century Fox brought in some cosplayers to be background characters.[34]

Six other members of the 501st Legion—John May, Steve Buckley, Ross Walmsley, Rob Ledsom, Steve Hill, and Gary Hailes—were likewise given an opportunity by Lucasfilm, which invited them to suit up as troopers in 2015's *The Force Awakens*.[35] In 2018, *The Mandalorian* creator Jon Favreau realized that they needed a number of stormtroopers for the show's season one finale and recruited dozens of 501st members to take part in the scene.[36]

But no other member has had quite the experience that Chris Bartlett had. He joined the 501st Legion in August 2001, and in 2005, he took an unconventional route to get his résumé before interviewers at Epic Games, deciding to suit up in his sandtrooper costume.

"I rode to the 6th floor and the doors opened. An Epic Games employee stood there, mouth agape. My trooper voice said, 'Scuse me sir, *click-shht*,' and I headed down the nearest hall, looking for any open office door. Another employee appeared and the trooper asked, 'Which way to Epic Games.' It wasn't a question. I was telling him to direct me. Because by now the sweat from my forehead brought on by the humid 95-degree weather was stinging my eyes and I needed to get this done. With a big smile he asks, 'Oh cool! Are you here for the meeting?!' "[37]

---

32   "DZ 418," by user Verona Blue, 501st Legion Costume Resources, accessed December 8, 2021, https://www.501st.com/members/displaymember.php?userID=219&costumeID=58.
33   "Verona Blue," IMDb, accessed December 8, 2021, https://www.imdb.com/name/nm4194431.
34   Steven Annear, "Here's Your Chance to Be an Extra In Ted 2," *Boston*, July 15, 2014, https://www.bostonmagazine.com/arts-entertainment/2014/07/15/ted-2-casting-call-boston-casting.
35   Ryder Windham and Adam Bray, Star Wars *Stormtroopers: Beyond the Armor* (New York: Harper Design, 2017), 131.
36   *Disney Gallery: The Mandalorian*, "Connections," Disney+, June 19, 2020.
37   Chris Bartlett, "Getting a Job as a Stormtrooper," TK409 (website), July 2005, http://www.tk409.com/gettingajob.html.

He ended up speaking directly with the studio's creative director, and then the CEO, and left an impression: he landed the job and eventually worked on a number of high-profile games, such as *Gears of War*, *Infinity Blade*, and *Fortnite*.

It was another costume that he put together that landed him bigger roles: C-3PO. Over its history, Lucasfilm has brought out its characters for high-profile events, such as the 1978 Academy Awards, when a couple of stormtroopers marched onstage to help present an award. Lucasfilm hired Bartlett to appear as C-3PO in a number of events, such as commercials for McDonald's,[38] O2,[39] Toyota,[40] and *Speechless*,[41] and award shows like the Oscars.[42]

The gig led Bartlett to other acting jobs as costumed characters, such as for *The Orville*,[43] and eventually he landed a high-profile series: *The Mandalorian*. In it he portrays a variety of costumed characters, such as the ferryman in the show's first episode, as well as the mercenary droid Zero in "Chapter 6: The Prisoner," and an RA-7 droid in "Chapter 7: The Reckoning." He's since gone on to play different droids in a handful of episodes of *The Book of Boba Fett*.

At the heart of these instances is an individual's performance as the character. The right moment on social media can lead people to specific roles within the franchises they admire. In cases like Bartlett's, Lucasfilm has had a useful person to bring in over the years when they needed a C-3PO for major events, or comparable roles, such as suited characters and droids. In other instances, the organization of groups like the 501st provides a pool of individuals to play the exact same role: one that they've been practicing for years.

---

38   "*Star Wars: [The] Clone Wars* UK McDonalds Commercial," YouTube video, aired in 2008, posted October 13, 2008, by Chris Bartlett, https://www.youtube.com/watch?v=MaKj1OoUK5s.
39   "*Star Wars: The Force Awakens* - 02 Priority Ad," o2ukofficial, YouTube video, November 20, 2015, https://www.youtube.com/watch?v=j5EeJhfou7c.
40   "2012 toyota prius phv cm japan 3 starwars (トヨタプリウスPHV)," The Car Commercial Jero316, YouTube video, https://www.youtube.com/watch?v=2cvTpM3Wpsw.
41   "Speechless 2x09 Promo 'S-T–STAR W–WARS W–ARS' (HD)," TV Promos, YouTube video, December 2, 2017, https://www.youtube.com/watch?v=mfl_SyQyRBI.
42   "*Star Wars* Droids at the Oscars," Oscars, YouTube video, March 23, 2016, https://www.youtube.com/watch?v=VkO62A_CycU.
43   Chris Bartlett (@chrisfbartlett), "Easter Egg: I appeared on #TheOrville this week! I'm the handsome one on the left," Twitter, February 24, 2019, 6:02 p.m., https://twitter.com/chrisfbartlett/status/1099806761811304448.

27 INFLUENCING CANON

ROSE BOWL PARADE

The 501st's moment in the spotlight came when Lucas was named the grand marshal for the Tournament of Roses Parade in 2007, in commemoration of the thirtieth anniversary of *Star Wars*' release in theaters. He wanted to make an impression and decided to invite the 501st Legion to march.

"I think George became aware of [the group] in the late 1990s," Steve Sansweet, Lucasfilm's former head of fan relations, told me.[1] While Lucas had heard about the group and seen pictures of its members in action, it was the Rose Parade that drove home the 501st's passion.

"We were all surprised that he agreed to do the Rose Bowl Parade," Sansweet recounted, "but it turns out that when George was a kid, he and his family would drive down to Pasadena to see the parade every year. It was something that was important to him personally. He was always tickled seeing his characters turned into physical manifestations all around the world. Anywhere he would go for a movie opening or for a premiere, he would be met by a cadre of costumed characters, and he appreciated that."

By this point, the Legion numbered in the thousands, and the company put out a call: they wanted members to submit videos of themselves marching in formation. Lucas wanted not just a squad of stormtroopers marching in the parade but a *legion* of them.

---

1 Steve Sansweet in conversation with the author, January 2020.

Albin Johnson stands at the corner of the 501st Legion's formation at the Rose Bowl Parade. The parade was an enormous public introduction of the group to mainstream America, and helped cement the club's status as a major organization within *Star Wars* fandom.

Image from the collection of Rancho Obi-Wan

Members of the 501st Legion assembled in California to take part in the Rose Bowl parade in 2007: it was one of the largest gatherings of troopers to date, and required several days of training to prepare for.

Image from the collection of Rancho Obi-Wan

Sansweet reached out to the 501st and invited them to audition. Home movies poured in from all around the world of troopers marching in formation, and soon, Sansweet and his colleagues had selected their marchers. Lucasfilm flew the volunteer troopers to California, where they spent a couple of days working with former military drill instructors on how to move as a formation, rehearsing on a football field. It was a grueling experience, but a rewarding one for those involved, who began to bond as a group.

The night before the parade, Lucas addressed the troopers at a banquet: "The big invasion is in a few days. I don't expect all of you to make it back. But that's okay, because stormtroopers are expendable."[2]

The next morning, the hundreds of troopers stepped off in three blocks: stormtroopers, a group of mixed troopers, and a group carrying flags from each of the Legion's home countries. They were accompanied by the Grambling State University's marching band, who were themselves decked out in Imperial officer costume. The sight of hundreds of stormtroopers marching in formation was a sensation and stunned the public. News commentators spoke in awe as the group walked by, noting that they were all volunteers who had made their own costumes. It was a major, visible piece of publicity for the Legion and helped to generate further interest in the group for years to come.

---

[2] "*Star Wars* Rose Parade 2007 Highlights," *Star Wars*, YouTube video, filmed January 1, 2007, https://www.youtube.com/watch?v=WW6cANKeCX0.

CANONIZED

The creation of the Legion and its success came full circle in 2004, when they went from fan group to part of the *Star Wars* canon. In 1991, book publisher Bantam Spectra had brought on science-fiction author Timothy Zahn to write a continuation of the *Star Wars* franchise. With no new films on the horizon, he wrote a spiritual "third trilogy" in *Heir to the Empire*, *Dark Force Rising*, and *The Last Command*, a powerhouse bestselling novel that opened the floodgates to more, keeping the franchise's torch alive. Zahn and others went on to write numerous original adventures within the franchise and often came in contact with 501st members who turned out to support book signings or other

LEFT: Members of the 501st Legion pose with Michael A. Stackpole, Timothy Zahn, and Aaron Allston at StellarCon in 2002. Zahn would later introduce the 501st Legion as a unit within the canon *Star Wars* universe, while Stackpole and Allston were best known for their X-Wing and Wraith Squadron novels. *Courtesy of Cheralyn Lambeth*

RIGHT: Bob Gouveia, a member of the 501st Legion's New England Garrison, poses at *Star Wars* Celebration V in Orlando, Florida, with his daughter Julia and Dave Filoni, the supervising producer of *Star Wars: The Clone Wars*, who was responsible for many of the designs that would later be re-created by the 501st. Gouveia is dressed in armor inspired by the animated series, while his daughter is dressed as Ahsoka Tano, one of the show's main characters. *Courtesy of Bob Gouveia*

related events. The Legion named Zahn an honorary member in 2002, and he soon returned the favor by writing the Legion into his novella *Fool's Bargain*, which followed a stormtrooper in the 501st Legion.

The appreciation for the Legion didn't stop with Zahn. In the final installment of the prequel trilogy, *Revenge of the Sith*, Lucas used the group's name as Anakin Skywalker/Darth Vader's personal legion of clone troopers. Moviegoers watched as rank upon rank of troopers clad in white-and-blue armor marched into the Jedi Temple at the end of the film.

When Lucas created the animated TV series *The Clone Wars* with Dave Filoni, the 501st Legion was front and center in the form of a major character, Captain Rex, who commanded the legion and was prominently featured in many of its episodes. Speaking at *Star Wars* Celebration in Orlando, Florida, in 2017, Filoni expressed his appreciation for the Legion members' enthusiasm, saying that they had inspired and pushed his design team to come up with new designs and variants of the armored troopers for them to build in person. "I love the cosplay," Filoni said during his panel. "To draw something on a piece of paper one day, then a year or so later have it come up to you and say hello—boom.

"I give a tremendous amount of thought to the costumes," he continued, "and it's something we were able to improve in part, especially on characters like Ahsoka, knowing that so many people were out there wearing that costume. I want to make sure to get it right, because I want you guys to have fun wearing this stuff."[3]

"Timothy Zahn is clearly the guy who started it all, and I can't give him enough credit," said Albin Johnson. "The fact that he found an easy way to go to the mother ship and say that he'd like to base a character on a real-life fan, that was enormous. There was a tremendous amount of faith on his part too, because what if we turned out to be a bunch of assholes?

"The idea that now we're in *The Mandalorian* is blowing my mind. I joked around the time *Attack of the Clones* came out that we were going to be invited to the production or to [the] set for a movie. And it was a great April Fool's joke! And then for *The Force Awakens*, we actually had members of the UK Garrison suit up at the invitation of Lucasfilm to come out and be on the set."

Fan-made creations have worked their way into other parts of the *Star Wars* universe as well. In one instance, 3D modeler Sean Fields noted that Lucasfilm had reached out to

---

3 Andrew Liptak, "Cosplayers Influenced the Costume Design in *Star Wars* Animated Shows," *The Verge*, April 13, 2017, https://www.theverge.com/2017/4/13/15293090/star-wars-celebration-2017-dave-filoni-clone-wars-cosplay.

him in the midst of *The Rise of Skywalker* to ask for permission to use the 3D print files that he'd developed for a B1 battle droid. The droid showed up in the background of a scene in Babu Frik's shop midway through the film. "So this means two things," wrote Fields. "One: My files are indisputably screen accurate. Two: . . . Since my files deviate from the established references, I have essentially introduced a new variant of Battle Droid. To put it another way, I have altered *Star Wars* canon."[4]

Lucasfilm has utilized fan work for even higher-profile screen time as well. For *The Force Awakens*, Lucasfilm recruited a pair of fans, Lee Towersey and Oliver Steeples, members of the R2-D2 Builders Club, to build droids for the film. The pair had met studio chief Kathleen Kennedy during Celebration Europe in 2012, and Steeples joked that they "were available if required." Kennedy later recommended that they join the film's creature effects team.[5]

Abrams also introduced a neat Easter egg into *The Force Awakens*. If you look closely as Han Solo, Finn, and Rey enter Maz's castle (right at the fifty-seven-minute mark), you'll spot a flag bearing the logo of the 501st Legion hanging in the courtyard.

Perhaps the biggest instance of studio-fan collaboration came in 2019, when a climactic scene in the final episode of *The Mandalorian* required a number of stormtroopers. During *Star Wars* Celebration, series creator Jon Favreau and director Dave Filoni revealed that they had turned to the 501st Legion to fill the roles. "In the production meeting there were only so many stormtrooper costumes they had. So we had to plan, has the 501st ever been on camera?" Favreau recalled.[6]

When *Star Wars* made the leap from film to live-action television with *The Mandalorian*, some fan-made parts made their way onto the screen. In one scene, the show's titular character hands someone a mythosaur skull pendant, which the Facebook page The Parts of Star Wars pointed out was made by an artist and sold on a fan site called Mostly Fantasy.[7] In another, it appears that the production might have utilized fan-made armor:

---

4   Project 842, "Now that the film is out, I suppose it's safe to post this . . . ," Facebook, December 22, 2019, https://www.facebook.com/Project842/posts/834997866932424:0.
5   Dan Brooks, "R2-D2 Is in *Star Wars: Episode VII*, and He's Fan-Made," *Star Wars* (website), November 19, 2013, https://www.starwars.com/news/r2-d2-is-in-star-wars-episode-7-and-hes-fan-made.
6   Ben Pearson, "501st Legion of *Star Wars* Fans Will Appear in *The Mandalorian*," *SlashFilm*, April 14, 2019, https://www.slashfilm.com/501st-in-the-mandalorian.
7   The Parts of Star Wars, "Mythosaur skull pendant . . . In this rare case, the production actually bought an existing fan made pewter pendant to use on the show. . . . ," Facebook, January 2, 2020, https://www.facebook.com/PartsofSW/photos/rpp.193037424152213/2468860606569872/?type=3&theater.

the pair of scout troopers seen in *The Mandalorian* were clad in armor that was made by a maker shop called Walt's Trooper Factory.

"The thing I know about *Star Wars* fans is that in all honesty a lot of the costumes you guys made are even better than what we see onscreen," Filoni added. "So I had no doubts that they would look great. And they act like stormtroopers. They know what to do."[8]

By 2019, more than two decades after its creation, the group had come around full circle: once inspired by the franchise they loved, they were now actively, officially contributing to it. It's a reciprocal relationship, one that seems to reinforce itself, the creative energy bleeding from the enthusiasm from fans into official projects, and back again.

THE RISE OF THE MERCS

"We've got the Mandalorian Mercs, here." Jon Favreau pointed out into the darkened auditorium to cheers. Beside him stood Dave Filoni, the writer, director, and producer who shepherded much of Lucasfilm's animated efforts, and the pair were about to unveil a first look at a highly anticipated project: the first-ever *Star Wars* live-action TV series, *The Mandalorian*. Fans packed the room, eagerly awaiting details about the project.[9]

Months earlier, the *Iron Man* and *Lion King* director had posted to Instagram, revealing the title and first details of his latest project: a series that would follow "a lone gunfighter in the outer reaches of the galaxy far from the authority of the New Republic."[10] The reveal was

A pair of Mandalorians stand guard at FAN EXPO Boston in August 2019.

Courtesy of Andrew Liptak

---

8   Ben Pearson, "501st Legion of *Star Wars* Fans Will Appear in *The Mandalorian*."
9   "*The Mandalorian* Panel – Sunday," *Star Wars* YouTube channel, April 14, 2019, https://www.youtube.com/watch?v=GrlTosbjylA.
10 Jon Favreau (@jonfavreau), "#starwars #TheMandalorian," Instagram, October 3, 2018, https://www.instagram.com/p/BofTUzhBtrZ/?utm_source=ig_embed.

INFLUENCING CANON

electrifying for fans: the Mandalorian culture has established itself as a major pillar of the *Star Wars* universe, aided by the effort of dedicated fans, cosplayers, and writers who have developed and expanded it. Without that passion, it's unlikely that the show would exist.

The Mandalorians have an unlikely origin: the 1978 San Anselmo Country Fair parade,[11] at which Lucasfilm editor Duwayne Dunham tested out a prototype Boba Fett costume months before the character appeared in the much-maligned 1978 *The Star Wars Holiday Special*, which introduced the character to the franchise.

The character had emerged out of George Lucas's development process. Early drafts of *The Empire Strikes Back* introduced several mercenaries to tie in with the plot about Han Solo's debt to Jabba the Hutt. "The Boba Fett character is really an early version of Darth Vader," Lucas recounted in *The Making of The Empire Strikes Back*. "He is also very much like the man-with-no-name from the Sergio Leone Westerns." The first hints that Boba Fett was part of a larger culture came in the film's novelization, in which Donald F. Gult described him as "dressed in a weapon-covered, armored spacesuit, the kind worn by a group of evil warriors defeated by the Jedi Knights during the Clone Wars."

In the years following the film's release, authors and artists tinkered with Fett's backstory and the Mandalorian culture from which he came. Marvel Comics brought the franchise's principal characters to Mandalore at one point, and Boba Fett's popularity meant that he didn't stay dead for long after his unceremonious end in *Return of the Jedi*. Fett's mysterious past hinted at a richer backstory and culture, and in his *Tales of the Jedi* comic series, Kevin J. Anderson delved into Mandalore's ancient history, establishing them as ancient crusaders and foes of the Jedi. The foundation for a new major culture within the *Star Wars* universe had been set.

With his first appearance in *The Empire Strikes Back* in 1980, Boba Fett was an immediate hit. In his book *How Star Wars Conquered the Universe: The Past, Present, and Future of a Multibillion Dollar Franchise*, Chris Taylor described him as "one of the most cultishly popular personalities in the entire *Star Wars* universe," noting that "the legions of devotees this character commands is out of all proportion to his screen time—less than 150 seconds in the original trilogy."

---

11   Brad Ricca, "The Real First Appearance of Boba Fett," *Star Wars* (website), July 8, 2014, https://www.starwars.com/news/the-real-first-appearance-of-boba-fett.

Immediately, fans like David Rhea went out and built their own versions of the costume after seeing the character in theaters. "I went and bought an old army helmet from the kids' store," he said, and he crafted the rest of the helmet out of cardboard and a wind guard from a motorcycle helmet.

Others wanted to make as exact a copy as they could manage. In the mid-1990s, Art Andrews, then a member of the Replica Prop Forum, began chatting about the character. His initial discussions "ran over the three-hundred-post limit four times in like two days," he said, which got him into some trouble with the site's owners, who had to pay for server space. He convinced them to "help [him] create [his] own site for Boba Fett." It was called The Dented Helmet.

The Dented Helmet became the definitive resource for all things Boba Fett costuming. Members did exhaustive research, tracked down all the parts that the costume designers reused, shared tips on paint schemes, sold one another parts, and worked to replicate the character's iconic costume for themselves. "The passion for Boba Fett is so crazy," Andrews notes. "I feel like that following—how many other *Star Wars* characters do you see an entire site dedicated to?"

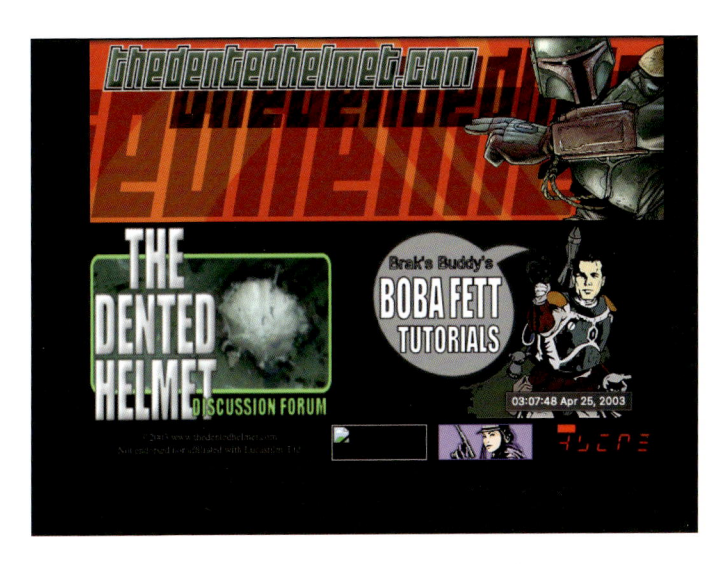

A screenshot of The Dented Helmet fan site in 2003. The site is one of the essential resources for anyone wishing to build a Boba Fett costume.

As Lucasfilm rereleased the original trilogy with a couple of extra seconds of Boba Fett footage in *A New Hope*, then the prequel trilogy (introducing Jango Fett and establishing that Boba was his clone), the *Star Wars* costuming scene exploded, leading to the rise of major cosplay groups like the 501st Legion, which included the character in its ranks.

Other fans liked the general appearance of Fett's armor but didn't want to be constrained by the strict rules that came with prop replicas: they wanted to make their own

INFLUENCING CANON

285

characters and color schemes. So, they went out and did that, drawing on the same design language to create their own unique characters, something that was well-suited for the sprawling culture that appeared throughout *Star Wars* canon.

One such individual was Tom Hutchens. Fett left a lasting impression on him when he first saw *Return of the Jedi* in theaters when he was five years old. "That's when I tell people I found my first love, but also experienced my first real death within a ten-second time frame," he explained. "It's probably the part of my childhood that I remember the most vividly."

Hutchens's love of Boba Fett stayed with him throughout school and a stint in the US Navy. In 2003, he began playing *Star Wars Galaxies*, where he ran a guild of Mandalorian bounty hunters. With his wife (they met through the game), Hutchens attended Dragon Con in Atlanta, Georgia, where he ran into a handful of Mandalorian cosplayers dressed in custom armor. "You had the 501st Legion table, and the Rebel Legion table, and [these guys] didn't really have a home of their own." After talking with them about their armor and their mutual love of Mandalorian culture, Hutchens caught the costuming bug: he went out and made his own set of custom armor. He was a former member of the Society for Creative Anachronism (SCA), he designed and built his own suit out of steel, which "looked just like my Mandalorian character in *Star Wars Galaxies*."[12]

A turning point for Hutchens came in March 2005 when Abel G. Peña published a feature in *Star Wars Insider*, "The History of the Mandalorians," which collected all the lore throughout the franchise and compiled it into a cohesive history. The article had an outsize impact in the fan community, essentially establishing the Mandalorians as a major component of the franchise. Hutchens explained that the article left a major impression, and that a detail about the ancient warriors turning to work as mercenaries allowed something to fall into place for him. "That is actually where the name of the Mandalorian Mercs costume club comes from."

Inspired by what he had seen at Dragon Con the year before, Hutchens set out to create an overarching group for the Mandalorian costumers who were appearing at conventions. There were some forums for custom characters, but nothing dedicated exclusively to Mandalorian costuming. "I set up a website, with pictures, an intro page, and a forum," Hutchens explained, noting that word of mouth from costumers brought new members. In 2007, he and several other Mandalorian costumers gathered at Adventure

---

12   Tom Hutchens in conversation with the author, January 2020.

Con in Knoxville, Tennessee: the first official Mandalorian Mercs event.[13] There, they came face-to-face with the actor responsible for their obsession: Jeremy Bulloch, a guest at the convention, who was suited up in his own set of armor. In the years that followed, the Mandalorian Mercs grew to include thousands of members across the world and would eventually be recognized by Lucasfilm. Their movement was underway.

At the same time, the Mandalorian culture was on the cusp of a major transformation within the franchise's canon. In 2004, author Karen Traviss published *Star Wars: Republic Commando: Hard Contact*, about a team of Republic commandos. In it and its sequels, Traviss took a particular interest in Mandalorian culture, reasoning that the clone army introduced in *Attack of the Clones* had to come from *somewhere*. "It was obvious that for a secret project like that, Jango would want to recruit some Mandalorians," she explained in 2006.[14] "I decided that Mando fighting skill was so much a part of their culture, language and philosophy that they'd teach all of that to their lads . . . they also saw Mando identity as being a really important spiritual thing to pass on to their trainees."

That world building, told through a series of other Republic Commando novels and articles in *Star Wars Insider*, further solidified the backstory of the culture, and established elements like the Beskar metal and color schemes the Mandalorians use in their armor. Traviss even expanded on the Mandalorian language that composer Jesse Harlin had developed in his score for the video game *Star Wars: Republic Commando*.

The Mandalorian Mercs "came about during Karen's time writing for *Star Wars*," Hutchens explained, noting that the club incorporated the lore and appearance based on what she created. "Our officer titles are all in Mando'a, the system of governance in the Mando Mercs is a sort of a meritocracy like how Mandos are, and of course the variations of the costumes and colors—the colors had meaning when she was writing, and we still kind of hold onto that a bit." That respect went both ways: Traviss wrote about her admiration for cosplayers, noting that she consulted with a fan about military operations and armor, leading her to name a character after him.

Most important was "the individualization, the whole sort of mercenary, bounty hunter

---

13 Tom Hutchens, "Heeding the Call: Rise of the Mandalorian Mercs," *Star Wars* (website), October 2, 2013, https://www.starwars.com/news/heeding-the-call-rise-of-the-mandalorian-mercs.
14 Jason D. Ivey, "Exclusive Interview with Karen Traviss, The Clone Gal," Boba Fett Fan Club (website), published August 5, 2006, updated March 8, 2021, https://www.bobafettfanclub.com/news/fettpedia/the-clone-gal-interview-with-karen-traviss.

attitude, and then the tenets that she had," Hutchens explained to me in an interview in January 2020. "We worked a little bit of that into how we function as an organization."[15]

It's that aptitude toward customization and individuality that attracted many members of the Mercs. At FAN EXPO Boston in 2019, Thorn Reilly told me that it was Traviss's books that got them interested in the armor. "Reading about it and having it in my head—there's no photos of these characters, but I can visualize them. Okay, what can I make? As a person who's a huge nerd for costume design, it was cool to be able to say I'm not one of three Princess Leias or Luke Skywalker. I can be like, 'I want racing stripes, and I could do that!'" they explained. "There's definitely a challenge inherent in replicating something so that it's screen accurate, but it was almost more fun for me because extrapolating that look was more appealing because I could put my own spin on it.

"Part of the fun of the Mandalorian Mercs is that everyone's character has a backstory—it's like your own Mando persona," they explained to me. "They have the same thing in the SCA, like, who is your character, roughly? Building the character backstory is a whole lot of fun. You don't have to go in depth with it, but you can go in depth with it."

That level of customization sets the Mandalorian Mercs apart from other established costuming groups within the sphere of *Star Wars* cosplay fandom. The 501st Legion, for example, is made up of members who replicate the costumes seen on the screen, which doesn't allow for customization or elaborate backstories. For that reason, the Mandalorian Mercs literally wear their creative streak on their bodies, coming up with endless variations on the T-visors and familiar armor plating. That creativity unlocks new possibilities for the culture that go beyond what's seen in the canon stories and lore.

In 2008, Lucasfilm launched a new major project: *The Clone Wars*, an animated television series for Cartoon Network. While the series initially focused on the fight between the Republic and the Separatists, it quickly folded Mandalorians into the plot, introducing a major story line with "The Mandalore Plot" in season two. With the series came a number of new canon characters for costumers to replicate, and new opportunities for Lucasfilm to build on the lore that they had been developing.

Speaking to *The Star Wars Show* a couple of years ago, Dave Filoni noted that his approach to fan service was to be intentional about it. "I've always leaned towards the—if we're going to create something, we should check and see if it existed already to the

---

15   Tom Hutchens in conversation with the author, January 2020.

ABOVE: Elly Madrigal poses as a Death Watch Mandalorian at Granite State Comic Con in Manchester, New Hampshire, in May 2011.

RIGHT: A cosplayer dressed as Sabine Wren poses in front of a mural at *Star Wars* Celebration in Chicago, Illinois, in April 2019.

Photos courtesy of Andrew Liptak

fans. Because it has way more value if we bring that in. Why would I just replace it with something new?"[16] *Star Wars* is notorious for recycling ideas, names, and design, something that appears throughout the franchise—especially the animated shows.

The Clone Wars amassed a huge following, bringing in new fans to the franchise and reinvigorating old ones. Groups like the Mandalorian Mercs and 501st and Rebel Legions suddenly found themselves with plenty of new characters to replicate, and Filoni was soon well aware of their work. Fans posed for pictures with him at conventions and sent him replicas of helmets that he helped create. Hutchens says that whenever the Mercs are at a *Star Wars* Celebration, Filoni is a standing guest for their club banquet, and that he makes time to attend. "He talks to everybody, he shakes everybody's hand. The reality of it is that he's just a huge fan himself. He's part of our family."

At the 2019 Celebration, Favreau recounted how his friendship with Filoni led to his involvement in the *Star Wars* franchise: by voicing a Mandalorian character named Pre Viszla in 2007. He went on to voice Rio Durant in *Solo: A Star Wars Story* and pitched his idea to Lucasfilm. "What happens after the celebration of the Empire falling?" he mused onstage. "The idea of the world after *Return of the Jedi* and what would happen and the type

---

16 "Dave Filoni Interview and More!" *The Star Wars Show*, *Star Wars* (website), accessed December 9, 2021, https://www.starwars.com/video/the-star-wars-show-episode-14.

INFLUENCING CANON

of characters that would survive until the New Republic took over."[17] The *Star Wars* underworld was particularly attractive, and the perfect place to bring in a Mandalorian warrior.

"If you want my honest opinion," Hutchens says, "I don't think the TV show would exist without the Mandalorian Mercs, or if it did, it wouldn't exist as it exists now."

"I see so much of what we've done over the last thirteen years woven into the stories of that show, and even when you go back and look at *The Clone Wars* and *Rebels*," Hutchens says. *The Clone Wars* TV series brought in its Mandalorians in 2009, just as Hutchens's Mandalorian Mercs were getting established. "But then when you get to seasons four and five," he notes, "you see the Death Watch looking more customized, and they're weathered and dirty, and you're starting to think that over the last few years, maybe we've had an impact. Then when you go to *Rebels*, you see things like the pilot helmets or helmets that people have had in the Mercs before that show was even thought up. And by the end of *Rebels*, when you see all the Mandos with all the different colors, and it's hard for you not to look at that and not think that you had something to do with that somehow. You don't really see that in past works, and it had to come from somewhere.

"I will almost guarantee that these things, even up to the *Mandalorian* series, are things that people have seen on Mercs members, and it's inspired artists to add those things. I think without us, it wouldn't have been the way it is."[18]

While looking back over his career at *Star Wars* Celebration 2019, Filoni pointed to the fan community as a driving force behind the projects that he's been involved with. "I think the voice of fans has really helped propel what I've done."[19] At the premiere of *The Mandalorian* in November, Lucasfilm invited members of the Mandalorian Mercs to the red carpet. Members brought their helmets to the screening and were called out by Filoni during the event's Q&A session. "When we were first starting this, I was telling Jon that there's a whole group of them out there. He's like, 'What are they like?' and I said, 'Well, they're pretty much like you'd think: they're Mandalorians.' They know the way, and really, we brought something to life onscreen that I see every summer at Celebration."[20]

---

17   "The Mandalorian Panel - Sunday," *Star Wars*, YouTube video, accessed December 9, 2021, https://www.youtube.com/watch?v=GrlTosbjylA.
18   Tom Hutchens in conversation with the author, January 2020.
19   "Dave Filoni Takes the Stage at SWCC 2019 | *The Star Wars Show* Live!" *Star Wars*, YouTube video, filmed April 13, 2019, https://www.youtube.com/watch?v=1PLMYhy5Qoo&t=564s.
20   "*The Mandalorian* | Live Stream Q&A," *Star Wars*, YouTube video, accessed December 9, 2021, https://www.youtube.com/watch?v=flsO_Wfxczw.

part five

Technology

The sun had long since set when I pulled into a sleepy town at the edge of Vermont's Northeast Kingdom in December 2016. I had driven an hour through dense forests. Trees drooped from the first snow of the season over small homes and trailers that sparkled with bright Christmas lights. It was an unlikely place to pick up a replica helmet from a *Star Wars* movie I hadn't even seen.

In the parking lot of the local supermarket, I met Jason. Tall, with a blond beard, wearing a thick, hooded sweatshirt, he could have easily passed for a member of a local biker gang. But online, he's gained a reputation among hard-core *Star Wars* fans and cosplay enthusiasts for his high-quality replica costumes. We engaged in small talk for a couple of minutes, then he handed me a plastic bag with the helmet. I'd been studying pictures of it online for months, but in the glow of the parking lot, finally holding it in my two hands, it left a grin plastered across my face.

When painted, the prop will look almost identical to the shoretrooper helmet introduced in *Rogue One: A Star Wars Story*, and later seen in episodes of *The Mandalorian* and *Andor*. Even though the film was just hitting theaters then, the new shoretrooper costume had been inspiring fans and artists for months as they scoured trailers and reference photos to design and create the most accurate replicas possible. While I'm writing this in 2021, a cosplayer has access to more source material, construction materials, tools, and community resources than at any point in history.

That's all possible due to the confluence of the latest digital modeling and printing technologies, and the rise of social media platforms that foster the communities of dedicated fans who support the entire hobby, all with one goal in mind: building the best costume possible and sharing your fandom with the rest of the world.

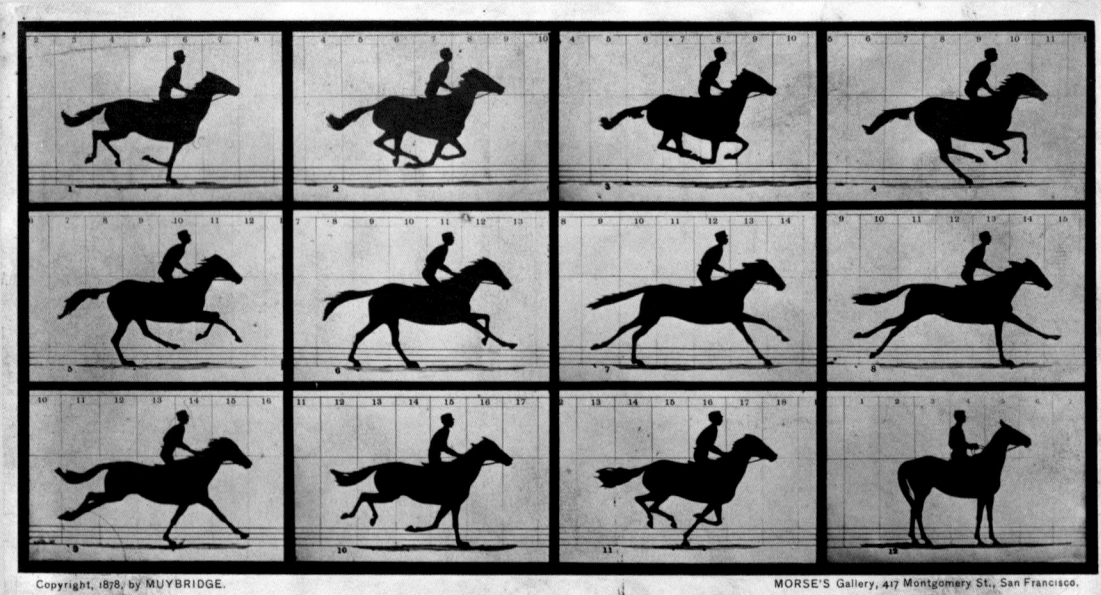

The Horse in Motion is an iconic series of images taken in 1872 that shows sequential movement, a key moment in the history of motion pictures.

Image: Eadweard Muybridge

28 HOLLYWOOD

Inevitably, technological advances opened up an entirely new avenue for the dramatic arts. One early example is celluloid. With the development of photography in the early 1800s, individuals could capture images, and some photographers realized that if they displayed a whole sequence of images, they could stretch out individual still photographs into a sequence that conveyed a longer moment. In 1878, California's former governor Leland Stanford commissioned photographer Eadweard Muybridge to take a sequence of images to settle a long-standing argument: Are all four of a galloping horse's hooves ever completely off the ground? The study resulted in a famous sequence: *The Horse in Motion*, which, when animated, showed the horse running at high speed. It was a photographic milestone, one that helped lead to an entirely new art form: motion pictures.

In her book *Hollywood Costume*, influential costume designer Deborah Nadoolman Landis (who's responsible for everything from Indiana Jones's iconic look to Michael Jackson's "Thriller" jacket) notes that as the public appetite for films grew, so too did the need for actors and costume designers. "Concurrent with this development was the migration of actors and costume designers from the theatre to the newly emerging cinema community," she writes, noting that it was a time of experimentation and exploration on the part of filmmakers.[1] Actors initially were largely responsible for providing their own

---

1 Deborah Nadoolman Landis, ed., *Hollywood Costume* (South Kensington, London: V&A Publishing, 2012), 13.

costumes, while some filmmakers relied on the costumes that they could rent from dedicated companies that catered to theaters.

Landis points to the 1910s as a time when studios began to implement new and innovative approaches to costume design. Relying on knowledgeable actresses, two dominant modes emerged: "Producer Adolph Zukor introduced Americans to the concept of the film costume designer as a creative artist, while director D. W. Griffith introduced the practice of creating costumes specifically for American-made films."[2]

Producers and directors began to realize the utility of costumes: they assisted with storytelling. By the end of the 1920s, costume departments had cemented their position within the larger Hollywood production machine: they were part of the filmmaking process, from beginning to end of production, and included designers, seamstresses, tailors, and more to develop and create the necessary costumes. In 1949, the Academy of Motion Picture Arts and Sciences gave out the first two Academy Awards for Best Costume Design, which went to Roger K. Furse for his work on *Hamlet* (black-and-white film category), while Dorothy Jeakins and Barbara Karinska earned one for their work on *Joan of Arc* (color film category).

The Second World War brought further changes to the film industry, as rationing limited the supply of fabrics available to designers. Landis credits one particular film designer, Irene Sharaff, for further advancing the film industry's approach to costuming. "Before Sharaff's arrival in Hollywood most film designers analyzed each script for the costumes they needed to design for individual actresses. But Irene Sharaff and Helen Rose, both designers with Broadway careers, introduced to Hollywood the concepts of an overall colour palette and the design integration of an entire cast of characters that were commonplace in the theatre."[3] The result was a further integration of the costume into the narrative of a film, which was baked in from the earliest days of various productions. Designers would create concept sketches, alter existing clothes, and consult and fit actors for stylistic choices.

Landis notes that while the field experienced a downturn amid studio turmoil throughout the 1950s and 1960s, the emergence of action, science-fiction, and fantasy films helped to re-elevate the role of costume designers. "Directors in these genres

---

2   Landis, *Hollywood Costume*, 14.
3   Landis, *Hollywood Costume*, 30.

required full partnership with a costume designer in order to accomplish their vision," and, following the success of films like George Lucas's *Star Wars*, "studios were willing to spend more money for a greater return on their investment. Directors were given the tools to allow their imaginations full reign."[4]

Close your eyes, and I'm willing to bet that you can picture Indiana Jones, Han Solo, Ellen Ripley, Alan Grant, Batman, Wonder Woman, and Harley Quinn in your mind. They are defined by their costumes as much as their heroics.

The role of the costume is front and center in any film or television show, enhancing a character by adding to their story subliminally, and at times providing them with an iconic outfit that is recognizable even outside of the shots they were made for. Those outfits leave an impression on moviegoers long after they leave theaters. They inspire fans—young and old alike—to dress up, cobbling together costumes from their existing wardrobes and parts they create themselves.

In doing so, they're expressing their love and appreciation of these stories that they've watched. It might be that they particularly love one character, because they're the most handsome or have the best lines. They might identify with them, recognizing something of themselves in that character. Or they might just love the look and feel of the costume, and want to imagine themselves in that world. Any way you cut it, that inspiration comes directly from the work that talented artists, costume designers, and makers put into those productions, which fans pick up on and make their own.

---

4   Landis, *Hollywood Costume*, 36.

29 OWNING A PIECE OF HISTORY

The 1990s ushered in more than just the internet. It was a decade that fostered a new generation of film enthusiasts—fans who had seen films like *Jaws, Close Encounters of the Third Kind, Star Wars,* and *Alien* as kids in theaters and were now entering a point in their lives where they could demonstrate their love for their favorite films in a new way: collecting.

The rise of genre films in the 1970s and 1980s brought about plenty of physical items to collect: action figures, toys, comic books, and, for the discerning collector, the props and costumes that appeared onscreen in those films.

Online forums like the Replica Prop Forum, as well as sales platforms like eBay, allowed for a new phenomenon to emerge: groups of fans who looked to own pieces of cinematic history. This was a huge shift in behavior, says Stephen Lane, who founded Prop Store in 1998.

Lane had started out collecting action figures, which eventually brought him into the world of collecting screen-used props and memorabilia. Action figures were cool, but props were better: "I can watch a movie and point to an object and say, 'I own that piece.'"[1]

"Props and costumes used in films and TV shows [were] a by-product of the filmmaking process," he told me by phone in January 2020. "There was never really any perception of an intrinsic value in the assets that were being manufactured, hired, rented in, or created for the shows. They were just there for the purpose for quite a short period of time, they

---

1 Andrew Liptak, "At San Diego Comic-Con, Movie Props and Costumes Are a Cottage Industry," *The Verge*, July 21, 2017, https://www.theverge.com/2017/7/21/16005346/prop-store-ceo-stephen-lane-of-collecting-costumes-sdcc-2017.

would be held on to until there was a lock on filming, and at that point, they'd go back to the rental companies, sold to crew members or for charity, or just thrown away."[2]

In that environment, a number of film props and costumes would circulate among rock music and popular culture auctions, science-fiction conventions, and private collectors, but they were rarely big-ticket items at the major auction houses. "People didn't know what to do with it," Lane says, noting that sellers would usually sell film props alongside other collectors' items, like toys and comics. Collectors would take pictures of their own collections and mail them back and forth, comparing notes and making offers. With the internet, all of that changed.

Prop collecting is a hobby that sits comfortably alongside cosplay. There are shared interests, like the fascination with movie memorabilia and nostalgia for one's favorite films. But the preservation of props is useful for cosplayers as well: it keeps the objects that they might want to replicate out of the trash and provides valuable source material from which they can work.

Fast-forward to the present day, and the scene has completely changed, says Lane. "Studios barcode and document their assets and track them from the start to finish of a production. The majority of big studios now have huge archives that have locked down a lot of this content, and they use it for marketing and promotional purposes."[3]

You might have seen some of these items on display: studios might bring them to a major convention for fans to take a look at even before a film has hit theaters. They also set up touring museums that travel the country or permanent ones that become destinations for fans to check out. Moreover, Lane notes, they've recognized the opportunity to capitalize on the ephemera that their productions generate, thanks in part to the growth of the collectors' market, and because of the work of people like Lane.

After getting his start as a collector, Lane started his company with an inventory of eight thousand items, ranging from production memorabilia such as hats and shirts to props and costumes that cost anywhere from $20 to $15,000. He now works closely with film productions to acquire costumes and props once productions wrap, as well as with collectors looking to downsize their collections.

An iconic prop or costume might run a collector hundreds of thousands or even millions of dollars. Lane's customers largely fall into three broad categories: serious film

---

2 Stephen Lane in conversation with the author, January 2020.
3 Stephen Lane in conversation with the author, January 2020.

buffs who are looking to preserve film history, investors looking for a collection that might grow in value with time, and cosplayers who are interested in procuring the most authentic costume available. One such example is for the film *The Chronicles of Riddick*, from which he acquired a large lot of costume armor. Lane said that he's seen them reappear at conventions as cosplayers suit up in them.

The purpose of the store, he explained, was to "educate people that these objects survive, and that anyone can own a piece of movie history." While the store serviced a wide range of buyers, they all had something in common: a shared love for film, and nostalgia for their favorite stories. Most people, he explains, will start with a small object and grow their collections with time and money.

Most importantly, Lane notes, the tendency for studios to simply junk their assets is largely a thing of the past, and to that end, collectors have played a vital role in preserving film history. "Thank goodness we saved all this stuff from *Superman*, *Batman*, and *Star Wars*, stuff [studios] didn't care about and was going to get thrown away or lost forever. They're culturally significant from a pop culture perspective, and look what's happened to pop culture in the last fifteen years. It's absolutely exploded."

Dana Gasser, the cofounder of costume company ANOVOS, linked the growing appeal of movie prop collectors to the early days of the cosplay movement. "It seems like science-fiction fans are collectors," he says. "Let's take a great TV show like *Modern Family*. But those people that are fans aren't collectors. They may buy something simple or basic, but we don't see them buying the same outfits they were wearing, and so forth.

"But if you go back and look at the science-fiction realm of it, what is there? There's always a group element of it—the team-up, or stormtroopers. *Star Trek*, everyone is wearing uniforms. *Ghostbusters*, you have a group of them. When you look at those realms, you see people wanting to dress up and wear those items, and collect them."[4]

The continued popularity of classic franchises from the 1970s and 1980s meant that there was a larger demand for film memorabilia. As the prices rose, fans naturally turned to the next best thing: if you couldn't own the original blaster that Han Solo used in *A New Hope*, you could at the very least get yourself a replica. The movie prop world was just one additional element that fed into the growth of the prop replica and costuming scene, allowing people to own a piece of the stories they loved.

---

4 Dana Gasser in conversation with the author, February 2020.

30 INTERNET FORUMS

Unless you're in a workshop or factory, the practice of prop or costume making is an inherently solitary one: a devoted and driven maker toiling in their basement, shop, or garage working out how to replicate or build a costume in the first place. While fandom had been connected through a variety of sources like fanzines, magazines, and conventions, it was the introduction of the internet that supercharged the hobby.

Prior to the introduction of the modern internet, early communities formed through groups on the Usenet system, which allowed users to trade messages back and forth with others around the world. Usenet eventually lost ground to what we think of as the internet in the early 1990s, as pioneers like America Online (AOL) grew in prominence, instituting its own set of dedicated internet discussion forums. These early forums were incredibly influential. The Internet Movie Database (IMDb) originated when a British programmer and film fan named Col Needham started up a Usenet group devoted to actresses with beautiful eyes, and grew to encompass a valuable resource: a living database that provides a comprehensive list of films, productions, crews, actors, and more.

Those early communities have become the foundation of the modern internet, and the forums that they utilized have proved to be an essential resource for cosplayers and fans around the world.

EARLY DAYS

In the early days of science-fiction fandom, fans would attend local or regional science-fiction conventions or share letters back and forth to keep in touch with one another. They developed the social infrastructure that has since coalesced into a broader movement: a worldwide group of like-minded people who love speculative fiction in all of its forms. Cosplay grew out of that framework, and over time, fans realized that simply talking with one another about their creative pursuits was a good way to brainstorm ideas and techniques. They met at conventions and in groups, such as the International Costumers' Guild, the Society for Creative Anachronism, and others. But for decades, science fiction and fantasy has been a bit of a taboo interest: rising from its pulpy origins, it was looked down on by mainstream culture, and as such, fandom was a bit more insular.

With the introduction of the early internet in the late 1980s–1990s, science-fiction fans—already interested in new and emerging technologies—recognized a new means for that kind of resource sharing and camaraderie. The first Usenet systems included watering holes for science-fiction and fantasy fans to gather and discuss their works. Those would be followed by specific email mailing lists and internet forums dedicated to these interests, costuming and prop replicas included. Forums allowed costumers and cosplayers to gather in friendly territory and share tips, tricks, and their mutual love of their favorite books, movies, and TV shows.

Within those forums, builders could work with one another to source materials, gather up reference photos, ask questions and give answers, and begin working on their costumes. One particular feature in this world is an ongoing, living document called the build thread. A builder would start a new topic in one of these forums, announcing that they were working on a new costume, and, in a step-by-step process, usually with pictures, they would document how they created their costume. These documents proved to be extremely useful to the community at large: well-trodden paths that people had taken to figure out how to build a costume. Now, instead of fumbling around in the dark, a maker could see what other builders did, and try something similar.

The ubiquitous build thread popped up in other places, too—on DIY sites and threads on Instagram and Twitter. But with the advent of video sharing, another type of resource appeared: real-time tutorials from builders who filmed themselves working.

Now, instead of reading about how to accomplish any given task (which, depending on the poster's writing ability, could leave details up to the imagination), you could watch someone do it.

When I was in high school, the computers in my school library became a gateway for meeting other fans through sites like TheForce.net and JediNet.com, as well as the brand's official website, StarWars.com, each of which had dedicated discussion forums that touched on every conceivable topic for the franchise—including costumes and regional groups with in-person meetings. That remained the case when I became interested in joining the 501st Legion.

After learning about the group and looking into joining, member Bob Gouveia encouraged me to visit the group's website and associated Yahoo! Group, and later, a private forum on the website itself, in which members discussed upcoming events; tips and tricks on assembling the costumes; detailed, step-by-step instructional build threads to document various costume types; and other sections for sharing the latest *Star Wars* news, funny pictures, and other general updates. The New England Garrison's forums served my local area, and other garrisons at the time put up their own websites and forums, each doing the same thing.

Full-fledged members were encouraged to sign up for another set of forums as well: the global site for the entire organization, which allowed members from around the world to talk to one another. A third network of sites called Detachments served another purpose: costume-specific discussion. It was here that members or aspiring members could dive down into the minutiae of individual costume types, allowing experienced members to share detailed information with newcomers and establish standards for the group at large.

These sites and forums were an essential centralized tool for the group's growth in the early 2000s: they allowed for the uniform distribution of information across the entire national membership. Garrisons essentially operated on a franchise model: they were beholden to the rules and regulations of the larger group but operated locally as a smaller representation. Thus, as new costumes were introduced to the group, members would have a—no pun intended—uniform appearance, no matter where you were in the world. All stormtroopers looked alike, meaning that not only would local troopers look the same but those troopers could travel to any other part of the country or world and fit right in.

Because the forums allowed for the efficient transfer of information from member to member via the larger organization, the Legion itself took on part of the burden on an individual member trying to build a costume. Whereas Albin Johnson and Tom Crews had once had to dig through obscure forums (and pay a fortune) to locate and assemble their stormtrooper costumes, a newcomer can now join one of hundreds of 501st-associated forums and access literally decades of the experience and knowledge of the members who came before. Build threads for individual costume types are just a search away for readers to learn how to construct a costume.

Forums often contain guides aimed at newcomers, telling them where to find the right kids or components of a costume, stockpiles of reference images, what specific kit types will fit certain body types, best practices for assembling a costume, what types of paints and glues to use, how to properly strap up a suit, and even the best types of boxes to store and transport finished costumes in. Once you've completed your costume, you'll also be able to find tips for maintaining and further modifying them. The forums also usually contain information educating cosplayers about the state of the community itself: guides for one's behavior and conduct, dos and don'ts of trooping and conventions, and planning threads for upcoming events.

The forums and the communities that they serve led to more accurate costumes, greased the wheels for ease of entry to new members, and provided the infrastructure for members in new areas to expand to places where the group didn't exist before.

THE REPLICA PROP FORUM

When it comes to fan props and replicas, one of the biggest sites on the internet is the Replica Prop Forum.

Art Andrews, the current owner of the RPF, first encountered *Star Wars* while *The Empire Strikes Back* was in theaters. "The first thing I saw was the [AT-AT] Walkers and they seemed impossibly tall. It captured my imagination," he said. "*Star Wars* has really defined a great deal of my life, my work, and my hobbies." While his friends grew out of *Star Wars* over the course of the 1980s and 1990s, he didn't.

In the late 1990s, Lucas announced that he would rerelease his original trilogy in celebration of the twentieth anniversary of their initial release, along with some updated special effects and scenes that he hadn't been able to film as desired when he'd first released them. Moreover, he would be returning to the universe with a new prequel trilogy, starting with *The Phantom Menace* in 1999. The excitement brought about a new wave of fan websites, which covered updates and provided message forums for fans to chat with one another: TheForce.net (launched in 1996), RebelScum (1996), StarWarz (1998), SWfans.net, and others.

"Of all things," Andrews told me in January 2020, the site "really got [its] start on a site called *Star Wars* vs. *Titanic*."

In 1995, a "loose collective of people" had started up a handful of prop replica discussion forums on AOL, which Andrews described as the forerunners to the RPF. Around the same time, Andrews explained, a teenage fan named Brandon Alinger, who later went on to work for the Prop Store and author *Star Wars Costumes: The Original Trilogy*, set up his own set of forums on a platform called BeSeen as a way for fans who didn't have access to those AOL forums to discuss replica props and other topics.

In 1999, with *The Phantom Menace* about to enter theaters, a *Star Wars* website called Jawa Fortress started up a forum thread called "starwarsvstitanic," which tracked the box office progress of the new *Star Wars* against James Cameron's *Titanic*. It grew quickly and became the official discussion forum for another fan site, SW-fans.net. Alinger was friends with the webmaster and migrated his own discussion forum over to it. In 2001, Alinger handed his discussion forums over to a pair of new owners, Nikki Burdett and Cliff Wright, who transferred them from SW-fans.net to their own set of forums, prop-planet.com.

By this point in time, the Replica Prop Forum had attracted hundreds of users, including Andrews. "It was somewhere between the special editions coming out and the prequels coming out that I really started looking into that stuff," he explained. "When I was a kid, I tried to build my own little wood guns and little costumes, but nothing serious. I didn't have the means to do that stuff."[1]

With *Star Wars* coming out again, he became interested in building props. "I found the RPF, and of all things, not actually for [movie] props," he says. "I was super into Pearl Jam and was looking for a jacket like Eddie Vedder wore. I first posted there, asking if anyone knew how to replicate the jacket, and nobody answered me at all."

Despite that minor setback, he was intrigued at what he found on the site. "I got interested in that and what they were doing there and saw all the things I wish I could have had as a kid: those people were making them. That just blew my mind."

---

1 Art Andrews in conversation with the author, January 2020.

He stayed with the forum and was inspired to begin a passion project that had been a childhood dream of his: a replica of Boba Fett's armor. He started up a thread in the RPF about the armor, which exploded with activity and prompted him to spin the discussion off into a dedicated forum of its own, The Dented Helmet.

By the early 2000s, the Replica Prop Forum had become a focal point for prop and costume making on the internet, extending beyond franchises like *Star Wars*. Members posted their progress in build threads for everything from scale models to Indiana Jones hats and accessories to Terminator busts. It wasn't the only major costuming forum out there: TheForce.net launched its own costuming subforum in its Jedi Council Forums in 2002, allowing its existing membership to provide much of the same support: tips on fabric types, how to build lightsabers, and a gallery to post pictures of the costumes that people were putting together.

The community provided makers with access to like-minded builders, a marketplace to sell props, and a space to talk about the stories and toys that they were most passionate about. As a result, the forums became a sort of incubator of talent throughout the late 1990s and early 2000s, attracting some high-profile users, such as Adam Savage, one of the hosts of the Discovery Channel's science reality series *MythBusters*.

While famous for his role as an energetic counterpart to his cohost, Jamie Hyneman, Savage had gotten his start acting as a child, and eventually turned his attention to building props and creating special effects, working as a model maker on films like *Flubber*,

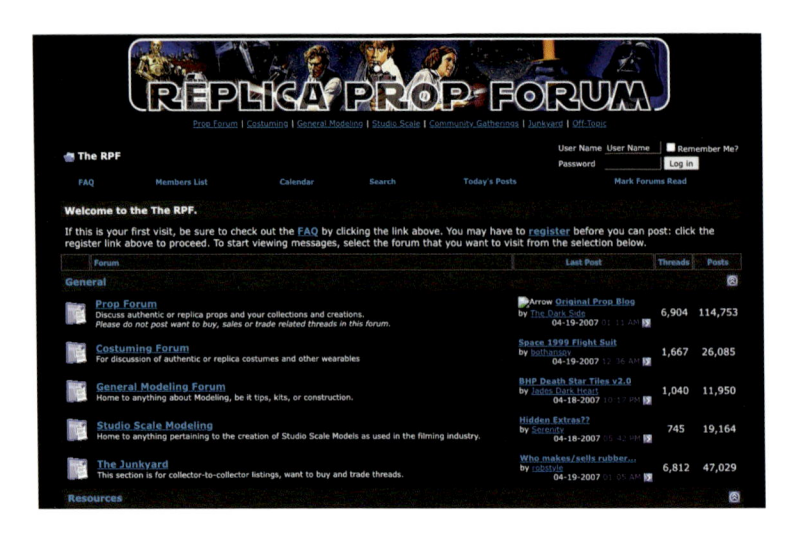

The Replica Prop Forum played a central role in the rise of the prop replica and cosplay community by providing a platform for builders to connect, share resources, and sell costumes.

Star Wars: The Phantom Menace and *Attack of the Clones, Bicentennial Man, The Matrix Reloaded* and *Revolutions*, and *Terminator 3: Rise of the Machines*.

"I was part of a kind of secret prop-building group online before the Replica Prop Forum called Toys for Big Boys," Savage says. "It was a short-lived list put out by a guy in the Midwest named John Pisarelli. It fell apart—I don't remember the social dynamics . . . but many of the people that were part of that group are still some of the most long-standing members of the RPF."

Savage notes that the RPF had an enormous impact on the fan costuming world. "A lot of people that were in those early forums were doing—it was an incubator, but it was also the brain trusts that became the foundation of Hollywood Collectibles Group and Master Replicas, all those guys came out of the Replica Prop Forum and Props Summit and GB Fans Forum, and the R2-D2 Builders Club."[2]

The RPF remains an influential hub of creativity and enthusiasm for anyone interested in building their own costume, and while it's not the only source of cosplay expertise on the internet, it's remained a major destination for makers of all stripes, containing entire tutorials and build threads for costumes; an online flea market for those looking for specialty parts; and a place for fans to find their enthusiastic counterparts as they look for inspiration for their next project.

ACP AND COSPLAY.COM

The RPF is one of several major online communities dedicated to cosplay and costuming. One other hub that popped up in 2000 is American Cosplay Paradise (ACP), originally a place for cosplayers to post pictures of their own costumes and connect with others to coordinate photo shoots at conventions. They could check out pictures of costumes at events that they missed, as well as share tips and build progress. In *Yaya Han's World of Cosplay*, Han described the ACP as the "first community site created for cosplay," and said that she was the thirteenth person to sign up when it launched. It quickly became a valuable resource for aspiring cosplayers.

"Whenever someone discovered a new technique or material," she wrote, "it spread like wildfire throughout the community and forum pages. The first cosplay tutorials were

---

2   Adam Savage in conversation with the author, December 2019.

Cosplay.com was one of the pivotal sites in the cosplay boom, providing a platform for cosplayers to meet one another and compare resources and techniques, and serving as a major launchpad for many of the community's biggest names.

created and shared this way," and allowed cosplayers to pioneer the techniques that are now commonplace.[3] Importantly, it highlighted specific cosplayers, allowing them to post updates to the site, host their own profiles in which they could show off their work, and provide their contact information so others could reach out. Those features were vital for establishing a community, where builders could collaborate and build alongside other members.

Other sites dedicated to cosplay formed around the same time, like Cosplay.com and Cosplay Lab. Founded in 2002, Cosplay.com became a major destination for cosplayers. The site's owner, Kyle Johnson, first founded the site because his partner was a cosplayer: "[I] pulled from my community experience and started Cosplay.com to have something to do while we were attending conventions together," he explained in the book *Cosplay World*.[4] The site offered a number of features for members, including forums, image galleries, calendars with upcoming conventions, and a blog that provided regular updates to the community. Cosplay.com quickly became a full-time job for Johnson, who opened a storefront there that allowed people to register for photo shoots online (and later, cosplay accessories), as well as a classifieds section and more. It became especially popular as traditional blogging sites like LiveJournal petered out, says Han, who noted that

---

3   Yaya Han, *Han's World of Cosplay: A Guide to Fandom Costume Culture* (New York: Sterling, 2020), 53.
4   Brian Ashcraft and Luke Plunkett, *Cosplay World* (Munich: Prestel, 2014), 41.

Cosplay.com became the go-to resource and community for anime cosplayers in particular. "It got really popular," says Han, "and was where everybody in the anime community gravitated towards, because they had really big forums that touched on all of these things. It was one of the first, biggest cosplay sites."

Han wrote that she sees this period as a "renaissance era of cosplay," and that while the community had its growing pains, it was an exciting period. Other cosplayers, like Kamui Cosplay, got their start by first reading and watching anime and manga, and attended their first convention in 2003 in Germany.[5]

The establishment and growth of sites like the RPF, the ACP, and Cosplay.com were instrumental in developing the social capital that forms the backbone of the modern cosplay movement. These online destinations helped to not only incubate talent and quickly spread information, they allowed cosplayers to connect with one another on even ground, fostering those relationships both in online and in-person settings.

But these sites also fostered very different communities from one another, highlighting the fact that the singular term "cosplay community" is a bit of a misnomer. The RPF and its associated sites dug into a specific tradition of costuming and props: the art of replication, fostering makers who were chiefly interested in trying to re-create the fixtures of their favorite films and TV shows. Cosplay.com and ACP came out of a separate, adjacent fan population that has its roots predominantly in animated and illustrated works. Both have their own vibrant internal cultures, norms, and quirks.

The RPF still exists and maintains its bustling community, and the ACP also remains up and running with active forums and resources for costumers. Cosplay.com has transformed over the years, seemingly fading out as cosplayers moved on to other resources and forums. As of September 2021, the site is in the midst of a relaunch that promises to bring back forums, picture galleries, and costume resources.

The forum is an instrumental element of the development and growth of the cosplay world, but it's not the only place in which these communities coalesce. Facebook and social media as a whole have since completely transformed the world of cosplay.

---

5   "Interview with Kamui Cosplay," The Cosplay Chronicles, YouTube video, October 30, 2014, https://youtu.be/4ymGzSzCIYA.

31 VIRTUAL COMMUNITIES

SMARTPHONES AND CAMERAS

The first permanent photograph was developed in 1825 by French inventor Joseph Nicéphore Niépce, after he exposed pewter coated with bitumen to form an image. From there, photographic technology steadily progressed as inventors shrunk down the devices and streamlined the required steps, transforming a cumbersome endeavor into a simple one. The original process was complicated: photographers exposed treated plates of glass or ceramic to light through their camera, which would require an extended amount of time to cure.

That changed in 1885 when inventor George Eastman developed a process that could capture photographs on paper, which he called Kodak. In 1888, he introduced a small handheld camera, a self-contained unit that allowed amateur photographers to shoot their images, send the box back to the factory, and get the finished images mailed back, along with new film. Writing in *Smithsonian* magazine, Clive Thompson explains that this was a watershed moment for the industry. "Suddenly, photography became unmoored in space. People took the camera out into the sunshine—and were immediately entranced by the ability to capture lively, goofy everyday motion."[1]

---

1 Clive Thompson, "The Invention of the 'Snapshot' Changed the Way We Viewed the World," *Smithsonian*, September 2014, https://www.smithsonianmag.com/innovation/invention-snapshot-changed-way-we-viewed-world-180952435.

Members of the 501st Legion's New England Garrison pose with an attendee at Boston's Walk Now For Autism event in 2009.   *Courtesy of Andrew Liptak*

Photography took off in American culture as Kodak offered up new, cheaper cameras. Thompson notes that by 1905, one-third of American homes had a camera. In the decades that followed, the technology improved—the Japanese optical company Asahi (later known as Pentax) developed the single-lens reflex (SLR) camera in 1954, while the instant camera, led by Polaroid, was introduced in the 1950s. The earliest digital cameras were introduced in the 1970s, but it wasn't until the 1980s and 1990s that they became widely available for a commercial audience. Similarly, the first camera phone appeared in 1999, and the market would steadily grow in popularity in the years that followed, especially as technology companies began releasing smartphones with better cameras.

The introduction of cheap cameras meant that a wider segment of the American public was able to take pictures of everyday life—including costumes. Pictures of cosplayers exist dating back to 1939 with the first images of Forrest Ackerman in the costume he wore to the first World Science Fiction Convention in New York, to be followed by plenty more of cosplaying fans in the following decades.

I first began appearing at events in public in stormtrooper armor in 2004, by which time digital cameras were common. Pedestrians who came across us would inevitably fumble around in a backpack, purse, or pocket and pull out their camera. They'd then have a companion or onlooker take their picture with me and go on with their day.

Around 2008 and 2009, I began to notice a shift in behavior: the proliferation of smartphones had begun to change bystanders' behavior. While some people still brought their cameras, others increasingly pulled out their phone instead. Rather than posed portraits, they began to take selfies with us. Now, it's a rare sight for someone to pick up a point-and-shoot digital (or even film!) camera to take pictures of us in armor. This caused a slight shift in the relationship between costumer and onlooker: whereas before, someone might take a picture of a cosplayer in a pose or a picture of themselves with a group of troopers, more people now take selfies with us, a photograph that is highly experiential, putting the photographer and cosplayer together in a single moment.

The explosive rise of digital photography has another advantage: one's pictures are now considerably easier to share with friends and followers via social media.

SOCIAL MEDIA

If communities laid the foundation for modern-day cosplay, social media supercharged it.

While you can attribute cosplay's popularity to factors like shifts in consumer taste in blockbuster films, television shows, and novels, the introduction of new production technologies such as foam production and 3D printing, it is the ease of distribution of visuals of the hobby in action and instructional documents that have changed the face of cosplay.

Some costumers had set up pages for themselves on early social media sites like Myspace, LiveJournal, and Friendster, which allowed them to interact and communicate with friends and cosplayers outside of forums. Lin Han points to LiveJournal as a major gathering point for cosplayers in the early 2000s. "It was less about cosplay and more about finding friends with similar interests," she says. "We kind of all started small together and it kind of filtered that way: people would costume with me, and we would grow closer together because we would plan things together."[2] Cosplayers would also set up their own websites on platforms like GeoCities, often with their own forums attached.

---

2   Lin Han in conversation with the author, February 2020.

But no site had quite the impact that Facebook did.

In 2004, Harvard student Mark Zuckerberg launched a student website called Face-Mash, which he'd built for his classmates to compare pictures of one another and judge their attractiveness using images scraped from various university sources. The site went viral and was later taken down, but the experience prompted him to launch a follow-up site: Facebook. This successor site allowed students to join, add pictures of themselves, provide basic information, and add friends. Initially, the site was limited to just college students, but in 2006, the company opened up registration to anyone over the age of thirteen.

Over the course of Facebook's life, it's added a slew of new features, like photo albums (and the ability to tag friends in pictures), Groups, News Feed, Events, reaction buttons, and Pages. For web-savvy costumers, Facebook represented a useful platform for organizing and self-promotion. Costumers had already been using a variety of social media platforms like Myspace and LiveJournal, taking advantage of their community-building functions. But Facebook deployed these features in new ways, not only allowing fans to connect with one another but recommending new people to follow based on networks of connected individuals. In the days after a convention or event, attendees could now upload their images and tag their friends, allowing others to see them. Facebook was—and is—ubiquitous, and with its scale of billions of users came some distinct social advantages: it reduced the emotional and mental load of keeping in touch with people on an individual level, allowing you to easily provide updates to your entire network, regardless of their role in your life.

The incremental features that Facebook introduced to keep people engaged proved a boon to cosplayers, by catering not only to distinct communities but also individuals. Facebook Groups allowed anyone to start up a closed group of like-minded people. It proved to be a useful tool for users to organize a local, in-person community, or a large, virtual one centered on a shared interest. This streamlined communication in many instances, because Facebook has grown to become such a prevalent part of our lives: members of a community could have an entire discussion under a single post without having to jump onto or through multiple forums.

When I began to organize a 501st squad in Vermont, Facebook was an important tool: we used a private group to stay organized and kept members apprised of updates (in addition to using email and our forums), set up a public-facing page to highlight our events and activities, and used the Events feature to invite members and the public to events that we were attending. It played a direct role in our recruitment efforts and public profile, leading to more events and a growing member base.

Groups have also become instrumental in the creation of pocket communities dedicated to individual costumes, like the Imperial shoretrooper. While most major film franchises have their own dedicated cosplayers, the *Star Wars* community is especially robust, thanks to large, established groups like the 501st and Rebel Legions, which collectively guide newcomers and veterans alike to build their costumes.

While there are well-established costumes like stormtroopers or Darth Vader, new stories present a fun challenge as builders work off of whatever details they can find to be among the first to complete their costumes ahead of the debut of said project. Before the release of the full film, new costumes demand collaboration, leaks, and an obsessive eye for parsing promotional materials like trailers and posters, which means it takes fans months to plot out their projects.

As interest in *Rogue One* began to build in 2016, Jason, my helmet dealer, created a private Facebook group—R1 Trooper Armory—as a forum for like-minded fans to discuss the new costumes they were interested in making. Jason is well-known in the prop-building community: his helmets are reputed for their detail and accuracy. His fame and talent quickly attracted both pro and amateur builders to the group. This and similar private groups like Shoretrooper Fam and Imperial Scarif Battalion became the heart of a vibrant movement to build not just any *Star Wars* costume but specifically the ones in *Rogue One*, which were based exclusively on marketing materials ahead of its December 2016 release.

When the first teaser for *Rogue One* arrived in early April 2016, it showed off a couple of totally new sets of armor: the tan-armored shoretrooper; the menacing, black-armored death troopers; and a trooper operating a tank.

But while trailers can give a general sense of a costume, fleeting shots and brief glimpses are no substitute for actual hands-on time with the real, official costumes. The break for those looking to create their own shoretrooper ensemble came in July during the official *Star Wars* Celebration convention in London. Lucasfilm brought along a group of screen-used costumes for display. Costumers turned out in droves to take photographs of the costumes from every angle, collecting close-ups of each piece of armor and detail, down to the weave of fabrics and the scuffs in the paint.

Fans in those dedicated Facebook groups identified the exact boots that were used in the costume because of the company logo on the heel—off-the-shelf Orca Bay Brecon Chelsea boots—and the company that sold them quickly ran out of stock as builders rushed to order their own pairs. The costume was also composed of other real-world items, ranging from parts of the ejection seat harness in a British warplane to a specific computer heat sink. Former trash became *Star Wars* treasure.

When it comes to building a screen-accurate costume, Jason explained to me, "reference is key," noting that he worked extensively off images from the trailers and the photos of displays, as well as images and dimensions supplied to him by friends and insiders. With that information in hand, he got started on his version of the helmet, beginning with a 3D-printed prototype, on which he constructed his final sculpt.

On the other side of the world, a different builder was tackling an even more ambitious project: a full suit of armor. Hailing from the Philippines, Jim (who also asked that we not use his last name) found it difficult in the past to get costumes and parts. So in 2014, he decided to make them himself. "No one was making a [helmet] from my favorite series of all time, so I had to have one," he says of his first costume, a clone trooper inspired by the 2003 animated TV series *The Clone Wars*. The costume was approved for use in the 501st Legion, and Jim has made props and sets of armor ever since.

With the shoretrooper, Jim's focus was on crafting the most accurate costume possible as quickly as possible, using all available reference materials as he sculpted each piece—first in foam, then in clay—with the end product cast in flexible fiberglass. Jim

A cosplayer dressed up as a shoretrooper poses for the camera at *Star Wars* Celebration in Chicago, Illinois. The costume is the central focus of a Facebook group called Shoretrooper Fam, which has helped to incubate interest, talent, and resources for those wishing to make the costume, helping to maintain its popularity, despite only appearing in the film *Rogue One* for a couple of minutes.

Courtesy of Andrew Liptak

began shipping out sets of his armor to members of the community on September 13, 2016—more than three months before *Rogue One* would open in theaters.

By December 1, 2016, the 501st Legion announced its official standards for the shoretrooper costume, providing a checklist for builders trying to get as close to the film version as possible. Like so many other *Star Wars* fans around the world, I had most of the elements already in place. Ever since I'd gotten my own fan-sculpted kit in October, I'd spent weeks trimming, gluing, and painting, and checking my work against that of a massive folder of images that I'd collected along the way. When I picked up that shoretrooper helmet on that snowy day in Vermont, the last piece of the puzzle was finally in my hands.

As I drove back home with my helmet buckled into the seat next to me, I reflected on what it took for this outfit to exist: an entire group of like-minded and collaborative fans singularly focused on bringing a costume to life from only a gallery of images online.

Since the release of *Rogue One* in 2016, Disney has released a number of *Star Wars* projects: *The Last Jedi*, *The Rise of Skywalker*, *The Mandalorian*, and *The Book of Boba Fett*, with plenty more on the way. Each of the unique costumes in those films—and in plenty of other franchises—has brought about its own dedicated group of builders working to replicate the costumes.

In 2007, Facebook launched Pages, a public-facing profile page for organizations that has also proved to be useful for cosplayers. It has enabled not only major, organized groups (like the 501st and Rebel Legions, 405th Infantry Division, Ghostbusters, and their affiliated chapters) to set up an online public presence, it also has allowed individual cosplayers to grow their followings, inviting the wider public to follow along, even if they weren't generally interested in participating in the community themselves. This has had a dual effect on the field. You can now easily find that one person you chatted with briefly at an event by looking through tags, pictures, or mutual friends. Users also spread the word about cosplay outside their immediate circle, so family, friends, and coworkers who weren't in the scene might see pictures of costumes and conventions. Even if they weren't particularly interested in participating, they were simply reminded that it existed by way of more than just judgmental snippets on the six o'clock news.

The introduction of social media sites had a curious impact on the workings of cosplay groups.

FACEBOOK GROUPS

Star Wars fans have always liked to dress up as their favorite characters, but high-quality costuming and cosplay have taken off in the last decade, aided by a variety of costuming websites, conventions, and the Facebook Groups feature.

In the years since *Rogue One* hit theaters, groups like Shoretrooper Fam and the costumes they're devoted to haven't withered away, even as general interest wanes and costumers move on to other projects. In fact, the opposite has occurred: they get new members every day as newcomers become inspired to make uniforms of their own. As with the internet forums that came before, these individuals each hold a wealth of knowledge and cumulative experience, supercharged when they form a group. Newcomers can—and do—ask existing members of these groups where to get started and share their progress as they go.

The shoretrooper costume, which originally appeared in *Rogue One*, has endured as a popular costume for cosplayers. It has several advantages: being from a film that's remained popular within *Star Wars* fandom, a *cool* look with several pieces you can find online, and an especially dedicated community behind it. While new *Star Wars* films have introduced their share of new costume types, you don't see the same devotion to the range trooper or jet trooper. Moreover, the costume is widely available thanks to the efforts of Sean Fields, who modeled and released files for anyone to print.

In a way, Shoretrooper Fam is a microcosm for the role that online communities have played in the cosplay world: a watering hole not only for useful advice to new costumers but for continuous enthusiasm for the costume, as well as ongoing research and study into what the original costume was composed of.

Several other costumes have drawn similar communities. Prior to the launch of *The Mandalorian*, fans began constructing their own costumes based on early photos and footage. As with the shoretrooper costume, they set up groups to trade information about its construction and formed a lasting, resourceful community. These groups will undoubtedly get a boost from this show's upcoming seasons (the titular character certainly having more screen time than the shoretroopers), on top of the massive mainstream following that the series has enjoyed thus far.

This model isn't limited to big franchises like Marvel, DC, or *Star Wars*. In 2017, a fan named Cricket Z. and her husband discovered Syfy's *The Expanse*, a series based on the novels by James S. A. Corey. Inspired by the costumes in the show, she set up the group Expanse Cosplay, hoping that she and her husband might meet other superfans of the series and get together with them at conventions. Boosted by word of mouth, the group grew, reaching more than 1,300 members at the time of this writing. In 2018, members gathered for their first meetup at VA Comicon in Richmond, and in the following months, segments of the group got together again at the Great Philadelphia Comic Con in Philadelphia; Shore Leave in Hunt Valley, Maryland; Dragon Con in Atlanta; and Arisia in Boston. When I met up with them in Atlanta in 2019, dozens of the group's members assembled in person, dressed up in the various costumes they'd come together to discuss virtually in the months and years before.

INSTAGRAM AND TIKTOK

Where forums and groups have provided valuable gathering points for cosplayers and builders to share tips and connect with one another, social media sites with an emphasis on visuals have proved to be exceptionally useful for cosplayers to show off their work and build massive followings. One of the largest of these platforms is the photo- and video-sharing app Instagram.

The platform was officially launched as an iPhone app in 2010 by two developers, Kevin Systrom and Mike Krieger, who had originally set out to produce a check-in app called Burbn. The idea was that as more people were carrying around smartphones, they'd be likely to check into their favorite places. Systrom built the app, began testing it, and started to chase venture capital funding, but he and his partner struggled to develop it and sell it to investors. The pair went back to the drawing board and tried to break the product down into its basic parts. As they did so, they kept coming back to photographs. They realized that they could set up a photo-sharing service that would allow users to upload pictures to the platform and "like" the ones that their friends uploaded. Then they added another instrumental feature: photo filters. Previously low-res (the iPhone 3GS had a 3 megapixel camera at the time, compared to the iPhone 13's pair of 12 megapixel primary lenses in 2021) photos could be turned into something a little more artistic, nostalgic, or black-and-white.

The app immediately took off. Within its first two years, the company's founders pulled in millions of dollars from investors, eventually attracting the attention of Facebook, which later bought the app for $1 billion, adding it to its suite of services.

LEFT: Jen Markham poses in front of her wardrobe at her home in New York City. Her cosplay videos on TikTok have earned her a massive following on the platform.

RIGHT: Jen Markham and her husband, Jeremy, prepare to shoot a new TikTok video. Her videos aren't off-the-cuff clips: she puts a considerable amount of preparation into their production.

Photos courtesy of Jen Markham

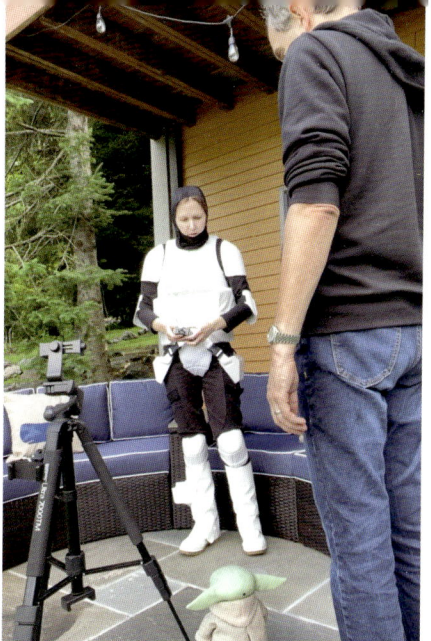

Writing in her book *No Filter: The Inside Story of Instagram*, tech reporter Sarah Frier notes that Instagram sees more than a billion users on the app each month, and that it was "one of the first apps to fully exploit our relationship with our phones, compelling us to experience life through a camera for the reward of digital validation."[3] Instagram has had a profound impact on the way we interact with people online: it's made celebrities accessible to the wider public without the professional filters of publicists or studios, and it's allowed creative individuals to build big followings through their pictures and short videos. People could go viral for a funny or well-captioned picture, spurred on by the app's features, like its "Popular" or "Explore" tabs.

Because Instagram is focused on pictures, it is a natural medium for cosplayers and cosplay influencers to show off their costumes, posting pictures of their in-progress builds, photo shoots of their finished costumes, snapshots from convention floors, or staged pictures of memes or funny moments—all for their followers to check out, like, and comment on. The platform helps users network by allowing them to tag their photos or videos with hashtags, and by recommending new users and posts to them. For cosplayers interested in looking at the work of others (either for inspiration or just for the pleasure of seeing new costumes), Instagram can be a bit like attending a 24-7 packed

---

3   Sarah Frier, *No Filter: The Inside Story of Instagram* (New York: Simon & Schuster, 2020), xvii.

VIRTUAL COMMUNITIES

convention hall, where you get to see all the vibrant costumes on display in an endless scrolling feed.

The platform isn't just a good fit for cosplay because of the ability to share photos; it's a platform that encourages self-marketing and projecting one's image into the world, which is something that cosplay inherently lends itself to. Frier notes in her book that "thanks to Instagram, life had become worth marketing—not for every Instagram user, but for millions of them."[4] For cosplayers looking to break into roles as spokespeople for the properties that they're informally representing, or into professions like modeling or becoming a nerd community micro—or in some cases macro—celebrity, the platform allows them to show off their work and their bodies for the world at large.

The social media landscape is enormously competitive, and plenty of other apps have made their mark on content sharing, like Snapchat or Vine, which both helped to popularize the public posting of photos or short videos via smartphones.

One relative newcomer has had a particularly huge impact on the world of cosplay: the video app TikTok. Founded in 2016 by a Chinese company called ByteDance, it allows users to post short video clips for their audiences. Users can edit their clips in the app, pair them with music or sounds, add captions or effects, apply filters, and, most importantly, share those videos with their friends and followers in a feed. As with Instagram, users can search through hashtags and recommendations. TikTok allows users to show off another dimension of their costumes: video brings those costumes to life in ways that pictures just can't do. Cosplayers can reenact moments of the movie or show where their character is from, lip-synch to popular songs, act out short skits, or simply jump onto trending memes in the community.

YOUTUBE

Traditional forums and social media sites like Facebook, Instagram, and Twitter played a major role in building up the cosplay scene, providing places for users to organize and coordinate efforts, whether that was building a single costume or prop or introducing an entire new wave of maker technology. Another media-sharing website proved an equally useful resource for builders: YouTube.

---

4   Frier, *No Filter*, 237.

Prior to 2005, watching videos on the internet was hit or miss: users generally depended on media players like Shockwave, QuickTime, or Windows Media Player to open and watch downloaded files. In 2004, Google had launched its own video streaming service, Google Video, but things drastically changed in 2006 when it purchased YouTube, a video-streaming platform set up in 2005 by a trio of PayPal employees: Steve Chen, Chad Hurley, and Jawed Karim. YouTube wasn't the only video-sharing site out there—in November 2004 Jake Lodwick and Zach Klein had launched Vimeo; while in March 2005 a pair of French programmers, Benjamin Bejbaum and Olivier Poitrey, set up their own site, Dailymotion.

These sites allowed a user to directly upload their own short videos, for viewing on the site or embedded in the user's personal website. Following its acquisition by Google and its ensuing partnerships with studios like NBC and CNN, YouTube's popularity exploded. In 2007, it launched a program that allowed users to be paid for their videos after a certain number of views, unlocking a new venue for content creators to make a living. The nature of YouTube and the work of cosplayers naturally dovetailed.

"The thing that I love about YouTube is how it is with the sharing ethos of cosplay," Adam Savage says. "YouTube is an incredible resource for that. There is no technique that I have needed that I haven't found [via] someone on YouTube."[5]

The visual nature of YouTube lends itself exceedingly well to instructional videos. "I love telling people now the kinds of machinations I would have to go through to find resources twenty-five years ago," Savage notes. "I'd have to find some listing for lightsabers in the back of a fanzine and find a guy in Texas who hand-machines Luke's lightsaber from *The Empire Strikes Back*—there was literally no other option unless you went to one of the early Celebrations, or to a *Star Trek* convention where someone happened to have them on hand."

Prior to YouTube, aspiring makers would have to reverse-engineer a prop on their own, or go through various forum build threads to make a prop. Those threads were often useful, containing a series of step-by-step instructions, but they were reliant on two things: the original user's descriptions and photographs, if they provided either. Video helped to cut out some of the ambiguity, as it would capture everything a maker did while building.

As a result, cosplayers realized that they could put together their own videos showing off how to build just about anything. Now, instead of writing down their documentation, they could simply film themselves.

---

5   Adam Savage in conversation with the author, December 2019.

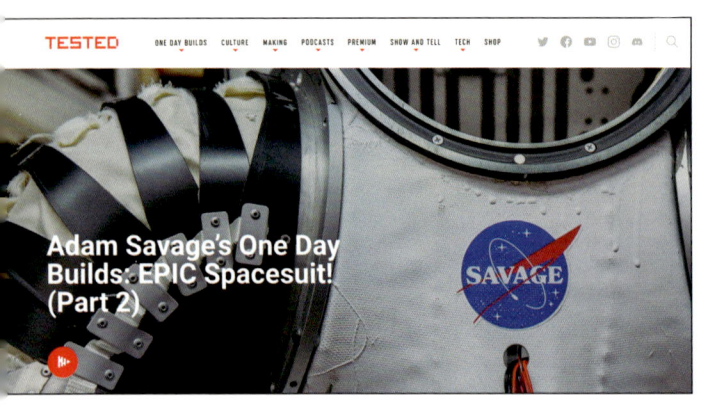

TOP: Created by Will Smith and Norman Chan in 2010, Tested was originally a platform dedicated to technology, and has since expanded into showcasing Adam Savage's builds, costumes, and tutorials.

BOTTOM: A screenshot of Punished Props Academy's YouTube channel. Creator Bill Doran uses the channel to showcase his builds and tutorials.

With YouTube's payment program, some cosplayers figured out how to fund an entire business based on their work as builders. Makers and cosplayers like Savage (Tested); Jessica Nigri; Bob Clagett (I Like to Make Stuff); Colin Furze; Bill and Britt Doran (Punished Props); Laura Kampf, Kamui Cosplay, and thousands of others set up channels in a growing subgenre of maker videos, covering everything from how to create foam armor and prop weapons to costume weathering and more. It allowed makers to rely on the sites for dedicated income, or as a place to showcase their props and costuming techniques.

Kamui Cosplay and Punished Props have a couple of the most dominant channels in cosplay tutorials. Bill Doran of Punished Props explained to me in February 2020 that he first became interested in the scene when some friends convinced him to show up to a local anime convention dressed as a character from *Team Fortress*. The experience blew him away, and he quickly began attending every event that he could in costume. "We did that for a few years, and I started publishing the work I did with the costumes I made," Doran explained. "I started with a blog on my website and got a lot of interest in what I was doing from people who wanted to know how to make these things."

In 2012, he decided that the next logical step was to film his process. "I started a YouTube channel, and it really was just for fun and for people who wanted to know how to make stuff," he says. "It started out super casual. I believe in the first year, I published twelve videos and got two hundred subscribers." But from that base, he and his wife, Britt, transformed their hobby into a business, selling their own tutorial books, patterns, knives, notebooks, and other merchandise while also producing hundreds of videos on costume guides, production tutorials, business advice, project plans, and tools.

Doran notes that a lot of effort goes into making each of the films that he and his wife produce. He handles the project while his wife does the filming. "Before we start, we figure out what we're going to make and what the story is going to be for the video." From there, they plan out the full build, making sure that they have all of the parts, tools, and materials that they'll need. "We figure all of that stuff out before we start filming, and we have the outline sitting on the table next to us while I'm building, then we cross things off the list." Once completed, they edit down the video and upload it to YouTube. "The hard part is figuring it all out ahead of time."[6]

He echoed the sharing ethos that YouTube facilitates for cosplayers. "People who got into this ten years ago learned a whole bunch of stuff along the way, and now they want to share that with others. People who got started a couple of years ago are now passing the knowledge along to the next person in line." With every video, cosplayers add to a much larger pool of knowledge that anyone can draw from, further enriching the field.

The popularity and sheer scale of YouTube does bring a few downsides with it. More videos mean more content that users have to wade through to find what they're looking for. Writing in *WIRED* magazine, Ryan Meith recounts trying to troubleshoot an issue on YouTube: "Recently, the voice chat on my Xbox crapped out, so I searched for helpful tutorials. What I found? Videos of charmless *children* all the way down. The top results redefined uselessness."[7] Searching for cosplay alone brings up a mixed bag of results: music videos, compilations scraped together from TikTok posts, and a handful of reviews for off-the-shelf products.

COSPLAY MUSIC VIDEOS

The upbeat song from singer Outasight plays in the background of filmmaker team Sneaky Zebra's 2018 music video from MCM London Comic Con, revealing a whirlwind

---

6   Bill Doran in conversation with the author, February 2020.
7   Ryan Meith, "Angry Nerd: YouTube Can't Help You," *WIRED* magazine, January 21, 2020, https://www.wired.com/story/angry-nerd-useless-youtube-advice.

of cosplayers. It's a catchy song and video, one that seems to capture the energy and spirit of what it's like at a convention.

While YouTube has become an extremely useful resource for costumers and makers showing off how they built something, it's provided another function to filmmakers and cosplayers alike: another venue for their performance. As others have done with photo-sharing sites and social networks, savvy filmmakers have established a niche genre on YouTube: the cosplay music video. Filmmakers from channels like mineralblu and Sneaky Zebra attend conventions with camera in hand and talk to the cosplayers that they come across. They work quickly, asking them to hold a pose or move like their character, whether it be a simple smile or an iconic pose or a large battle scene, then shoot a couple of takes.

Once the convention is over, they take the footage to the editing room and assemble a short video set to music, sometimes tying together the characters and lyrics. It is generally composed of several cuts of cosplayers reenacting very brief scenes from their shows. The effect is greater than that of even a professionally shot picture, and these videos can serve as a trailer of sorts for the season's cosplay and convention scene.

Creators on YouTube release a range of similar projects on the platform. YouTuber acksonl posts a variety of convention clips set to music, along with shorter videos called "Cosplay Featurettes" showing several scenes that highlight a character in action, set to music that captures the mood—be it whimsical or action-packed—yet stopping short of a proper fan film, which would have a longer story and plot. These instead act as more of a character study.[8]

FRAGILE INFRASTRUCTURE

While the internet has been an essential resource for costumers, the infrastructure that fosters such communities is deceptively fragile. While any picture you post to the internet might well stay on there forever, the meticulous documentation, images, and build threads are reliant on a vast patchwork of volunteers, owners, and cheerleaders to ensure that they remain a useful resource.

In its earliest days, the owners of the Replica Prop Forum had to pay for their own

---

[8] "Horizon Zero Dawn: Aloy [Cosplay Featurette]," acksonl, YouTube video, September 17, 2019, https://www.youtube.com/watch?v=efKwae-Ipf8.

server. "Back then, it was a big deal how much data you took up," Art Andrews recounted. "So they wouldn't allow threads to go beyond three hundred posts. They would shut them down, and after a certain period of time, they would delete threads."

Andrews noted that while there were intentional deletions to save server space, there were also accidental data purges. Before he took over the forum, "there were several server migrations that lost so much." He explained, "You still go out there, and it's one of my greatest sadnesses; that there is so much great data gone."

Another major issue surfaced in June 2017, when popular photo-sharing website Photobucket announced in a blog post that it was introducing a payment tier for its users. Launched in 2003, it was once one of the most popular websites on the internet, and by 2017, it found that it couldn't keep operating under its free model. Previously with a free account, users could upload their images, and from there, provide links to online retailers, personal websites, or forum posts. But now, if someone wanted to hotlink an image that they'd uploaded to the site onto another site, they'd have to pay $399 a year for the privilege.[9]

It was understandable overall, but the company didn't warn users before eliminating its free tier and ended up automatically blocking users from reposting images on other websites. The result was disastrous, particularly for costumers, who had for years used Photobucket as a place to store all the images they'd taken of costumes and props they were building. For users who didn't pay, each hotlinked image was replaced by a gray box with an illustration of a speedometer and the header: PLEASE UPDATE YOUR ACCOUNT TO ENABLE 3RD PARTY HOSTING.[10]

"Don't think this doesn't affect you because you don't use Photobucket," wrote Ian Billings of Norvic Philatelics after discovering the change of terms. "This still affects you if you look at any site which uses images stored [there]."[11] Once-useful build threads and tutorials were now filled with pages of the warning image, rendering them largely ineffective. Andrews noted that it was a problem right away on the RPF. "You get so many great

---

9   Natt Garun, "Photobucket Accused of Blackmail after Quietly Requiring Users to Pay $400 a Year to Hotlink," *The Verge*, July 4, 2017, https://www.theverge.com/2017/7/4/15919224/photobucket-broken-images-amazon-ebay-etsy-paid-update.
10   Matthew Humphries, "Photobucket Breaks Image Links Across the Internet," *PCMag*, June 30, 2017, https://www.pcmag.com/news/photobucket-breaks-image-links-across-the-internet.
11   Ian - Norvic, "PHOTOBUCKET ALERT! A New Sort of Ransom!" Norvic Philatelics (blog), June 30, 2017, https://blog.norphil.co.uk/2017/06/photobucket-alert-new-sort-of-ransom.html.

things that are like, 'Hey, here's how to do something, look at the pictures,' and there are no pictures, well, that makes people upset and the thread totally useless."

Some users ponied up the money to get their images back online. But Photobucket had been around for nearly a decade and a half, with millions of users: if people had moved on from the hobby, didn't care, or simply couldn't afford to pay the fee, those images remained broken across the internet. A year later, the company course corrected, bringing on a new CEO and reducing the prices on its paid tiers.[12] Most importantly, it dropped the speedometer image, although the stand-in image remained watermarked to encourage users to subscribe. "Photobucket hurt very badly," Art Andrews explained. "They finally got that corrected, but by the end, so many people had gone and deleted their account anyway. That stuff is lost forever."

Following the issue, Andrews notes that he and his web team implemented a bit of a backstop to protect against other issues. "One of the things we do now is when anybody links to an external image, the software automatically moves that image to our site, so those things can't be lost."[13]

Photobucket wasn't the only site to change how it did business. In April 2018, photo-sharing site SmugMug purchased one of its rivals, Flickr, which had previously offered a generous free tier. But by November, it became clear that that model couldn't be sustained, and it introduced the new Flickr Pro tier for fifty dollars a year. While the site would keep free accounts, they would limit them to only a thousand images.[14] While some users opted to pay the annual fee, others couldn't or wouldn't, and were about to lose years of images. Moreover, SmugMug has said that despite the shift, it is still not a profitable business and has encouraged users to subscribe.[15]

This isn't an issue limited to just service platforms like Photobucket or Flickr. In 2001, Yahoo! introduced a new feature: Yahoo! Groups, a cross between an internet

---

12 Greg Avery, "Photobucket Drops Pricing that Angered Millions (And New CEO Hopes to Unbreak the Internet)," *Denver Business Journal*, May 17, 2018, https://www.bizjournals.com/denver/news/2018/05/17/photobucket-drops-pricing-that-angered-millions.html.
13 Art Andrews in conversation with the author, January 2020.
14 "Flickr Announces New Photographer-Centric Improvements to Flickr Pro, Free Plans," *BusinessWire*, November 1, 2018, https://www.businesswire.com/news/home/20181101005328/en/Flickr-Announces-New-Photographer-Centric-Improvements-Flickr-Pro.
15 Nick Statt, "Flickr Owner SmugMug Says it Needs More Money to 'Keep the Flickr Dream Alive,'" *The Verge*, December 19, 2019, https://www.theverge.com/2019/12/19/21030795/flickr-pro-smugmug-don-macaskill-open-letter.

forum and email listserv. Users could sign up for a group and participate in discussions on the site or via email digests. It became a major early platform for fan and costuming groups looking to organize their activities.[16]

In October 2019, Yahoo! announced that it was going to sunset the service: users wouldn't be able to add new postings to groups, and starting in December, it would begin deleting everything.[17] While the company said that users could download their data and keep in touch with community members, the collective body of how-tos and resources contained in those groups would be lost. In 2009, Yahoo! had pulled a similar move when it closed down GeoCities—a once-popular platform from which users could build their own websites—eliminating millions of websites and user content.[18]

The plight of the two sharing sites highlights an issue with how the cosplay community is set up. While dedicated forum owners can keep their platforms running, users often depend on the viability of third-party services. Photo-sharing sites can go down, go out of business, or change how they operate, impacting the data that cosplayers have come to rely on. YouTube videos can be taken down, Twitter and Instagram users can be banned from the service or delete their profiles, and information can simply get lost.

Furthermore, as top social media platforms have grown in prominence, much of the activity transitioned to them from other platforms, they decimated the online traffic to the traditional forums that costumers had been organizing on for years. Forums do still exist today, but they're not as vibrant as they once were, their usefulness reduced from a means to facilitate a community to an archival resource.

In many ways, Facebook's features have taken over the role that forums like the RPF have traditionally played: providing gathering points for fans to share information. In particular, they've become pop-up incubators for interested fans with the release of new science-fiction and fantasy films and TV shows. Facebook's Groups feature has led to an interesting development within the cosplay community: pop-up groups dedicated to a single costume type, allowing members to not only share the resources needed to build

---

16   "F-Costume," Fanlore (website), accessed December 9, 2021, https://fanlore.org/wiki/F-Costume#cite_note-owner-2.
17   Jordan Pearson, "Yahoo Groups Is Winding Down and All Content Will Be Permanently Removed," *Vice Motherboard*, October 16, 2019, https://www.vice.com/en_us/article/8xwe9p/yahoo-groups-is-winding-down-and-all-content-will-be-permanently-removed.
18   Leena Rao, "Yahoo Quietly Pulls the Plug on Geocities," *TechCrunch*, April 23, 2009, https://techcrunch.com/2009/04/23/yahoo-quietly-pulls-the-plug-on-geocities.

it but also provide comradery to keep people engaged, even if the film or television show said costume appears in came out years ago.

But what happens when Facebook decides that the Groups feature no longer makes sense and eliminates it? Facebook has made major systemic changes to its architecture over the years, and users have no say in how these platforms operate. Even if some are able to download their information and content, much will likely be lost forever. While it's easy to point and laugh over an obsolete platform like Yahoo! Groups going under (I mean, really, who used Yahoo! Groups when they could use Facebook Groups?), if it happens again, a newcomer entering the field won't be able to find the valuable information that a group or thread might have once held—they could be forced to start from scratch or simply give up.

Facebook, like other sites that can change the algorithm for how users see their content (including Google, Instagram, and Twitter), doesn't even need to do something as drastic as removing a key product to make an impact: they would only have to tweak how their content is distributed. In 2015, Facebook rolled out a change to how pages would be seen by followers, noting that "Pages that post promotional creative should expect their organic distribution to fall significantly over time," while at the same time encouraging page owners to buy ads to increase their reach.[19] The result was a major reduction in how many people a page owner could organically reach. In 2018, cosplayer Jessica Nigri told *Business Insider* that her official page registered around 4.7 million followers—a sizable number. But with the change, her reach through Facebook was "decimated."[20] Nigri, and other cosplayers who rely on social media to make a living, have since shifted to other platforms like Patreon or YouTube, where they may have smaller followings but bring in a more reliable income.

The rise and fall of major community sites isn't the only thing to be concerned with: regular domains, blog posts, articles, and documents regularly fall off the internet due to run-of-the-mill restructuring, alterations, deletions, and other changes to websites and platforms. Someone's house might catch fire, destroying costumes or physical

---

19   "An Update to Facebook News Feed: What It Means for Business Pages," Meta for Business (f.k.a. Facebook for Business), accessed December 9, 2021, https://www.facebook.com/business/news/update-to-facebook-news-feed.
20   Nathan McAlone, "Cosplay Superstar Jessica Nigri Talks about Turning Her Passion into a Full-Time Job, and How Facebook's Algorithm Changes Have Affected Her," *Business Insider*, January 30, 2018, https://www.businessinsider.com/jessica-nigri-cosplay-star-talks-business-facebook-new-rooster-teeth-documentary-2018-1.

photos of older conventions. Individuals with specialized knowledge of a build technique or the history of the scene might suddenly pass away—as did happen in the midst of researching this book—leaving certain pieces of information unrecoverable. Indeed, Cosplay.com appears to have restructured itself over the years, and while some of its content is preserved by the Internet Archive (which deploys web crawlers to take snapshots of pages), there's a lot that doesn't get backed up. This phenomenon isn't limited to only the internet, either: countless fanzines, works of fan fiction, cosplay pictures, and more have been lost to the sands of time because of age, wear-and-tear, moves, fires and natural disasters, or just plain old discarding in trash bins. What remains is often the result of devoted and passionate fans who recognize a creation's importance to the community and take it upon themselves to preserve it.[21]

Even keeping a community afloat can be a trying experience. Organizations like the 501st and Rebel Legions are complicated bodies, and interpersonal drama can burn out a dedicated webmaster or specialist. Andrews noted that the RPF might have met an early end without his intervention. When the original owners of the site decided that they wanted to move on, they asked him if he wanted to take the reins. "They ran out of people to run it, and because I had done The Dented Helmet for so long, they came and asked me. I initially turned them down, and they finally were like, 'If you don't do it, it could close.'" Andrews took over ownership of the site and introduced an advertising and paid member system, which has since kept the site running. Had he not been there to step in? It very well could have vanished, one more relic in the vast internet graveyard. One way to prevent this from happening? A robust community that preserves that legacy.

SHARING IS CARING

But despite the potential pitfalls that online infrastructure brings with it, these different platforms do one thing: ease the flow of information from person to person, whether it's pictures, tutorials, videos, or discussions. As sites and forums such as the Replica Prop Forum, Cosplay.com, TheForce.net forums, Dewback Wing: ASAP, and Facebook

---

21 Jay Castello, "The Race to Save Kirk and Spock's Fanfiction Legacy," *Polygon*, September 23, 2021, https://www.polygon.com/features/22684381/kirk-spock-fanfic-archive-of-our-own-star-trek.

Groups demonstrate, these gathering points act as force multipliers for cosplayers, imparting not only enthusiasm but the techniques and tutorials that allow people to construct costumes at an ever-lower cost.

This reduction of cost is key to the rise of cosplay as an activity, as is the reduction of the time needed to build something. If one person pioneers a technique, they might be the only person who can do that. But when that technique is shared, the cosplayers who follow don't have to invest the same amount of time into puzzling together the same thing; they only need to follow along and replicate. "In the early parts of our careers," Savage notes, "our labor was free and materials cost a crap ton, while later in our career, our labor is the most expensive part of the equation. Materials that support our labor are literally minute expenses comparatively. I love how much the sharing economy of cosplay has lowered the threshold to entry as deeply as it can."[22]

Moreover, information is hard to contain once it's out there, meaning the techniques that cosplayers rely on won't likely be limited to one or two builders. This has an impact on the social and cultural dynamics of the scene—the RPF was once heavily male-dominated, but the increase in access to foam-building techniques and a handful of popular influencers grew the forum's female population. "The gatekeeping of middle-class white guys is legendary," Savage noted. "Certainly, there is some institutional racism. Certainly, there's gatekeeping; certainly, there's 'This is my hobby, not yours.' "[23]

At its worst, the internet codifies these behaviors, but when everything works out, it can democratize the flow of information, eliminating those boundaries and barriers and allowing anyone who's interested in cosplay to take part. Those who can't afford to spend thousands of dollars on a top-of-the-line, screen-accurate Boba Fett can still make their dream of being the silent bounty hunter a reality with the techniques, tools, and tricks they learn from the community; and by embracing that, fandom as a whole gets a bit stronger and more resilient.

Where forums first incubated communities and allowed people to pool their knowledge, social media acts as the hobby's best distributor to the wider world. Before, where members might have been connected with person-to-person relationships through conventions, letters, fanzines, or forums, they can now share those pictures and experiences

---

22 Adam Savage in conversation with the author, December 2019.
23 Adam Savage in conversation with the author, December 2019.

with the wider world. The infrastructure and ubiquity of platforms like Facebook and Instagram means that groups that were once fairly isolated are now able to break out beyond the walls of those gated communities.

One can now be part of both the costuming world and the world at large, with cosplay accomplishments sitting alongside "regular" life updates like new jobs, trips, relationships, and moves. Posting pictures to Facebook after a convention means that you are sharing them with not only your other cosplay friends but also potentially your aunt, grandmother, childhood/high school/college friends, and coworkers. Not only that, but they can see the reactions and comments that those poses rack up, as well as the cultural ephemera that these communities create among their practitioners. As this happens, a hobby that once seemed mysterious or strange becomes a little more standard. Someone who hadn't been all that interested in attending a convention might realize that they, too, happened to like that recent blockbuster film or hit sci-fi TV show and look into it more in-depth. As a result, anyone who's posted their cosplay pictures to social media has become a sort of unofficial ambassador or conduit for someone new to step through and check it out. Social media acts as a force multiplier for the entire vocation of cosplay, and, as such, it's probably the most important piece of technology for its survival and growth, helping not only to establish and reinforce the culture online but also to recruit new costumers into its ranks.

32 COSPLAY AND COVID-19

Science fiction has long imagined the many ways in which a world-ending pandemic might spread across the world: one need look no further than Stephen King's *The Stand*, John Scalzi's novella *Unlocked*, Emily St. John Mandel's *Station Eleven*, Ling Ma's *Severance*, or Steven Soderbergh's 2011 film *Contagion*. Our globalized world has increased the chances of a rapidly spreading pandemic, and in early 2020, SARS-CoV-2 proved to be the right virus for the job with its long incubation period and transmission through the very air we breathe—meaning every cough, sneeze, and spoken word is a risk—and it is deadlier than the common flu.[1]

When COVID-19 cases began to mount in the United States and the rest of the world in January and February that year, it became increasingly clear that governments and people around the world weren't doing enough to stop the spread of the virus. Faced with a huge spike in cases, Italy instituted a nationwide lockdown in early March, and other nations around the world followed suit. Schools closed, workers were encouraged to stay home (if they were able), bookstores and restaurants and museums closed their doors. When it came to the world of fandom, conventions weren't spared the consequences: they also began to shut down, citing the risk of exposure.

---

1 Kristina Sauerwein, "COVID-19 Patients at Higher Risk of Death, Health Problems than Those with Flu," Washington University School of Medicine in St. Louis, December 15, 2020, https://medicine.wustl.edu/news/covid-19-patients-at-higher-risk-of-death-health-problems-than-those-with-flu.

If you've been to a convention, you'll know that they're a prime breeding ground for illnesses of all types. The country's biggest conventions draw hundreds of guests, celebrities, and cosplayers into one location over the course of a single weekend, all packed into tight quarters. Walkways are often hard to navigate as you dodge cosplayers posing for pictures, con-goers stopping to chat or buy something from a vendor, or bystanders simply gawking at the spectacle of it all. Everyone breathes the same air, and in many cases, they'll head home with more than a collectible, memory, or autograph: they'll come down with what's colloquially known as "con flu," an annoying amalgamation of whatever illnesses people brought with them onto the con floor. In a COVID-19 era, a convention is the perfect super-spreader event, one that could infect hundreds or thousands of people from a huge geographic area. This has already happened: in November 2021, Anime NYC was an early focal point for a new variant of the COVID-19 virus, Omicron, which saw cases spread among its 53,000 attendees, then again in their home communities after they left the convention.[2]

Faced with this new problem, conventions around the world began to contend with some difficult decisions: Do they cancel and lose out on that year's revenue and disappoint everyone who was planning to attend, or do they hope that it isn't so bad and that a brief set of lockdowns will solve the problem? The first high-profile cancellation was South by Southwest in Austin, Texas, which was soon followed by others: Costume-Con 38 in Canada; ACE Comic Con in Boston; River Region Comic Con in Montgomery, Alabama; and more.[3] Conventions were often forced to wait to cancel until the force majeure clauses in their contracts were triggered by their host convention centers, allowing them to escape crushing financial penalties.

As COVID-19 showed no sign of abating over the course of the spring and into the summer, major conventions began to shut down, including San Diego Comic-Con, *Star Wars* Celebration, and New York Comic Con.

Conventions are the lifeblood of cosplay, and their sudden absence represented a huge change for the community as a whole: cosplayers who had planned on meeting

---

[2] Beth Mole, "Anime Convention of 53k Is First US Case Study for Omicron Spread, CDC Says," *Ars Technica*, December 7, 2021, https://arstechnica.com/science/2021/12/officials-trying-to-contact-all-53k-anime-convention-attendees-in-omicron-probe/.
[3] Andrew Liptak, "Coronavirus: The Sci-Fi/Fantasy Conventions Canceled So Far," *Tor*, March 15, 2020, https://www.tor.com/2020/03/15/coronavirus-the-sci-fi-fantasy-conventions-canceled-so-far.

friends and fellow cosplayers now wouldn't get to show off their work to admirers and photographers on the convention floor. Furthermore, with movie theaters shuttered because of the pandemic, an entire year of new films—and potential costumes—were put on hold. Some of the year's most-anticipated movies, like *Wonder Woman 1984*, *Black Widow*, *Mulan*, *Ghostbusters: Afterlife*, *Tenet*, *The Eternals*, and *Dune*, faced delays, pushing the anticipation off for months or even a year. Some ended up not hitting theaters at all but went directly to streaming services. Over the course of the spring, cosplayers lamented those cancellations: they missed the community, their friends, and the sense of celebrating all things pop culture with thousands of fellow fans.

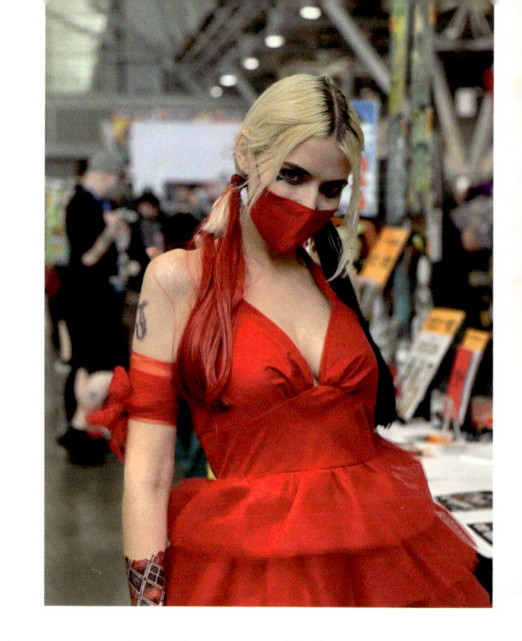

While conventions came to a screeching halt in the spring, organizers quickly figured out that you didn't have to be clustered in a convention center to attend it: cosplay contests and panel discussions for movies and television shows eventually made their way online as cons like San Diego Comic-Con, the World Science Fiction Convention, and others figured out how to retrofit their events for an online audience. While not optimal for those hoping to see long-absent friends, the online nature of these conventions did open the doors to people who might not have ordinarily attended a convention—it was much easier to tune in via their computer.

Cosplayers are resourceful, though, and while conventions are an important part of the larger community, they aren't the only part. Faced with lockdowns, cosplayers found other ways to keep themselves occupied. Many used their now-freed-up time to finish the projects that they had been wanting to work on. Others turned their skills toward making cloth masks for friends, family members, or buyers, or used their 3D printers and design software to design and create personal protective equipment like face shields, mask holders, or respirators. Some, recognizing the depressive impact that the lockdowns had on their neighbors, suited up in costume to simply stand on the street to wave at people driving by, hoping to bring a brief moment of joy to those who saw them.

The pandemic also helped highlight the importance of social networking platforms like Facebook, Instagram, TikTok, and Twitter to the cosplay community. Cosplayers set

ABOVE, FROM LEFT:

1: A cosplayer dressed as Harley Quinn from *The Suicide Squad* poses at FAN EXPO Boston in September 2021. She added a mask to her costume because of COVID restrictions, matching the fabric to the costume.

2: A cosplayer dressed as Cyborg from the DC Comics universe integrated a mask into his costume at FAN EXPO Boston in September 2021.

3: A cosplayer dressed as Cinderella wears a blue mask to match her costume at FAN EXPO Boston in September 2021.

4: One of several Loki cosplayers at FAN EXPO Boston in September 2021. She created a mask to match the look and feel of her costume.

Photos courtesy of Andrew Liptak

up their cameras to record group memes or short videos of their costumes. One notable example that came out of the lockdowns was the "Pass the Brush" challenge, in which a cosplayer in plain clothes would pick up a makeup brush (or in some cases, a group challenge coin), pretend to brush the camera lens, and pull the brush back to reveal themselves in costume, before handing, tossing, or throwing the brush to the next cosplayer down the chain. These collaborative projects kept cosplayers connected to one another and provided a way to have a bit of fun online.

As of now, as I write this a little more than two years since the start of the pandemic, it still isn't over; but conventions have begun to trickle back into existence, and as they do so, organizers are figuring out how to bring people together while ensuring a baseline level of safety. In some cases, those conventions are requiring proof of vaccination or a negative test before they attend: Dragon Con 2021 was one of the first to issue such a requirement, telling guests that in light of the spread of a highly infectious variant called Delta, they'd need to either be vaccinated or show proof of a negative test taken within seventy-two hours of the convention.[4] Other conventions didn't ask for proof of vaccination or a negative test, but instead required attendees to wear masks the entire time, and encouraged people to wash their hands frequently and to maintain social distancing.[5] In all likelihood, some of these measures will remain in place: handwashing or sanitizing stations, the encouragement to wear masks or to stay home if ill will remain fixtures of conventions to come. When I attended FAN EXPO Boston in September 2021, I noticed that cosplayers had integrated masks into their cosplays, matching the fabric or making them look otherwise congruent with the rest of their costumes; or they just wore protective masks under their headpieces. Celebrities greeted fans and posed for pictures with guests separated by a barrier.

But things won't go back to the way they were exactly, including within the cosplay community. A year's worth of social distancing guidelines will likely mean that major events will include harder caps on attendance, and will likely also come with plenty of health measures, like temperature checks and handwashing stations at cons. Attendees might need to show that they've been vaccinated and boosted against COVID-19 in order to enter the convention hall, and it seems more than likely that someone will be turned away by convention staff if they're showing signs of illness.

Cosplayers will adapt to these changes. They might focus on costumes that include masks, like the technicians from HBO's *Westworld*, Sister Night from HBO's *Watchmen*, a Fremen in a stillsuit from *Dune*, or even something as simple as a biohazard suit—real or imagined.[6] But while some cosplayers are eager to return to the convention floors to have their pictures taken, there will be others who will hold off, weighing the risks and deciding that the chance of catching something just isn't worth it. But cosplay is a resilient calling, and it will continue on for years to come, pandemic or no.

---

4   Myrydd Wells, "Dragon Con Announces its 2021 Covid-19 Guidelines: Vaccine or Negative Test and Masks Required, No Public Parade Spectators," *Atlanta*, August 1, 2021, https://www.atlantamagazine.com/news-culture-articles/dragon-con-announces-its-2021-covid-19-guidelines-masks-on-no-public-parade-spectators.
5   "Fan Expo Boston COVID-19 Guidelines," FAN EXPO Boston (website), accessed December 9, 2021, https://fanexpohq.com/fanexpoboston/health-safety.
6   Andrew Liptak, "The Perfect Costumes for Conventions in a Post-Coronavirus World," Cosplay Central (website), September 21, 2020, https://www.cosplaycentral.com/topics/covid-19/feature/the-perfect-costumes-for-conventions-in-a-post-coronavirus-world.

33 THE FUTURE

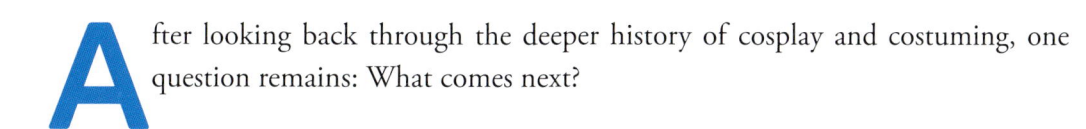

After looking back through the deeper history of cosplay and costuming, one question remains: What comes next?

▬ MEDIA

In 2019, *Avengers: Endgame* took home $2.79 billion at the worldwide box office. Other films that cracked the $1 billion mark that year included *The Lion King* ($1.65 billion), *Frozen II* ($1.42 billion), *Spider-Man: Far from Home* ($1.14 billion), *Captain Marvel* ($1.12 billion), *Toy Story 4* ($1.073 billion), *Joker* ($1.071 billion), *Aladdin* ($1.05 billion), and *Star Wars: The Rise of Skywalker* ($1.04 billion).[1] While attending cons that year, I personally saw costumes from every one of those projects: Elsas and Annas, Captain Americas and Captain Marvels, Spider-Men, Jokers, and more all walked through hotels and convention centers, celebrating the films that they loved.

In the coming years, we'll see plenty of other blockbuster films, and the flood doesn't appear to be slowing. At San Diego Comic-Con in 2019, Marvel announced ten new

---

1 "2019 Worldwide Box Office," Box Office Mojo, accessed December 9, 2021, https://www.boxofficemojo.com/year/world/2019.

film and television projects[2] and added on several more in the months that followed. Disney has a bunch of *Star Wars* projects in the works for film and streaming. Then there's James Cameron's *Avatar*, which is projected to have four sequels hitting theaters starting in 2022. Other studios have packed slates as well: Warner Bros. will release a number of DC Comics films and a potential franchise based on Frank Herbert's *Dune*, and Sony is trying to get its own Spider-Man universe going. That's to say nothing of the other countless projects that will enter development and production in the years to come. Some of which will be huge hits, while others might garner only meager audiences. There's someone out there now who will eventually cosplay something from them.

That's just what we already know to be arriving in theaters in the coming years. Streaming services like Amazon Prime Video, Apple TV+, CBS All Access, Disney+, HBO Max, Hulu, Netflix, and Peacock all have robust rosters of new genre projects in the works: big-budget adaptations or continuations of classic science-fiction properties like *Star Trek*, *Star Wars*, *The Lord of the Rings*, *Dune*, *The Wheel of Time*, and *Foundation*, to name just a few. And there will be countless new books, comics, cartoons, memes, webcomics, and more. Anime in particular has become a growing segment of the entertainment world, and streaming services like Netflix have dumped billions into creating new animated shows to fuel their subscriber growth.[3]

All of this is to say that fans will not be wanting for inspiration when it comes time to plan for their next convention or Halloween in the coming years. If the last decade and a half is any indication, what we watch and read will inspire countless new costumes.

This isn't limited to fans attending conventions, either. According to the National Retail Federation, American consumers spent more money on Halloween candy and costumes, hosted or attended more Halloween parties, and carved more pumpkins in 2019 than they had in 2009.[4] Moreover, foot traffic at major conventions like San Diego Comic-Con and New York Comic Con has risen exponentially in just a few years.

These combined factors signal that costuming will remain popular: the endurance

---

2   Richard Newby, "The Promise Behind Marvel's Phase 4 Slate," *Hollywood Reporter*, July 21, 2019, https://www.hollywoodreporter.com/heat-vision/marvel-phase-4-lineup-revamps-mcu-1225925.
3   Nick Statt, "Netflix Plans to Spend $8 billion in 2018 to Help Make Its Library 50 Percent Original," *The Verge*, October 16, 2017, https://www.theverge.com/2017/10/16/16486436/netflix-original-content-8-billion-dollars-anime-films.
4   "Halloween Shopping Trends: Then and Now," National Retail Federation, October 2, 2019, https://nrf.com/blog/halloween-shopping-trends-then-and-now.

of Halloween as a pop culture holiday and the sheer volume of content to get costume ideas from means that there's no shortage of inspiration for kids. Some of those kids will discover that they love dressing up in costume, continuing to do so into their adult lives. And as long as science-fiction, fantasy, and other genre projects remain in the pop culture zeitgeist, we'll see people expressing their appreciation and love of those properties by sharing and discussing them, as well as producing fan art, fan fiction, and of course, their very own costumes. And new stories are always working their way through the minds of creators, through meetings at studios, and on computers and film sets, destined to end up in the hands of fans, who will put their own spin on the characters, worlds, and moments that they most connect with.

▰ TECHNOLOGY

Only a decade ago, it was unfathomable that I might have a 3D printer in my house. My Snapmaker sits on my workbench, and I've used it for a wide variety of activities, from making small toys for my children to small components for costumes that I wouldn't have been able to easily make otherwise. Friends of mine own similar printers of their own, as does my local library and other local makerspaces. This is due in part to the dramatic drop in price that these devices have undergone, making them more affordable for more people. In the last year or so, the cost for a resin 3D printer rapidly dropped, meaning that we'll see more of them entering households and workshops. With more innovation in this particular field, it seems likely that we'll see more printers come onto the marketplace that'll be faster, cheaper, and better than their predecessors.

As they do so, they'll be accompanied by other advances. A couple of years ago, I struggled to 3D-print a simple shape to replace the broken handle on my freezer: the free software that I was using simply wasn't user-friendly or intuitive, the product of an established industry of professionals. Fast-forward a couple of years, and with more widespread adoption, companies have already started to develop better, more intuitive programs that'll allow people to more easily design their own creations for their printers. As that skill barrier drops, a greater swath of the population will put it to good use.

Moreover, while 3D printing has been around for decades, it is "becoming faster and producing larger products," writes Mark Zastrow in *Nature*. "Scientists are coming up with innovative ways to print and are creating stronger materials, sometimes mixing multiple materials in the same product."[5] Other new advances are on the horizon: the ability to print objects that are flexible, leading to new possibilities for costumes. Those improvements will allow for better prints and better products, including props for film and television projects and for cosplayers.

When it comes to costumes themselves, the cosplay boom has led to constant innovation and experimentation in the field. Makers add lights, sounds, and smoke effects to their characters, bringing them to life in new ways every day. Devices like the open-sourced, single-board computer Raspberry Pi have brought about a programming revolution for tinkerers, and we'll likely see widespread adoption on the part of cosplayers to introduce more special effects and interactivity to their costumes. In 2014, when Lucasfilm unveiled the first trailer for *The Force Awakens*, fans quickly assumed that the rolling droid BB-8 was an entirely digital creation. But months later, that assumption was dashed when Lucasfilm rolled one onstage. Fans quickly reverse-engineered the character, and you can frequently find one roving around a convention floor. Fans are creative, intuitive people who can often figure out how to make something that seems implausible at first. The possibilities are endless.

CORPORATE ENCOURAGEMENT

As we've seen throughout the history of cosplay, the scene is heavily dependent upon several factors: spaces for cosplayers to organize, and the licensors of the various properties tolerating and encouraging the activity. While some companies take a harder stance on fan art and fan-made prop replicas, others remain mostly hands-off, allowing their respective fan scenes to flourish and contribute. The recent history of cosplay has shown that when studios recognize the benefits that enthusiastic fans play in the success of their properties, these properties tend to hit it big.

Relationships like those between the 501st Legion and 405th Infantry Division and their respective corporate IP holders represent how those companies recognize the power that fandom holds for their properties. The licensors allow the fan communities to flour-

---

5   Mark Zastrow, "The New 3D Printing," *Nature*, vol. 578, February 6, 2020, https://www.nature.com/magazine-assets/d41586-020-00271-6/d41586-020-00271-6.pdf.

ish, while also providing them with a body of well-constructed costumes from which to draw on for corporate or just good PR.

Within the last couple of years, some studios have taken a step further, recognizing that cosplayers will inevitably make their own costumes based on franchise characters. Film and television studios will release images ahead of time or even bring screen-used costumes to conventions for fans to check out up close like what Lucasfilm did in 2016 for the shoretroopers, allowing them to take detailed pictures and measurements to use for their own costumes.

And increasingly, some IP holders are actively aiding cosplayers by providing them with detailed tutorials and models. In 2016, Blizzard Entertainment released an official cosplay guide for its upcoming game *Overwatch*. The guide included tutorials for each of its twenty-one launch characters, which had images of the characters and their accessories from a variety of angles, as well as detailed logos and color codes for each character's outfit.[6] The guide worked, as the game's characters appear frequently at conventions. While Blizzard appears to have abandoned the effort for *Overwatch*,[7] it has unveiled similar guides for other games, like *Heroes of the Storm*[8] and *World of Warcraft*.[9]

Other companies have taken a cue and launched similar efforts. Ubisoft released a guide for the Warden for its game *For Honor*,[10] and in 2017, developer Piranha Bytes teamed up with German cosplayer duo Lightning Cosplay to produce an official guide for its game *ELEX*.[11] Sony released a guide for its game *God of War* (featuring detailed reference shots of the main character's armor and tattoos),[12] Gearbox released a cosplay guide for its game *Borderlands 3* in 2019 (highlighting character details and official col-

---

6   Andy Chalk, "Blizzard Releases Crazily Detailed *Overwatch* Art and Cosplay Guide," *PC Gamer*, January 5, 2016, https://www.pcgamer.com/blizzard-releases-crazily-detailed-overwatch-art-and-cosplay-guide.
7   "What Ever Happened to the Cosplayer Reference Kits?" asked by user brokenstyli in Blizzard Forums, April 2019, https://us.forums.blizzard.com/en/overwatch/t/what-ever-happened-to-the-cosplay-reference-kits/328483.
8   "Introducing: Cosplay Reference Kits," Blizzard, https://news.blizzard.com/en-us/heroes-of-the-storm/19881985/introducing-cosplay-reference-kits.
9   Blizzard Entertainment, "Cosplay Guide: Becoming Illidari," *World of Warcraft* (website), May 5, 2017, https://worldofwarcraft.com/en-us/news/20724770/cosplay-guide-becoming-illidari.
10 "The Warden Cosplay Reference Guide," Ubisoft, https://www.ubisoft.com/da-dk/game/for-honor/news-updates/1zr5xVsPcnR2IkSIhSzFJx/the-warden-cosplay-reference-guide.
11 "Official ELEX Cosplay Guide," Lightning Cosplay, accessed December 9, 2021, https://www.lightningcosplay.com/official-elex-cosplay-guide.
12 "God of War Cosplay Guide," Sony, https://secure.cdn.us.playstation.com/god-of-war/cosplay/god-of-war-cosplay-guide.pdf.

ors),[13] and Naughty Dog released an official guide for a character from *The Last of Us Part II*.[14] Lucasfilm released one for its animated series *Star Wars: The Bad Batch*,[15] and others have followed suit as well. Most recently, 343 Industries released an exhaustive, in-depth guide for its latest installment of the *Halo* franchise, *Halo Infinite*, which runs more than a hundred pages, and specifically praises the cosplay community: "*Halo* has been incredibly blessed to have such a massive and engaged cosplay community, with dedicated members all over the world pouring their heart, soul, and skills into bringing the universe to life."[16]

CD Projekt RED appears to have been on the early end of this trend: it released cosplay guides for its character Ciri from *The Witcher* and for various characters from the *Cyberpunk 2077* game,[17] and also launched a cosplay contest for fans of both.[18, 19]

In another instance, when *District 9* and *Elysium* director Neill Blomkamp launched his experimental film production company, Oats Studios, he noted that one of his goals was to provide fans with its digital assets to fool around with on their own.[20] Blomkamp explained that if cosplayers were able to use 3D models directly from a studio, "the results would be heads and shoulders above old techniques," because they would have that screen-accurate lineage. Since the launch of Oats, he notes that he's seen some cosplayers use his studio's models as the basis for costumes.

These guides or assets all tend to contain the same information: detailed reference images of the character from various angles, the finer details of their outfits and accessories,

---

13   "Vault Hunter Cosplay Guides Now Available," *Borderlands* (website), May 9, 2019, https://borderlands.com/en-US/news/2019-05-09-vault-hunter-cosplay-guides.
14   "The Last of Us Part II Ellie Cosplay Guide," Sony, https://www.playstation.com/en-us/games/the-last-of-us-part-ii-ps4/outbreakday/ellie-cosplay-guide.
15   Kristin Baver, "Cosplay Command Center: The Bad Batch," *Star Wars* (website), April 15, 2020, https://www.starwars.com/news/cosplay-command-center-the-bad-batch.
16   Andrew Liptak, "Microsoft Releases New Halo Cosplay Guide for the Mark VII Armor," Cosplay Central (website), June 15, 2021, https://www.cosplaycentral.com/topics/cosplay/news/microsoft-releases-new-halo-cosplay-guide-for-the-mark-vii-armor.
17   "Cosplay Guides," Cyberpunk.net, accessed December 9, 2021, https://www.cyberpunk.net/en/cosplay-contest/#guides.
18   "The Witcher Cosplay Guide – Ciri," CD Projekt RED (website), August 13, 2014, https://en.cdprojektred.com/news/the-witcher-cosplay-guide-ciri.
19   "Official Cyberpunk 2077 Cosplay Contest Announced!" CD Projekt RED, June 27, 2019, https://www.cdprojekt.com/en/media/news/official-cyberpunk-2077-cosplay-contest-announced.
20   Andrew Liptak, "*District 9* Director Neill Blomkamp on Why He's Starting His Own Movie Studio," *The Verge*, June 3, 2017, https://www.theverge.com/2017/6/3/15703414/neill-blomkamp-oats-studios-short-films-sci-fi-district-9-chappie-elysium-rakka.

and the proper colors. These are the details that cosplayers would normally acquire by playing the game and taking screenshots. What the studios do is remove some of that effort on the part of their fans, often providing it ahead of a game's release.

By doing this, studios take some of the guesswork out of the equation. This saves fans time and helps to fire them up, as well as the added bonus of turning them into walking advertisements for the game ahead of its release.

COSPLAY LITE

For decades, a key part of a nerd's wardrobe has been the branded T-shirt. On it might be an in-joke or catchphrase, a film's official logo, or a piece of art focused on one character or element of a franchise. These play an important role in the geek community, telegraphing to the world: I AM A FAN OF #INSERTPROPERTYHERE. Walking down the street these days, it's not uncommon to come across people wearing clothing with the Zelda Triforce, the *Star Wars*/Flash/Batman/Nintendo insignia, or another form of corporate branding.

As these properties become more popular, companies are releasing not just T-shirts or other apparel with their branding but clothing that edges closer to the appearance of a costume.

One example is Eckō Unltd., a fashion company founded by Marc Ecko in 1993 that specializes in urban fashion. In 2007, it picked up a license to produce a line of *Star Wars* apparel and released several high-end sweatshirts that made the wearer look like Boba Fett or an Imperial stormtrooper.[21] These weren't simply sweatshirts with the features printed on: they were detailed garments, with different panels of fabric sewn together to resemble the various plates of armor on the two characters. While they wouldn't pass as a costume, they certainly looked more like casual cosplay than your run-of-the-mill sweatshirt. The company also produced some *Halo*-branded garments in 2009 that replicated the look of Master Chief's armor.[22] Additionally, sportswear company Columbia released its own line of costume-inspired gear over the years: jackets inspired by the crew

---

21 "Marc Ecko's Boba Fett Hoodie," *TechCrunch*, October 1, 2007, https://techcrunch.com/2007/10/01/marc-eckos-boba-fett-hoodie.
22 "Ecko Halo Hoodie," The Awesomer (website), September 23, 2009, https://theawesomer.com/ecko-halo-hoodie/19411.

in *The Empire Strikes Back*,[23] a set inspired by *Rogue One*,[24] and another for *The Mandalorian*.[25]

Another fashion company called Musterbrand has released its own branded garments over the years. In 2015, it created a line of *Halo*-themed clothing licensed from Microsoft: jackets and T-shirts that featured detailing that vaguely resembled character costumes. It worked closely with the company to decide on styles, fabrics, colors, patterns, and labeling for the items with an eye toward making the products wearable in everyday situations.[26] It followed up with a license from Nintendo for *The Legend of Zelda: Breath of the Wild*, releasing a series of costume-like jackets, hats, shirts, and accessories,[27] as well as similar items for *Assassin's Creed*,[28] *Borderlands*, and *Black Panther*.

Her Universe, a clothing brand founded by *The Clone Wars* actress Ashley Eckstein, likewise sells clothing inspired by a number of franchises. In addition to its own branded clothing, the company has released pieces that take cues from the costumes themselves,

Dan Celik, Nicholas Norton, Eeka Thaxton, and Andrew Liptak pose in cosplay-esque clothes at the Vermont Sci-Fi & Fantasy Expo in October 2021. From left to right: a Mark Ecko Boba Fett Hoodie, Musterbrand's *Breath of the Wild* knitted hoodie, Her Universe's Rose Tico jacket, and Columbia's *Rogue One* Cassian Andor Jacket.

Courtesy of Andrew Liptak

---

23   Dan Brooks, "How Rare *Empire Strikes Back* Crew Gear Inspired Columbia's Amazing New Parka," *Star Wars* (website), December 3, 2018, https://www.starwars.com/news/columbia-star-wars-empire-crew-parka.
24   Catrina Dennis, "Behind the Seams of Columbia's Beautiful *Rogue One* Jackets," *Star Wars* (website), December 9, 2016, https://www.starwars.com/news/behind-the-seams-of-columbias-beautiful-rogue-one-jackets.
25   Dan Brooks, "Better than Beskar: Inside Columbia's New *Star Wars* Collection Inspired by *The Mandalorian*," *Star Wars* (website), November 30, 2020, https://www.starwars.com/news/columbia-the-mandalorian.
26   Xbox Wire Staff, "Xbox and Musterbrand Team Up to Bring *Halo* into the World of High Fashion," *Xbox Wire*, November 5, 2015, https://news.xbox.com/en-us/2015/11/05/xbox-musterbrand-halo.
27   Sean Fallon, "*The Legend of Zelda: Breath of the Wild* Gets a Stylish Clothing Line," ComicBook.com, November 9, 2017, https://comicbook.com/gaming/2017/08/31/botw-clothing-line.
28   Anthony Taormina, "Musterbrand Debuts *Assassin's Creed Unity* Clothing Line," GameRant, September 23, 2014, https://gamerant.com/assassins-creed-unity-clothing-musterbrand.

such as a romper based on Wonder Woman's Themyscira outfit. And if you go online to any number of quick pop-up shops, you can find tons of unlicensed, screen-printed hoodies, shirts, and other garments that replicate the look of just about anything you can think of, from Iron Man to an Apollo space suit.

Adults aren't the only target audience for these types of clothes: costume-inspired outfits for children do much the same thing. When my son was four years old we got him a Darth Vader–inspired hoodie that featured details as extensive as a cape, plus a Spider-Man–style shirt with a hood that formed a sort of mask resembling the character's.

Dallas Nagata White says that she thinks we'll see more of this as companies wake up to the potential that these types of products have. Certainly, people show off their fandom with everything from branded T-shirts to cosplay, and it stands to reason that this middle ground will capture some appeal. Some fans might not want to go through the full effort of making a costume but still want to embody the character in their everyday lives or simply want a casual, costume-like garment in which to go about their day.

▰ A PRECARIOUS EXISTENCE

Even in instances where there isn't a formal group, the costuming world largely relies on the cooperation (or at the very least, acceptance) of the corporate intellectual property owners. In the late 1990s and early 2000s, studios would go after makers and cosplayers in a variety of ways: ordering vendors like eBay to remove listings for props and costumes or issuing cease and desist notifications to makers who were making the props, or issue stringent regulations to cosplayers who wanted to appear as their characters.

We've seen instances where the environment has chilled following a studio's actions: look no further than Paramount's lawsuit against the *Axanar* project. Whether or not you look at the film as a purely fan-made project (some *Star Trek* fans have grumbled about it, pointing to its slick production and cast of professional actors), Paramount's response was heavy-handed: issuing strict regulations that limited what fans could create, something particularly unfortunate, given the reach that platforms like YouTube afford young filmmakers, and the ease with which a fan film can be made in 2020, as opposed to 1999, 1989, or 1979.

Other studios haven't taken the same approach: Lucasfilm works fairly closely with the 501st and Rebel Legions, but it wouldn't take much for them to change their mind and work to shut down the organizations or make life difficult for them. As it stands now, the flexibility that the 501st and Rebel Legions once enjoyed in their early days has diminished considerably: the groups are required to get approval for some categories of events—like concerts or major sporting events, while others—like appearing at a store to promote the release of a book, Free Comic Book Day, or a home media release—are generally prohibited, with certain exceptions around major merchandising periods in the holiday shopping season.

Should a studio decide that the benefits that cosplayers bring to their brand in raw enthusiasm and creative talent isn't worth it, it's not inconceivable that makers and prop shops would receive official warnings from legal departments; have their listings on Amazon, Etsy, or eBay removed; or face other pressures that would slowly extinguish the passion of cosplayers.

Hopefully that won't happen. It wouldn't be a good look in terms of public relations. There's no story quite like that of an underdog.

34 WHY WE TROOP

A number of years ago I was with a troop at a now-defunct Toys"R"Us in Williston, Vermont. The event was a tie-in for Toys for Tots, and a couple of us troopers had assembled to raise some awareness for the charity. I remember standing near the entrance when a woman passed me, and under her breath—but loud enough for anyone next to her—she muttered, "Creepy."

That moment has stuck with me ever since—any time I don a costume for a public-facing event—because it's a good reminder that what I do in the 501st is sometimes seen as something strange or bewildering by the general public. As much as phenomena like *Game of Thrones*, *Iron Man*, Comic-Con, and cosplay are seen as mainstream fixtures, there's still a good portion of the general public that will purposefully look ahead and avoid eye contact when they see us out in public walking around on the street.

Over the years I've pondered a single question—sometimes while trying to deal with a passive-aggressive colleague asking vague questions about fascism and stormtroopers, and other times while I'm suiting up and marveling at the sheer strangeness of the hobby itself—why do I, and other cosplayers, do this? Why do we dress up as superheroes, as plastic spacemen, as robots, wizards, secret agents, and everything in between? Why do we risk public ridicule, weird glances, questions, and expense? Why do we spend years perfecting a costume, getting every detail just right?

There are as many answers to that question as there are cosplayers. The cosplayers that I've spoken with over the years point to their appreciation of their favorite movies, the ability to give back to the community through charitable work, the reactions from the people they interact with while in costume, a desire to show off their craftsmanship, a sense of belonging in the fandom communities, the enjoyment of entertaining themselves, and plenty of other reasons.

Ultimately, I think that there's one deeper answer that links all of us together: We love to imagine ourselves as the characters that we idolize onscreen, in comic books, or in the stories we read, because of how much we love the worlds that they inhabit. In costume, we get to take a small piece of that world and bring it back into our own, and even share it with everyone else. We do so in many ways, whether that's a convention, Halloween, a visit to a sick child in a hospital, a special day at a park, or just because it's something we feel like doing.

Cosplay is a way of sharing our fandom and love for a story with each other and the rest of the world, in the hope that we'll recognize another fellow companion or introduce someone to one of the places that we care about. By dressing up, we bring a part of that world to life, even if just for a brief moment—for a quick photograph or a flick of a screen to the next picture on an app. There's something special and magical in that moment, and those instances where we see that glimmer of recognition and the squeal of delight from a bystander are ones that we live for.

If there's one lesson to glean from the history of cosplay, it's that people will find ways to celebrate the stories that they love. Cosplay brings joy, and for all the technological advances that allow us to make more complicated and detailed costumes, it's all still in the service of something very simple: dressing up in an act of fandom.

We are inherently storytelling creatures, and over this period of time, we've found new and innovative ways to show off our appreciation for stories, whether it's sewing a garment or 3D-printing a complicated prop. At the core of this hobby is a deep love— for a story and its characters, for building and creating, for the community that comes together around that shared attraction, and for bringing what was once fictional to life for those around us.

Despite the social stigma that anime shows, superhero comics, and science-fiction and fantasy stories have carried for decades, despite the many times that an evening news program has mocked people dressing up for fun, and despite the setbacks that global events like the COVID-19 pandemic have thrown in the way of fans, cosplay has endured and even flourished. It's a way to escape one's world, to take part in a fictional one, and to gather and celebrate with friends. No matter what next direction the entertainment world follows, or the changes that we might see with the internet, I firmly believe that cosplay is here to stay. It will change and evolve as a community and split off into subgroups and new traditions to account for any number of cultural shifts, but it's still something that will continue to grow for years to come as we discover new stories and decide that it's worth stepping into the shoes of their characters for a little while.

Everything that cosplay brings with it—the skills required to build costumes; the networks that cosplayers form with one another; the introduction to new stories, characters, and worlds—are all things that we desperately need. We go to these characters because we need comfort—a light in the dark or just a friend to hold on to. Cosplay brings these characters and stories to life. It's a way to play in a world that isn't ours.

Since I bought my very first set of armor in 2003, I've slowly added to the pile and worked to share my favorite stories with my children and friends. Halloween has become a time when I not only figure out a fun costume for my kids to wear but teach them a way of appreciating the stories they're growing to love. The upcoming calendar of conventions is an opportunity to look forward to seeing what everyone else has been working on, and a time to revel in the stories that we collectively love. Time in my workshop is time that I spend learning to bring something new into the world, and the moment I step into a room in armor is one that I can make what was unreal real for just a moment.

So when you find that story, that character that you love, look into what it might take to dress up as them. Trust me, it's a lot of fun.

ABOVE, FROM LEFT:

1: A cosplayer poses as Leeloo at Dragon Con in Atlanta, Georgia, in September 2019. Cosplayers often seek to bring to life their favorite film for bystanders and con-goers, posing for pictures or reciting lines from the story from which they come.

2: A cosplayer portraying Spider-Man poses at FAN EXPO Boston in August 2019.

3: A cosplayer portraying Ripley from *Alien* poses at Rhode Island Comic Con in 2019.

4: Ashley Wilde-Evans poses for a picture at Star Wars Celebration in 2019. She painted her Clone Trooper armor to match that of an upcoming appearance in the then-forthcoming final season of *The Clone Wars* animated series.

Photos courtesy of Andrew Liptak

ACKNOWLEDGMENTS

There are so many people who I'm indebted to when it came to writing this book. First and foremost, my wife, Megan, son, Bram, and daughter, Iris, for their ideas and cheerleading from start to finish, for all of the times I vanished for weekends to visit a convention, the interviews that stretched late into the night, and the hours behind the computer typing away. Thanks as well to my mother and father, Ellen and Alan; siblings/in-laws Dan and Kate, Keelia, and Derek; and my grandmother Gloria for their endless support, enthusiasm, and encouragement along the way.

This book has been a journey unto itself, one that got its start when editor Joe Monti got in touch with me out of the blue to ask if I wanted to write a book about the people who dressed up as stormtroopers. He saw the initial germ of a story that this book became and was instrumental in shaping its early vision.

Thanks are also in order to my agent, Seth Fishman, who wrangled this book and helped bring it to Saga/Gallery, and who's been a fantastic guide throughout this entire process. Thanks to my editor, Amara Hoshijo, who took over the project, hammered out all of the dings and scratches in my early drafts to mold it into something presentable, came up with idea behind the book's fantastic cover design, and quite a bit more. I also have to thank my copyeditor, Jaime Costas, who caught all my little mistakes and helped turn this from a manuscript into a *book*. Thanks to Mackenzie Hickey, Kayleigh Webb, and especially Lucy Nalen for their enthusiasm in tackling the challenge of telling the world about this book and putting up with all my wild ideas along the way. To Eunice Wong, for expertly bringing my words to life in audio.

By my account, this book dates back to February 2016, and between now and then, I've worked and spoken with some incredible people who've helped fundamentally shape my approach to this history: Bryan Bishop, Laura Hudson, and Kwame Opam, you've each changed how I look at cosplay, entertainment, and writing, not just as an activity but as something that tells us how we interact with the rest of the world. I'm a better writer for your mentorship and friendship, and this book wouldn't have happened without either.

I've had help along the way from other writers and friends, as well: Katherine Arden, Christopher Brown, August Cole, Myke Cole, F. Brett Cox, Amanda Gustin, Ken Liu, Kristen Lomasney, Maureen Ogle, Adam Savage, Peter Singer, and Brian Staveley, who've provided invaluable advice along the way. My local writers' collective, Kristin Dearborn, Nate Herzog, Daniel Mills, and Aimee Picchi, who've been great friends and champions along the way. My nerd friends Eric Barber, Sam Gallager, Blackwell Hird, and Jesse Tidd, who have been geeking out with me for decades.

And then there are the people I spoke with for this book. Thanks to Ashley Wilde-Evans, the very first person I interviewed and photographed for this project; Amie Dansby, who told me everything I wanted to know about 3D printing and more; Adam Baker-Siroty, who let me crash in his hotel room at Dragon Con; Albin Johnson, for indulging my questions about his role in creating the 501st (and, you know, for creating it in the first place), Brian Anderson for his insights into costume-making; Bob Gouveia for his stories and thoughts about sculpting and cosplay culture; Jack and Jenni Durnin, Lin Han, Cheralyn Lambeth, Art Andrews, Astrid Bear, John L. Coker III, Carol Resnick, Dallas Nagata White, and more for their insights, pictures, and stories. Special thanks are also in order to the folks behind the Fanac Fan History Project, which has dutifully preserved the documents and history of fandom, and which remains a valuable resource.

For my local 501st and Green Mountain Squad family: Brian and Jodi Anderson, Mike Anton, Mike and Jamie Brunco, Bob Cassell Jr., Dan Celik, Gordon and Heather Gravelese, Craig Hahn, Katie Henderson, Ben Higgins, Lara Keenan, Mike King, Divvy Kuy, Andrew MacLeod, Nicholas Norton, Patrick and Katie Ormiston, Mark Poutenis, Brock Preston Viv Pustell, Thorn Reilly, Erich and Ann Marie Schafer, Kevin Snow, Eeka Thraxton and Mary Humphrey, and a whole bunch of others: y'all are beautiful weirdos, and are why I've stuck with this strange, crazy hobby for as long as I have. I look forward to seeing you at the next troop.

And finally, thanks to Sylvia Allen, my high school librarian, who provided so much guidance and encouragement in my budding days as a writer and historian, and who is undoubtedly the reason I've become a writer in the first place. I miss you every day and wish I could give you a copy of this to read.